A-level Accounting

Edited by M A Nardone
BA (Econ), FCA

Revised and updated by Sally Fishburn

Twelfth Edition

HLT Publications

HLT PUBLICATIONS
200 Greyhound Road, London W14 9RY

First published 1979
Twelfth edition 1996

© The HLT Group Ltd 1996

ISBN 0 7510 0250 X

British Library Cataloguing-in-Publication.

A CIP Catalogue record for this book is available from the British Library.

Printed and bound in Great Britain

Contents

A-level Accounting

Foreword by Brian Heap

A-level work, comprising two, three or even four subjects, is a challenging course of study. It follows a period of general education leading to the GCSE in which you have experienced a 'taster' course of up to ten subjects presented to you in a highly structured teaching system. Thereafter, it becomes necessary to make a choice of specialisms for a more concentrated period of two years in which more time will be spent in 'private study' – literally, teaching yourself.

Inevitably, private study is a new experience for most students and the time normally allocated is rarely used to the best advantage. The assimilation of facts while working on your own can be difficult since it also necessitates identifying the important issues from a range of books and a wealth of information. The framework of your course is naturally vital, not simply in terms of passing your A-level examinations but also in achieving the right grades you need to enter the university or college degree course of your choice.

My A-level series therefore aims to provide you with this essential framework. This book will give you the support you need to work through your syllabus and to reinforce the knowledge you will need to be sure of success at the end of your school or college career.

Brian Heap

Preface

This textbook covers the core syllabus of all the examination boards offering A-level accounting. It is also a valuable text for those taking AS level accounting and students who are taking the subject as part of a professional qualification. The student taking an examination with accountancy bodies, such as the Institute of Bankers, and also BTEC courses at Higher and National levels would find the content useful as a course companion.

The textbook is designed to enable students to understand basic accounting concepts, and as far as possible to apply these to the latest information and policy changes. The early chapters deal with general accounting issues, whilst others cover more specific topics. In an attempt to cope with the difficulty of students sometimes having problems appreciating parts of the subject matter without understanding the whole, some use of cross-referencing has been made. There is also treatment of many of the new issues in current accounting practice and, as far as possible in such a rapidly changing subject, this textbook aims to provide the student with up-to-date coverage of the theory and practice which is at the heart of modern accounting.

In addition, at the end of most chapters, past examination questions are provided, to enable students to check their understanding and recall of the contents of each chapter. These questions should firstly be attempted without reference to the suggested solutions in chapter 30.

Acknowledgement

All material reproduced from official publications is used by permission of the Controller of Her Majesty's Stationery Office or the Office for Official Publications of the European Communities.

Cover

The authors and publishers would like to thank The Chartered Insititute of Management Accountants, The Institute of Chartered Accountants of Scotland, The Chartered Association of Certified Accountants, The Chartered Institute of Public Finance and Accountancy and The Institute of Chartered Accountants of England and Wales for the loan of the pictures and permissions to reproduce on this cover.

Key

1	The Chartered Insititute of Management Accountants (Logo)
2	The Chartered Insititute of Management Accountants
3	The Institute of Chartered Accountants of England
4	The Institute of Chartered Accountants of Scotland
5	The Institute of Chartered Accountants of Scotland (Logo)
6	The Chartered Association of Certified Accountants (Logo)
7	The Chartered Association of Certified Accountants
8	The Chartered Institute of Public Finance and Accountancy (Logo)
9	The Institute of Chartered Accountants of England and Wales (Logo)

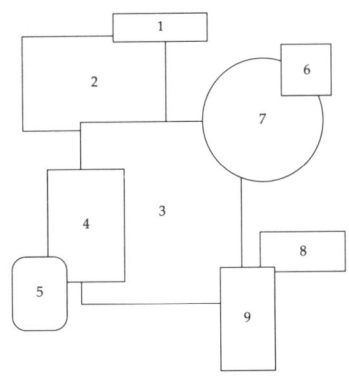

Introduction | 1

Historical background

Accounts have been kept as records of wealth and transactions for as long as personal property has been recognised. Though the first accounting records predate the invention of money by several thousand years, it seems that financial accounting records became widespread in ancient Greece and Rome around 600 BC.

Accounts are now universally prepared using the double entry system of accounting, originally developed in Italy around AD 1400. However, the early Italian accounts did not cover any specific period of time, as accounts do now. Instead a separate set of books was kept for each 'venture' undertaken by a merchant.

From Italy, the double entry system spread to the rest of Europe in the early sixteenth century, mainly through the publication of Luca Pacioli's basic text on the subject.

By the nineteenth century the spread of industrialisation meant that in most enterprises the cycle of operations was continuous, unlike the separate trading ventures of old. It therefore became necessary to produce 'periodic' financial statements of the business, in place of the old 'venture' accounts.

Legislative provision for producing periodic accounts was first introduced for UK companies in 1844, and the Companies Act of 1888 first made it compulsory for these accounts to be examined by suitably qualified auditors. The published accounts of UK companies are now regulated by the Companies Acts 1985 and 1989 and by Statements of Standard Accounting Practice and Financial Reporting Standards, produced by the UK accounting profession.

The work of an accountant

Qualified accountants are concerned with five main areas of work:

a Preparation and interpretation of accounting information *within* a business organisation.

b Auditing – reviewing accountancy work carried out by others.

c Taxation.

} Often referred to as 'compliance' work.

d Investigation of a business for some special purpose such as advising a client on the purchase of a controlling share holding in a company.

e Management consultancy.

Other specialised areas include insolvency work, administration of trusts and, for some, accountancy education.

Preparation and interpretation of management information

This is one of the largest areas of employment for accountants. Virtually all companies, apart from the smallest, will employ at least one qualified accountant.

Frequently there will be an accountant on the board of directors, either in a full-time executive capacity or as a part-time adviser. This also applies increasingly to public sector organisations, such as schools and hospitals, as a result of the recent move towards the introduction of commercial principles into the management of these organisations.

The work may consist of:

a   financial accounting: dealing, among other things, with cash, debtors, creditors and preparation of periodic financial statements;

b   cost accounting, concerned with calculation and control of production costs; and

c   management accounting, concerned with providing information for decision-making.

Increasingly, these areas are integrated to form a single unit.

Auditing

Many accountants are partners in or employees of professional firms, who offer their services as independent experts to businesses and other organisations. Much of their work is auditing – that is, examining and reporting upon accounts produced by the client. Companies registered under the Companies Act are required by law to have qualified auditors to examine their records and accounts and report in statutory terms to the members. The main function of the independent audit of a company is to satisfy the shareholders (owners) that the accounts presented to them each year by the Directors give a 'true and fair' view of the company's transactions.

Employees of a company may carry out audit checking of the work of others. Such an audit is called an internal audit. Its main object is to ensure that the company's control procedures are being followed. It is emphasised that the scope, approach and responsibility of the internal auditor is somewhat different from that of the statutory (or 'external') auditor.

Taxation

The ever increasing complexity of tax legislation has resulted in specialisation in taxation by accountants. Five main taxes require to be considered:

a   corporation tax on company profits;

b   income tax on incomes of individuals (including partners) and trusts;

c   capital gains tax on realised capital profits;

d   inheritance tax on assets transferred by an individual on death and, in some circumstances, during the life of individuals;

e   value added tax ultimately charged on consumers on the provision by a business of most goods and services.

Investigations

Investigation of a business being considered for purchase will require accounting expertise which may be available in the purchasing company or provided by a professional firm.

Management consultancy

An accountant will often be required to give advice on aspects of proposed business decisions. One of his main tasks may well be to calculate the cost effectiveness of the proposal and of any alternatives. For example, at the time of writing, the large supermarket chain of Sainsbury's appointed management consultants to advise on staffing levels.

Financial control and accounting

It has already been explained that an important aspect of an accountant's work is preparation and interpretation of accounting information.

A small business may operate profitably without much in the way of financial controls. A trader may base his business decisions on intuition or calculations made on the back of an envelope!

However, as soon as a business reaches a size at which it is no longer possible for one person to control directly all its activities the introduction of formal financial controls and comprehensive records becomes essential. If a business is carried on by a 'company' the provisions of the Companies Act 1989 requiring proper recording of transactions and the production of annual accounts apply.

The object of financial control in a business is to enable it to function in a proper and efficient manner and achieve its profit objectives.

This will be achieved by providing management with information for decision-making. The accountant will interpret information for management where necessary, and will frequently be involved in the decision-making as a member of the board of directors of the company.

The following diagram illustrates the cycle of financial accounting and decision-making within a business:

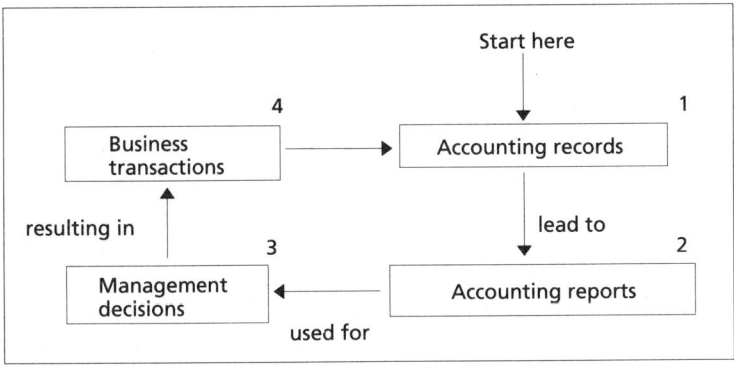

Areas covered by accounting reports to management include:

a Periodic summaries of performance 'profit and loss accounts' and financial position 'balance sheets'.

b Budgets and forecasts.

c Costing of products or proposed products.

d Capital project evaluation and control.

e Special investigations including take-over possibilities.

f Liquidity, including debt collection, stock control, and cash budgets.

Book-keeping and accounting

It is essential to grasp at an early stage in your studies the distinction between 'book-keeping' and 'accounting'.

Book-keeping is the simple *recording* of transactions.

Accounting is the use of the information recorded by the book-keeping operation to produce reports for management, owners and others.

Financial accounting is concerned with the external requirements of creditors, shareholders, prospective investors, the Registrar of Companies, the Inspector of Taxes and persons *outside* the management, as well as with the *internal* requirements of the management. Book-keepers record in the appropriate books, the revenue received and expenditure incurred by the company, so that its overall trading position can be ascertained at any point in time. The financial accounting system classifies, records and interprets, in terms of money, transactions and events of a financial character.

Basic accounting concepts | 2

Introduction

Finance and accounting are specialist subjects. This does not mean that they are incomprehensible, or even very difficult to understand, but it does mean that they have their own special language and method which must be grasped firmly right at the beginning of your studies. Without this framework, it is like trying to learn a new language without ever being told what the basic vocabulary is – all that is seen is a meaningless jumble of rules!

The underlying structure of accounting consists of a few basic principles and concepts, a set of relationships among the elements which make up the accounting system, a terminology, and rules for the application of the principles to specific situations.

Some general considerations

Who needs accounting data – and for what purpose?

a The management – to control, plan and make decisions concerning the running of the business.

b The owners – to see how profitable the business is and to assess the performance of management.

c The employees and unions – to assess job security and wage negotiations.

d The Inland Revenue – to assess and collect taxation.

e Providers of finance – to assess the credit-worthiness of the business.

Other interested parties might include research institutes, competitors, environmental protection organisations, customers and potential purchasers of the business. All the above groups are sometimes known as the 'stake holders' in a business.

It will be obvious that the same set of figures will not necessarily be of equal interest or usefulness to all parties, and indeed there may sometimes be a conflict of interest, for example, the directors of a company might be very reluctant to allow the employees to have details of individual director's pay, on the grounds that it might lead to accusations of unfairness and higher wage claims. Similarly, the management, who have control of the day-to-day running of the firm need more detail than the shareholders who are more specifically interested in the end profit figure and the dividends they are to receive.

Accounting figures are approximations

It should be remembered that accounting figures are often approximations, and that in practice the ability to quantify a figure to the last penny is usually a spurious accuracy. Businesses are complicated organisms which include many very different elements – money, buildings, morale, machines, incentives, materials, policies and so on – not all of which can be readily quantified. There can be no precise way of adding these diverse parts together to form a completely accurate numerical picture of the firm. Financial information is usually seen to be useful if it is reasonably accurate for the purpose, even if it is not 100 per cent correct.

In addition, the problem is further complicated by the wish of management to have information as soon as possible. A rough approximation today working with the incomplete data available now is usually much more use than more precise information in three months time.

What the basic accounting principles do is to provide a framework of rules so that anyone who knows these basic principles knows what can be relied on in a set of accounts, how they have been prepared, what will have been left out and what degree of approximation there is likely to be in various areas.

Basic accounting concepts

Accounting is often referred to as the language of business, and one of the greatest difficulties of really getting to grips with the subject is being able to distinguish between the accounting meaning of a term and the meaning it may have in everyday use. For example, the words 'profit', 'cost', 'depreciation' and 'capital' are all used in everyday language, but in accounting they sometimes have another, slightly different, meaning. To complicate matters even further, the meaning may change according to the context – 'capital' does not mean quite the same in 'share capital' as it does in 'capital expenditure'; and the words 'profit' and 'cost' have several different definitions according to the use they are being put to.

Like a language, accounting procedures have been evolved over time and certain rules and conventions have come to be accepted. This acceptance usually depends on how well a rule meets the criteria. The rule must be:

a Useful – it must result in information which is meaningful and helpful.

b Objective – the information must not be influenced by any personal judgment or bias on the provider.

c Feasible – it must be possible to implement the principle without undue complexity or cost.

Seven of the most widely accepted basic principles are outlined below.

The money measurement concept

In accounting a record is only kept of facts that can readily be measured in money terms. For example, it is possible to know what an item of machinery cost, therefore it is recorded. It is not, however, possible to place any money value on, say, the existence of good relations with the work force, so that is not recorded. It is important to note that this does *not* mean that this relationship does not exist, or that it is of no value to the firm, merely that as it is so difficult to value with any degree of accuracy that no attempt is made in the accounting system, and no record of it would be expected by anyone reading the accounts, who would have to make his own judgment on this aspect.

This concept provides a common denominator by which facts about a business can be expressed in terms of numbers that can be added, subtracted, multiplied and divided.

The business entity concept

The business is regarded as an entity in its own right, quite distinct from the owner, management, or any other person associated with it. One important implication is that 'private' transactions are not reflected in the business accounts.

It should be noted that this concept holds true for the accounts of all businesses, not just those which do in fact have a separate identity in law (such as companies).

The going concern concept

Unless there is evidence to the contrary, accounting reports assume that the business is going to continue operating. This has particular importance in valuing the assets.

Consider, for example, a major UK car manufacturing business. This will have a large amount of expensive and specialised machinery. As long as this business is a 'going concern' these assets will be recorded at a value based on their cost. Suppose, however, the business were threatened with permanent closure and that there is no other car manufacturer in the UK at present who needs or could use the extra capacity. There would be no market for the machinery which would therefore have perhaps only scrap metal value – a fraction of its cost. This would obviously make a radical difference to the value of the business.

Similarly, if an asset is bought on hire purchase, legally it does not belong to the purchaser until the final payment has been made. However, as it is being used in the purchaser's business, it makes sense to show the commercial reality – the purchaser has acquired an asset and has chosen a particular method of paying for it – rather than the technical legal position. If, however, there is any doubt about the business being able to continue trading, then the legal position becomes very important and the asset would no longer be classified as belonging to the business.

The cost concept

Resources owned by a business are called 'assets'. They are normally entered on the accounting records at the price paid for them, that is, at *cost*. It is important to realise that although the *value* of an asset, or what it could be sold for on the open market, may change quite dramatically over time, the accounting records will not necessarily be adjusted – they do not show the current value of the assets (except systems which specifically set out to show the effects of inflation). This cost figure will be reduced gradually by an amount known as depreciation, which will be discussed in detail later. Nonetheless, it should be noted immediately that the 'book' amount of the assets (based on their cost) may have only the slightest resemblance to the market value.

This concept is intended to comply with the requirements that accounting principles should be objective – cost is a provable fact (market value far more a matter of opinion), and feasible – even if it were possible to establish a market value for the assets, it would involve much work and research to obtain it.

The accruals or matching concept

The need for this concept arises from the fact that accounting reports are produced at regular but essentially arbitrary intervals – most commonly once a year. Obviously the business does not just stop dead at this point so there has to be some rule for tying up all the unfinished loose ends.

To take a simple example, suppose a trader bought an item for £100, delivered it to a customer and received £150 for it. It would seem that he has made a profit of £50. However, the matching or 'accruals' concept requires that all expenses incurred in earning revenue should be set against that revenue, so if in order to take the item to the customer he hired a car which cost £10, that £10 must be set against his profit even if he has not yet had to pay it. His profit is therefore £40 not £50.

The objective is to match income with these expenses which have been incurred in order to earn that income, and not merely to compare 'cash in with cash out'. This is most clearly seen in the case of the purchase of a major asset – a new factory, for example.

Consider the following situation. A business makes sales for the year of £500,000, expenses are £300,000 and the purchase price of a new factory £450,000. On a simple 'cash in less cash out' basis the business would appear to have made a 'loss' of £250,000, but this is obviously not the case, as the factory will still be available for use next year and for many years thereafter. All that should be set against the revenue of the year is the amount out of the £450,000 which it is estimated has been 'used up' in earning the year's sales.

It should, however, be stressed that 'cash in less cash out' (cash flow) has recently received increasing attention as an important accounting measure. We shall deal with 'cash flow statements' later.

The realisation concept

This states that revenue is considered to be earned only on the date when it is realised. That is on the date when goods or services are made available to the customer in exchange for some consideration. This need not actually be cash – a legally enforceable promise to pay cash in the future (a 'debtor') is equally good consideration.

This concept is needed in order to prevent excessive optimism by traders. For example, suppose a businessman manufactured a new type of pen which he was convinced would sell for £5 each, but which cost only £3 to make. If he made 10,000 pens he might then say he had a 'profit' of £20,000. That profit, however, depends on the customers actually buying the pens, and if he recorded the profit in 1995, say, before actually selling any, he might find himself unable to continue running the business for lack of cash in 1996 if it turned out that there was in fact no market for the pens. If he had already spent the money in anticipation there would be no way of getting it back.

The dual aspect concept

This concept states that every transaction has two effects, which are equal and opposite in nature. This is the basis of the system of double entry book-keeping which is dealt with in detail in Chapter 3.

Accounting conventions

The above concepts are modified in practice by certain widely accepted accounting conventions. The accounting data recorded should be:

a *Consistent* – once a policy has been decided on it should not be changed without good reason, otherwise it becomes very difficult to compare one year's results with another.

b *Material* – accounting data should be concerned with important and significant factors and not trivia. There is no universally accepted criterion for 'important'; judgment must be used. An amount of £500 might well be material for a corner shop, but would be completely insignificant in the accounts of British Airways. Indeed, most large companies publish their records in round £'000s or even £ millions.

c *Conservative* – when there is a reasonable choice between amounts or methods, the most conservative (ie the one showing the lowest profit) should be used.

It should be noted that these accounting concepts and conventions differ slightly in headings and emphasis from those laid down by the accounting bodies in the Statement of Standard Accounting Practice No 2. This statement refers particularly to published sets of accounts, and will be dealt with in Chapter 14.

Problems

Examination questions have been set in this area and the following problems are illustrative.

Problem 2.1

Discuss, using examples, the use and significance of the following generally accepted rules in drawing up accounts:

a Consistency.   (6 marks)

b Prudence (also known as conservatism).   (7 marks)

c Going concern.   (6 marks)

d Materiality.   (6 marks)

Problem 2.2

Given below are four unconnected transactions by different companies and the proposed treatment of those transactions in the accounts of the companies concerned:

a Last year depreciation on plant and machinery was provided at the rate of 20 per cent on cost. This year because profits have slumped it is decided to provide depreciation on the same assets at a rate of 10 per cent on cost.

b In the current year a television advertising campaign has cost £250,000. It is proposed to spread this heavy cost over the present year, and the following four financial years.

c A company has bought a very specialised piece of scientific equipment which it intends to use for a number of years. It is proposed to charge the total cost against this year's profits on the grounds that if the company went into liquidation, the machine will not have any resale value.

d A company has sold for £750,000 a freehold property which cost £300,000 many years previously. It is proposed to credit the surplus to the profit and loss account as part of the year's trading profit.

Required:

a Explain, for each of the above proposals, which generally accepted accounting conventions and principles are being followed or violated in each case.

(16 marks)

b Indicate, with a brief reason, how you would treat each transaction.

(4 marks)

Principles of double entry book-keeping | 3

Objects of book-keeping and accounting

The main object of accounting is to provide management and owners of a business with information about its transactions. The primary information required is whether the business is profitable and capable of meeting its liabilities as and when they fall due. This information is provided by periodic statements of profit earned (profit and loss accounts), financial position statements (balance sheets) and day-to-day control information, such as the balance of cash in hand, amounts due to the business by customers who have bought goods on credit, or amounts owed for goods and services received.

Secondary objects include provision of information to third parties, such as the Inland Revenue or potential investors.

Book-keeping exists to provide the data base from which accounting reports can be prepared.

The accounting equation – stage one

We shall introduce the techniques involved in double entry book-keeping by means of the 'accounting equation'. This equation emphasises the crucially important point that all business transactions involve two aspects (hence the term 'double entry').

As a starting point a number of items of terminology need to be introduced and defined:

a An *asset* is a resource used by a business and recognised to be of value to that business (eg cash, motor vehicles, stocks of goods for sale to customers).

b A *liability* is a claim on those resources by parties other than the owners of the business (eg loans from a bank, amounts owed to suppliers for goods and services provided).

c *Capital* is the amount owed by a business to the owners of that business. It represents the amount initially invested in the business by its owners plus any profits accumulated in that investment.

The accounting equation can now be stated in its initial form as follows:

Assets = Liabilities + Capital

or, using standard abbreviations:

$A = L + C$

This equation simply states the point which a moment's thought should indicate is obvious – the assets (resources) of a business are all provided from one of only two sources, ie the owners (capital) and outsiders (liabilities).

We can now show how the accounting equation can be used to record the 'double entry' effect of a range of business transactions.

Paul has recently won £20,000 on the football pools and decides to use his winnings to start his own accountancy practice. He undertakes the following initial transactions:

a On 1 January 1995 he pays £12,000 for a computer and general office equipment. His accounting equation after this first transaction will show:

		£
Assets:	Equipment	12,000
Capital introduced		£12,000

The two impacts of this transaction are:

Assets increase by £12,000
Capital increases by £12,000

b Paul then pays the balance of his winnings into a newly-opened business bank account on 2 January 1995. The accounting equation will now show:

		£
Assets:	Equipment	12,000
	Cash	8,000
		20,000
Capital introduced		£20,000

The two aspects of this transaction are:

Assets increase by £8,000
Capital increases by £8,000

c On 3 January 1995, Paul buys a new car for visiting his clients. The car costs £10,000 and a local bank lends the purchase price to the business on a loan. The accounting equation shows the following position on 3 January:

		£
Assets:	Equipment	12,000
	Car	10,000
	Cash	8,000
		£30,000
Liabilities:	Loan	10,000
Capital introduced		20,000
		£30,000

In this case, assets (car) have increased by £10,000 and liabilities (loan) have increased by £10,000. It is important to notice that, here, there has been no change in Paul's capital – the additional asset was provided by the bank, not by Paul himself.

d On 4 January Paul decides to use part of his winnings previously paid into the business bank account to treat himself to a holiday cruise. He therefore withdraws £2,000 from the business bank account to pay for the cruise. The equation now becomes :

		£
Assets:	Equipment	12,000
	Car	10,000
	Cash	6,000
		£28,000

Liabilities: Loan		10,000
Capital introduced		18,000
		£28,000

The double entry effect here is as follows:

Assets (cash) reduced by £2,000
Capital reduced by £2,000

A withdrawal of capital by the owner of a business is often referred to as 'drawings'.

The accounting equation – stage two

Our accounting equation now requires some expansion if it is to able to record the impact of all possible types of business transactions. This expansion needs to recognise that a business will need to be able to record income (or 'revenue') from goods or services sold to customers or clients and also expenses incurred in the course of earning that revenue.

Revenue earned by a business belongs to the owner and therefore can be seen as an addition to the owner's capital invested in the business. Expenses will, of course, have the opposite effect and can therefore be shown as reducing the owner's capital.

If we also incorporate the concept of drawings referred to above, the expanded accounting equation becomes:

Assets = Liabilities + Capital introduced + Revenue – Drawings – Expenses

In order to make the equation as easy as possible to use, it can be rearranged as follows (don't worry about the maths involved!):

Assets + Drawings + Expenses = Liabilities + Capital introduced + Revenue
or,
A + D + E = L + C + R

This expanded version can be used to record the impact of *all* business transactions.

We left Paul's equation as at 4 January 1995 showing the following position:

		£
Assets:	Equipment	£12,000
	Car	10,000
	Cash	6,000
		£28,000
Liabilities:	Loan	10,000
Capital introduced		18,000
		£28,000

We shall go on to record a further series of transactions affecting Paul's accountancy practice.

a On 5 January 1995 Paul deals with some tax points on behalf of his first client, Claire. Paul bills Claire the agreed amount of £300 for this work, having agreed that Claire will pay in seven days time. The accounting equation will now show:

		£
Assets:	Equipment	12,000
	Car	10,000
	Debtor (Claire)	300
	Cash	6,000
		£28,300
Liabilities:	Loan	10,000
Capital introduced		18,000
Revenue:	Fees	300
		£28,300

The transaction is a source of (revenues) income to the practice and also generates an asset in the form of a debtor (the amount owed by Claire until she pays in seven days time).

b On 9 January 1995, Paul buys office stationery from a local supplier for £100. The supplier's normal trading terms allow Paul to pay for these items after fourteen days. The accounting equation will now show:

		£
Assets:	Equipment	12,000
	Car	10,000
	Debtor	300
	Cash	6,000
Expenses:	Stationery	100
		28,400
Liabilities:	Loan	10,000
	Creditor	100
Capital introduced		18,000
Revenue:	Fees	300
		£28,400

An expense of £100 has been recorded and a liability to pay for this expense of £100 has also been recorded.

c On 12 January 1995, Paul undertakes a number of transactions as follows:

£300 due from Claire is received in cash
£100 due to the stationery supplier is paid by Paul
Paul pays £200 for the services of a part-time secretary
Paul pays £600 off the bank loan
Paul sends bills to a number of clients totalling £2,000

Follow through these transactions carefully and see whether you can arrive at the following accounting equation:

		£
Assets:	Equipment	12,000
	Car	10,000
	Debtors	2,000
	Cash	5,400
Expenses:	Stationery	100
	Wages	200
		£29,700

Liabilities: Loan	9,400
Capital introduced	18,000
Revenue: Fees	2,300
	£29,700

A summary of the effect of each transaction is now given:

£300 reduce debtors; increase cash
£100 reduce cash; reduce creditors
£200 increase expenses; reduce cash
£600 reduce loan; reduce cash
£2,000 increase revenue; increase debtors

From the accounting equation to debits and credits

Although it is true to say that the accounting equation can be used to record all business transactions (it is indeed the basis of the system used by many computer programs used for accounting applications) it is a rather clumsy and time-consuming system for the manual recording of a large number of transactions.

We therefore now introduce a more practical method of recording which, of course, still retains the essential 'double entry' impact of all transactions but uses 'ledger accounts' as the recording medium rather than the accounting equation. Once again, some terminology needs to be introduced:

An 'account' is simply a record of transactions. The record may take any one of many forms:

a a loose-leaf sheet of paper or card;

b a page in a bound book;

c part of a computer's stored data.

A 'ledger' is a set or collection of accounts.

We are going to look at the process of recording transactions by means of making entries in ledger accounts. An account will be opened for each type of item which requires recording and will therefore follow the same broad categorisation of items as we have already seen in our use of the accounting equation, ie there will be accounts for each asset, each liability, each item of revenue, each expense, for capital and for drawings.

The form which ledger accounts take is by no means standardised but, for the purpose of this text we shall adopt the following format:

DR			Name of Account		CR
Date		£	Date		£

You will note that the account format shown above has two 'sides', each with columns headed 'date', 'detail' and 'amount'. In practice, ledger accounts may also show 'reference' or 'folio' columns, but theses are generally not relevant for examination purposes and hence are not shown here.

The left-hand side of the account is used to record 'debit entries'. The right-hand side of the account is used to record 'credit entries'. The terms 'debit' and 'credit' will be explored more fully shortly, but we shall deal firstly with the information to be recorded in each of the three columns shown above.

Date – it is often important to know the precise date on which a transaction takes place. The date of a transaction dictates the accounting period in which the transaction is recorded, ie does the item of revenue earned affect the profit of 1994 or of 1995? Dates should always be recorded (where the relevant information is provided) in preparing ledger accounts.

Details – this column gives a brief description of the item being recorded, together with a note of the ledger account in which the other impact of the transaction (the other 'side' of the double entry) will be found. This information is useful for checking that entries have been made completely and accurately.

Amount – the money amount of the transaction is recorded here, in practice in pounds and pence but pounds only are usually adequate for examination purposes.

We have already introduced the terms 'debit' and 'credit' in describing the above format used for ledger accounts. We now consider how these terms are used in making entries in ledger accounts.

These two terms, which are part of the fundamental language of book-keeping, developed from the Latin verbs meaning 'to give' and 'to receive'. This, however, is not significant in developing our understanding of the use of the terms in book-keeping. We can explore the concepts of debits and credits by referring back to the accounting equation with which you should now be fully familiar.

The expanded version of the accounting equation shows:

$$A + D + E = L + C + R$$

This equation has been arranged such that all the items on the left-hand side (assets, drawings and expenses) obey one set of book-keeping rules, whereas those on the right-hand side (liabilities, capital and revenue) obey a second set of rules. This arrangement means that we can develop a series of simple rules which enable us to record any transaction in ledger accounts by means of debit and credit entries.

Items on the left of the accounting equation
Entry in ledger account to record:

	Increase	Decrease
Assets	Debit	Credit
Drawings	Debit	Credit
Expenses	Debit	Credit

Items on the right of the equation

Liabilities	Credit	Debit
Capital	Credit	Debit
Revenue	Credit	Debit

These rules must be thoroughly learned and practised – they are fundamental to most aspects of accounting. You should also be fully aware of the following key point:

The golden rule of double entry book-keeping is that for every debit entry there must be a credit entry (or several credit entries) totalling the same amount as the debit entry.

This is, in fact nothing more than a restatement of the principle we established earlier – that all transactions have two impacts.

As we have seen, ledger accounts give us a practical means of recording business transactions. However, many businesses enter into a large number of transactions, particularly those affecting cash. It is clearly important therefore not only to be in a position to record transactions, but also to be able to see the overall result of these transactions. In the case of cash payments and receipts, the business will want to know its balance of cash available (if any!) at appropriate intervals – the end of the day, week, month etc.

This overall summary of the affect of a period's transactions on an account is achieved by the process of 'balancing off' an account.

The process can be illustrated by considering the simplified cash account (or cash book) shown below:

DR		Cash Accounts		CR
	£			£
Sales	6,000	Rent		500
Debtors	2,000	Insurance		800

The balancing off process is as follows:

a   Add up the side of the account showing the greater total and write in this total at the foot of the column. In this case, the debit side shows the greater total, ie £8,000.

b   Write in the same total (£8,000) at the foot of the other side of the account.

c   Make this other side (here the credit side) add to the total which you have written by including a 'balancing figure'.

In our case, the balancing figure to be included on the credit side of the account would be £6,700 at the end of the period under review.

An inspection of the cash account above shows that the debit entries (cash receipts on the left-hand side) exceed the credit entries (cash payments on the right-hand side). This means that the balancing figure of £6,700 is a debit balance – the business has an asset, £6,700 of cash left at the end of the period.

Of course, if there is an asset in the form of cash of £6,700 at the end of this period, the same amount of cash must also exist at the beginning of the following period. This point is reflected by showing the balance at the end of the first period (or the balance carried down) as the opening balance (or balance brought down) for the second period.

The final, balanced account would appear as follows:

DR		Cash Accounts		CR
	£			£
Sales	6,000	Rent		500
Debtors	2,000	Insurance		800
		Balance c/d		6,700
	£8,000			£8,000
Balance b/d	6,700			

The normal balances you would expect to find on various types of accounts are as follows:

Items on the left-hand side of the accounting equation:

assets, drawings, expenses – show a debit balance

Items on the right-hand side of the accounting equation:

liabilities, revenue, capital – show a credit balance

Worked example (Kitchener)

There follows a comprehensive example illustrating the recording of business transactions by debit and credit entries. The example is subsequently taken further to illustrate additional aspects of book-keeping and accounts preparation.

Kitchener started business on 1 January transferring £1,000 into a business bank account which he opened immediately. During January he had the following transactions all of which went through his business bank account. His business was trading in 'white goods' – cookers, refrigerators, freezers and washing machines.

Date		£
Jan 2	Purchase of 6 washing machines for	600
	Rent of showroom for month in advance	100
Jan 3	Purchase of 6 refrigerators for	250
Jan 7	Sold 4 washing machines @ £150 each and	
	2 refrigerators @ £100 each	800
Jan 12	Purchase of 9 cookers for	700
Jan 15	Paid sundry expenses	40
Jan 20	Sold 2 cookers @ £150 and I refrigerator @ £100	400
Jan 25	Sold 2 washing machines @ £120, 3 refrigerators @ £70,	
	4 cookers @ £125 and 3 cookers which had been	
	badly damaged for spare parts @ £50 for all 3	1,000
Jan 31	Paid wages of sales assistant for January	100
	Drew cash for personal use	200

Stage one, in answering our progressive example, is to *record* Kitchener's transactions in the bank account. You should try this before referring to our solution.

You should have the following answer:

DR			Bank Account			CR
Date		£	Date			£
Jan 1	Kitchener – capital introduced	1,000	Jan 2	Purchase of washing machines		600
Jan 7	Sales	800		Showroom rent		100
Jan 20	Sales	400	Jan 3	Purchase of refrigerators		250
Jan 25	Sales	1,000	Jan 12	Purchase of cookers		700
			Jan 15	Sundry expenses		40
			Jan 31	Wages of salesman		100
				Drawings – Kitchener		200
				Balance c/d		1,210
		£3,200				£3,200
Feb 1	Balance b/d	1,210				

In practice the bank transactions of a business are kept in a separate book known as the 'cash book' rather than on a 'bank account'. The ruling will be devised to suit the requirements of each particular business. The term 'cash book' will be used in future in this text. A 'book' is used for cash transactions because of their large volume.

We have now completed stage one.

Stage two is the completion of the *double entry* in respect of these transactions, which require the creation of further 'accounts' as shown below. Remember our golden rule:

For every *debit entry* there must be an equal *credit entry*.

By observing this rule you can see that if a debit (DR) entry has been made in the cash book you will need to make a credit (CR) entry in some other account to complete the double entry. Conversely, if a CR entry has been made in the cash book a DR entry will be required in another account.

The first transaction, the purchase on Jan 2 has been entered for you. The double entry is:

DR	Purchases account	£600
CR	Bank account	£600

You should now complete the rest of the transactions – without reference to the suggested solution.

DR			Kitchener – Capital Account		CR
Date		£	Date		£

DR	Kitchener – Drawings Account		CR
Date	£	Date	£

DR	Purchase Account		CR
Date	£	Date	£

DR	Sales Account		CR
Date	£	Date	£

DR	Rent Account		CR
Date	£	Date	£

DR	Salaries Account		CR
Date	£	Date	£

DR	Sundry Expenses Account		CR
Date	£	Date	£

When you have finished turn the page for the answer.

DR		Kitchener – Capital Account			CR
Date		£	Date		£
			Jan 1	Bank	1,000

DR		Kitchener – Drawings Account			CR
Date		£	Date		£
Jan 31	Bank	200			

DR		Purchase Account			CR
Date		£	Date		£
Jan 2	Bank	600			
Jan 3	Bank	250			
Jan 2	Bank	700			

DR		Sales Account			CR
Date		£	Date		£
			Jan 7	Bank	800
			Jan 20	Bank	400
			Jan 25	Bank	1,000

DR		Rent Account			CR
Date		£	Date		£
Jan 2	Bank	100			

DR		Salaries Account			CR
Date		£	Date		£
Jan 31	Bank	100			

DR		Sundry Expenses Account			CR
Date		£	Date		£
Jan 15	Bank	40			

After completing this double entry exercise we have the information necessary to compute Kitchener's profit or loss for January and to prepare a balance sheet showing his financial position.

First it is necessary to balance off all the above ledger accounts. Having done this we can summarise the 'balances' on the various accounts we have created. This is done in a 'trial balance', which is a list of all the balances on the ledger accounts, separating the debit balances from the credit or balances.

Your next exercise is to prepare a trial balance for Kitchener by completing the blank layout below.

Trial Balance, 31 January

Name of Account	DR £	CR £

You should notice something interesting about the totals of the two sides!

The completed trial balance as you should have it appears on the next page.

Kitchener
Trial Balance, 31 January

Name of Account	DR £	CR £
Cash book	1,210	
Capital		1,000
Drawings	200	
Purchases	1,550	
Sales		2,200
Rent	100	
Wages	100	
Sundry expenses	40	
	£3,200	£3,200

The two totals balance because every transaction has been recorded *twice* in the book-keeping system, once on the debit side and once on the credit side.

The trial balance may now be used to prepare the two principal financial statements:

a a trading and profit and loss account – showing the results of activities for the period;

b a balance sheet, showing the financial position as at the end of the period

Kitchener
Trading and Profit & Loss Account
for the month ended 31 January

	£	£
Sales		
Less: Purchases		2,200
		(1,550)
Gross profit		650
Less: Operating expenses		
Rent	(100)	
Wages	(100)	
Sundry	(40)	(240)
Net profit		£410

Kitchener
Balance Sheet as at 31 January

	£
Assets: Cash	1,210
Capital	1,000
Profit	410
	1,410
Less: Drawings	(200)
	£1,210

You should note the following points about these two important statements.

a The heading for the profit and loss statement is 'Trading and Profit & Loss Account'. The 'Trading Account' is the first section, in which the *gross* profit emerges, and the 'Profit & Loss Account' is the second, in which expenses are deducted from gross profit to produce the net profit. Gross profit is simply the difference between revenue from sales and the cost of the goods which are sold.

b Drawings are in effect the withdrawal of anticipated profits for a period. Profit increases capital and strictly speaking drawings, as a withdrawal of capital, should be debited to the capital account. However, as drawings are usually made regularly throughout an accounting period this would involve many entries in the capital account, which is not a recommended practice. In order to avoid this situation, drawings are collected in a separate account and then at the end of a period transferred to the capital account.

c You will note that Kitchener has no stock left. He has sold exactly the number of items purchased.

d To complete the book-keeping exercise we need to recognise that the profit of £410 belongs to Kitchener and should be credited to his capital account, whereas the drawings reduce his capital and should be debited to his capital account. This has effectively already been done on the balance sheet above, but, as a matter of good practice, the entries should be made in the capital account. Kitchener's final capital account is shown below, together with the drawings account.

DR			Kitchener – Capital Account		CR
Date		£	Date		£
Jan 31	Transfer –		Jan 1	Cash	1,000
	drawings a/c	200	Jan 31	Profit & Loss a/c	410
	Balance c/d	1,210			
		£1,410			£1,410
			Feb 1	Balance b/d	1,210

DR			Kitchener – Drawings Account		CR
Date		£	Date		£
Jan 31	Cash	£200	Jan 31	Transfer –	
				Capital a/c	£200

A book-keeping system

The Kitchener example above shows how a short series of simple transactions are recorded and then summarised to produce the main financial statements – a profit and loss account and a balance sheet. We now turn our attention to the way a book-keeping system fits together and the functions of the various elements which make up such a system. It should be stressed that the detailed mechanics of book-keeping systems can vary significantly, but all systems will contain, in some form or other, the same main features – it is these features which we are now interested in exploring. We start with an overview of the structure of a book-keeping system and then deal with each main element in more detail.

The overall structure of a book-keeping system can be represented diagrammatically as follows:

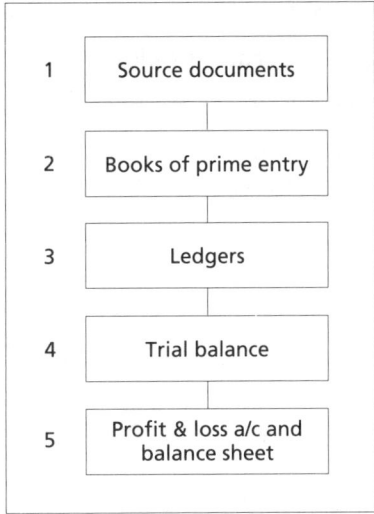

Source documents

Most everyday transactions are evidenced by an appropriate source document. These documents often form the starting point for the recording process. A typical book-keeping system will be made up of a number of sub-systems each of which will have its own source documents, as follows:

Sub-system	Source documents
Sales system	Sales invoices
Purchase system	Purchase invoices
Payroll system	Time sheet/clock cards
Cash receipts	Cheques received/Remittance advices
Cash payments	Cheques paid

Books of prime entry

So far we have assumed that the first recording of any transaction is that made in the ledger accounts. In practice, however, the first recording of many transactions are made in a 'book of prime entry'.

Over the years a number of these books of prime entry have developed, often one for each of the sub-systems referred to above. These will be considered later. At this stage we are solely concerned with the original book, the *journal*.

The journal is a form of diary used for recording all transactions as they occur. For every transaction the following details will be recorded:

a   the date;

b   the name of the account(s) to be debited and the amount(s);

c   the name of the account(s) to be credited and the amount(s);

d   a description of the transaction, called the narrative;

e   frequently a folio number, referring to the accounts involved will be included.

For examination purposes, however, this can usually be omitted.

The reasons for using a journal are as follows:

a it eliminates the need for reliance on the book-keeper's memory;

b some transactions are of a complicated nature. The narrative of the journal will describe fully the transaction, consequently the ledger entries can be expressed in fairly simple terms;

c with a change of book-keeper the absence of a journal could leave many unexplained items in the accounts;

d errors, irregularities and fraud are more easily effected when entries are made direct to the ledger;

e the risk of omitting transactions altogether, or of making only one side of an entry is reduced.

Nowadays the journal is mainly used for recording transactions of an irregular or complicated nature such as:

a the purchase and sale of fixed assets;

b the correction of errors;

c the issue of shares.

These are typically transactions which do not fall within any of the main sub-systems. The actual operation of the journal is demonstrated in the following illustration. You should carefully study the presentation of the journal entries, noting in particular:

a the journal is titled;

b each entry is underlined;

c each entry has a brief explanation ('narrative').

Journal entries are often asked for by examiners so you must learn the layout thoroughly – they are a very good test of your double entry ability.

F Jones who had personal savings of £2,000 decided to set up business as a market stall holder. During the month of March the following transactions were made:

a Mar 1   commenced business with £2,000 capital;

b Mar 2   bought a stall for £400 cash;

c Mar 3   bought a cash box for £50 cash;

d Mar 7   bought sundry items for resale for £250 cash;

e Mar 31   cash sales for the month of £400;

f Mar 31   withdrew £50 cash from the till for his own personal use.

The related journal entries would appear as follows:

The Journal of F Jones

Date	Narrative	Folio	DR £	CR £
Mar 1	Cash		2,000	
	F Jones Capital			2,000
	Being the introduction of capital			
	on commencement of business			
Mar 2	Stall		400	
	Cash			400
	Being purchase of stall			
Mar 3	Equipment		50	
	Cash			50
	Being the purchase of a cash box			
Mar 7	Purchases		250	
	Cash			250
	Being purchase of goods for resale			
Mar 31	Cash		400	
	Sales			400
	Being cash sales for March			
Mar 31	Drawings		50	
	Cash			50
	Being personal drawings for March			

Ledgers

We have already defined a ledger as a set or collection of accounts. Clearly, even a relatively small business may find it necessary to open up a large number of separate accounts in order to maintain adequate records of all assets, liabilities, capital, drawings, revenue items and expense items relevant to the business. This point is particularly relevant to those businesses which buy and sell on credit, which is of course normal practice where one business sells to another. Businesses such as these will usually maintain a separate account for each debtor and for each creditor – there could be hundreds or possibly thousands of such accounts.

It is therefore normal practice for a business to allocate accounts to appropriate ledgers, typically:

Sales ledger – a set of accounts, one for each customer to whom the business sells on credit.

Purchase ledger – a set of accounts, one for each supplier from whom the business buys on credit.

General/ Nominal ledger – a set of all accounts other than those contained in the sales and purchase ledger.

We shall deal with the workings of the sales and purchase ledger in detail later.

Profit and loss account and balance sheet

These have already been introduced in the Kitchener example and will be dealt with again at a later stage. At this stage we will just emphasise some important basic features of these three statements:

a They represent the basic minimum in terms of financial statements and will be prepared by all business and also, in a slightly different form, by many non-business organisations, such as clubs and societies.

b The profit and loss account is a 'dynamic' statement. It shows the size of flows of revenue and expenses *during* a stated period of time. It is a statement showing the basic performance of the business in terms of profit or loss.

c The balance sheet is a 'static' statement. It shows a summary of the financial position of a business *at the end of a stated period of time*. The balance is widely used as a basis for evaluating the financial health of a business.

Trial balance

The trial balance will detect many mistakes made in recording transactions. Errors in additions, errors in posting the incorrect amount to an account and, of course, errors in preparing the trial balance itself by, for example, omitting to list an item, will all be detected by the fact that the trial balance fails to balance.

However, there are several types of error which may exist without affecting the agreement of the trial balance totals. These types of errors are:

a Error of *omission* – a transaction has not entered in the book-keeping system at all, ie neither a debt nor a credit entry has been made.

b Error of *commission* – the posting of the correct amount to the incorrect account in the ledger. An example would be cash received from customer J Smith posted in error to the account of K Smith.

c Error of *principle* – this is a sub-type of (b) above in which the error affects the recorded profit because a profit and loss item is recorded in a balance sheet account or vice versa. Example: the purchase of a car mistakenly debited to motor expenses account.

d Error of *original entry* – a transaction is entered incorrectly. Double entry is made correctly but the wrong figure is used, eg a sale of £37 is incorrectly entered throughout as £370.

e *Compensating* errors – two or more errors counteract each other so the trial balance stays in balance.

f *Reversal* of entries – the correct accounts are used but entries are made on the wrong side of each account.

Purchases and sales on credit

We have already noted that normal commercial practice includes businesses trading between themselves on 'credit' terms, ie payment is allowed to be made within a defined period after the goods or service have been purchased.

Up to now, we have concentrated on 'cash' transactions, with sales and purchases on credit being introduced at only a very straightforward level. The accounting for credit transactions can be complex and hence we now deal with this topic in more depth.

Let us start by summarising some basic accounting entries:

Cash sales:	DR	Cash a/c
	CR	Sales a/c
with the value of the sale		

Credit sales:	DR	Customers' a/c (debtors)
	CR	Sales a/c
with the value of the sale		

This entry is made when the sale is made.

Later, when the customer pays, the business will make the following entry:

	DR	Cash a/c
	CR	Customers' a/c
with the amount of cash received		

Cash purchases:	DR	Purchases a/c
	CR	Cash a/c
with the amount of the purchase		

Credit purchases:	DR	Purchases a/c
	CR	Suppliers' a/c (creditors)
with the value of the purchase		

The payment to a supplier is recorded by:

	DR	Suppliers' a/c
	CR	Cash a/c

In practice each customer and supplier would be given a personal ledger account. These are maintained in the sales and purchase ledgers respectively. Remember:

a A debtor is a person who owes money (ie our customers who have not yet paid).

b A creditor is a person who is owed money (ie our suppliers who have not yet been paid).

Let us now look at a worked example. A business sells goods on credit to a customer, X, on 8 January for £40. X pays for the goods on 28 February. Show the entries necessary to record the transaction in the books of the seller.

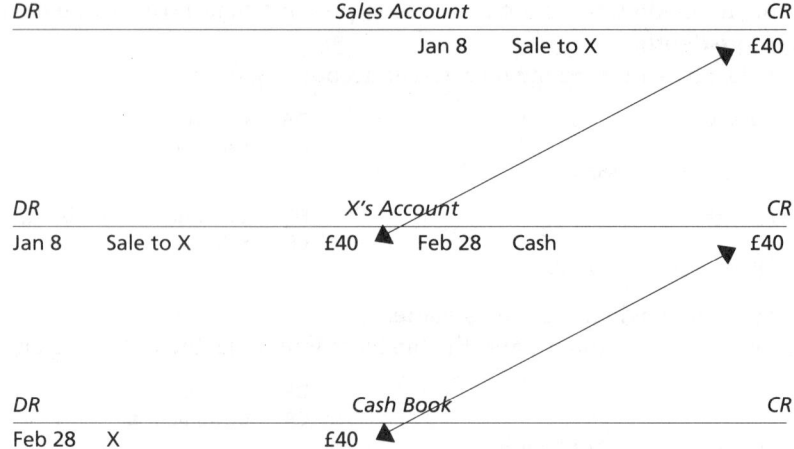

Similarly, accounts for suppliers will be maintained to record credit purchases.

Example:
A business buys goods on credit from Q Ltd on 15 January for £120. The goods are paid for on 25 February. Show the entries necessary to record the transactions in the books.

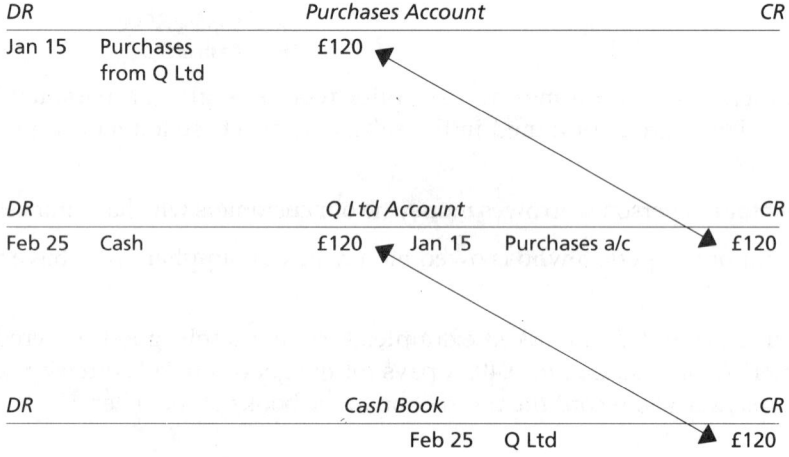

Trade discounts and cash discounts

a   *Trade discounts*. It is the custom in many trades to offer goods for sale at a standard price less a variable discount percentage. The discount may vary according to the quantity sold or relationship with the purchaser. Such a discount is termed a trade discount. Normal book-keeping practice for both seller and purchaser is to record the net price only (ie the price after deducting the discount) in the book-keeping system.

b *Cash discounts*. A company may also offer a cash (or 'settlement') discount for prompt payment of the account. This is recorded separately and referred to as 'discounts allowed'. One method of recording cash discount allowed to customers is shown in the example below.

A business sells goods to R Ltd on 8 January for £100 less trade discount of 20 per cent and a cash discount for settlement within seven days of 5 per cent. R Ltd pays the account on 12 January.

Show the entries necessary to record the transaction in the company's books.

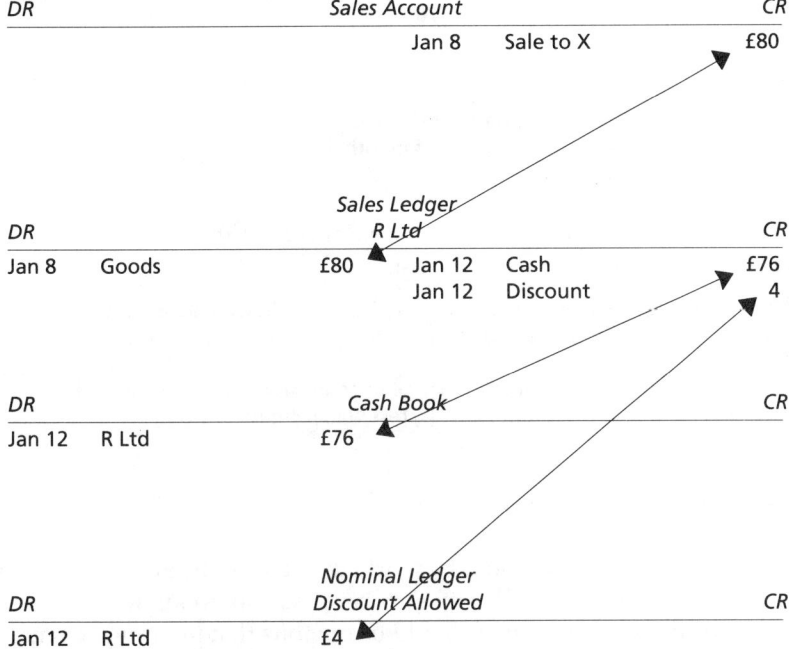

DR		Sales Account			CR
			Jan 8	Sale to X	£80

DR		Sales Ledger R Ltd			CR
Jan 8	Goods	£80	Jan 12	Cash	£76
			Jan 12	Discount	4

DR		Cash Book			CR
Jan 12	R Ltd	£76			

DR		Nominal Ledger Discount Allowed			CR
Jan 12	R Ltd	£4			

There is an alternative method of recording which eliminates the need for a separate transfer from each sales ledger account to the discount allowed account for every transaction. Cash discount must always be associated with the cash book. We can therefore introduce a further column into the cash book to record all cash discounts allowed. The discount is transferred to the ledger account at the same time as the transfer of the cash entry, but only the *total* of the discount column is debited to the discount account, usually monthly. *This is the method normally used in practice*. Similar entries in reverse deal with discounts received on payments to suppliers.

The alternative method is illustrated overleaf using the data above.

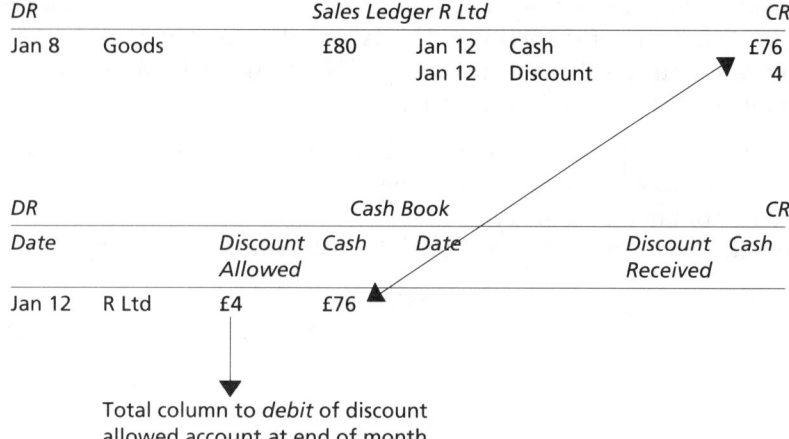

Total column to *debit* of discount
allowed account at end of month

At the end of the trading period the balances on the discount accounts are transferred to the profit and loss account:

DR   Profit and loss account   ⎫   ie discounts allowed are an expense,
CR   Discounts allowed account   ⎬   reducing profit
and
DR   Discounts received account   ⎫   ie discounts received is a source of
CR   Profit and loss account   ⎬   revenue, increasing profit

The treatment of stock

The Kitchener example previously worked, was made artificially simple to illustrate fundamental principles by ensuring that no goods were left unsold at the end of the period. However, it should be obvious that in normal circumstances a business is likely to have the following items to deal with in relation to stock:

a   stock at the beginning of the period (*opening stock*);

b   stock at the end of the period (*closing stock*);

c   purchases from suppliers;

d   returns to suppliers (returns *out*);

e   sales to customers;

f   returns from customers (returns *in*).

Opening and closing stocks on hand

Let us consider another situation. Suppose Kitchener went on to buy ten driers at £50 each during February, and had sold seven of them at £100 each. On the lines of what we have seen so far, the trading account might be thought to look like this:

Trading Account

	No of machines	£
Sales	7	700
Less: Purchases	10	(500)
Gross profit		£200

This, however, is obviously wrong. Kitchener is making £50 gross profit on each machine he sells, he has sold seven, therefore his gross profit must be £350, not £200. This situation arises because there is closing stock, and because we are not observing the matching concept. We have compared the sales of seven machines with the purchase of ten, which is incorrect in principle. What is required is the matching of the sales proceeds of seven machines against the cost of seven machines, that is, we need to find the *cost of sales*. (Sometimes referred to as 'the cost of goods sold'.)

Trading Account

	No of machines	£	£
Sales	7		700
Deduct: Cost of sales			
Purchases	10	500	
Less: Closing stock	(3)	(150)	350
	7		
Gross profit			£350

Let us now go one stage further and look at what might happen in the next accounting period – March, in this case.

In March Kitchener bought a further 12 driers, still at £50 each, and sold nine at £100.

If he sold nine machines and made a gross profit of £50 on each, his gross profit for the period must come to £450.

Trading Account

	No of machines	£	£
Sales	9		900
Deduct: Cost of sales			
Opening stock	3	150	
Add: Purchases	12	600	
(Note l)	15	750	
Deduct:			
Closing stock	(6)	(300)	(450)
	9		
Gross profit			£450

Note 1: the 15 machines at a total cost of £750 represent the total *available for sale* during the period. Closing stock must then be deducted to arrive at the cost of the nine machines actually sold.

Let us now consider the next trading period, April. Let us assume Kitchener buys a further 15 machines at £60 each, and sells 13 at £110 each. His trading account might look like this:

Trading Account

	No of machines	£	£
Sales	13		1,430
Deduct: Cost of sales			
Opening stock	6	300	
Purchases	15	900	
	21	1,200	
Less: Closing stock	(8)	(480)	(720)
	13		
Gross profit			£710

Several important points need to be noted here. Kitchener had in total 21 machines available for sale during the period. As he sold only 13, he would have had eight left. But which eight? Some of his machines cost him £50, some £60. We have assumed in the above trading account that the ones he sold first were the ones he bought first, ie his closing stock was composed of the items he had bought most recently (at £60). This basis is known as the FIFO basis – First In, First Out, and is one of the most commonly used bases.

Another possible basis is the average price, this is not simply the average of £50 and £60, as numbers bought have to be taken into account. In this case, there were:

6	@ £50	=	£300
15	@ £60	=	£900
Total			£1,200

The average price is therefore:

$$\frac{£1,200}{21} = £57 \text{ (approx)}$$

This is known as a 'weighted' average, since numbers of units are reflected in the figure.

The closing stock would then become £456 which would mean that the cost of sales was £744, and the gross profit £686.

Another possible basis is LIFO – Last In, First Out. If this basis were used, it would be assumed that of the 15 new machines, 13 were sold, leaving as closing stock two at the new price of £60 and all the original six at £50, giving a closing stock figure of £420 and therefore a cost of sales figure of £780 and a gross profit of £650.

Finally, of course, Kitchener might have kept a note of the serial numbers of his machines and therefore know exactly what their original costs were – perhaps he might have three of the old stock and five of the new giving a closing stock of £450, a cost of sales of £750 and a gross profit of £680. This would be an *actual* valuation. However, although this might seem the most sensible it is really only appropriate for large items – it would not be possible to apply it to tons of sugar, or nuts and bolts, for example.

The four methods mentioned have given the following gross profit figures:

FIFO:	£710
Average:	£686
LIFO:	£650
Actual:	£680

The largest difference is between FIFO and LIFO – a discrepancy of £60, which is nearly 10 per cent of the stock figure.

It is not possible to say that any of these methods are right or wrong – merely that they give different profit figures. If the level of stocks remains stable, then when averaged out over two or three years the profits will be the same; as although the lower LIFO stock figure decreases the gross profit in April, April's closing stock is May's opening stock, and a lower opening stock will increase the gross profit. The point where it will make a substantial difference is in the year or period of change from one method to another, which is why it is so important to adhere to the accounting convention of consistency; or if a change is made, then a note should be added to the accounts explaining the reason for the change and the effect it has had on the profit figure.

This effect on the profit figure is something you should note very carefully. Any change or error in the closing stock will affect the gross profit, and therefore the net profit, by exactly the same amount. It is for this reason that so much emphasis is placed in practice on obtaining an accurate stock valuation. It is normal to have a physical stocktake at the year end. The reason for this is that the stock is going to be included as an asset on the balance sheet, and therefore the figure which appears must be the stock which is actually owned by the business, not what should be owned. For example, if Kitchener had discovered that he in fact had only seven machines at the end of May then only seven would have been valued as closing stock. Stock may deteriorate or become obsolete or be stolen – this is why it is essential to value the stock at the year end and not just rely on the book records.

The physical location of stocks is not important, for example, some goods may have been sent out on a sale-or-return basis. If the customer has not taken up title to the goods, then they should be included as closing stock. On the other hand, if goods have been sold but not yet despatched, they should not be included (if they have been sold then the double entry DR Debtor CR Sales will have gone through the books, and it would be double counting to include the goods as asset Stock as well as having the asset Debtor in relation to the same goods).

One final word about stock at this stage, to bring us back to double entry. You may have noticed that none of our book-keeping examples have used a 'stock' account – where we have purchased goods for resale (ie 'stock') we have debited a purchases account. This system is the one that the majority of businesses use in practice – and which examiners tend to use in setting their questions. On this basis, the stock figure we have used in the trading account and the closing balance sheet is arrived at by physically counting stock at the end of the period and valuing that stock.

We should, however, stress that everything in a book-keeping system has a double entry effect and thus applies to the stock figure just as to anything else.

The 'double' impact of closing stock is as follows:

DR   Closing stock on the balance sheet, ie closing stock is an *asset* on the business
CR   Closing stock in the trading account, ie closing stock *reduces* purchases to match units purchased with units sold

Have said that regular entries are made in a purchases account not in a stock account, we should add that the spread of computer based accounting systems allows businesses to maintain a constantly updated stock account, especially with 'point-of-sale systems' as widely used by supermarkets. This concept is, however, not normally recognised in examination questions.

Returns in and returns out

Returns to suppliers (returns out)
When stock is returned to a supplier the effect is to reduce the amount we owe to the supplier and to reduce the amount of purchases made. However, normal practice records these returns out in a separate account, rather than in the purchases account itself.

To record the return of stock it is necessary to open a returns out account which will be credited with the value of goods returned. The corresponding debit entry will be made in the supplier's personal account.

At the end of the trading period, the balance on the returns out account is transferred to the trading account, being shown as a deduction from 'purchases'.

Returns from customers (returns in)
When stock is returned by a customer the effect is to reduce the amount the customer owes us and to reduce the amount of sales made but, again, we normally use a separate returns inwards account.

To record the return of stock, it is necessary to open a returns in(wards) account which will be debited with the value of goods returned. The corresponding credit entry will be made in the supplier's personal account.

At the end of the trading period the balance on the returns in account is transferred to the trading account, being shown as a deduction from 'sales'.

Follow through the following example, using data for a specified trading period:

Opening stock	£250
Purchases (on credit)	1,250
Returns out	100
Sales (on credit)	1,800
Returns in	60
Closing stock	240

The ledger accounts and trading account for the period would appear thus:

DR	Purchases Account		CR
Creditors	£1,250	Trading account	£1,250

	Returns Out Account		
Trading account	£100	Creditors	£100

Creditors Account

Returns out	£100	Purchases	£1,250
Balance c/d	1,150		
	£1,250		£1,250

DR		Sales Account	CR
Trading account	£1,800	Debtors	£1,800

DR		Returns In Account	CR
Debtors	£60	Trading account	£60

DR		Debtors Account	CR
Sales	1,800	Returns In	60
		Balance c/d	1,740
	£1,800		£1,800
Balance b/d	1,740		

Trading Account for the period

	£	£
Sales, less returns (£1,800 – £60)		1,740
Cost of sales		
Opening stock	250	
Add: Purchases, less returns (£1,250 – £100)	1,150	
	1,400	
Less: Closing stock	(240)	(1,160)
Gross profit		£580

There follows a brief summary of accounting entries for some of the transactions dealt with in recent sections.

	Transaction	Debit	Credit
1	Purchase of goods on credit	Purchases	Creditors
2	Purchase of goods for cash	Purchases	Cash
3	Sale of goods on credit	Debtors	Sales
4	Sale of goods for cash	Cash	Sales
5	Return of goods purchased on credit	Creditors	Returns out
6	Return of goods purchased for cash	Cash	Returns out
7	Return of goods sold on credit	Returns in	Debtors
8	Return of goods sold for cash	Returns in	Cash

Accruals and prepayments

It was established earlier that accounts are prepared on an accruals basis, not a cash basis. At the end of the accounting period, therefore, it is necessary to examine all the expense accounts to ensure that the transfer of the profit and loss account is correct. Consider the following situation.

Example:

Jones started up in business on 1 January 1994. He paid electricity bills as follows:

Quarter to 31 March 1994	£78	Paid 30 April
Quarter to 30 June 1994	£53	Paid 30 July
Quarter to 30 September 1994	£48	Paid 30 October

He received the bill for the quarter to 31 December 1994 for £75 on 20 January 1995 and paid it on 31 January 1995.

His electricity account would show:

DR		Electricity Account		CR
Date	£	Date		£
1994				
30 April Cash	78			
31 July Cash	53			
30 Oct Cash	48			
	£179			

At this point the electricity account shows £179 worth of electricity has been paid for, but this does not comply with the accruals principle. It is necessary that the revenue of 1994 be charged with *all* the expenses incurred in order to earn that income, and that means that *four* quarters' electricity must be charged, whether or not they have been paid for, and even if no bill has yet been received.

In this case, if Jones were drawing up his accounts before 20 January he would not know how much the bill would be for the final quarter. This does not mean it can be ignored; an estimate would have to be made. This might turn out to be incorrect, but not by a great amount. It is evident that the bill for a winter quarter would be likely to be in the region of £60–£80, and a figure in this range would be selected, as any error would not have a material effect on the profits. If he waited until after 20 January then the exact amount would be known and could be inserted.

This does *not* imply that accounts should not be drawn up until all the information is available – it may be far more use to the management to have slightly inaccurate information promptly than more precise accounts months later.

In order to estimate the correct charge to the profit and loss account, therefore, an amount of £75 needs to be added on to the amount actually paid, and carried down into the next period as a balance owing:

DR			Electricity Account		CR
Date		£	Date		£
1994			1994		
30 Apr	Cash	78			
31 Jul	Cash	53			
30 Oct	Cash	48			
31 Dec	Balance c/d	75	31 Dec	Profit & loss a/c	254
		£254			£254
			1995		
			1 Jan	Balance b/d	75

The profit and loss account has been debited with an extra £75. As in the case of stock, this means that a corresponding credit has to be entered; this is an 'accrual' (current liability) on the balance sheet.

Where an account has been *overpaid*, or paid in advance, then the principles are the same, but the balance is on the other side and is known as a *prepayment*. Examples might be business rates which are normally paid in advance.

Example:
Smith started business on 1 April 1994. He made up his first set of accounts to 31 December 1994. On 20 May he paid rates of £1,800 for the year to 31 March 1995.

In this case, only nine months revenue is being taken into the accounts to 31 December 1994 so only nine months expenses should be debited. The correct charge to the profit and loss account therefore is:

$$\frac{9}{12} \times £1,800 = £1,350$$

and the balance is carried down to the next period and shown on the balance sheet as a current asset (a prepayment).

The ledger account for business rates would show:

DR			Business Rates Account		CR
Date		£	Date		£
1994			1994		
20 May	Cash	1,800	31 Dec	Profit & loss a/c	1,350
			31 Dec	Balance c/d	450
		£1,800			£1,800
1994					
31 Dec	Balance b/d	450			

The same principle applies to any item of either expense or income – the question which should be asked is, 'What is the correct charge/credit to the profit and loss account?' and the relevant adjustment put through. The objective is always to match X month's revenue with X month's expenses. In fact, the same principle can be applied in other situations, including stocks not for resale. Examples of such items include stationery and fuel.

The book-keeping entries when stocks such as these are purchased are:

DR   Appropriate *stock* account (eg fuel)
CR   *Cash/bank* or *creditors* account

(Notice the difference in treatment from stocks purchased for resale, which are debited to 'purchase account'.)

Like the other expenses of running a business, it is the amount of such stocks *consumed* in the period which should be *debited* to the profit and loss account, *not* the amount *purchased*.

Example:

A Smith commenced trading on 1 January 1994. During the year he purchased stationery as follows:

1 Jan	£50
6 Mar	£100
12 Sep	£150
5 Dec	£100

At 31 December 1994, he estimated that stationery to the value of £75 remained unused.

A Smith's stock of stationery account for 1994 would appear as:

Stock of Stationery

Date		£	Date		£
1994			1994		
1 Jan	Cash	50			
6 Mar	Cash	100			
12 Sept	Cash	150	31 Dec	Balance c/d	75
5 Dec	Cash	100	31 Dec	Profit & loss a/c	325
		£400			£400
1994					
31 Dec	Balance b/d	75			

The debit balance of £75 represents the stock of stationery remaining at 31 December 1994, it must therefore be included in the balance sheet. It appears under current assets, probably as a 'prepayment'.

Summary

Candidates are frequently required, in examinations, to prepare final accounts (ie trading and profit and loss accounts and balance sheet), from a given trial balance. However, it is often necessary to adjust the trial balance before the final accounts can be prepared. The following is a list of the actions you should take, to deal with prepayments etc, when answering such questions.

Item		Action to be taken
Prepaid expenses (expenses paid for but not yet incurred)	1	Deduct amount of prepayment from the expense figure in trial balance (CR)
	2	Enter amount of prepayment in current assets in balance sheet (DR)
Accrued expenses (expenses incurred but not yet paid for)	1	Add amount of underpayment to the expenses in trial balance (DR)
	2	Enter the amount of underpayment in current liabilities in balance sheet (CR)
Income in advance (deposits received on goods to be sold next period)	1	Deduct amount of excess income from figure in trial balance (DR)
	2	Enter amount of excess income in current liabilities in balance sheet (CR)
Income in arrears (similar to 'debtors')	1	Add amount of imcome in arrears to income figure in trial balance (CR)
	2	Enter amount of income in arrears in current assets in balance sheet (DR)
Stocks of goods not for resale	1	Deduct closing stock from opening stock + purchases in trial balance (CR)
	2	Enter amount as current asset in balance sheet (DR)

Bad and doubtful debts

Bad debts

If a business sells to customers on credit, it may find that a few of these customers will fail to pay. When a debt is considered to be irrecoverable it is referred to as a *bad debt* and must be taken out of the sales ledger. The cost of reducing the value of debtors in this way must be borne by the business as an expense. Periodically therefore, the balances in a sales ledger must be reviewed and bad debts transferred out to a *bad debts account*. The total of bad debts account will be transferred to profit and loss account at the end of a trading period along with the other expenses. The process of eliminating a worthless debt from the sales ledger is termed 'writing off' the debt – a bad debt is *not* an asset of any value and is therefore removed from debtors.

Book-keeping entry to write off a debt:

    DR   Bad debts account   (P/L)
    CR   Debtors' account   (B/S)

If the debt should subsequently prove to be 'good' and the debtor pays this account, the receipt is credited to a 'bad debts recovered account' and thence to profit and loss account and, normally, debited to cash.

Doubtful debts

As well as bad debts there will probably be some overdue balances in the sales ledger which are regarded as suspect when annual accounts are prepared. It is usual to make a *provision* for the estimated loss which may arise in future periods. This provision may be *specific*, that is, related to individual doubtful items, or *general*, often based on a percentage of total debts. A 'provision', as the term is used here, means an amount used to reduce the value of an asset on a balance sheet.

Book-keeping entries and procedures

Examination questions often require you to deal with both 'bad' and 'doubtful' debts in the same question. The approach should be as follows.

a Write off any 'bad' debts

DR   Bad debts accounts
CR   Debtors account

b Assess the required provision for doubtful debts.

It is important to note that a provision account is a balance sheet account. It is used to reduce the value of an asset. Balance sheet accounts are *cumulative*, ie they may have *opening* as well as closing balances. The procedure for recording doubtful debts provision therefore involves the following:

	EG (1)	EG (2)
Required provision	£2,000	£2,000
Existing (opening) provision	1,500	(3,000)
Difference ('movement')	£500	£(1,000)

In EG (1), the opening provision needs to be increased by £500 to give the required closing provision. We therefore require an entry as follows:

DR   Doubtful debts   (P/L)   500
CR   Provision   (B/S)   500

In EG (2) the opening provision exceeds the provision we now require by £1,000 – this opening provision is to be reduced, ie:

DR   Provision   (B/S)   1,000
CR   Doubtful debts   (P/L)   1,000

It is acceptable for the profit and loss account entries for both bad and doubtful debts to be combined in a single ledger account. Also, remember that the provision account is a balance sheet item, the closing balance being deducted from debtors on the balance sheet.

Consider the following example:

Year ending	Bad debts written off	Provision required for doubtful debts
31 December 1991	846	240
31 December 1992	1,020	280
31 December 1993	1,208	310
31 December 1994	1,220	260

There was no provision for doubtful debts before 31 December 1991. Show the entries in the bad and doubtful debts expense account and the provision account for each year.

Bad and Doubtful Debts Expense

	£		£
1991		1991	
Debtors	846	Transfer to P/L	1,086
Provision (increase)	240		
	£1,086		£1,086
1992		1992	
Debtors	1,020	Transfer to P/L	1,060
Provision (increase)	40		
	£1,060		£1,060
1993		1993	
Debtors	1,208	Transfer to P/L	1,238
Provision (increase)	30		
	£1,238		£1,238
1994		1994	
Debtors	1,220	Provision (decrease)	50
		Transfer to P/L	1,170
	£1,220		£1,220

Provision for Doubtful Debts

	£		£
1991		1991	
		Balance b/d	Nil
Balance c/d	240	Expense	240
	£240		£240
1992		1992	
		Balance b/d	240
Balance c/d	280	Expense	40
	£280		£280
1993		1993	
		Balance b/d	280
Balance c/d	310	Expense	30
	£310		£310
1994		1994	
Expense	50		
Balance c/d	260	Balance b/d	310
	£310		£310
1995		1995	
		Balance b/d	260

You should take particular note of the following:

a In 1994, the required provision is lower than that recorded at the end of 1993. This entails a debit entry in the provision account and a credit entry in the expense account.

b At each year end the balance on the provision account (eg 1994: £260) is deducted from debtors in that year's balance sheet.

Division of the ledger and use of day books

Division of the ledger

The examples considered so far have recorded the transactions within the framework of the cash book and ledger system. In practice it is found that in all but the smallest of businesses it is more convenient to divide 'the ledger' into at least three separate sections, a *sales ledger* containing all accounts of credit customers, a *purchases ledger* (or bought ledger) containing the accounts of credit suppliers, and a *nominal ledger* containing the remaining accounts which deal with expenses, income, assets and liabilities. This concept has already been introduced at a preliminary level in our look at book-keeping systems. We now look at the area in more depth.

Day books

It is found that it is not particularly convenient to make an entry in the sales account or purchases and expense account every time a sale or purchase on credit is to be recorded. Two further books are introduced into the system to *list* credit sales and credit purchases. Every credit sale is recorded in a *sales day book*. This book has two functions, firstly to provide the total credit sales for a period obtained by totalling the listed items, and secondly to provide a convenient source for making the entries individually to the debit of each customer's account. Similarly, credit purchases are entered in a *purchases-day book* (sometimes called a bought day book).

The sales day book and purchases day book are two further examples of 'books of prime entry', as such they are often referred to as the sales journal and purchases journal. We introduced the concept of the journal generally in the previous section on book-keeping systems.

If customers return goods, it is necessary to reduce the amount of their debt by crediting their account. Credits of this kind are entered in a *returns inwards book*. The normal procedure is for the company to issue a sales *credit note* which is listed in the returns inwards book in the same way that invoices for sales are listed in the sales day book. The individual items in the returns inwards book are credited to the customers' accounts and the total is debited to returns in account at the end of the month. A returns outwards book is maintained to deal with goods returned to suppliers. The book-keeping entries for purchases returns are the opposite to those for the return of goods from customers.

Both the returns inwards and returns outwards books are 'books of prime entry' and as such they are often referred to as the returns inwards journal and returns outward journal.

Summary

Sales ledger
Purchases ledger
Nominal ledger
Cash book
} All contain 'accounts' and are part of the double entry system

Sales day book
Purchases day book
Returns inwards book
Returns outwards book
} Books of prime entry. These are 'listing devices' to save the relevant accounts from unnecessary detail – they do not normally form part of the double entry system

Block diagram

There follows a diagram of a book-keeping system similar to, but showing more detail than that given in the previous example. Make sure you understand it!

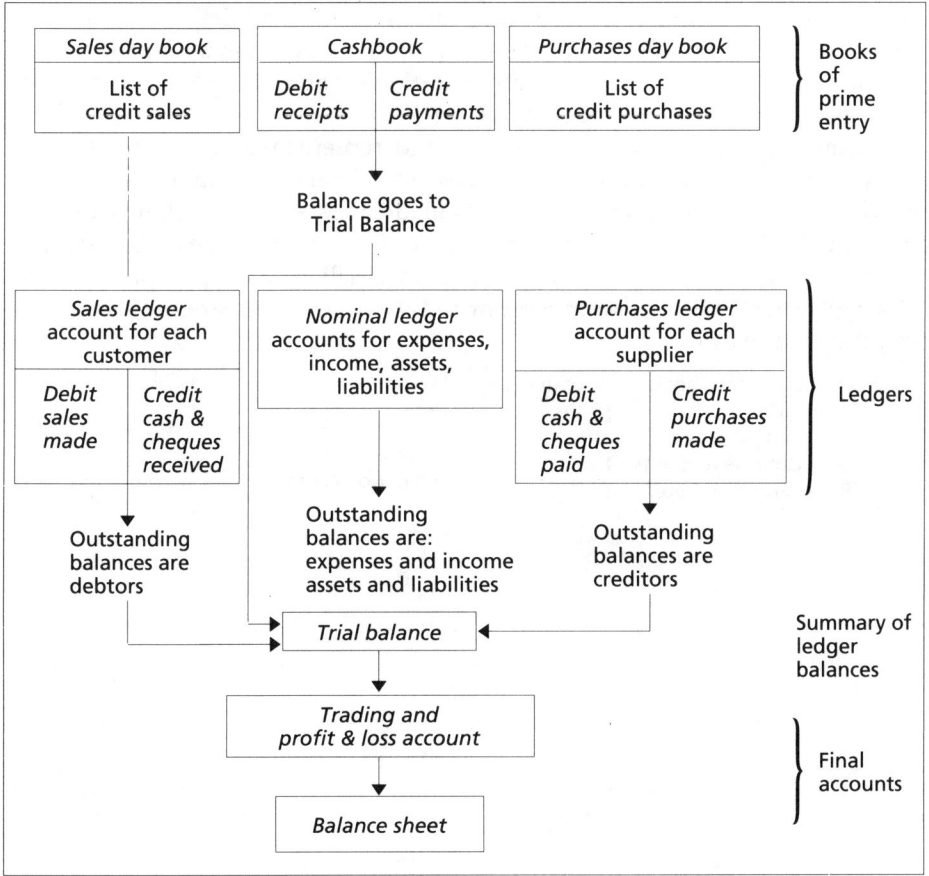

You should note particularly the following:

a The diagram shows only a 'selection' of the books of prime entry which a business may use. We have already mentioned that there will probably also be books listing returns in (sales returns) and returns out (purchase returns).

b The cash book is shown as a book of prime entry – it lists receipts and payments, one by one – but the cash book is also, effectively, a nominal ledger account. The balance represents an asset (or liability) of the business and is therefore listed in the trial balance and appears in the balance sheet.

Similar comments apply to the petty cash book dealt with in the next section.

Petty cash book

The cash book of the business will usually record transactions on the business bank account, ie cheques paid and received or cash amounts withdrawn from or paid into the bank account. Inevitably the need for small cash payments for sundry expenditure on postage, travelling, office stationery and the like will arise. Such minor cash payments are recorded in the *petty cash book*.

A 'cash-float' is drawn from the bank and replenished as necessary, often weekly. It is customary for the weekly drawing to be the amount of the *petty cash expenditure*. In this way the opening float is made up again to the original amount. This method is known as the *imprest system*. We show below a typical format for a petty cash book, but clearly the analysis headings will vary, as appropriate.

The petty cash book is a ledger account and part of the double entry system. The accounting entries are:

DR	Petty cash book	} with cash paid to petty cashier – drawn from
CR	Cash	} the bank account
	and	
DR	Expense accounts	}
CR	Petty cash book	} with expenses (in periodical totals)

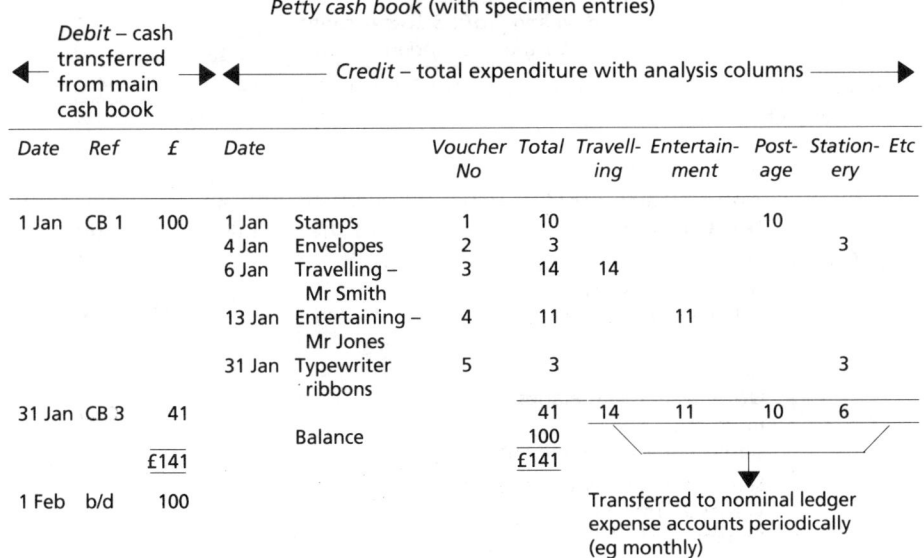

Petty cash book (with specimen entries)

Date	Ref	£	Date		Voucher No	Total	Travell-ing	Entertain-ment	Post-age	Station-ery	Etc
1 Jan	CB 1	100	1 Jan	Stamps	1	10			10		
			4 Jan	Envelopes	2	3				3	
			6 Jan	Travelling – Mr Smith	3	14	14				
			13 Jan	Entertaining – Mr Jones	4	11		11			
			31 Jan	Typewriter ribbons	5	3				3	
31 Jan	CB 3	41				41	14	11	10	6	
				Balance		100					
		£141				£141					
1 Feb	b/d	100									

Transferred to nominal ledger expense accounts periodically (eg monthly)

Debit – cash transferred from main cash book

Credit – total expenditure with analysis columns

Pro-forma financial statements

This chapter has covered a lot of ground. It you have understood its contents you should now be able to record, by double entry, a wide range of transactions. By way of conclusion, we look here in more detail at the 'end result' of all our recording – the final financial statements of the business.

There follows an outline trading and profit and loss account and balance sheet suitable for use in answering examination questions. We suggest you master these formats and use them in your examination.

Name
Trading and Profit & Loss Account
for the Year Ended ...

	£	£
Sales (net of returns)		X
Cost of sales		
Opening stock	X	
Add: Purchases (net of returns)	X	
Less: Closing stock	(X)	(X)
Gross profit		X
Add: Discounts received		X
Other non-trading income		X
		X
Less: Administration expenses		
Office wages and salaries	X	
Insurance	X	
Depreciation of equipment	X	(X)
Selling and distribution expenses		
Wages and salaries	X	
Commissions	X	
Advertising	X	
Transport and carriage out	X	(X)
Financial expenses		
Discounts allowed	X	
Bad debts	X	
Bank interest and charges	X	(X)
Net profit		£X

Balance Sheet as at ...

	Cost	Depn	£
Fixed assets			
Intangible assets			
Goodwill			XXX
Tangible assets			
Freehold land and buildings	XXX	XX	XXX
Leasehold land and buildings	XXX	XX	XXX
Plant and machinery	XXX	XX	XXX
Vehicles	XXX	XX	XXX
	XXX	XX	XXX
Investments			XXX
Total fixed assets			XXX
Current assets			
Stock		XXX	
Debtors and prepayments		XXX	
Cash at bank and in hand		XXX	
		XXX	
Less: Current liabilities			
Trade creditors	(XXX)		
Accruals	(XXX)	(XXX)	(XXX)
Net current assets			XXX
Less: Long-term liabilities			(XXX)
Financed by			XXX
Capital account			£XXX

Problems

Problem 3.1

A property of a business was rented at £250 per month payable monthly. The rent was three months in arrears on 31 December 1993 and five months in arrears on 31 December 1994. The rates were £1,200 per annum payable half yearly in advance on 1 April and 1 October in each year. At 31 December 1993 the rates for the half year to 31 March 1994 had not been paid, but these arrears were cleared and rates for 1994 were paid when due.

Required:

a Explain the nature of 'accruals' and 'prepayments' in preparing final accounts. Why may such adjustments be necessary?

(12 marks)

b From the information above prepare the *combined* rent and rates account for the year ended 31 December 1994 showing the figures that would appear for rent and rates in the profit and loss account and the figures in the balance sheet at 31 December 1994.

(8 marks)

Associated Examining Board – updated

Problem 3.2

Tom Thumb commenced a new venture on 1 July 1993, as a distributor of Kimples, a patented piece of household equipment.

The selling price of a Kimple has been fixed for 1993 and 1994 at £60. Tom Thumb has decided to prepare trading and profit and loss accounts for each three monthly period commencing with the three months to 30 September 1993. However, Tom Thumb is undecided as to the method of stock valuation he should use, whether it should be first in first out (FIFO) or last in first out (LIFO). It appears that he will be attracted to the method which shows 'the higher profit'.

Transactions for the first nine months of the venture are summarised as follows:

Date	Number of Kimbles	
	Purchases	Sales £
1993		
July	20 @ £10 each	
August	10 @ £12 each	
September		15
October	30 @ £14 each	
November		40
December	35 @ £15 each	
1994		
January	40 @ £16 each	
February		35
March	No purchases or sales	

Overhead expenses amounted to £100 each calendar month.
Required:

a Trading and profit and loss accounts for each of the first three accounting periods to 31 March 1994, using:

i first in first out stock valuation;

ii last in first out stock valuation.

b An objective comparison of the two methods of stock valuation used in this question and a reasoned recommendation to Tom Thumb concerning the method he should use.

(26 marks)
Associated Examining Board – updated

Problem 3.3

Ben Bow commenced trading as the sole distributor of Bangos in Maytown on 1 January 1993. During the succeeding two years Bow's dealings in Bangos were as follows:

Bangos		Purchases	Sales
1993	January	100 @ £100 each	
	May	60 @ £120 each	
	July		80 @ £200 each
	November	70 @ £130 each	
1994	March		40 @ £220 each
	April	50 @ £140 each	
	October		90 @ £230 each
	December		All remaining Bangos sold @ £240 each

Bow incurred expenses (including part time staff) for the operation of the Bangos exercise of £2,000 in each of the years 1993 and 1994.

In 1993 Bow was assisted by Peter Plow and in 1994 by Roger Roe; it is Bow's intention to pay a bonus to Plow of 25 per cent of the gross profit and bonus to Roe of 10 per cent of the gross profit in the year of their respective involvements.

In preparing his trading and profit and loss accounts for the years ended 31 December 1993 and 1994, Bow has decided to utilize the method of stock valuation which will give him the higher overall net profit. The methods of stock valuation to be considered are Last In First Out (LIFO) and First In First Out (FIFO).

In view of the Bangos distribution project, Bow decided against the purchase of a yacht costing £10,000 in December 1992. Instead, the £10,000 was used for the Bangos project. However, Bow now wishes to buy a yacht (same model as he considered in December 1992) and has been advised that the current cost is £15,000.

In becoming the sole distributor of Bangos Ben Bow had to discontinue his managerial post carrying a salary of £9,000 per annum.

Note: ignore taxation.
Required:

a Ben Bow's trading and profit and loss accounts for the years ended 31 December 1993 and 1994, using the following stock valuation methods:

  i   Last In First Out.

  ii First In First Out.

b A report addressed to Ben Bow advising him whether, on financial grounds, it has proved to be a wise decision to defer his yacht purchase. The report should be supported by appropriate computations.

Associated Examining Board – updated

Problem 3.4

Jack Jackson makes up the annual accounts of his business to 31 August in each year. It proved impossible to take stock on 31 August 1994, but a physical stock take was carried out on 10 September 1994 at which date the total stock, as shown on the stock sheets was £9,870, valued at cost. All sales were made at cost price plus 20 per cent; the following information is also relevant:

a Goods costing £360 were received from suppliers between l and 10 September 1994.

b Sales for the same period were £1,500 out of which goods, with a selling price of £150, were returned on 9 September.

c A figure of £680 had been carried forward to the next stock sheet as £860.

d One stock sheet had been overcast by £100 and another had been undercast by £40.

e Stock purchased in August 1994 for £760 was found to be unsuitable and returned to the suppliers on 3 September 1994.

f Goods with a selling price of £450 had been sent on 15 August to Clappers Ltd on a sale or return basis. They had not been included in the stock figure at 10 September and Clappers Ltd had not indicated whether or not they intended to buy the goods.

g Items which cost £120 had been in stock for several years and were now considered valueless.

h In April 1994, the firm bought 120 silk shirts at £10 each. By 31 August, 80 had been sold at £12 each; Jackson had taken two for personal use and three shirts could not be accounted for. The remaining shirts were included in stock valued at cost. The shirts had now gone out of fashion and their net realisable value was expected to be £8 each.

Required: prepare a statement to show the figure at which stock should be included in Jackson's accounts at 31 August 1994.

(15 marks)
Associated Examining Board – updated

Problem 3.5

During the year ended 30 September 1992 Silas Tapp had many problems trying to get his debtors to pay more promptly. The business is successful but Silas felt he should give more attention to the control of his debtors. He decided to establish a provision for doubtful debts at 30 September 1992.

Silas Tapp's debtors at 30 September 1992 totalled £39,321; after a careful examination of the list of debtors it was decided to make a specific doubtful debts provision for all the following debts.

T Barnes	264
A Camache Ltd	45
H Singh Ltd	72
M Grimmett	96
F Ming	60
K O'Reilly	184

In addition to the specific provision at 30 September 1992, a provision for doubtful debts of 4 per cent of the balance of debtors as at that date was created.

During the year ended 30 September 1993 the following events took place.

a T Barnes paid his debt in two equal instalments and has since paid all accounts promptly and is no longer considered to be a doubtful debtor.

b H Singh Ltd is in liquidation and a first and final dividend of 75p in the £ was received.

c M Grimmett has been declared bankrupt, however an interim payment of £56 has been received and a full settlement of the balance due is expected shortly.

d The liquidator of A Camache Ltd has informed creditors that it is very unlikely that they will receive any monies.

e The £184 due from K O'Reilly was paid in full.

f An agreement has been reached with F Ming that he will pay the outstanding debt during the year ended 30 September 1994. In spite of this agreement, Silas Tapp has decided to make a specific doubtful debt provision at 30 September 1993 for the £60 due.

g At 30 September 1993 R Viljoen and U McDuff Ltd, who owe £94 and £176 respectively, are now considered to be in difficulties and they will be added to the specific group of doubtful debtors.

h K Smit Ltd £70 and Q Toni £98 have been written off as bad debts.

i A bad debt of £52 relating to E Pancho written off during the year ended 30 September 1992 has been recovered.

j At 30 September 1993 it was felt that it would be a sound policy to maintain the specific doubtful debts provision as part of the overall doubtful debts provision. In addition a provision for doubtful debts was made of 4 per cent of the debts totalling £36,400 for which specific provision was not considered necessary.

Required:

a A calculation of the provision for doubtful debts at 30 September 1992 and 30 September 1993 using the basis indicated.

(16 marks)

b Prepare the bad debts account for the year ended 30 September 1993 (include bad debts recovered).

(6 marks)

c Prepare the provision for doubtful debts account for the year ended 30 September 1993.

(6 marks)

d State what you consider are the features of good control of debtors.

(8 marks)

e What are the likely adverse consequences if creditors are paid slowly?

(8 marks)

(44 marks)
Associated Examining Board
November 1993

Accounting for fixed assets | 4

Introduction

Fixed assets may be defined as assets which are acquired for use in the business. Current assets, by contrast, are assets acquired for resale (eg stock), or they result from the resale of assets (cash, debtors). The balance sheet presented at the end of 'Disposal of assets' (above) indicates that fixed assets may be tangible (they have a physical existence) or intangible (no physical existence) or investments.

Depreciation

Depreciation is an amount charged annually in the profit and loss account against the cost of an asset such that the asset is 'written off', ie reduced in book value to nil, by the end of its useful life.

There are a number of different ways of regarding depreciation. One is the layman's approach. If asked what 'depreciation' means he is likely to reply in terms of the fall in value of, say, his car between one year and the next. Another approach is to describe depreciation as a means of spreading the cost of the asset over its useful life. The accounting profession is now in favour of the latter, ie depreciation is seen as the allocation of the cost of fixed assets over the periods expected to benefit from its use – it is therefore an application of the accruals concept. Let us examine this in more detail.

Depreciation as a matching process

Depreciation is now regarded simply as an example of the accruals or matching concept. The object of owning fixed assets in a business is the contribution they make to its efficient running. Sometimes there is an element of choice in ownership, sometimes it is essential. For example, a mail order firm might decide not to have any delivery vehicles itself but to rely on the postal services, but it is difficult to see how a coal merchant could do so. From this it would follow that if the mail order firm sets its postal charges against its income for the year, so should the coal merchant set a proportion of the cost of his delivery vehicles. The only real difference is that the mail order firm operates on a pay-as-you-go basis whereas the coal merchant paid in advance. At the end of the day they will both just have expired costs. From this point of view, then, depreciation is charged against each year's profits because the income of each year benefits from the firm's possession of the assets, and therefore it would not be appropriate for any one year to bear a disproportionate share.

The book-keeping entries for depreciation are very simple:

DR   Profit and loss account (depreciation expense)
CR   Provision for depreciation account (or 'accumulated depreciation')

with the depreciation for the year. Here, as with doubtful debts earlier, we are seeing the use of a provision account as a means of reducing the value of an asset on the balance sheet. The principal methods of calculating what the depreciation is for a given year are now outlined.

Equal instalment ('straight line') method

This method spreads the depreciation equally over the period of anticipated use. The formula for calculating the annual depreciation is:

$$\frac{\text{Cost price} - \text{estimated residual value}}{\text{estimated life of asset}}$$

Example:

Plant details	£
Cost	500
Residual value	50
Expected life	9 years
The annual depreciation charge is:	£500 – £50
	9
=	£50 per year

Reducing balance method

This method spreads the provision by annual instalments of diminishing amount computed by taking a fixed percentage of the book value of the assets as reduced by previous depreciation. It involves heavier charges in the earlier years and relatively light charges in the later years.

Example:

Delivery lorry details		£
	Cost	15,000
	Estimated rate of depreciation	20% reducing balance
Year 1	Cost	15,000
	Depreciation	3,000
	Written down value (WDV)	£12,000
Year 2	WDV	12,000
	Depreciation (20% x £12,000)	2,400
	WDV	9,600
Year 3	WDV	9,600
	Depreciation (20% x £9,600)	1,920
	WDV	£7,680

Although a Nil balance is never reached if this method is strictly followed, it is normal procedure to write off the balance remaining at the end of the estimated life.

Merits of reducing balance v straight line methods

The arguments in favour of the reducing balance method are as follows:

a It most nearly accords with reality – generally speaking, any item loses value faster in the first year. This is particularly obvious in the case of cars – it makes a very substantial difference in the price whether a car is brand new or one year old, but very little difference as between ten and 11 years old. The higher charge in the early years of the reducing balance method reflects this.

b The lower charge in the later years helps even out the total expense of running a piece of equipment, as in later years although the depreciation charge is lower, repairs and maintenance expenditure will be higher.

c Assets tend to be more efficient earlier in their life – the higher charge in earlier years reflects the fact that the business derives more benefit from use of the asset.

In favour of the straight-line method:

a It is arithmetically very simple, which results in time-saving particularly when computing accumulated depreciation on disposal (see below).

b If each year's profit benefits equally from the ownership of the asset, then an equal charge should be made in each year. A five-year-old lorry may perform the delivery function just as adequately as a one-year old-lorry.

c The straight line method can be used for almost all assets, whereas the reducing balance method, even if suitable on the grounds of argument (b) in its favour in respect of plant and machinery, is not suitable for, say, leases, which amortise on a straight line basis. The straight line method saves complication, error and confusion without incurring any conceptual faults.

Other methods

Usage method
If it is possible to know the hours involved, this can be appropriate to certain types of machinery. If in one year a machine is used twice as much as in the next, depreciation could be apportioned in the ratio 2:1. Similarly, if it is accepted that a car deteriorated purely with the mileage covered in a year, depreciation could in theory be calculated accordingly.

Example:

Cost of machine	£9,500
Estimated residual value	£1,500
Estimated life	8 years
Estimated annual running hours	2,000 hours
(ie 50 weeks x 40 hours)	

Estimated life in running hours = 8 years x 2,000 hours = 16,000 hours

Depreciation rate for operating hour:

$$= \frac{\text{Original cost minus residual value}}{\text{Estimated life in running hours)}}$$

$$= \frac{£9,500 - £1,500}{16,000}$$

= £0.50 per operating hour

Assume that the machine is worked for more than 40 hours per week on average, because of shift work, overtime etc, and consequently it has a life of only five years. The depreciation charges might be calculated as follows:

Year	Actual operating hours £	Annual depreciation charge @ £0.50 per hour £
1	2,400	1,200
2	2,800	1,400
3	4,000	2,000
4	3,600	1,800
5	3,200	1,600
	£16,000	£8,000

Revaluation method

This is used mainly for such assets as loose tools, and is basically the difference between value at the beginning of the year plus additions less value at the year end:

	£
Valuation 1 Jan	2,500
Additions in year	1,250
Total	3,750
Actual value 31 Dec	3,000
Depreciation	£750

Sinking fund method

This method, which is very rarely used in practice, has far more in common with the concept of depreciation meaning building up funds for replacement.

Each year an amount is set aside from profits and invested, normally outside the business in government stocks etc, such that the annual amounts plus the interest received and re-invested equal the costs (or replacement price, if the firm is operating a system of inflation accounting) of the asset by the end of its useful life.

The double entry is as follows.

Annually:

DR	Profit and loss account
CR	Sinking fund

} with amount set aside

DR	Sinking fund investment account
CR	Cash book

} with amount withdrawn from general cash and invested outside the firm

When interest and dividends received:

DR	Sinking fund investment account (or sinking fund cash)
CR	Sinking fund

The sinking fund and the sinking fund investment account should always be equal and opposite amounts.

Depletion

In the case of mines, oilwells, quarries etc depreciation is usually charged on the amount taken out in the year (or, in the case of cemetaries, filled in!).

Description in the balance sheet

In a simple case, just cost, accumulated depreciation (do not confuse this with the depreciation for the year) and written down value would be shown, as illustrated below:

	Cost £	Depreciation £	WDV £
Plant and machinery	5,000	(1,000)	4,000
Fixtures and fittings	2,000	(500)	1,500
Motor vehicles	6,000	(2,500)	3,500
	£13,000	£(4,000)	£9,000

In a more complicated example a full schedule of cost, depreciation, additions and disposals would be needed. This would normally be given as a separate note to the accounts and merely a single figure transferred to the face of the balance sheet.

Disposal of assets

When an asset is disposed of there are five stages necessary to record its disposal and the resultant profit or loss:

a open a sale of asset account (sometimes called 'disposal account' or 'disposal of asset account');

b transfer the asset sold, at cost, to the sale of asset account (DR the disposal account; CR the asset account);

c record the receipt of cash (if any) in the sale of asset account (DR cash; CR the disposal account);

d transfer the accumulated amount of depreciation charged on the asset disposed of, from the provision for depreciation account to the sale of asset account (DR the provision for depreciation account; CR the disposal account);

e transfer the balance on the sale of asset account to the profit and loss account. This balance is the profit or loss made on the disposal.

Example:
XY commenced business on 1 January 1992. Plant was purchased as follows:

1992	1 Jan	£8,000
1992	1 Jul	£4,000
1994	1 Apr	£6,000

Depreciation is charged using the straight line method at a rate of 10 per cent on cost.

On 30 September 1993 the plant purchased on 1 July 1992 was sold for £2,400.

Accounts are prepared to 31 December.

Show the plant account, provision for depreciation account and sale of asset account for the three years.

The ledger accounts and calculations now follow. Ensure you understand exactly what has occurred and follow the double entry.

Plant account – open the plant account and enter all transactions.

DR			Plant Account		CR
Date		£	Date		£
1992			1992		
1 Jan	Cash	8,000	31 Dec	Balance c/d	12,000
1 Jul	Cash	4,000			
		£12,000			£12,000
1993			1993		
1 Jan	Balance b/d	12,000	30 Sep	Sale of asset a/c	4,000
			31 Dec	Balance c/d	8,000
		£12,000			£12,000
1994			1994		
1 Jan	Balance b/d	8,000	31 Dec	Balance c/d	14,000
1 Apr	Cash	6,000			
		£14,000			£14,000
1995					
1 Jan	Balance b/d	14,000			

Provision for depreciation account

a Calculate the depreciation charge for the first year (1992):

£8,000 x 10%   £800

$£4,000 \times 10\% \times \frac{6}{12}$ *   200

                          £1,000

b Calculate the depreciation charge applicable to the asset being sold, for the second year (1993):

$£4,000 \times 10\% \times \frac{9}{12}$ *   £200

c Calculate the accumulated depreciation charged in respect of the asset being sold:

£200 + £300   =   £500

(1992) (1993)

d Calculate the depreciation charge for the second year (1993) on the remaining asseting:

£8,000 x 10%   £800

e Calculate the depreciation charge for the third year (1994):

£8,000 x 10%   £800

$£6,000 \times 10\% \times \frac{9}{12}$ *   450

                          £1,250

* It is advisable in an examination to calculate the depreciation on a monthly basis unless the question states otherwise. This strictly follows the accruals or matching concept.

Frequently, both in examinations and in practice, a full year's depreciation is charged in the year of acquisition and none in the year of disposal, which on the straight line (though not the reducing balance) method, more or less averages out to the correct overall charge.

DR			Provision for Depreciation Account			CR
Date		£	Date			£
1992			1992			
31 Dec	Balance c/d	1,000	31 Dec	Profit & loss a/c		1,000
1993			1993			
30 Sep	Sale of asset a/c	500	1 Jan	Balance b/d		1,000
31 Dec	Balance c/d	1,600	30 Sep	Profit & loss a/c		300
			31 Dec	Profit & loss a/c		800
		2,100				2,100
1994			1994			
31 Dec	Balance c/d	2,850	1 Jan	Balance b/d		1,600
			31 Dec	Profit & loss a/c		1,250
		£2,850				£2,850
1995			1995			
			1 Jan	Balance b/d		2,850

Sale of plant account:

a DR with cost price of asset being sold, £4,000.

b CR with accumulated depreciation in respect of asset being sold, £500.

c CR with cash received, £2,400.

d Transfer balance to profit and loss account.

DR		£	Sale of Asset Account		CR
Date		£	Date		£
1993			1993		
30 Sep	Plant a/c	4,000	30 Sep	Provision for	
				depreciation a/c	500
				Cash	2,400
				*Profit & loss a/c	
				(loss)	1,100
		£4,000			£4,000

*You will see also this profit (loss) sometimes described as of 'over(under)-provision of depreciation in previous years'.

Revaluation of fixed assets

Assets that increase in value over a period of time (eg land and buildings) may be incorporated into the accounts at the revalued amount. This is a departure from the usual historic cost concept, but is allowed under the alternative accounting rules of the Company's Act.

On revaluation the difference between the new valuation and the carrying value (net book value) at the date of valuation is transferred to a revaluation reserve.

Fixed assets with a finite useful life are still depreciated although they are increasing in value. This may seem inappropriate until you remember that depreciation is the allocation of *cost/valuation* of the asset over the accounting periods expected to benefit from its use. The new depreciation charge is based on the new valuation which is allocated over the remaining useful life of the asset.

Example:
Freehold premises are purchased in 1992 at a cost of £70,000, comprising land £20,000 and buildings £50,000. The buildings have an estimated useful life of 25 years, and no residual value. After five years the land and building are professionally revalued at £160,000, comprising £70,000 for the land and the balance of £90,000 for the buildings. At this date the buildings have a remaining useful life of 20 years. After a further five years the land and buildings are sold for £200,000.

Depreciation is charged on buildings only, in full in the year of acquisition, with no depreciation in the year of sale.

Calculate:

a The annual depreciation charge for each year up to the date of revaluation and then for the years up to the date of sale;

b the revaluation surplus to be transferred to the revaluation reserve;

c the profit/loss on sale; and

d the balance sheet value of the land and buildings at the end of each year.

Solution:

a Depreciation charge: depreciation for the five years *prior to revaluation* is calculated as the *cost* of the buildings £50,000 spread over the *estimated useful life of 25 years* (£50,000/25 years) ie £2,000 per annum. Depreciation for the period *after revaluation* is calculated as the *valuation* of the building £90,000 spread over the *remaining useful life* (£90,000/20 years) ie £4,500 per annum.

b Revaluation surplus: this is calculated as the difference between the new valuation of land and buildings and the carrying value at the date of revaluation.

		£	£
New value			160,000
Net book value at end of year 5:	Land	20,000	
	Buildings	40,000	
(£50,000 less £10,000 depreciation)			60,000
Revaluation surplus			£100,000

The revaluation surplus is shown on the balance sheet as a revaluation reserve. If it arises in an unincorporated business it must be shown with capital.

c Profit/loss on sale: this is the difference between the proceeds of sale and the carrying value (net book value) at the date of sale.

	£	£	£
Proceeds of sale			200,000
Net book value at the end of year 10	Land	Building	
Valuation	70,000	90,000	
Acc depreciation	–	(22,500)	
Net book value	£70,000	£67,500	(137,500)
			£62,500

The profit on sale is credited to the profit and loss account as usual.

d Balance sheet net book value:

Year	Cost/Valuation £	Depreciation £	NBV £
1	70,000	2,000	68,000
2	70,000	4,000	66,000
3	70,000	6,000	64,000
4	70,000	8,000	62,000
5	70,000	10,000	60,000
6	160,000	4,500	155,500
7	160,000	9,000	151,000
8	160,000	13,500	146,500
9	160,000	18,000	142,000
10	160,000	22,500	137,500

Summary of book-keeping entries for revaluation and sale

	£	£
Revaluation of asset:		
Fixed asset – increase in value	90,000	
Provision for depreciation – eliminate	10,000	
Revaluation reserve		100,000
Depreciation after revaluation:		
Depreciation expense (profit & loss) } years 5 to 10	4,500	
Provision for depreciation (balance sheet) }		4,500
Disposal of asset:		
Fixed asset – transfer to disposal a/c		160,000
Provision for depreciation – transfer		
to disposal a/c	22,500	
Disposal a/c (160,000 – 22,500)	137,500	
Disposal a/c – transfer proceeds/profit	62,500	200,000
Profit & loss a/c		62,500

FRS 3 Reporting financial performance

Chapter 16 together with the section on published accounts for companies deals with the requirements of FRS 3 in more detail. However, it should be noted that the revaluation surplus calculated in the example above is to be shown in a new *statement of recognised gains and losses*, described as an *unrealised surplus*, in accordance with FRS 3. In addition, a new note to the accounts called *note of historical cost profit and losses* must be prepared by companies who choose to revalue fixed assets. This shows the profit before and after tax adjusted to add back the extra depreciation arising because of the revaluation and the adjustment for the extra profit that would be charged in the profit and loss account if the asset had not been revalued.

Annually, as the asset is depreciated and, finally, when the asset is sold, a proportion of the unrealised revaluation reserve becomes realised. This realisation can be demonstrated by making a transfer from the revaluation reserve to the profit and loss reserve in the balance sheet. (They are not disclosed in the profit and loss account itself.)

However, at this stage in your studies it is sufficient for you to be aware that revaluation of assets will reappear in Chapter 16, and that if you have any difficulties at that stage you should return to this chapter and study the calculations demonstrated above.

Problems

Problem 4.1

Bennie Ltd was formed on 1 January 1992 with an issued capital of 500,000 ordinary shares of £1 each. The company reported profits for the years to 31 December 1992 and 1993 of £60,000 and £75,000 respectively and draft accounts for the year to 31 December 1994 show a profit of £70,000. A dividend of 12 per cent on the ordinary share capital was paid late in December each year. The company's fixed assets, all of which were bought on 1 January 1992 and which are still held at 31 December 1994 were:

	£	Estimated life in years (from 1 January 1992)
Freehold land	50,000	indefinite life
Buildings	200,000	indefinite life
Plant	160,000	10 years
Vehicles	70,000	5 years

Depreciation where appropriate, was provided in the accounts on a straight line basis on assets in use at the year-end, ignoring the possibility of any resale or scrap value.

Before finalising the 1994 draft accounts (which had been prepared on the same basis as in earlier years) the company reviewed its depreciation policy and decided that as from the 1994 accounts onwards, buildings would be depreciated at 2 per cent per annum on the straight line basis, and that vehicles should be depreciated at 30 per cent per annum on the reducing balance basis.

Required:

a Calculate the revised depreciation charge for 1994 and show how the effects of the change in accounting for depreciation should be dealt with in the company's published accounts.

(9 marks)

b Calculate the increase in the company's working capital in each of the years 1992, 1993 and 1994.

(6 marks)

c Explain *three* implications of the decision to change depreciation policy.

(9 marks)

Associated Examining Board – updated

Problem 4.2

S and P Manufacturing Co Ltd has recently purchased new plant and machinery which cost £58,000. Delivery and installation of the new machinery cost £5,000. The company expects to use the machinery for four years after the end of which it will be sold for scrap. The following estimates have been agreed concerning its operation and year end valuation:

Year	Running hours	Market value £
1	9,500	40,000
2	12,000	25,000
3	8,000	12,000
4	10,500	3,000 equal to scrap value

You are also informed that the company could invest funds temporarily outside the company during the four year period at 10 per cent interest per annum. In order to accumulate sufficient funds for replacement the company would have to set aside £12,928 at the end of each of the four years.

Required:

a Calculate for each of the four years the annual depreciation charge, using each of the following methods:

i Reducing balance (reducing instalment) method using a rate of 40 per cent.

ii Usage (units of service) method.

iii Revaluation method.

iv Sinking fund method (including interest on the sinking fund).

(12 marks)

b Discuss the view that there is no 'right' method of providing for depreciation, and that depreciation is rarely adequate to provide for the replacement of fixed assets.

(8 marks)

Associated Examining Board – updated

Problem 4.3

Chefs and Co operate a small private catering business for domestic and other social occasions. The company commenced business on 1 March 1990 when it purchased a specially designed food delivery van (G 11 ABC) for £12,000. A depreciation rate of 25 per cent using the reducing balance method is applied.

As trade expanded it was agreed to replace the existing delivery van by an improved model and in addition, a smaller ordinary van was to be purchased. On 1 March 1992 a quotation for a nearly new improved model (J 22 CBC) was received. The details were as follows:

	£
Basic cost	19,782
Number plates	12
Comprehensive insurance	238
10 gallons of diesel fuel	26
Delivery charge	56
Road fund licence	200
Specially fitted food containers for the van	1,200
Service and parts	110
Sign-writing on van	150
	21,774
Trade-in allowance for G 11 ABC	£6,200

The other small van (J 33 CBC) was quoted at an 'on the road' price of £9,620. This figure, apart from the basic cost only included the road fund licence of £120.

Both quotations were accepted and the vehicles concerned were purchased on 1 March 1992.

Required:

a The following ledger accounts for the period 1 March 1990 until 28 February 1993:

   i   vehicles at cost account;

   ii   depreciation provision on vehicles account;

   iii disposal of vehicles account.

(20 marks)

b The relevant extracts in the profit and loss account for the year ended 28 February 1993 showing the effects of *all* the transactions involved.

(6 marks)

c The relevant extract in the balance sheet as at 28 February 1993 relating to the vehicles.

(4 marks)

d Explain what is meant by the term 'depreciation' and why it is necessary to provide for it.

(18 marks)

(48 marks)
Associated Examining Board
Summer 1993

Accounting for debtors and creditors | 5

Introduction – control accounts

An accounting system might consist of many hundreds of accounts involving the entering of perhaps thousands of transactions. It needs only one transaction to be entered incorrectly to cause the trial balance not to balance, and in those circumstances a great deal of searching, checking, and delay could occur in order to correct the error. What is needed is a system whereby the ledger system can be divided into sections and each section balanced independently thereby localising errors. This localisation of errors is one of the main functions of control accounts which normally apply to debtors and creditors but are sometimes encountered in other contexts.

The advantages of control accounts are:

a They enable each sales and purchases ledger to be balanced independently of the other ledgers, thereby localising errors. Ledgers may be divided alphabetically, geographically etc.

b The trial balance can be balanced even though there may be errors within the sales or purchases ledgers. This is because the trial balance will include the control accounts totals, and not the individual sales or purchases ledger balances.

c The fact that sales or purchases ledgers do not balance with their respective control accounts need not delay the preparation of final accounts.

d The control accounts keep a running total of trade debtors and trade creditors.

e Sales and purchases ledger accounting sections can be operated independently with a high degree of control. One employee may operate the sales ledger, another the control account.

A control account is a total account. The general principle of operating a control account is that transactions which are entered into individual accounts within the ledger being controlled must also be entered in total within the control account.

We should stress at this stage that, although accounting systems vary, it is normally the control account in the nominal ledger which is part of the double entry. The ledgers being controlled are 'memorandum' records not normally part of the double entry system.

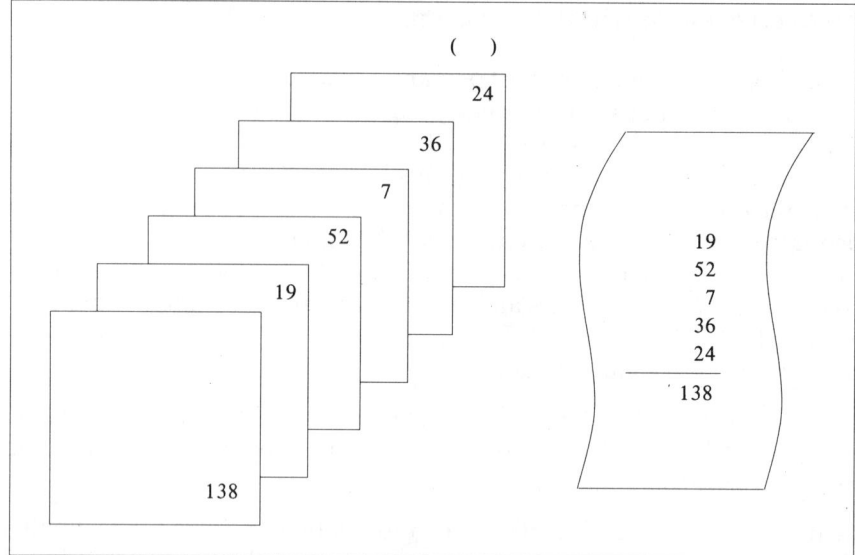

The diagram illustrates a purchases ledger together with its control account. A batch of invoices have been listed in the purchase day book and have been posted to the credit of individual suppliers accounts. The batch total is posted to the credit of the purchases ledger control account.

If this principle is followed reliably then at any time the sum of the balances on the individual ledger accounts should agree with the balance on the control account.

Example – sales ledger of Sellit Ltd

Week commencing 2 April 1995

Date	Narrative		£	
Monday 2nd	Sold goods to	J Smith	900	
		A Brown	1,000	
		D Jones	600	
Tuesday 3rd	Sold goods to	B Green	500	
		G Davis	400	
Wednesday 4th	Sold goods to	M Black	200	
		F White	300	
Thursday 5th	Received cash from	J Smith	400	on account
		A Brown	950	(5% discount allowed)
Friday 6th	B Green returned goods to the value of		100	
	Sold goods to F White		200	

Sales Day Book

Date		£	£
2.4.95	J Smith	900	
	A Brown	1,000	
	D Jones	600	2,500
3.4.95	B Green	500	
	G Davis	400	900
4.4.95	M Black	200	
	F White	300	500
5.4.95			
6.4.95	F White	200	200
			£4,100

Returns Inwards Day Book

Date	£
6.4.95	100

In this illustration it is assumed that Sellit Ltd is a new business, and that the list of transactions at the beginning represents the first week's trading. We are dealing only with the sales side here, although exactly the same principles apply to purchases. Sellit Ltd will initially record the sales in the sales day book, which, as has already been mentioned, is used to save the labour of recording every single sale in the sales account in the nominal ledger, as only the total sales figure for the year is required for entry into the trading account, and for this purpose a daily, weekly or even monthly total is perfectly adequate. The sales day book will not normally be a handwritten book; it will usually be composed of carbon copies of the sales invoices sent to the customer with daily, weekly or monthly add-list totals, or, increasingly, it may be a computer-produced listing.

Provided that the sales day book is complete and accurate, the postings to the ledgers can wait until the book-keeper has time to deal with them. When the postings are done, the debit entry for each item of sales will be to the personal account of the customer in the sales ledger; so, for example, the first entry in the sales day book was goods worth £900 to J Smith; £900 will be debited to J Smith's account, and similar entries made for the other sales on the 2nd, 3rd, 4th and 6th of April. These as we have mentioned are 'memorandum' entries, not part of double entry. If Sellit Ltd is using a control account, the double entry is completed with the *total* sales (£4,100) being debited to the control account and credited to the sales account.

On 5 April cash is received from two customers.

The receipts are listed in the cash book (this, you will recall is part of the double entry system) and a credit entry is made in the relevant customer's account. Periodically, receipts are totalled in the cash book and the total credit to the debtors control account, thus completing the double entry.

Sellit Ltd's cash book might be structured as follows:

DR	Sellit Ltd – Cash Book (debit side)			
Date	Discount allowed	Sales ledger	Other	£
5.4.95				
J Smith		400		400
A Brown	50	950		950
Rent of garage sub-let			100	100
	£50	£1,350	£100	£1,450

In this example the debit side of the cash book has, in addition to the ordinary total column, firstly a column which indicates which of the receipts relate to the main selling business of the company, as opposed to miscellaneous other receipts such as VAT refunds, investment or rental income, or sales of fixed assets, all of which are peripheral to the main trading concern. (There would be similar, though normally more extensive, analysis columns on the payments side of the cash book.) Secondly, there is a column for recording discounts allowed to customers. It is convenient to record these discounts here, as it is only when the customer actually pays for the goods that the firm knows whether or not he intends to take advantage of the discount offered. It must be emphasised at this point that this column does not form part of the double entry, it is *memorandum* only. It is, in fact, effectively a discounts allowed day book, and the daily, weekly, or monthly totals can be posted easily to the debit of the discounts allowed account in the nominal ledger, with the credit entry being recorded in the debtors control account.

This, then, is how the entries in the customers' accounts in the sales ledger are built up – sales are debited individually from the records in the sales day book, returns credited similarly from the returns inwards day book. Cash and discounts are picked up from the debit of the cash book, and posted to the credit of the customer's account.

Sellit Ltd – Sales Ledger

DR			A Brown			CR
Date		£	Date			£
2.4.95	Goods	1,000	5.4.95	Cash		950
				Discount allowed		50

DR			M Black			CR
Date		£	Date			£
4.4.95	Goods	200				

DR			G Davis			CR
Date		£	Date			£
3.4.95	Goods	400				

DR			B Green			CR
Date		£	Date			£
3.4.95	Goods	500	6.4.95	Returns		100

DR			D Jones		CR
Date		£	Date		£
2.4.95	Goods	600			

DR			J Smith		CR
Date		£	Date		£
2.4.95	Goods	900	5.4.95	Cash	400

DR			F White		CR
Date		£	Date		£
4.4.95	Goods	300			
6.4.95	Goods	200			

These same records can now be used to build up a control account that will help verify the figures in the final accounts.

The week's total sales of £4,100 have been credited in total to the sales account in the nominal ledger; what is also done is to post this total figure to the debit of the sales ledger control account. Remember, another name for control accounts is 'total accounts' and this is exactly what they are – a summary or totalling, of all the items which would appear *individually* on the accounts in the personal ledgers. The total of £100 on the returns inwards day book is posted to the credit of the sales ledger column and discount allowed column in the cash book.

DR			Sellit Ltd – Sales Ledger Control Account		CR
Date		£	Date		£
2.4.95	Balance b/d	Nil	W.E. 6.4.95	Returns (2)	100
				Cash (3)	1,350
W.E. 6.4.95	Goods (1)	4,100		Discounts allowed (4)	50
				Balance c/d	2,600
		£4,100			£4,100
6.4.95	Balance b/d	2,600			

(1) From sales day book.
(2) From returns inwards day book.
(3) From sales ledger column in cash book.
(4) From discounts allowed column in cash book.

DR		Sales Account		CR
	£			£
			W.E. 6.4.95	
			Debtors control a/c	4,100

What has been achieved? Firstly, it is very easy to find the debtors figure as at 6 April – only one account has to be balanced to arrive at the figure of £2,600 whereas without this control account it would be necessary to balance off each account in the sales ledger and then list the balances thus:

A Brown – nil, M Black – £200, G Davis – £400, B Green – £400, D Jones – £600, V Smith – £500, F White – £500; total £2,600. This is not too arduous here where there are only seven accounts, but it would be very time consuming if the sales ledger occupied seven volumes, which in a large company it might well do.

More important, however, is the situation that would occur if the two totals did *not* agree at £2,600. Suppose that the sale to G Davis had been posted to his account as £40 in error instead of £400. On receiving his monthly statement, G Davis *might* have pointed out the error, but human nature being what it is, he is far more likely to pay the £40 and keep quiet; and then only by accident would the company discover its loss. If a control account is kept, however, it will immediately be seen that the control account balance is £2,600 but the total of the list of balances would be £2,240, which would immediately locate the difference to the sales ledger, thereby considerably reducing the amount of detailed checking to be done.

To take another example, suppose the total in the sales day book had been miscast, that is, added up wrongly, and £4,200 had been posted and not £4,100. Then the list of balances would have totalled £2,600 but the sales ledger control £2,700. On checking the error would be found and the misposting (which would have affected not only the sales ledger control account but also the sales account in the nominal ledger and therefore the trial balance) could be corrected.

The sales ledger control account contains in total everything that appears on any individual debtor's account, so, for example, in addition to the entries already described you must remember to enter on the credit of the sales ledger control such items as bad debts, credits or allowances for faulty goods, and on the debit such entries as dishonoured cheques. You should also bear in mind that in most businesses there will be a few debtors who in fact have *credit* balances – customers who pay in advance, for example. You may well find, therefore, that there is both a debit and a credit balance brought down and to carry down on the control account. You should not net these off, this should only be done where there is a legal right of set-off which will not normally be the case.

Purchase ledger

Everything we have seen so far relates to the sales ledger and the sales ledger control account. The purchase ledger control account works in exactly the same way.

Example:

DR	Buyit Ltd – Purchase Ledger Control Account		CR
	£		£
Balance b/d	300	Balance b/d	20,000
Cash (2)	380,000	Purchases (1)	400,000
Discounts received (3)	10,000		
Returns outwards (4)	15,500		
Balance c/d (5)	14,650	Balance c/d (6)	450
	£420,450		£420,450

(1) From purchases day book.
(2) From analysis column in cash book.
(3) From memorandum column in cash book.
(4) From returns outwards day book.
(5) Trade creditors at year end.
(6) Suppliers overpaid at year end.

The purchase ledger control account looks very similar to the sales ledger control – except that most of the entries are on the opposite side. Totals will be entered daily, weekly or monthly from the purchases day book to the credit of the control account; cash and discounts from the analysis columns on the credit of the cash book to the debit of the control account; returns outwards totals from the returns book to the debit of the account. At the end of the period the balances carried down represent suppliers to whom money is owed at the end of the year, and also any who have been overpaid. As with the sales ledger balances, these should not be netted off – the £450 debit balance should be included with debtors on the balance sheet, and any credit balances on the sales ledger should be included with creditors.

You may, by the way, be confused by some of the terms used in practice by businesses: the sales ledger is also known as the debtors ledger, and the purchase ledger is often called the bought ledger or creditors ledger. Control accounts are also frequently described as total accounts – unfortunately, terminology is not standardised.

Contras

Occasionally you will find items called 'contras' in control accounts. A contra entry is made when the same firm is both a debtor and a creditor. In the illustration below for instance a firm, Bolts Ltd, manufactures nuts and bolts. It buys its raw materials from Steel Ltd, and therefore Steel Ltd has an account in the purchase ledger. On 1 March, Bolts Ltd buys goods to the value of £6,000 from Steel Ltd and duly enters this in the ledger (and control account). Subsequently on 15 March Steel Ltd buys a quantity of nuts and bolts to the value of £4,500, thus becoming a debtor. As at 31 March, when the monthly statements go out, Steel Ltd will ask Bolts Ltd for £6,000 while Bolts Ltd will ask Steel Ltd for £4,500. It is much simpler for everyone if Bolts Ltd just sends Steel Ltd the net balance of £1,500 rather than both parties writing cheques for the full amount. In other words, the £4,500 is 'contra'd out' between the two by crediting the sales ledger and the sales ledger control, and debiting the purchase ledger and purchase ledger control. Note that the entry must be recorded in *both* the control accounts and in the personal accounts.

Bolts Ltd
Sales Ledger
Steel Ltd

DR					CR
Date		£	Date		£
15.3	Goods	4,500	31.3	Contra	4,500

Purchase Ledger
Steel Ltd

DR					CR
Date		£	Date		£
31.3	Contra	4,500	31.3	Goods	6,000
	Cash	1,500			

Specimen question

Questions involving correction of errors on control accounts are an excellent test of your grasp of the principles of double entry. An example of such a question appears below:

Illustration

W Simpson keeps a sales ledger control account. At 30 June the debit balance of £3,940 did not agree with the list of balances extracted from the sales ledger. Investigation revealed the following errors:

a A transfer of £25 was made from A Evans' account in the sales ledger to clear part of the amount owing to him in the purchases ledger. This transfer had not been recorded in the control accounts.

b The sales day book had been overcast by £10.

c £30 owing by D Brown had been omitted from the list of balances extracted from the sales ledger.

d The total of the discount allowed column in the cash book had been undercast by £1.

You are required:

a to prepare the necessary journal entries to correct the errors;

b to enter the balance of £3,940 in the sales ledger control account, and record the adjustments arising out of the corrections;

c to calculate the effect of the above errors on net profit for the year.

Answer:
a

Narrative	DR	CR
	£	£
Purchase ledger contol account	25	
Sales ledger control account		25
Contra entry re A Evans		
Sales account	10	
Sales ledger control account		10
Correction of overcast of sales day book		
Discount allowed account	1	
Sales ledger control account		1
Correction of undercast of discount allowed		

Item (c) does not require a journal entry – it is not part of the double entry system.

b

DR	Sales Ledger Control Account		CR
	£		£
Balance b/d	3,940	Purchase ledger contra	25
		Sales account	10
		Discount allowed	1
		Balance c/d	3,904
	£3,940		£3,940

c

	£	£
Additions to profit		nil
Deductions:		
Reduction in sales	10	
Increase in discounts	1	11
Net decrease in profits		£11

Problems

Problem 5.1

The following information relates to the debtors' and creditors' control accounts for the month of April 1995 and is taken from the books of a trading company.

(Note: You are advised that not all the following information affects the control accounts.)

Balances at 1 April	£
Debtors' ledger (debit)	65,200
Debtors' ledger (credit)	900
Creditors' ledger (credit)	37,400
Creditors' ledger (debit)	100
Credit sales	213,500
Credit purchases	106,700
Cash sales	71,200
Provision for doubtful debts	3,500
Cash received from debtors	179,800
Cash paid to creditors	87,100
Purchases returns	1,500
Sales returns	2,300
Discounts received	2,050
Bad debts written off	700
Bills payable accepted	3,300
Discounts allowed	3,400
'Contras' between debtors' and creditors' ledger	1,200

Balances at 30 April	£
Debtors' ledger (credit)	700
Creditors' ledger (debit)	150

Required:

a Prepare for the month of April 1995 either the debtors' ledger control account or the creditors' ledger control account.

(6 marks)

b Explain the advantages of control accounts and say how 'contra' items may arise.

(6 marks)

Associated Examining Board – updated

Problem 5.2

The accounting staff of Jura Ltd have found it increasingly difficult to supervise and monitor the large number of debtors and creditors of the company. As a consequence of this problem the accountant has decided to introduce control accounts.

The first step was to extract the total balances from the personal ledgers and these were subsequently confirmed. The sales ledger at 1 October 1993 revealed debit balances amounting to £63,010 and credit balances of £130. Similarly the purchases ledger contained debit balances totalling £85 and credit balances of £41,530.

During October 1993 the following transactions occurred:

	£
Cash sales	1,518
Credit sales	309,079
Credit purchases	209,196
Cash purchases	614
Administration expenses	4,700
Cash overpaid refunded by supplier	168
Carriage outwards	2,416
Amounts received from debtors and paid into the bank	335,426
Debtors' cheques returned marked 'Refer to drawer'	683
Returns inwards	4,342
Purchases returns	3,529
Recoverable transport costs paid on behalf of customers	700
Amount paid to creditors	217,934

A further scrutiny of the transactions during October revealed the following errors and adjustments:

a In the amounts received from debtors was a cheque for £48 relating to commission receivable.

b A purchase invoice for £103 had been processed as a sales invoice.

c Discounts received and discounts allowed were totalled in the cash book and amounted to £390 and £145 respectively.

d Two bad debts of £60 and £117 were revealed and were required to be written off.

e A credit customer, Tiree Ltd, has been given a monthly rebate of 5 per cent. Their purchases in October were £800. This is to be taken into account on 31 October.

f At 31 October there were credit balances totalling £36 in the sales ledger, but there were no debit balances in the purchases ledger.

g Debit balances totalling £1,562 in the sales ledger were offset against credit balances in the purchases ledger.

Required:

a Prepare a sales ledger control account and a purchases ledger control account for the month ended 31 October 1993.

(26 marks)

b What are the benefits of operating control accounts?

(6 marks)

(32 marks)
Associated Examining Board
November 1993

Receipts and payments accounts | 6

Definition

A receipt and payments account is a summary of *actual* cash *received and paid* during the period:

a   prepared by clubs, associations and non-profit-making organisations who do not prepare income and expenditure account and balance sheet;

b   also used as a basis for preparing accounts from incomplete records.

A receipts and payments account can be viewed as a summarised cash book.

General

Receipts and payments accounts leave little scope for skilful arrangement. The principal aim is to show the receipts and payments of an organisation in as much detail as is in keeping with the simplicity of such an account.

The opening and closing balances must be included in order to balance the account but, if possible, they should be entered in such a way that they do not become included in the totals of receipts and payments for the year.

Where there are both receipts and payments in respect of one function or aspect of the organisation's work, eg a raffle or a disco, then one should be deducted from the other so that the *net* result is shown.

Contents

a   Opening bank (or cash) balance.

b   Summary of amounts *actually* received or paid during the period. No adjustment is made for accrued income and expenses – this is, you will recall, a summarised cash book.

c   Receipts entered on the debit side.

d   Payments entered on the credit side.

e   Closing balance represents the bank balance (or cash in hand).

You should note that *non-cash* items (eg depreciation) are not included. Also, no distinction is made between capital transactions (eg a purchase of a fixed asset) and revenue items (eg maintenance or repairs).

Example

The analysed cash book of the County Social Club shows the following receipts and payments for the year ended 31 December 1994.

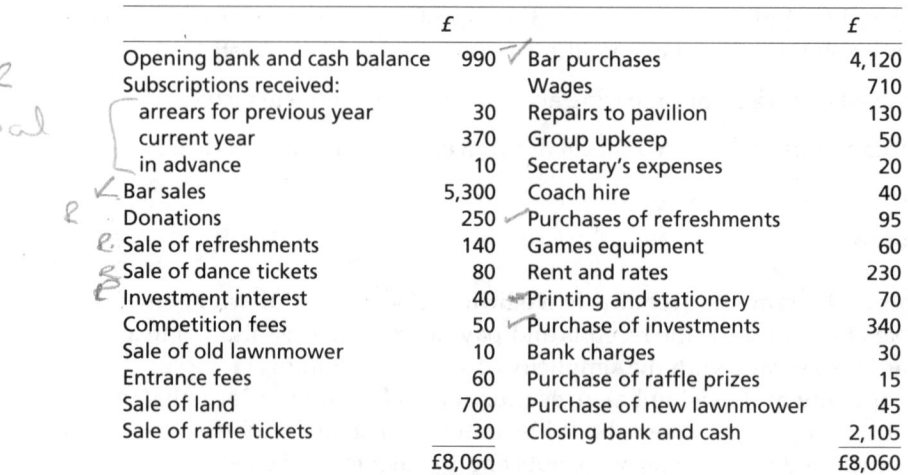

	£		£
Opening bank and cash balance	990	Bar purchases	4,120
Subscriptions received:		Wages	710
arrears for previous year	30	Repairs to pavilion	130
current year	370	Group upkeep	50
in advance	10	Secretary's expenses	20
Bar sales	5,300	Coach hire	40
Donations	250	Purchases of refreshments	95
Sale of refreshments	140	Games equipment	60
Sale of dance tickets	80	Rent and rates	230
Investment interest	40	Printing and stationery	70
Competition fees	50	Purchase of investments	340
Sale of old lawnmower	10	Bank charges	30
Entrance fees	60	Purchase of raffle prizes	15
Sale of land	700	Purchase of new lawnmower	45
Sale of raffle tickets	30	Closing bank and cash	2,105
	£8,060		£8,060

In order to submit the above facts to the club members and management in a more intelligible form, the analysis can be presented in the form of a receipts and payments account as follows:

The County Social Club
Receipts and Payments Account for the Year Ended 31 December 1994

	£	£		£	£
Opening balance		990			
Subscriptions:			Wages		710
arrears for last year	30		Repairs to pavilion		130
current year	370		Group upkeep		50
in advance	10	410	Secretary's expenses		20
			Coach hire		40
Donations		250	Games equipment		60
Competition fees		50	Rent and rates		230
Entrance fees		60	Printing and stationery		70
Sale of land		700	Bank charges		30
Bar sales	5,300		Purchase of investments	340	
Bar purchases	(4,120)	1,180	Investment interest	(40)	300
Sale of refreshments	140		Purchase of new		
Purchase of refreshments	(95)	45	lawnmower	45	
Sale of raffle tickets	30		Sale of old lawnmower	(10)	35
Purchase of raffle prizes	(15)	15			
Sale of dance tickets		80	Closing balance		2,105
		£3,780			£3,780

Limitations

As it is a cash book summary, no account is taken of accrued expenditure or prepayments, increases or decreases in stocks, depreciation, or capital as opposed to revenue expenditure. All it can show is the excess of receipts over payments, or vice versa, which is not the same as the profit or loss. As such, it is only really suitable for organisations that operate purely on a cash basis and have no assets of any material value.

Except therefore in the smallest and simplest case a receipts and payments account, by itself, can never be a fully satisfactory form of annual account. It can, in fact, be positively misleading, unless it is read with a full appreciation of its limitations. For example, it might disclose an excess of receipts over payments, due to a delay in paying certain items of expenditure the payment of which may reveal an excess of expenditure over income.

However, current accounting practice requires companies to prepare and publish a cash flow statement, to supplement their balance sheet. This statement is, in effect, a receipt and payments account in a prescribed form.

Incomplete records | 7

Introduction

The term 'incomplete records' can refer to any shortcomings in the system of double entry book-keeping, as a result of which double entry records have not been kept, ranging from a total absence of any records whatsoever to a failure to complete certain final entries. We will first look at the extreme situation where there are no written records at all.

No written records available

Illustration:

Shiner is a window cleaner who keeps no records of his receipts or expenditure. On 1 January 1994 he had net assets estimated at £4,000. You ascertain the following:

a He gives his wife £40 per week for housekeeping.

b He has a car for which the estimated weekly running costs are £10 (excluding depreciation). He does not use the car for business purposes.

c During the year he took his family on a holiday costing £900.

d During the year he won £400 in a lottery.

e On 31 December 1994 his net assets are estimated at £8,000.

Shiner, as a window cleaner, has very little need to keep written records. All his takings are in cash paid over immediately, so he has no need of a sales ledger. He probably purchases what few materials he needs for cash over the counter and is unlikely to keep receipts, and his assets, other than perhaps his car, are likely to be too little in value to be worth recording. Therefore any estimate of his profits during the year has to be made by way of examining the movements on his net assets.

This estimate is made by drawing up a balance sheet or statement of affairs at the beginning and end of the period. If his net assets have increased during the year then he must have made a profit, unless there is evidence of capital coming from elsewhere – a legacy, say. This should be clear if you remember the basic accounting equation: capital equals assets minus liabilities. The difference in net assets between the beginning and end of the year must be represented by the difference between the opening and closing capital. After adjusting for any other changes in capital during the year the balance must be caused by profits earned during the year.

The profit will not, however, simply be the full increase in assets – the trader must have been drawing cash to live on during the year and the increase in net assets is really equivalent to savings made. Therefore, an estimate has to be made of his drawings during the year, taking into account such factors as the size of his house, whether he runs one or more cars, whether his wife works, how many children he has and so forth. When this figure has been calculated it is added to the increase in assets to find his total profit for the year.

	Shiner		
Calculation of profit for year ended 31.12.94		£	£
Net assets at end of period			8,000
Add: Drawings			
Housekeeping (£40 x 52 weeks)		2,080	
Motor expenses (£10 x 52 weeks)		520	
Holiday		900	
		3,400	
Less: Capital introduced		400	3,000
			11,000
Deduct: Net assets at beginning of period			4,000
Estimated profit for period			£7,000

So, in the illustration, the computation starts off with Shiner's net assets on 31 December 1994. To this figure of £8,000 we add back those amounts we know have been spent during the year – housekeeping of £40 per week, motor expenses at £10 per week and the holiday, less the money won on the lottery, giving a net expenditure out of cash takings of £3,000. In total, then, Shiner has had access to £11,000 of assets during the year. He started off with only £4,000, so during the year his excess of receipts over business expenses – his profit, in other words – must have been £7,000.

This could be checked by looking at his capital account, remembering capital = net assets:

DR				CR
	£			£
Drawings	3,400	Opening balance		4,000
		Profit		7,000
Closing balance	8,000	Capital paid in		400
	£11,400			£11,400

Partial written records available

Assuming the business is not a newly commenced one there will presumably be a copy of last year's final accounts available. From last year's balance sheet we can pick up the opening figures for the current year – opening capital, debtors, creditors, cash and assets. The other information usually available is the bank statements and/or a cash book. In practice the analysis of the bank statements into trade purchases and the various categories of expense payments takes some time, but in an examination a bank statement summary is normally given in the question, and from this point onwards the process resembles that of putting together a jigsaw puzzle, by constructing working accounts and filling in the missing figures, either solely from the bank statement information or by the additional and often purely verbal information given by the proprietor.

Very often we may need to find figures for sales and purchases. Let us consider purchases. This is found by constructing a 'total purchases account' such as is shown below. The total purchases account is very similar to a purchase ledger control account except that it includes cash purchases. The opening balance of creditors brought forward will be picked up from the previous year's balance sheet; the cash purchases from the estimates given by the proprietor, or from a rough cash book, or petty cash book if there is one. The discounts received figure will again be an estimate by the proprietor, but the bank purchases figure will come from the analysis of the bank statements. The balance carried down will be either estimated by the proprietor or found by examining invoices paid in the month or so after the year end to see if any of them relate to the current year.

Illustration:

DR		Total Purchases Account	CR
	£		£
Cash	1,800	Balance b/d	700
Discounts received	70	Missing figure =	
Bank	4,000	Purchases	5,770
Balance c/d	600		
	£6,470		£6,470

It is *vital* that you complete the double entry as you go along, otherwise it is almost impossible to produce a correct answer.

The technique relies on your basic knowledge of double entry. Accounts must balance, hence if I know all figures except one (here purchases) affecting an account, I can derive that missing figure.

The figure most often omitted by students is the cash purchases figure, because the double entry is to another working account, the total cash account, as shown in the next illustration.

Illustration:

DR		Total Cash Account (or 'Till' Account)	CR
	£		£
Balance b/d	50	Banked	9,000
Missing figure =		Casual labour	156
Cash takings	12,812	Repairs	24
		Postage	104
		Cleaning	78
		Drawings	2,000
		Purchases	1,400
		Balance c/d	100
	£12,862		£12,862

The reason for having a total cash account is that very few small traders know exactly how much money they have taken on any individual day, let alone an entire year. The trader may not have a proper till, or he may not always ring up the amounts when he makes sales. Nor is it possible just to count the cash and cheques in the till at the end of each day, because most traders take cash out of the till during the day to pay various expenses or as drawings. In drawing up a total cash account we add together on the credit side all the items which went *out* of the till – cash banked, expenses paid in cash, cash purchases and drawings by the proprietor. Given that we know how much the trader started off with in the till (the cash in hand picked up from the previous year's balance sheet), how much he has expended and banked from the till and how much he has in hand at the end, we can work out what he must have taken in cash in order to have been able to make those expenditures and bankings. This is the figure of cash sales. If there are no credit sales then this amount can go straight onto the trading account as the sales figure. If there are also credit sales then we need to draw up another working for the total sales account.

You may like to think of this total cash account as a 'till' account.

DR		Total Sales Account		CR
	£			£
Balance b/d (opening debtors)	500	Cash takings (from cash a/c)		12,812
		Bank		950
Missing figure =		Balance c/d (closing debtors)		600
Sales	13,862			
	£14,362			£14,362

The cash takings amount has been transferred from the debit of the total cash account to the credit of the total sales account in order to collect together all the sales, cash and credit, in one working. It is important to note that the bank figure relates only to customers who have made their payments *directly* into the trader's bank account – in other words, if they have sent their cheques to his shop, the cheques would have gone through the till and therefore would already have been included in the *cash* takings figures, so to include them again in the total sales account would be to double-count. The balance carried down, the debtors at the year end, will, like the year-end creditors, probably be estimated by the proprietor.

From these three workings, therefore, the key missing figures of purchases and sales have been obtained. One point, however, needs to be more fully explained. In 'our total cash account' illustration we said that the balancing figure was the amount of cash takings. In 90 per cent of cases, this is true. Occasionally, though, the examiner gives the amount of cash takings, and in that case he does not normally give the drawings figure, which then is taken as the balancing figure on the cash account. But what happens if the examiner gives *neither* the cash takings *nor* the drawings? Obviously, one cannot have two unknowns in one account so the examiner gives a means of working out the sales figure, and this is by using the gross margin or, alternatively, the mark-up.

Mark-ups and margins

Mark-ups

When profit is expressed as a percentage, or fraction, of the cost price it is known as the mark-up. When a uniform rate of mark-up is used in a business compiling final accounts from incomplete records can be made easier.

Illustration 1:
The following figures relate to the year 1994.

	£
Opening stock	2,000
Closing stock	3,000
Purchases	9,000

A uniform mark up of 25 per cent is used. Find the gross profit and sales figures for the year.

So, cost of goods sold = opening stock plus purchases less closing stock:

= £2,000 + £9,000 – £3,000
= £8,000

And £8,000 + mark up = sales:

£8,000 + 25% = ?
£8,000 + £2,000 = £10,000 sales

Therefore: gross profit = £2,000 (10,000 – 8,000).

Margins

When profit is expressed as a percentage, or fraction, of the selling price, it is known as the margin. If a uniform rate of margin is used in a business, compiling final accounts from incomplete records can be made easier.

Illustration 2:
The following figures relate to the year 1994:

	£
Opening stock	1,000
Closing stock	2,000
Purchases	4,000

A uniform rate of margin of 50 per cent is used. Find the gross profit and sales figures for the year.

So, cost of goods sold = £1,000 + £4,000 – £2,000
= £3,000
and   £3,000 = sales – margin
£3,000 = ? – 50%
£3,000 = £6,000 – £3,000

Therefore: gross profit = £3,000
and sales = £6,000 (£3,000 + £3,000).

Use of formula

Given other pieces of information the two formulae used above can, of course, be used to find missing figures other than gross profit and sales. For example, if you are given the sales figures, the margin and the opening and closing stocks, by re-arranging the formula you could easily establish the cost of goods sold, and consequently, the purchases.

Relationship between mark-ups and margins

If the mark-up is known the margin can be calculated by:

a taking the margin's numerator to be the same as the mark-up's numerator;

b taking the margin's denominator to be equal to the sum of the mark-up's numerator and denominator.

Illustration 1:
Mark up is three-fifths ($\frac{3}{5}$). What is the margin?

        Numerator   = 3
        Denominator = 3 + 5 = 8

Therefore the margin is $\frac{3}{8}$ ths.

Likewise, if the margin is known, the mark-up can be calculated by:

a taking the mark-up's numerator to be the same as the margin's numerator;

b taking the mark-up's denominator to be equal to the margin's denominator less its numerator.

Illustration 2:
Margin is $\frac{3}{7}$ ths. What is the mark-up?

        Numerator   = 3
        Denominator = 7 – 3 = 4

Therefore the mark-up is $\frac{3}{4}$ ths.

Example

Johnson is a grocer trading from a rented shop. He makes up his accounts to 30 June each year. On the 30 June 1994 his shop and all records were destroyed by flooding. His balance sheet as at 30 June 1993 was:

	£	£	£
Capital			8,400
Represented by:			
Fixed assets:			
Fixtures at WDV			1,920
Current assets:			
Stock		2,300	
Debtors		380	
Prepayment – rates		72	
Balance at bank		5,504	
Cash in hand		280	
		8,536	
Deduct: Current liabilities			
Trade creditors	1,880		
Accruals: electricity	32		
accounting	144	2,056	
Net current assets			6,480
			£8,400

An analysis of copy statements obtained from the bank yielded the following summary:

	£
Purchases for resale	43,160
Rent	1,500
Rates	288
Electricity	184
Accountancy	168
Sundry trade expenses	184
Drawings	1,800
	£47,284

Total bankings during the year were £49,004.

Johnson supplied the following additional information:

a Cash payments from till before banking:

i shop assistant's wages, £60 pw;

ii casual wages, £2 pw;

iii sundry expenses, £3 pw;

iv cash purchases, £40 pw;

v drawings between, £60 and £80 pw.

b During the year he had gambling winnings of £600 which had been paid into his bank account.

c £104 was received during the year for rent of storage space above the shop. This was not banked.

d The following amounts were outstanding at 30 June 1994:

		£
Debtors		440
Trade creditors		2,040
Accruals:	electricity	40
	accountancy	272
	rent	500
Prepayments – rates		80
Cash in hand		340

e During the year a debtor owing £100 went bankrupt. No payment is expected.

f The insurance company has agreed to pay out £1,800 for the fixtures and £1,700 for the stock.

g For the past five years Johnson's gross margin has been static at 20 per cent.

There follows a detailed description of how to answer this question. You should follow it through carefully, step by step and then compare your final answer with ours.

The first step in any question is to head up the required accounts – the trading and profit and loss account and the balance sheet and the major working accounts nearly always required in an incomplete records question, that is, the total sales, purchase and cash accounts.

Now we see what figures need to be picked up from the opening balance sheet. The capital at 30 June 1993 can be put straight on the balance sheet as opening capital. The letters or numbers in the margins of the solution given refer to the source of the final figure on the accounts. The next figure is that of the fixtures and fittings £1,920. These were destroyed and the insurance company have agreed to pay out £1,800 for them. Therefore there is a loss on the fixtures and fittings of £120 which must be debited to the profit and loss account, while the claim for the £1,800 will be a debtor as at 30 June 1994.

The stock figure is the opening stock which can be written immediately on the trading account, the debtors will be debited to the total sales working, while the prepayment on the rates will affect the amount to be debited to the profit and loss account and needs to be noted in a working. The question does not actually give the closing balance at bank, so this needs to be calculated in working (5) and the cash in hand is debited to the total cash account. On the liabilities side, the trade creditors form the opening balance on the total purchases working and the accruals are noted in workings (6) and (7) respectively. At this point then all the figures on the opening balance shall have been transferred either direct to the final accounts or on to a working, and we can now deal with the bank analysis. The purchases figure will be debited to the total purchases account; the rent, rates, electricity, accountancy and sundry trade expenses to their respective workings and a note needs to be made of the drawings from the bank (working 10) so they can be later added to cash drawings. The total payments £47,284 need to be credited to the bank account, while the bankings are debited to the bank account, credited to total cash account.

The double entries for the bank summary having been completed, the next step is to deal with the additional information given by the proprietor.

The assistant's wages and casual labour should be credited to the total cash account, and can be debited directly to the profit and loss account, as there are no adjustments to be made for accruals or prepayments. The sundry expenses are credited to the cash account, debited to the relevant working, and the cash purchases credited to cash, debited to total purchases. Cash drawings are not known – all that is known is that they should be within the range £60 to £80 per week. The cash drawings figure, therefore, will be the balancing figure on the total cash account and it should fall between £3,120 and £4,160 for the year.

What do we do about point (b) – the gambling winnings? This figure will have been included with bankings in the total cash account, and would therefore inflate the figure of cash takings; or, in this case *decrease* the balancing figure of drawings. It is not, however, a trading item, it is in fact extra capital introduced, so to reflect the correct position we need to debit the cash account which will effectively remove it from the cash takings figure, and credit the capital account on the balance sheet. A similar principle applies with point (c) – the rent received. Although this was not banked, presumably it was available in the till for paying the various other cash outgoings, and so the effect on the balancing drawings figure would be the same as the gambling winnings. The correct double entry is to debit cash account, and credit rent receivable in the profit and loss account. The various outstanding amounts now need to be debited or credited to their various working accounts and the total accruals – £40 plus £272 plus £500 – inserted on the balance sheet under current liabilities with the trade creditors; and the prepayment of £80 and the trade debtors under current assets. The cash in hand is carried down on the total cash account and put under current assets on the balance sheet.

· The bad debt needs to be credited to total sales account, debited to the profit and loss account, and the amount owing from the insurance company is a debtor on the balance sheet. The £1,700 for the estimated stock is the only available figure we can use for the closing stock figure on the trading account, so it is inserted there to enable the cost of sales figure to be calculated.

All the information on the question has now been used, and the remainder of the process involves closing off each of the workings in turn and transferring the balancing figures to the trading and profit and loss account, the balance sheet or another working.

Let us take the bank account (working 5) first. The balancing figure, £7,224, is the cash at bank at 30 June 1994 and is put under current assets on the balance sheet. Next the various expense accounts are closed, rates, electricity, accountancy, sundry trade and rent. The balances on these accounts represent the amounts to be transferred to the debit of the profit and loss account.

The next account to be closed off is the total purchases account. The balance, £45,400 is debited to the trading account, and we are now in a position to find the cost of sales figure – £46,000. From this we can find the sales figure, because although we were not told the mark-ups, only that the gross margin was 20 per cent or one-fifth, we know that if the margin is one-fifth, the mark-up must be one-quarter. One-quarter of £46,000 is £11,500 so by inserting this figure as the gross

quarter. One-quarter of £46,000 is £11,500 so by inserting this figure as the gross profit in the trading account, we can see that the sales figure must be £57,500.

Now that the sales figure is known it can be inserted into the debit of the total sales account, and now the only missing figure from that account is the cash takings – the balancing figure of £57,340, which is a credit in the total sales account and is debited to the total cash account. This means that the missing figure of cash drawings must be £3,520, which is between the upper and lower limits given, and can therefore be taken as probably correct. This is added to the drawings (working 10) from bank.

All the working accounts are now complete and all that remains is to carry down the gross profit, work out the net profit, which comes to £5,052 and add it to the capital account on the balance sheet. Deducting drawings of £5,320 gives capital employed of £8,748 which agrees with the net assets.

Your worked solution should show the following: check it carefully!

OBS = Opening Balance Sheet Q = per information given in Question
W = workings

Johnson
Trading and Profit & Loss Account
Year ended 30 June 1994

		£		£
OBS	Opening stock	2,300	Sales	57,500
W 2	Purchases	45,400		
		47,700		
	Deduct: Estimated closing stock	1,700		
	Cost of sales	46,000		
	Gross profit (20% of sales or 25% of cost of sales)	11,500		
		57,500		57,500
Q	Wages and casual labour	3,224	Gross profit b/d	11,500
Q	Bad debt	100	Rent receivable	104
W 9	Rent	2,000		
W 4	Rates	280		
W 6	Electricity	192		
W 7	Accountancy	296		
W 8	Sundry trade expenses	340		
	Loss on fixtures and fittings	120		
	Net profit	5,052		
		£11,604		£11,604

Balance Sheet as at 30 June 1994

		£	£
OBS	Capital at 30.6.93		8,400
Q Add:	Capital introduced	600	
	Profit for year	5,052	5,652
			14,052
	Deduct:		
W 10	Drawings		5,320
			£8,732

Represented by:

		£	£	£
	Current assets			
Q	Debtor – Insurance claim		3,500	
Q	Trade debtors		440	
Q	Prepayment – rates		80	
W5	Balance at bank		7,224	
Q	Cash in hand		340	
			11,584	
	Deduct: Current liabilities			
Q	Trade creditors	2,040		
W	Accruals	812	2,852	£8,732

Workings

(W 1) Total Cash Account

		£			£	
OBS	Balance b/d	280	Banked		49,004	Q
Q	Capital introduced	600	Wages		3,120	Q
Q	Rent receivable	104	Casual labour		104	Q
W3	Cash takings	57,340	Sundry expenses		156	Q
			Purchases		2,080	Q
			Balance =			
			Drawings		3,520	
			Balance c/d		340	Q
		£58,324			£58,324	

(W 2) Total Purchases Account

		£		£	
Q	Bank	43,160	Balance b/d	1,880	OBS
Q	Cash	2,080	Balance =		
Q	Balance c/d	2,040	Purchases	45,400	
		£47,280		£47,280	

(W 3) Total Sales Account

		£		£	
OBS	Balance b/d	380	Bad debt	100	Q
	Sales	57,500	Balance =		
			Cash takings	57,340	
	Balance c/d			440	Q
		£57,880		£57,880	

(W 4) Rates Account

		£		£	
OBS	Balance	72	Profit & loss a/c	280	
Q	Bank	288	Balance c/d	80	
		£360		£360	

(W 5) Bank Account

		£		£	
OBS	Balance	5,504	Payments	47,284	Q
Q	Cash	49,004	Balance c/d	7,224	
		£54,508		£54,508	

(W 6) Electricity

		£		£	
Q	Bank	184	Balance c/d	32	OBS
Q	Balance c/d	40	Profit & loss a/c	192	
		£224		£224	

(W 7) Accountancy

		£		£	
Q	Bank	168	Balance b/d	144	OBS
Q	Balance c/d	272	Profit & loss a/c	296	
		£440		£440	

(W 8) Sundry Trade Expenses

		£		£
Q	Bank	184	Profit & loss a/c	340
Q	Cash	156		
		£340		£340

(W 9) Rent

		£		£
Q	Bank	1,500	Profit & loss a/c	2,000
Q	Balance c/d	500		
		£2,000		£2,000

(W 10) Drawings   1,800 + 3,520 = 5,320

Examination technique

The following procedure should be adopted when dealing with this type of question:

a Study the examiner's requirements.

b Open up accounts required by the examiner which will normally be:

   i   trading account and profit and loss account;

   ii   balance sheet.

c Glance through the rest of question to gain a general picture of its structure and content.

d Adjust the summary of bank statements for errors, omissions, outstanding cheques and uncredited items;

e then work through the question *line by line*.

f Reconstruct the opening balance sheet. Even if the *capital* figure is given, other figures may have been omitted, eg stock. Record each item in the opening balance sheet.

g Use the summary at (d) above to post into the accounts, adjusting for opening or closing accruals at the same time.

h Where the figures require difficult adjustments, use rough ledger accounts on the working sheet.

i It is nearly always essential to open up a cash account in order to deal correctly with cash position.

j Always aim at 'building up' the whole of the answer, on a simultaneous basis rather than completing one account at a time.

k *Always* submit your workings.

Problems

Problem 7.1

Tom Blunderbus, sole trader, has never kept more than the most scanty accounting records. It is only with the patient assistance of an accountant each year that final accounts are prepared for the business.

Tom's summarised balance sheet at 31 August 1993 is as follows:

	£		£
Capital	19,000	Fixed assets: at net book value	18,900
Bank overdraft	3,400	Stock in trade: at cost	5,000
Trade creditors	3,500	Trade debtors	2,000
	£25,900		£25,900

Note: the fixed assets were all bought in 1991 at a cost of £27,000.

After much research, the following information has been produced for the year ended 31 August 1994:

	£
Additions to fixed assets	3,000
Cost of goods sold	45,000
Cost of goods withdrawn from stock for own use	2,000
Cash drawings	4,000
Payments to suppliers for purchases	51,500
Purchases	51,000
Establishment expenses	6,000
Administrative expenses	2,000
Loan received from J Jones on 31 August 1994	8,000
Trade debtors at 31 August 1994	1,500
Legacy from deceased aunt paid into business bank account	7,000
Sales and distribution expenses	one-twelfth of sales
Gross profit	one-quarter of sales

Depreciation is provided annually on fixed assets at the rate of 10 per cent per annum on the cost of assets held at the end of each financial year and charged to establishment expenses.

Required:

Tom Blunderbus's trading and profit and loss account for the year ended 31 August 1993 and a balance sheet at that date.

(26 marks)

Associated Examining Board – updated

Problem 7.2

Carter owns and operates a small retail shop. From the few records he keeps, the following information is available for the beginning and end of his accounting year:

	30 June 1994 £	30 June 1995 £
Cash in shop till	70	105
Bank overdraft	695	1,350
Stock	2,000	4,600
Owed by customers	920	2,540
Owed to suppliers	2,180	3,730
Loan from wife	2,000	1,500

Additional information:

a Carter tells you that during the year and before making the weekly bankings of takings he took from the till:

   i   £50 a week for his personal needs; and

   ii £40 a week for his assistant's wages.

b Paid cheques show that all payments from the bank account were to suppliers except:

   i   a payment of £110 to an insurance company being £80 for the insurance of the shop and £30 for the insurance on Carter's private house; and

   ii a payment of £750 for furniture for Carter's own house.

c During the year Carter had paid business expenses of £600 through his separate private bank account.

d Although no record of it is kept, Carter owns the retail shop, having purchased it on 1 July 1990 for £12,000 and shop fixtures bought on the same date for £3,000. It is agreed that fair rates of depreciation are 5 per cent per annum on cost for the shop and 10 per cent per annum on cost for the fixtures.

Required:

a A detailed calculation of Carter's profit for the year ended 30 June 1995.

(7 marks)

b A statement of the financial position of his business at 30 June 1995.

(8 marks)

Associated Examining Board – updated

Problem 7.3

Ben Dover owns and operates a 'hot-dog' stall in the local market. He buys the sausages at 4p each and bread rolls at 3p each. Rolls are purchased daily and any not used by the end of the day are thrown away. The sausages will keep for several days and there is no wastage. The cost of garnish, ie onions, sauces etc, is estimated by Ben at 1p per 'hot-dog', and the 'hot-dogs' are sold at 15p each. He does not keep any accounting records and all his business is conducted on a cash basis. However, the suppliers of the sausages and bread rolls pay him a six-monthly rebate based on the total purchased from them, and he has received the following amounts:

Rebate on purchase of sausages – 5 per cent rebate.

Received 3 February 1995 for the 6 months to 31 December 1994	£140
Received 1 August 1995 for the 6 months to 30 June 1995	£160

Rebate on purchase of bread rolls – 3 per cent rebate.

Received 20 January 1995 for the 6 months to 31 December 1994	£72
Received 10 August 1995 for the 6 months to 30 June 1995	£81

The stall is rented from the Council at £10 per week, and gas used for cooking has cost £230 in the year ended 30 June 1995.

You may assume that one sausage and one bread roll, plus garnish, are the ingredients of each 'hot-dog'.

Required:

Prepare a revenue statement for the year to 30 June 1995, showing clearly the cost of rolls thrown away.

(22 marks)

Associated Examining Board – updated

Problem 7.4

C Jay has operated a small business for several years without any proper accounting records. He has visited an accountant in order to put his financial affairs in order.

The following information has been given to the accountant relating to the year ended 30 April 1993:

a A full set of bank statements from which the accountant has discovered that the opening bank balance at 1 May 1992 was £3,000 and that the receipts and payments for the year were:

	£		£
Receipts:		Payments:	
Takings banked	31,250	Business rates	1,700
C Jay's life assurance		Rent	2,800
endowment policy proceeds	3,250	Delivery van (2/5/92)	11,200
		Telephone expenses	550
		Payments to suppliers	20,250
		Light and heat	1,100
		Drawings	3,750

b A list of the other assets and liabilities which includes:

	at 1 May 1992 £	at 30 April 1993 £
Fixtures at cost (bought 10/1/92)	4,000	4,000
Stock	7,750	8,500
Creditors	1,750	3,000

c An allowance of £1,200 had been received against the cost of the new delivery van when the old van, estimated to be worth £2,000, had been traded in.

d The accountant suggested and it has been agreed that it would be wise to depreciate the fixtures at a rate of 15 per cent using the reducing balance method and to give a full year's depreciation for the year ended 30 April 1992. The delivery van will be depreciated at 20 per cent using the straight line method.

e All the business sales were for cash only and prior to banking the takings, it was noted that the following cash payments had been made:

	£
Wages (part-time staff)	6,700
Van expenses	1,050
Insurances	310
Drawings	2,625

f The proprietor had drawn goods costing £1,500 from the business for personal use.

g A cheque for £1,100 for purchases had been posted to a supplier on 20 April 1993 but did not appear on the April bank statement.

The accountant indicated to C Jay that advice relating to establishing sound accounting records was available.

Required:

a Prepare a statement of affairs for C Jay as at 1 May 1992.

(4 marks)

b Prepare a trading and profit and loss account for the year ended 30 April 1993.

(14 marks)

c Prepare a balance sheet as at 30 April 1993.

(14 marks)

d State what are the possible dangers to a business due to inadequate records.

(12 marks)

Associated Examining Board
November 1993

Accounts of clubs and societies | 8

Introduction

The limitations of a receipts and payments account (see Chapter 5), can be remedied by preparing an account that is not restricted to just receipts and payments but shows the actual *income and expenditure* appropriate to a given period.

Such an account, logically enough, is termed an *income and expenditure account*. This amplifies the receipts and payments account in that it records *all revenue* transactions during the period.

An income and expenditure account is simply the profit and loss account of a concern, such as a club, whose main source of income is not from trading. The only differences are that instead of a profit or loss being credited or debited to a capital account, the excess of income over expenditure or excess of expenditure over income is credited or debited to an account normally called the accumulated fund, which replaces the capital account.

It is possible to prepare an income and expenditure account from whatever records are available; it is, however, more usual to take the receipts and payments account, where it exists, as the starting point. Turning this into an income and expenditure account involves:

a separating capital from revenue items;

b making provisions for accrued expenditure;

c accounting for prepayments;

d providing for depreciation of assets.

Any capital transactions are recorded in a balance sheet.

Comprehensive example

The following were the assets and liabilities of the County Sports Club on 30 June 1994:

	£
Assets:	
Furniture and fixtures	260
Sports pavilion	300
Sports equipment	120
Stock of stationery	20
Investments	95
Subscription in arrears	5
Balance at bank	105
Cash in hand	15
Liabilities:	£
Subscriptions received in advance	10
Electricity accrued	15
Telephone accrued	10

An analysis of the treasurer's cash book reveals the following in respect of the year ended 30 June 1995:

Receipts	£	Payments	£
Opening balance	120	Wages of groundsmen	400
Subscriptions:		Electricity	65
Current year	700	Postages, stationery, telephone	102
Previous year	5	Purchase of sports equipment	35
Next year	15	Purchase of investments	15
Sale of dance tickets	130	Affiliation fees	10
Donations	20	Match expenses	7
		Dance expenses:	
		Hire of hall	20
		Hire of band	60
		Refreshments at dance	12
		Closing balance	264
	£990		£990

You are required to prepare the Club's income and expenditure account for the year ended 30 June 1994, and a balance sheet as at that date, taking into account the following information and instructions:

a the net profit or loss from the dance is to be disclosed as an identifiable figure;

b subscriptions in arrears were £20 at 30 June 1995;

c stock of stationery at 30 June 1995 was £22;

d repairs to pavilion invoiced but not paid amounted to £13;

e the sports equipment in hand at the end of the year was valued at £140;

f accounts outstanding at the end of the year were:

electricity £19

telephone £14;

g depreciation on assets is to be provided at 10 per cent.

Method:
Firstly, it is useful to construct a balance sheet at the beginning of the year in order to find out what the opening balance on the accumulation fund was. Taking the information given in the question the following can be drawn up:

Balance Sheet as at 30 June 1994

	£	£
Fixed assets:		
Sports pavillion		300
Furniture fixtures		260
Sports equipment		120
Investment		95
		775
Current assets:		
Stationery	20	
Debtors (subs in arrears)	5	
Bank	105	
Cash	15	
	145	
Current liabilities:		
Electricity	15	
Telephone	10	
Creditors (subs in advance)	10	
	35	
Net current assets		110
Accumulated fund (balancing figure)		£885

Note: unless the examiner asks for this question calculation of opening accumulated fund to be done in the form of a balance sheet it is perfectly acceptable to calculate it using a simple list of figures.

From this it is obvious that the balance on accumulated fund at the beginning of the year was £885. This accords with the accounting equation capital = assets less liabilities. Next it is necessary to sort out the receipts and payments.

Subscriptions need careful consideration. Because there were and are some subscriptions in arrears and some paid in advance, the actual cash received is not the amount due in the year. A working account is therefore set up in which all the available information is collected together, and the balancing figure transferred to the income and expenditure account. Remember, income and expenditure accounts follow normal accruals accounting principles.

DR		Subscription Account	CR
	£		£
Balance b/d		Balance b/d	
subscriptions in arrears	5	subscriptions in advance	10
		Cash received in the year	720
Therefore transfer to income		Balance c/d	
and expenditure a/c	730	subscriptions in arrears	20
(balancing figure)			
Balance c/d			
subscriptions in advance	15		
	£750		£750

The balance carried down will be added to the current liabilities and current assets figures as creditors and debtors in the year end balance sheet.

It is important to note that:

a subscriptions in arrears are a debtor due to the club – an asset;

b subscriptions received in advance are future income – or a liability – of the club.

Working accounts can be opening for other expense items.

DR		Secretarial Expenses Account	CR
	£		£
Stock of stationery b/d	20	Amount owing for	
Cash – postage, stationery		telephone b/d	10
and telephone	102	Income & expenditure a/c	104
Balance (amount owing c/d		Stock of stationery c/d	22
for telephone)	14		
	£136		£136

DR		Electricity Account	CR
	£		£
Cash	65	Balance b/d	15
Balance c/d	19	Income & expenditure a/c	69
	£84		£84

DR		Repairs Account	CR
	£		£
Balance c/d	13	Income & expenditure a/c	13
	£13		£13

DR		Sports Equipments Account	CR
	£		£
Balance b/d	120	Income & expenditure a/c	15
Cash	35	Balance c/d	140
	£155		£155

The purchase of investments is a capital item and needs to be added to the opening balance on investments.

The closing cash goes directly to the balance sheet.

Do not forget to provide depreciation. The requirements of the question must be read carefully to ascertain whether new assets are depreciated by a full year in the year of acquisition or on a pro rata basis. Similarly, depreciation may or may not be chargeable in the year of disposal.

You will note that the technique adopted here is essentially the same as that used in the incomplete records example (Johnson) in the preceding section.

Solution:

The County Sports Club
Income & Expenditure Account for the Year Ended 30 June 1995

	£	£	£
Subscriptions			730
Donations			20
Profit on dance			
Sale of tickets		130	
Less: Expenses		92	
			38
			788
Secretarial expenses		104	
Electricity		69	
Repairs		13	
Groundsman's wages		400	
Affiliation fees		10	
Match expenses		7	
Depreciation:			
Sports equipment	15		
Sports pavilion	30		
Furniture	26		
		71	
			647
Excess of income over expenditure			£114

Balance Sheet as at 30 June 1995

	Cost	Depn	£
Fixed assets:			
Sports pavilion	300	30	270
Furniture and fixtures	260	26	234
Sports equipment (valuation)	140		140
	500	56	644
Investment:			110
Current assets			
Stationery		22	
Debtors (subs due)		20	
Bank and cash		264	
		306	
Current liabilities:			
Creditors for repairs		13	
Creditors for subs		15	
Accruals		33	
		61	
Net current assets			245
			999
Accumulated fund:			
Opening balance			885
Excess of income over expenditure			114
			£999

Tutorial notes:

a Subscriptions in arrears in examination answers tend to be treated as debtors, but in practice, in view of the doubtful nature of such debts they may be excluded altogether.

b Where an annual event such as a garden party or dinner and dance takes up much of the book-keeping it is often better to have a separate income and expenditure account for it, only the net balance being transferred to the main income and expenditure account. Similarly, where much of the income comes from a bar, it is usual to keep a separate bar trading account, the profit or loss again being transferred to the main income and expenditure account.

Examination techniques

The following is suggested as a method of tackling income and expenditure account questions in examination.

a Draft an opening balance sheet (sometimes called 'statement of affairs'), to establish opening accumulated fund balance.

b Open up an income and expenditure account and a closing balance sheet.

c Enter the opening accumulated fund balance, calculated in (a) above in the closing balance sheet.

d Go through the receipts and payments account or cash book analysis and adjust revenue items for prepayments and accruals, where necessary.

e Enter revenue amounts (adjusted where necessary), in the income and expenditure account and enter prepayments and accruals in the closing balance sheet as debtors or creditors as appropriate.

f Calculate the depreciation charge. Enter the amount in the income and expenditure account and enter the accumulated depreciation in the closing balance sheet.

g Balance the income and expenditure account and transfer the excess income over expenditure or expenditure over income to the closing balance sheet, as an addition/deduction to the opening accumulated fund.

h Calculate changes in capital items and enter adjusted totals in the closing balance sheet.

Problems

Problem 8.1

The following receipts and payments account and other information have been supplied by the treasurer of the Tuff Road Rugby Club for the year ended 31 August 1995.

Receipts	£	£	Payments	£	£
1994			**1995**		
1 Sep			**31 Aug**		
Balances at bank:			Groundsman's salary		2,700
Current a/c	450		Rent, rates, insurances		1,840
Deposit a/c	700	1,150	Repairs to pavilion		425
			Petty cash		75
1995			New rugby equipment		500
31 Aug			Travelling expenses		2,870
Subscriptions		9,230	Printing and stationery		560
Bar takings		15,510	Cash register		400
Collections at matches		1,280	Bar purchases		11,730
Donations		5,000	Balances at bank:		
Interest on deposit a/c		480	Current a/c	4,250	
			Deposit a/c	7,300	11,550
		£32,650			£32,650

Other information is as follows:

	31 August 1994 £	31 August 1995 £
Club pavilion, cost £16,000 depreciated by 5% annually	4,800	4,000
Bar stocks at cost	1,250	960
Amount due for bar purchases	850	1,910
Amount due for subscriptions	460	720
Subscriptions received in advance	40	55
Petty cash float	30	15

a The donations are the result of an appeal for funds to build an extension to the club premises, and the proceeds have been placed on deposit account.

b Petty cash expenditure is mainly on postal expenses.

c It is the club's policy to write off the cost of rugby equipment as soon as it is purchased. The cash register is to be depreciated by 25 per cent.

d Collections made at matches go towards meeting the revenue expenses of the club.

Required:

a An account to show the profit or loss on the bar for the year to 31 August 1995.

(5 marks)

b The club's income and expenditure account for the year to 31 August 1995.

(12 marks)

c A balance sheet at 31 August 1995.

(8 marks)

Associated Examining Board – updated

Problem 8.2

The Chaucer Theatre Club performs a number of plays every year in the premises which they own in Austenville. In addition to these plays the Club organises a variety of other arts functions, which means that their premises are actively used throughout the year.

The Club's membership is composed of individuals and business organisations. Several of the businesses give additional funds to sponsor productions.

The honorary treasurer of the Club has prepared the following receipts and payments account for the year ended 31 March 1994.

	£		£
Rents charged	3,900	Balance brought forward	880
Sponsorship	12,500	Light and heat	3,960
Subscriptions:		Insurances	1,890
Individual	4,000	Club advertising	1,560
Business	1,700	Copyright costs	1,504
Programme advertising	320	Caretaker's wages	8,016
Ticket sales from plays	52,880	Printing and stationery	1,575
		Postages and telephone	610
		General expenses	6,772
		Play performance costs	27,800
		Repairs and maintenance	6,318
		Equipment and costume hire	3,725
		Balance carried forward	10,760
	£75,300		£75,300

The following information is available.

a The premises were purchased on 1 April 1984 for £85,000 and are being depreciated at a rate of 4 per cent per annum on cost. The Club also owns a variety of fixtures which originally cost £16,000 and upon which depreciation of £6,200 up to 1 April 1993 has been charged. The rate of depreciation on fixtures is 10 per cent per annum using the reducing balance method.

b A cash float of £100 has been maintained but it was decided during the year to increase this to £150. The additional £50 was taken from ticket sales before the takings were banked.

c Individual members pay annual subscriptions of £20 each and business organisations pay £100 per annum. At 31 March 1993 four individual members were in arrears but three businesses had paid in advance. On 31 March 1994 seven individual members had not paid but six had paid for the year 1994/95. Those individual members who had been in arrears at 31 March 1993 have subsequently paid up.

d At 31 March 1993 the following amounts had been outstanding – printing £390 and repairs £170 whilst at that date insurances of £190 had been prepaid.

e At 31 March 1994 a telephone bill of £85 and one for electricity of £510 were unpaid but copyright expenses of £195 had been prepaid.

f The Club committee agreed to grant an honorarium of £100 each to the secretary and treasurer for the year ended 31 March 1994.

Required:

a A statement showing the calculation of the accumulated fund of the Chaucer Theatre Club as at 31 March 1993.

(10 marks)

b Prepare an income and expenditure account for the Club for the year ended 31 March 1994.

(19 marks)

c Prepare the balance sheet of the Club as at 31 March 1994.

(13 marks)

d Discuss the benefits and drawbacks of sponsorship from the point of view of

i   the business sponsors;   (6 marks)

ii   the Club.   (6 marks)

Associated Examining Board
Summer 1994

Correction of errors 9

Introduction

The examiner often requires the student to correct errors appearing in a set of accounts. There is no one way of approaching these problems except to be very knowledgeable in accounting. It is a very good test of your understanding.

Consequently, this section contains a worked illustration, together with problems for you to solve.

Illustrations

Dubious and Hazardous

Dubious and Hazardous are partners in a small trading company, sharing profits and losses in the ratio 2:1. They have little idea of accounting and have submitted their books to their accountant presenting figures of £8,720 and £4,360 as their respective profits for the period 1 April 1994 to 31 March 1995.

The accountant discovers that during the year ended 31 March 1995:

a Sales of £3,500 have not been entered in the books;

b the closing stock figure of £6,875 has been added to purchases;

c repairs to motor vehicles includes an item of £316 for the overhaul of a car owned and used privately by Dubious;

d no entries have been made in the accounting records of the partnership for goods taken from the business for their private use by Dubious and Hazardous costing £734 and £627 respectively;

e no adjustment has been made for an advertising account of £72 unpaid at 31 March 1995;

f during the year ended 31 March 1995, depreciation has been charged on delivery vehicles at 15 per cent on the reducing balance method instead of on the straight line method;

g repairs to premises amounting to £917 have been entered in the premises, at cost, account, but the charge for depreciation on premises for the year ended 31 March 1995 has been computed correctly;

h deductions from profit have been made for discounts received of £458;

i only one month's interest has been provided for on a loan of £1,200 received on 1 April 1994;

j an accrual for carriage outwards of £43 has been added to profit.

Additional information:

a The delivery vehicles owned by the partnership cost £9,300 and the provision for depreciation at 31 March 1994 was £2,500.

b Interest is payable on the loan received on 1 April 1994 at the fixed monthly rate of 1.75 per cent.

Required:

A computation of the corrected profits of Dubious and Hazardous for the year ended 31 March 1995.

(15 marks)

Associated Examining Board Specimen paper – updated

Solution:

Restatement of Profit

		£	£
Balance b/d	D		8,720
	H		4,360
			13,080
Sales	(1)		3,500
Closing stock adjustment	(2)		
(6,875 x 2)			13,750
Repairs for private car	(3)		316
Goods for own use	(4)		1,361
(734 + 627)			
Advertising accrual	(5)		(72)
Depreciation adjustment	(6)		(375)
(working 1)			
Repairs to premises	(7)		(917)
Discounts received error	(8)		916
(working 2)			
Loan interest	(9)		231
(working 3)			
Carriage outwards error	(10)		(86)
(working 4)			
Revised profit, divided between			£31,242
Partners as	D (⅔)	20,822	
	H (⅓)	10,414	
		£31,242	

Workings:
(1) Depreciation

Originally charged: 15% (9,300 – 2,500) = £1,020
Should have been charged 15% x 9,300 = £1,395
Additional charge   375

(2) Discount

This should have been added not deducted.
Therefore the adjustment is 458 x 2 = 916

(3) 1,200 x 1.75% x 11 = £231

(4) £43 should have been deducted not added therefore 43 x 2 must be deducted now.

Problems

Problem 9.1

The draft accounts for the year ended 30 September 1994 of Lowden Dealers Ltd are as follows:

Lowden Dealers Ltd
Trading and Profit & Loss Account for the year ended 30 September 1994

	£	£
Sales		121,200
Cost of sales		92,900
Gross profit c/d		28,300
Establishment expenses*	9,700	
Administrative expenses	9,000	
Distribution expenses	6,000	
		24,700
Net profit		3,600
Proposed dividends		2,000
Retained profit for year		1,600
Retained profit b/f		8,000
Retained profit c/f		£9,600

*Includes depreciation of fixtures and equipment.

Balance Sheet at 30 September 1994

	Cost	Depn	£
Fixed assets:			
Freehold property	15,000	–	15,000
Fixtures and fittings	17,000	9,700	7,300
	£32,000	£9,700	22,300
Current assets:			
Stock		9,100	
Debtors		7,200	
Bank		1,200	
		£17,500	
Current liabilities:			
Creditors		3,200	
Proposed dividend		2,000	
		£5,200	
Net current assets			12,300
Total assets less current liabilities			£34,600
Ordinary share capital			20,000
Share premium a/c			5,000
Profit & loss a/c			9,600
			£34,600

After the preparation of the draft accounts, the following information becomes available:

a Goods received in August 1994, from Thompson and Son Ltd, on a sale or return basis and 'costing' according to a pro-forma invoice £1,000, were still held by Lowden Dealers Ltd at 30 September 1994. Although these goods have not been passed through the purchases day book, they were included in the company's stock taking at 30 September 1994.

Lowden Dealers Ltd have not yet decided whether or not to buy these goods.

b Goods sent in September 1994 to T Goon, on a sale or return basis and unsold at 30 September 1994, have been inadvertently regarded as sold to T Goon in the draft accounts of the year under review. The sales value of the goods concerned is £1,200.

c The company had its freehold property revalued in December 1993, and it was then decided that the property would be shown in the accounts at its revalued figure of £30,000.

d On 28 September 1994, a cheque was prepared for £400 in favour of P Fitzpatrick, a trade creditor. The cheque was recorded in the company's cash book, but was never despatched. The company has now decided to settle the account in December 1994 when further goods, completing a contract, are received; in these circumstances, it has been decided to cancel the cheque.

e The purchase of fixtures and fittings in January 1994, at a cost of £3,000 has been debited to purchases.

Notes:

a Ignore tax.

b The company invariably obtains a gross profit of 25 per cent on its sales.

c In the accounting treatment of all items during the financial year under review, the company wishes to maintain retained earnings at the highest possible level.

d Depreciation is provided annually on fixtures and fittings at the rate of 10 per cent on cost of assets held at the end of each financial year.

Required:

a A corrected trading and profit and loss account for the year ended 30 September 1994, and a balance sheet at that date.

b The journal entries required for items (b) and (d) above.
Note: narratives are not required.

(24 marks)
Associated Examining Board – updated

Problem 9.2

The draft balance sheet at 30 September 1994 of Red Holly Ltd is as follows:

	Cost	Depn	£
Fixed assets:			
Freehold property	20,000	–	20,000
Plant and machinery	64,000	15,000	49,000
	£84,000	£15,000	69,000
Current assets:			
Stock		11,000	
Debtors		7,300	
Bank		2,500	
		£20,800	
Current liabilities:			
Creditors		9,000	
Proposed dividends		4,800	
		£13,800	
Net current assets			7,000
Total assets less current laibilities			£76,000
Ordinary shares			40,000
8% preference shares			10,000
Share premium			5,000
General reserve			8,000
Profit & loss a/c			13,000
			£76,000

The following information subsequently becomes available:

a All the plant and machinery held at 30 September 1994, had been bought during the financial year ended 30 September 1993. The company's policy of providing for depreciation at the rate of 12 ½ per cent per annum on the cost of plant and machinery held at each accounting year end had been wrongly interpreted as the reducing balance method.

b The company's board insists on proposing a dividend for the year ended 30 September 1994, of 10 per cent on ordinary shares in issue on that date.

c The acquisition in June 1994 of a new machine for the workshop at a cost of £4,000 was debited to purchases.

d A cheque for £1,000 received by the company from L King, debtor, was dishonoured on 22 September 1994, but no entry has been made in the company's books of account.

e The directors have decided that there should be a provision for doubtful debts of 5 per cent of trade debtors at 30 September 1994.

Note: there is already a credit balance of £500 on the provision for doubtful debts account.

f An advertising charge of £3,000 for a new product to be launched in 1995 has been debited in the profit and loss account for the year under review instead of being treated as deferred revenue expenditure.

Required:

The corrected balance sheet at 30 September 1994, of Red Holly Ltd.

(25 marks)
Associated Examining Board – updated

Manufacturing accounts | 10

Introduction

So far we have only considered trading entities which purchase goods from a manufacturer and then sell them to the customer. In the situation where the business actually manufactures the product that it sells it is necessary to reflect the manufacturing costs in detail in a 'manufacturing account'. The various costs involved must be classified and presented in a meaningful way and this is usually done by splitting the factory production cost into 'direct' and 'indirect' expenses. Direct expenses are those that relate specifically to the product being made, ie raw materials consumed and wages, and these are described on the manufacturing statement as 'prime costs'. Indirect expenses are those incurred in the factory, but of a more general nature, ie factory light and heat, plant depreciation, factory supervisor's wages etc, and these are listed on the manufacturing statement after the prime cost.

Nature of manufacturing operation

Consider the steps of manufacturing any product:

a The firm buys raw materials – if the company manufactures desks it will need wood, screws and varnish at least.

b The firm employs labour (people) to work on the raw materials and to make it into a product which it can sell. In the case of our desk manufacturer the labour cuts the wood to size, makes it smooth, assembles it using the screws and finally varnishes it.

c The firm expends other costs in the manufacturing process. It must have foremen (overseers) for the workers, cleaners for the factory, oil to lubricate its machines, electricity or other energy to power its machines, the rent or rates on the factory where the goods are produced, depreciation on its machines etc. This list can be endless. These costs are overheads and have several names: factory costs; factory overheads; production costs or overheads.

Manufacturing costs

It can be seen from the above that the firm has three basic types of manufacturing cost which must be incurred before the product can be brought to a 'finished' state ready to be sold. These costs are:

a raw materials;

b manufacturing labour;

c manufacturing overheads.

Manufacturing stocks

The manufacturing process does not stop simply because the accountants decide to use a particular date for our year end. It is a continuous process. Consequently at the balance sheet date the firm will have on hand:

a Raw materials (RM) stocks: these are the stocks which are ready for the manufacturing process.

b Work-in-progress (WIP) stocks: these are the products which have had some work done on them but which have not yet been completed or finished.

c Finished goods (FG) stocks: the finished items which have not yet been sold.

Manufacturing account preparation

A manufacturing account is prepared before the usual trading and profit and loss account, in order to show the calculation of 'cost of goods manufactured'. A pro-forma showing the exact format to be used is set out below:

Pro-Forma Manufacturing Account

	£	£
Opening stock of raw materials		4,200
Purchases		29,500
		33,700
Closing stock of raw materials		(5,200)
Cost of materials consumed		28,500
Manufacturing wages		21,800
Prime cost		50,300
Factory overheads		
Supervisory wages	6,300	
Repairs and maintenance	3,100	
Power	5,200	
Light and heat	1,600	
Factory rent, rates and insurance	3,000	
Depreciation of plant and machinery	4,000	23,200
Cost of all production		73,500
Opening stock of work-in-progress	1,500	
Closing stock of work-in-progress	(3,000)	(1,500)
Cost of completed production (transfer to trading a/c)		£72,000

	£	£
Sales		XXXX
Opening finished goods stocks	XXX	
Purchases of finished goods	XXX	
	XXX	
Closing finished goods stocks	XXX	
Cost of sales		XXX
Gross profit		XXX

For the manufacturing firm its trading account will be as follows:

Trading Account

	£	£
Sales		XXX
Opening stock of FG	XXX	
Cost of manufacturing FG during year	XXX	
	XXX	
Less: Closing stock of FG	XXX	
Cost of sales		XXX
Gross profit		XXX

The cost of manufacturing that year's additions to finished goods is computed in the manufacturing account and the total transferred to the trading account.

As already stated this cost is comprised of three elements:

a raw materials;

b manufacturing (or 'direct') labour;

c factory overheads.

Let us take a company which had opening raw material stocks of £4,000, purchases of raw materials during the year of £25,000 and closing raw materials stocks of £6,000.

The raw materials cost is easy to work out and and the manufacturing account begins with this:

Manufacturing Account for year ended …

	£
Opening RM stocks	4,000
RM purchases	25,000
	29,000
Less: Closing RM stocks	6,000
Cost of RM consumed (used)	£23,000

The manufacturing labour is easy too. Suppose the firm had factory wages of £5,000. The manufacturing account would continue as follows:

	£
Cost of RM consumed	23,000
Factory wages	5,000
Prime cost (RM cost plus manufacturing labour)	£28,000

Factory overheads are not difficult either. Suppose the firm paid rent and rates of £1,500 and depreciation on factory machines of £2,500. The manufacturing account continues:

	£	£
Prime cost		28,000
Factory overheads:		
Rent and rates	1,500	
Depreciation	2,500	4,000
(This total does not really have a name)		£32,000

Finally there is the problem of work-in-progress. If the firm had opening WIP stocks of £5,200 and closing WIP stocks of £4,200 then some adjustments must be made in the manufacturing account.

Rule:

a If the closing WIP is lower than the opening WIP, the difference must be added into the manufacturing account.

b If closing WIP stock is higher than opening WIP stock, the difference must be deducted from the manufacturing account.

Thus the manufacturing account ends with:

	£	£
WIP adjustment		32,000
Opening WIP stocks	5,200	
Closing WIP stocks	4,200	1,000
Factory (production) cost of finished goods		
manufactured transferred to trading account		£33,000

The trading account is then normal:

	£	£
Sales		56,000
Opening FG stocks	700	
Manufacturing account	33,000	
	33,700	
Closing FG stocks	900	
Cost of sales		32,800
Gross profit		£23,200

Rewritten, so as to see the whole, the manufacturing and trading accounts appear as follows:

Manufacturing and Trading Accounts for the year ended ...

	£	£
Opening RM stocks		4,000
RM purchases		25,000
		29,000
Closing RM stocks		6,000
RM consumed		23,000
Factory wages		5,000
Prime costs		28,000
Factory overheads:		
Rent and rates	1,500	
Depreciation	2,500	4,000
		32,000
WIP adjustment:		
Opening WIP stocks	5,200	
Closing WIP stocks	4,200	1,000
Factory cost		£33,000

	£	£
Sales		56,000
Opening FG stocks	700	
Manufacturing account	33,000	
	33,700	
Closing FG stocks	900	
Cost of sales		32,800
Gross profit		£23,200

Try this illustration, but take into account the following:

a The firm has only just commenced business, therefore no opening stocks of any kind.

b The prime cost is given, therefore purchases will have to be worked out.

c No closing WIP stocks, therefore no adjustment.

d Administration and selling expenses appear in the profit and loss account.

Note: requirement (b) is really part of 'breakdown analysis' in the section on costing but try it anyway!

Illustration:
Briar Ltd commences business on 1 July 1994 selling a single product. The following forecasts are made in respect of the first year of operations:

a 400 units of the product will be sold at £75 each.

b The prime cost of each unit will be:

	£
Material	11
Direct labour	22
	£33

c 700 units will be produced (normal capacity).

d Overheads will be:

	£
Factory: Power	3,000
Depreciation	7,000
General expenses	4,000
Administration and financial expenses	3,500
Selling expenses	2,500

and these overheads are not expected to vary with either the number of units produced or the number sold.

e Material stocks will amount to £550 at the end of the financial year and there will be no work in progress on that date.

Required:

a A budgeted manufacturing, trading, and profit and loss account for the year to 30 June 1995 for each of the following situations:

    i   finished goods in stock are valued at prime cost;   (10 marks)

    ii finished goods in stock are valued at total factory cost.   (10 marks)

b If finished goods are valued at prime cost and are sold at £75 each, a calculation of the number to be sold so that net profit is nil.

                                                        (10 marks)

                                      Associated Examining Board – updated

Solution:

a

Briar Ltd
Budgeted Manufacturing, Trading and Profit & Loss Account
for the year 30 June 1995

		situation (i)		situation (ii)	
	£	£	£	£	
Material purchases (by balance)		8,250			8,250
Less: Closing stock of RM		550			550
RM consumed 700 x £11		7,700			7,700
Wages 700 x £22		15,400			15,400
Prime cost		23,100			23,100
Factory overheads: Power		–	3,000		
Depreciation		–	7,000		
General		– –	4,000	14,000	
Transfer to trading a/c					
(cost of producing 700 units)	£23,100			£37,100	
Sales (400 x 75)		30,000		30,000	
Manufacturing account	23,100		37,100		
Less FG stock $\left(\dfrac{23,000}{700} \times 300\right)$	9,900				
$\left(300 \times \dfrac{37,100}{700}\right)$			15,900		
Cost of sales		13,200		21,200	
Gross profit		16,800		8,800	
Less: Expenses					
Power	3,000				
General	4,000				
Administration etc.	3,500		3,500		
Selling	2,500		2,500		
Depreciation	7,000		–		
		20,000		6,000	
Net profit/(loss)		£(3,200)		£2,800	

b

		£	£
Selling price			75
Prime cost:	Material	11	
	Labour	22	33
Contribution			£42

Where net profit = nil

the number to be sold will be total fixed cost ÷ contribution/unit or $\dfrac{20,000}{42}$

which is 477 (rounding to the next highest).

Note: selling 477 actually produced a profit of £34 and selling 476 a loss of £8. As one cannot sell a fraction of a unit the answer is taken to be the one which produces the smallest profit (ie 477).

Transfer prices

Not all life is as simple as the foregoing section.

Let us consider the firm which manufactures desks. It could probably buy the desks complete from someone else and is thus taking extra profit from manufacturing the desks itself. This profit comes from the manufacturing process and firms occasionally wish to reflect this.

One way of reflecting this is to transfer the goods from manufacturing to trading at a price higher than factory goods. This is known as a transfer price. It is usually set at a rate somewhere equivalent to the price at which the merchandising (trading) section could buy the product from an independent supplier.

When a firm does this it will create a situation where it has two types of FG stocks:

a FG stocks in the factory waiting for delivery to the warehouses. These will be valued at factory cost.

b FG stocks in the warehouses awaiting sale. These will be valued at the transfer price and will thus include a proportion of the manufacturing profit.

At the balance sheet date the FG stocks at the transfer price include the manufacturing profit. This profit has not been realised and must therefore not be taken into account.

Taking the previous example, but now assume that in addition to a factory cost of £33,000 the firm has FG stocks at factory cost as follows:

Opening	£9,000
Closing	£6,000

and FG stocks at the transfer price (which is factory cost plus 25 per cent) of:

Opening	£2,000
Closing	£3,000

the manufacturing account will end as follows:

	£	£
Factory cost of production		33,000
FG (at factory cost) adj.		
Opening	9,000	
Closing	6,000	3,000
Factory cost of FG transferred to warehouse		36,000
Factory gross profit (25% of factory cost)		9,000
Trading account transfer		£45,000

The trading account will appear as follows:

	£	£
Sales		56,000
Opening FG stocks (at transfer price)	2,000	
Manufacturing account	45,000	
	47,000	
Closing FG stocks (at transfer price)	3,000	
Cost of sales		44,000
Trading gross profit		£12,000

The firm also has manufacturing gross profit and thus the profit and loss account will continue:

	£
Trading gross profit	12,000
Manufacturing gross profit	9,000
	21,000
Adjustment for unrealised profit in stock	200
	20,800
Expenses	XXX
Net profit for year	£XXX

The adjustment for unrealised profit is computed in the following way:

DR	Provision for Unrealised Profit in Stock Account		CR
	£		£
	Opening balance b/f		400
	($\frac{1}{5}$ x 2,000)		
	Transferred to Profit & loss a/c		
Closing balance c/d	600	(by balance)	200
($\frac{1}{5}$ x 3,000)	£600		£600
	Opening balance b/d		600

The balance sheet will also reflect these figures, as follows:

	£	£
Current assets:		
Stock – finished goods – at cost		6,000
at transfer price	3,000	
Less: Provision for unrealised profit	600	2,400
WIP stocks		4,200
RM stocks		6,000
		£18,600

Problems

Problem 10.1

The manufacturing and trading accounts of Orange Ltd for the year to 30 September 1994 are as follows:

		£000	£000	£000
Raw materials:	Stock, 1 October 1993	45		
	Purchases	310		
		355		
	Stock, 30 September 1994	(55)	300	
Manufacturing wages			160	
Factory overhead:	Indirect labour	38		
	Indirect materials	14		
	Depreciation of plant	50	102	
			562	
Work-in-progress:	1 October 1993	139		
	30 September 1994	(141)	(2)	
			560	560
Stocks of finished product at factory cost:				
	1 October 1993	70		
	30 September 1994	(30)		40
				600
Factory profit				150
Transfer price of output from factory to warehouse				750
Sales			1,000	
Warehouse stock	1 October 1993	80		
Transferred from factory		750		
		830		
Warehouse stock	30 September 1994	(60)	770	
Warehouse profit			£230	

Required:

a Calculate the total gross profit on sales for the year. You may assume that profit margins have not changed from the previous year.

(8 marks)

b Show how all stocks, including work-in-progress, should appear on the company's balance sheet at 30 September 1994.

(6 marks)

c Calculate the stock turnover ratios for each of the four types of stock.

(5 marks)

d Explain the purpose of transferring goods from the factory to the warehouse at a price higher than factory production cost.

(3 marks)

Associated Examining Board – updated

Problem 10.2

Panchem plc produces a range of chemical products, some of which are dangerous.

The following balances were extracted from the company's ledger at 31 March 1994, which is the financial year end:

	£000
Stocks at 1 April 1993:	
Raw materials	470
Work-in-progress	323
Finished goods	398
Indirect materials	54
Purchases of raw materials	376
Power charges	59
Indirect materials purchased	82
Chemists' and production directors' salaries (factory)	48
Manufacturing wages	209
Non-production wages	81
Office expenses	127
Selling expenses	53
Business rates and insurances	49
Internal transport costs (factory)	34
Safety and protective measures expenses (factory)	12
Depreciation for 1993/94: Plant	60
Buildings	20
Customs duties on raw material purchases	8
Office (£55,000) and selling staff (£36,000) salaries	91
Sales	1,436
Canteen expenses	40

The following additional information is available.

a Details of pre-payments and accruals at 31 March 1994 are:

	£
Pre-payments	
Office expenses	3,000
Selling expenses	4,000
Insurances and business rates	1,000
Accruals	
Power	21,000
Office expenses	6,000
Selling expenses	5,000

b Various items of expenditure and depreciation are to be apportioned as follows:

	Manufacturing expenses %	Office expenses %	Selling expenses %
Insurances and business rates	75	12 ½	12 ½
Canteen	60	30	10
Depreciation: plant and buildings	90	5	5

c Closing stocks at cost at 31 March 1994 were:

	£
Raw materials	420,000
Work-in-progress	370,000
Finished goods	450,000
Indirect materials	51,000

Required:

a Prepare manufacturing, trading and profit and loss accounts for Panchem plc for the year ended 31 March 1994

(34 marks)

b Identify and discuss *four* limitations of manufacturing accounts.

(8 marks)

Associated Examining Board
Summer 1994

Partnership accounts | 11

Introduction

A partnership usually comes into existence for one or both of two reasons. A businessman may have an idea which he thinks may be profitable but is unable to exploit it on his own (which would be the most profitable course for him) because he lacks either the necessary skills or the necessary capital. He will therefore look for one or more people to join in his venture contributing their talents or their capital or both. It is essential to the definition of a partnership, that this combination should be with a view to making a profit. The venture may, in fact, make losses but the partners must at least have intended to try and make a profit.

Unlike limited companies, partnerships do not have to comply with stringent legal requirements. This is because the partners are presumed to be competent businessmen capable of looking after their own interests on an equal footing with the other partners, as opposed to shareholders who may well have little or no knowledge of business and therefore need more protection by the law.

The most obvious difference between a partnership and a limited company is that of liability. The law has to be drawn very tightly around companies as there is no access to individual shareholders assets, should the company fail and the creditors be left unpaid. In a partnership, on the other hand, the partners normally have unlimited joint and several liability; that is a creditor can sue any or all of the partners to the limit of both their business and personal assets, until his debt is satisfied. A partnership may have limited partners, that is partners whose liability does not extend beyond a stated amount, but every partnership must have at least one partner whose liability is unlimited. Another difference between a partnership and a limited company is in the number of members – with a public company at least, there is no limit, but a partnership may not have more than twenty members, except for certain professional partnerships such as accountants, lawyers, and doctors who may not operate as limited companies. Obviously, if a partner has unlimited liability he will want to have a say in the management of the firm and with more than 20 partners this would be difficult if not impossible.

Legal considerations

The following table outlines the principal points to be found in a partnership agreement.

Item	Agreement specifies	In no agreement – Act specifies (Partnership Act 1890)	Remarks
Capital	The amount of capital to be contributed	That all partners are entitled to contribute capital equally	
Profits/losses	The ratio in which profits/losses are to be shared	That profits/losses are shared equally	
Interest on capital	a Whether interest is to be allowed on capital before calculation of divisible profits b If allowed, the rate	That a partner is not entitled to interest on capital	
Interest on drawings	a Whether interest is to be charged on drawings before calculation of divisible profits b If charged, the rate	No provision	
Capital and current account	a Whether or not capitals are to remain fixed, or b If drawings/ profits etc are to be adjusted through capital accounts	No provision	Generally profits etc are adjusted through current accounts, the capital accounts remaining fixed
Remuneration for services	Whether or not partners are to be allowed salaries for acting in the partnership business	Partners are not allowed salaries	Salaries are not charged before calculation of profit
Loans to the business	a If loans in excess of capital contribution are to be permitted b If allowed, the rate of interest that they will attract	That if a partner contributes in excess of his capital, he is entitled to 5% interest	Interest on loans is treated as an expense of running the business and is *not* an appropriation of profit

Note that column (3), the Partnership Act of 1890 only applies if there is no specific agreement by the partners on a particular item.

Absence of any agreement to the contrary

The partners may vary any or all of the conditions – indeed it is rare for a partnership to have all partners contributing and sharing profits and losses exactly equally. A partnership agreement does not have to be written – a verbal agreement is sufficient, or even just acceptance over a period of time of a certain way of conducting the business. For examination purposes, though, you *must* remember that the profit sharing ratio is *equal*, unless the examiner tells you to the contrary. You should *not* assume the profit sharing ratio is the same as the ratio of fixed capitals – this will only happen by coincidence. Similarly, do not assume any interest on capitals or salaries unless the examiner quite clearly tells you that they are to be given.

Partnership accounting

To move from generalisations about partnerships to the specific accounting problems, in what ways do partnership accounts differ from sole trader's accounts? The differences start after the net profit has been ascertained, because at this point, in a sole trader's accounts, the entire net profit belongs to the proprietor and is therefore credited direct to his capital account. In the case of a partnership, however, the net profit must be shared out between the partners and for this purpose the *appropriation* account is used.

Illustration 1:

X, Y and Z are in partnership sharing profits in the ratio: 3:2:1. Their fixed capitals are:

   X £20,000   Y £10,000   and Z £4,000.

Y and Z are entitled to salaries of £2,000 and £1,600 respectively, and all partners are entitled to interest on fixed capital at 6 per cent per annum. The partners have current account balances as follows: X £3,000; Y £1,200 and Z £300. The net profit for the year ended 31.12.94 was £30,000 and the partners had made drawings of £11,000, £6,000 and £4,500 respectively.

Solution 1(a):

Profit & Loss Appropriation Account

	£	£
Net profit		30,000
Salaries:		
Y	2,000	
Z	1,600	(3,600)
Interest on capital:		
X (20,000 x 6%)	1,200	
Y (10,000 x 6%)	600	
Z (4,000 x 6%)	240	(2,040)
		24,360
Balance in profit sharing ratio:		
X (³⁄₆ x 24,360)	12,180	
Y (²⁄₆ x 24,360)	8,120	
Z (¹⁄₆ x 24,360)	4,060	(24,360)

The profit and loss appropriation account follows immediately after the profit and loss account, much as the profit and loss account follows the trading account. Just as the gross profit is carried down to the credit of the appropriation account. Where some or all of the partners are entitled by the partnership agreement to salaries or interest on capital these are debited to the appropriation account. In example 1 Y and Z are entitled to salaries of £2,000 and £1,600 respectively, so these amounts are debited to the account. All the partners are entitled to 6 per cent per annum interest on their fixed capitals so X is entitled to £20,000 @ 6 per cent or £1,200, Y to £600 and Z to £240. Only when the prior charges have been debited will the balance of £24,360 be shared between the partners in their profit sharing ratio. Now we need to consider the other side of the double entry. Remember, the appropriation account is part of the double entry system, just as the profit and loss account is. With the accounts of a sole trader, the final entry is to debit the profit and loss account with the net profit and credit the proprietor's capital account, so in a partnership the debits on the appropriation account must be matched by credits on the capital accounts.

This raises a problem. We were told that the partners were entitled to 6 per cent per annum interest on their *fixed* capital accounts, but if salaries, interest and profits are credited to their capital accounts annually, they can hardly be described as fixed. Moreover, calculating interest on a fluctuating balance is difficult and time consuming unless the business is computerized. To overcome this, the partners' capital accounts are split into two component parts – the capital accounts, which record their permanent investment in the business, and the current accounts which record the fluctuating balances. To the current accounts we credit the salaries, interest on capital and share of profits, and debit drawings and interest on drawings (if there is any). So in illustration 1 the capital accounts are left untouched, and the salaries, interest and profit share credited to the current accounts, while drawings are debited to the current account. You should be careful to remember that the double entry for drawings is credit cash, debit current account, since as for some reason many students seem to have an irresistable temptation to put drawings through the appropriation account, which is completely wrong. Interest on drawings will be credited to the appropriation account but not the drawings themselves.

It is not always necessary to open current accounts as well as capital accounts; in an examination you should open current accounts if, firstly, the examiner asks for them, secondly, if the question makes any reference to fixed capitals and, thirdly, if there is interest on capital. In other circumstances a combined capital and current account is acceptable. You should also note the columnar form used in the solution to illustration 1 – this saves time in the examination.

Capital Accounts

	X £	Y £	Z £	Details	X £	Y £	Z £
	25	24	24	Balance b/d	20,000	10,000	4,000

Current Accounts

	X £	Y £	Z £		X £	Y £	Z £
Drawings	11,000	6,000	4,500	Balance b/d	3,000	1,200	300
				Salaries		2,000	1,600
Balance c/d	5,380	5,920	1,700	Interest on capital	1,200	600	240
				Profit for year	12,180	8,120	4,060
	£16,380	£11,920	£6,200		£16,380	£11,920	£6,200
				Balance b/d	5,380	5,920	1,700

So in illustration 1, the first figure is the £30,000 net profit brought down from the main profit and loss account. This is the profit to be shared between the partners according to the partnership agreement. Firstly, we give the salaries to the partners who are so entitled, in this case Y and Z. Debit the profit and loss account with £2,000 and £1,600 and credit the current accounts of Y and Z respectively. Next the interest on fixed capitals – 6 per cent of £20,000, £10,000 and £4,000 respectively for X, Y and Z is debited to the appropriation account, credited to the partners' current accounts. Of the £30,000, £5,640 has now been shared out leaving £24,360 to be divided between the partners in their profit sharing ratios – X one-half, Y one-third, Z one-sixth. The appropriation account is debited with the amounts, the current account credited. What would have happened if the profit had been £3,000 instead of £30,000? It is possible that the partnership agreement would say that salaries and interest on capital might not be payable in years where the profits were below a certain figure; but what would normally happen is that the salaries and interest would be regarded as prior charges, and debited to the appropriation account and credited to the current accounts as before. In the present example, this would mean that the appropriation account would show a deficit of £2,640 after salaries and interest, and this figure would be split between the partners in their profit sharing ratio and *debited* to their current accounts.

Complications can arise where the partnership agreement is varied during the year. Suppose that in the year to 31 December 1994 Z retired – on 1 September, say, if the profit for the year was £33,000 the situation would be as shown in solution 1(b).

Solution I(b):

Profit & Loss Appropriation Account
for the year ended 31 December 1994

	8m to 31.8.94 £	£	4m to 31.12.94 £	£		8m to 31.8.94 £	4m to 31.12.94 £
Salaries					Net profit		
Y	1,333		667		b/d	22,000	11,000
Z	1,067	2,400		667			
Interest on capital							
X	800		400				
Y	400		200				
Z	160	1,360		600			
Balance in PSR							
X	9,120		5,840				
Y	6,080		3,893				
Z	3,040	18,240		9,733			
		£22,000		£11,000		£22,000	£11,000

For eight months of the year – January to the end of August – there were three partners, and for four months only two. (*Note:* take great care when counting up the number of months, in particular it is very easy to confuse the lst of the month with the 31st.) The net profit for the year is £33,000; assuming this accrued evenly over the year, two-thirds of it or £22,000 related to the first period and one-third or £11,000 to the second. The net profit can be assumed to accrue evenly unless the problem clearly indicates otherwise, but students should scan the trial balance and any additional information carefully for items which occurred on a particular date – for example, repairs done to remedy damage caused by a storm in a particular month. Where this sort of event is mentioned, it may be necessary to apportion the figures in the profit and loss account.

Gross profit is apportioned on a time basis unless the turnover figures for the relevant months are known; rent, rates, light and heat, wages and salaries and depreciation will all be on a time basis; but salesmen's commission and sometimes bad debts, may be based on turnover. Repairs will either be due to a specific event on a particular date or be apportioned on a time basis. You should be particularly careful about interest payable to a retiring partner: as soon as he ceases to be a partner any interest payable to him from the date of retirement becomes an ordinary financial expense of the business and will, therefore, be charged in the main profit and loss account.

In this illustration, however, we will assume that the net profit has accrued evenly through the year, and can therefore be split on a simple time basis. Y then is credited, and the profit and loss account debited, with $\frac{8}{12}$ of his £2,000 salary, or £1,333; Z with $\frac{8}{12}$ of £1,600. X, Y and Z then receive $\frac{8}{12}$ each of their interest on capital leaving £18,240 to be split between the partners in their profit sharing ratio.

After the retirement of Z whose balances on capital and current accounts are transferred to a loan account, X is credited and the profit and loss account debited with $\frac{4}{12}$ of his annual salary; Z is no longer a partner and is therefore no longer entitled to any share in the profits, whether in the form of salary, interest or percentage share. X and Y are then credited with $^4/_{12}$ of their annual interest on capital, and the balance of £9,733 is split between X and Y in the ratio 3:2. You should bear in mind that there is no reason why the new profit sharing arrangements should have any resemblance to the old – in the present example X and Y could have decided to discontinue salaries and interest on capital and simply split the £11,000 between them in whatever ratio they felt was fair.

Capital Accounts

	X	Y	Z		X	Y	Z
	£	£	E		£	£	£
1.9.94				Balance b/d	20,000	10,000	4,000
Transfer to							
loan a/c			4,000				4,000

Current Accounts

	X	Y	Z		X	Y	Z
	£	£	E		£	£	£
Drawings (say)	10,000	8,000	2,000	Balance b/d	5,380	5,920	1,700
9.94 Transfer				Salaries		1,333	1,067
to loan a/c			3,967	Interest	800	400	160
				Profit for			
				period	9,120	6,080	3,040
				Salaries		667	
			£5,967	Interest	400	200	£5,967
				Profit for			
Balance c/d	11,540	10,493		period	5,840	3,893	
	£21,540	£18,493			£21,540	£18,493	
				1.1.95			
				Balance b/d	11,540	10,493	

DR		Loan Account – Z		CR
Date	£	Date		£
		1.9.94	Capital a/c	4,000
			Current a/c	3,967
				£7,967

There is one other topic which occasionally crops up with relation to profit appropriation, and that is the minimum guarantee. Suppose two partners, A and B, sharing profits equally, admit a new partner 'C' on the basis of a profit split of 2:2:1 but subject to a minimum guarantee of £2,000 pa. In the new partnership's first year's trading they make a profit of only £4,000. According to the profit sharing ratio, therefore, C would be entitled to only £800. However, as he has been guaranteed £2,000 pa A and B must make up the difference from their shares according to how they share profit. So instead of A getting £1,600, B £1,600 and C £800, A and B will have to pass over to C £600 each to make up his guaranteed £2,000 leaving them with only £1,000 each. You should, of course, remember to scale down the guaranteed amount if the new partner has been in the partnership for less than a year.

Changes in the partnership – goodwill

We now need to look at a major problem which arises on any major change in a partnership, whether this change is the admission of a new partner, the retirement of a partner, the amalgamation of two firms or even simply a change in the profit sharing ratio. This is the problem of goodwill. The term 'goodwill' as used in business had a variety of meanings before it became part of accounting terminology. One of the more common meanings of the word in a non-accounting sense refers to the benefits to be derived by a business enjoying a favourable reputation among its customers. From an accounting viewpoint, however, goodwill has a wider meaning than that of customer relationship. One definition by a judge was 'the tendancy of a customer to return to a place where he has done business before', but to accountants a closer definition would be 'the difference between the value of a business as a whole and the fair value of its separable net assets'. (This is based on Statement of Standard Accounting Practice No. 22.)

Although one can think of a business 'building up' goodwill, in accounting terms it only comes into existence when either the whole or a part of a business is sold for more than the fair market value for the tangible assets sold. That fact that the purchaser of the business is willing to pay more than the sum of the values of the tangible assets shows that he is paying for some other intangible benefits as well, and this extra amount paid is called goodwill. Goodwill exists when the rate of average net profit earned is in excess of the average for the industry. Excess profits in past years are important to a prospective purchaser only insofar as he believes that those excess earnings will continue in the future. If he believes this will happen, then he may be willing to pay a premium for the business. The premium he pays will represent the cost of purchased goodwill, and he may properly record it in the accounting records, in a goodwill account.

Illustration 2:

	Company A £	Company B £
Tangible assets	250,000	250,000
Average rate of return for industry	15%	15%
Anticipated profits	37,500	37,500
Actual profits	37,500	50,000

Two businesses, Company A and Company B are similar in size and in the same industry, and the average return on capital employed in that industry is 15 per cent. Both companies have visible net assets, other than goodwill, of £250,000, so one would expect to see average profits of 15 per cent of £250,000 or £37,500. The average profits over the past few years, however, show that although Company A has profits of £37,500 as expected, Company B has average profits of £50,000 or £12,500 pa above the average.

It should be obvious that a prospective purchaser will both be expected and willing to pay more for Company B than for Company A, because Company B has a superior earnings record which will presumably continue for some time in the future. Or, in other words, Company B has goodwill while Company A has not, and anyone thinking of purchasing Company A, other things being equal, will be unwilling to pay more than £250,000 as a maximum price. The amount that a purchaser would be prepared to pay for Company B would depend largely on how long excess profits could be expected to continue.

It should be noted that goodwill should *only* be incorporated in the accounting records of a business when it has been *paid for*, and there is an assumption that the excess earnings will continue under the new ownership.

There are several methods of valuing goodwill both for practical purposes and in examinations. The first is arbitrary agreement between purchaser and vendor, in which case the value must be given. A second possibility, popular with examiners, is to take a multiple of average profits of past years. For example, if a business has earned £50,000 on average for the past five years, then goodwill might be valued at, say, two years purchase of the average profits, or £100,000. This method is open to the criticism that it completely ignores the concept of excess earnings as a basis for estimating goodwill – the business might be less profitable than the average for the industry and still, on this method, be credited with having goodwill.

To avoid this criticism, a third method uses a multiple of the amount by which average earnings exceed the average for the industry. So, as in the original example, company B has excess earnings of £12,500 a prospective purchaser might be willing to pay a multiple of say, 4 times giving a goodwill figure of £50,000.

There is a more sophisticated variation of this, which starts with the excess earnings, but which then, instead of using a fairly arbitrary multiple, uses the average return on capital employed for the industry. So, in this case, as the average return is 15 per cent the excess earnings of £12,500 would be multiplied by $^{100}/_{15}$ giving a goodwill figure of £83,333. What this approach really means is that in this industry assets produce a return of 15 per cent. The return in this particular business is £50,000, which is the return we would expect from a business with £333,333 of assets. We can only see assets of £250,000, so we assume there must be further invisible assets of £83,333 and the invisible assets we call goodwill.

We can now consider how this asset, which will be unrecorded in the books of the partnership unless it was purchased from a previous owner, affects the book-keeping when there is a change in the partnership.

Illustration 3:
Brown, Jones and Green set up partnerships many years ago, and now, as at 31 December 1994, Green wishes to retire. The partners share profits in the ratio 2:1:1.

Brown, Jones and Green
Balance Sheet as at 31 December 1994

		£	£
Fixed assets:	Freehold land and buildings		9,000
	Plant and machinery		4,000
	Motor vehicles		2,000
			15,000
Current assets:	Stock	3,000	
	Debtors and cash	2,000	
		5,000	
Creditors		(2,000)	3,000
			£18,000
Capital accounts:	Brown	4,000	
	Jones	6,000	
	Green	8,000	
			£18,000

Green's capital is £8,000 and on the face of it, this is the amount owing to the fundamental accounting concept that capital equals net assets; it can be seen that Green will only be entitled to £8,000 if the shares and liabilities on the balance sheet are accurately stated. If the asset values are wrong, then so will be the partners capital accounts.

As the business has been in existence for many years, it is reasonable to assume that the partners have built up a certain amount of goodwill among their customers; and if they were to sell the business as a going concern they would expect a payment for this goodwill. There is no figure on the balance sheet for this intangible asset, as it is not considered good accounting practice to show assets which are not capable of valuation with any reasonable degree of accuracy. This does not mean, however, that the asset does not exist – merely, that it is not shown. Let us say that in this case goodwill is valued at £12,000. If Green now leaves the partnership taking only his capital of £8,000, he will be leaving a partnership which has an asset which belongs partly to him and from which the remaining partners will benefit if the business is eventually sold. To be fair, Green should be allowed to take from the partnership payment for his share of the goodwill he has helped to create; and so a journal entry is put through which records the asset of Goodwill as a debit; and the credit goes to the people who worked to create that asset – the partners – in the ratio in which they share profits, ie Brown £6,000, Jones £3,000, Green £3,000.

Green can now leave the partnership with the £11,000 which accurately represents his share of the business's true assets. Unfortunately, there is now an asset figure of £12,000 in the books representing Goodwill and we have already seen that it is not good accounting practice to have this asset on the balance sheet.

The next step, therefore, is to write it off. This involves *crediting* the goodwill account and *debiting* the remaining partners. Let us assume that Brown and Jones agree to share profits from now on equally. They will both then be debited with £6,000 in order to write off goodwill, and the balance sheet will show their new capital balances.

Solution:

	DR	CR
	£	£
Journal: Goodwill account	12,000	
Capital accounts: Brown		6,000
Jones		3,000
Green		3,000
Capital accounts: Brown	6,000	
Jones	6,000	
Goodwill account		£12,000

Capital Accounts

	Brown	Jones	Green		Brown	Jones	Green
	£	£	£		£	£	£
Transfer loan account			11,000	Balance	4,000	6,000	8,000
Balance c/d	10,000	9,000		Goodwill	6,000	3,000	3,000
	£10,000	£9,000	£11,000		£10,000	£9,000	£11,000
Goodwill				Balance b/d	10,000	9,000	
written off	6,000	6,000					
Balance c/d	4,000	3,000					
	£10,000	£9,000			£10,000	£9,000	
				Balance b/d	4,000	3,000	

You will notice that the first journal entry debits Goodwill account with £12,000 and the second credits Goodwill with £12,000. As these two effectively cancel each other out, the journal entry is often contracted to:

credit the *old* partners in the *old* profit sharing ratio
debit the *new partners* in the *new* profit sharing ratio.

This rule applies whenever there is a change in the partnership – retirement, admission change in profit sharing ratio or amalgamations.

DR			Balance Sheet 1 January 1994		CR	
	£	£			£	£
Capital a/c:			Fixed assets:			
Brown	4,000		Freehold land & bldgs			9,000
Jones	3,000	7,000	Plant & machinery			4,000
			Motor vehicles			2,000
Loan a/c: Green		11,000				15,000
			Current assets:			
Current liabilities:			Stock		3,000	
Creditors		2,000	Debtors & cash		2,000	5,000
		£20,000				£20,000

We have now looked at the problems raised by having a balance sheet which does not accurately reflect the true asset value of the partnership in particular relation to goodwill. The same problems, however, arise with any asset which is incorrectly valued.

Illustration 4:
There follow the balance sheets of two partnerships as at 31 December 1993:

Black and White	£	Red and Yellow	£
Land and buildings	7,000	Land and buildings	6,000
Plant	2,000	Plant	5,000
Current assets	2,000	Current assets	5,000
	£11,000		£16,000
Capital: Black	5,000	Capital: Red	9,000
White	6,000	Yellow	7,000
	£11,000		£16,000

The two partnerships wish to amalgamate ('combine') as at 31 December 1994.

Black and White shared profits in the ratio 2:1.
Red and Yellow shared profits equally.
The new profit sharing ratio is to be: Black $\frac{1}{3}$rd, White $\frac{1}{6}$th, Red $\frac{1}{3}$rd, Yellow $\frac{1}{6}$th.

The following asset values were agreed by all parties:

	Black and White £	Red and Yellow £
Goodwill	12,000	6,000
Land & buildings	13,000	10,000
Plant & machinery	3,500	4,000

Black and White are about to amalgamate with Red and Yellow. Before this can be done, however, it is necessary that the capital account of each of the partners accurately reflects his ownership of the true asset value of the firm. In the case of Black and White we are told that goodwill is worth £12,000. It is not recorded on the balance sheet, so we temporarily debit a goodwill account with £12,000 and credit Black with two-thirds or £8,000, White with £4,000. Similarly, with Red and Yellow the goodwill figure of £6,000 is divided between the partners, in this case equally. The next figure is land and buildings. Although this item is on the balance sheet of both firms, in both cases it is undervalued, and the effect is exactly the same as with unrecorded goodwill. Land and buildings are undervalued by £6,000 in the case of Black and White, so we put through the entry *debit* land and buildings £6,000, *credit* Black £4,000, White £2,000 – splitting the revaluation in the profit sharing ratio. Red and Yellow's land and buildings are undervalued by £4,000, so we debit their land and buildings account with £4,000 credit, Red £2,000, Yellow £2,000, as they share profits equally. When we come to plant and machinery, again for Black and White we need to debit plant and machinery account with the revaluation of £1,500, credit Black £1,000, White £500; but in the case of Red and Yellow we find that the plant and machinery is *over-valued* on the balance sheet by £1,000. We need, therefore, to reverse the usual entries and *credit* plant and machinery account with £1,000 to reduce it to its true value, and *debit* Red and Yellow with £500 each to reflect their reduced share of the asset value.

Once these adjustments have been made, the amalgamation takes place simply by aggregating all the asset values. First, however, goodwill must be eliminated from the books of the new partnership; so the total goodwill of £18,000 is debited to the new partners in their new profit sharing ratios. Black is therefore debited with £6,000, White £3,000, Red £6,000 and Yellow £3,000. The new firm's balance sheet can now be prepared showing the new asset values and the new capital balances. You should note that it is not usual to write the assets back to their original values – where the assets are tangible they are left at the revalued amounts. It is normally only goodwill which is written off.

Solution:

Black and White Capital Accounts

DR	Black £	White £		Black £	White £	CR
Balance carried into			Balance b/d	5,000	6,000	
new partnership	18,000	12,500	Goodwill	8,000	4,000	
			Land & buildings	4,000	2,000	
			Plant & machinery	1,000	500	
	£18,000	£12,500		£18,000	£12,500	

Red and Yellow Capital Accounts

DR	Red £	Yellow £		Red £	Yellow £	CR
Plant & machinery	500	500	Balance b/d	9,000	7,000	
Balance carried into			Goodwill	3,000	3,000	
new partnership	13,500	11,500	Land & buildings	2,000	2,000	
	£14,000	£12,000		£14,000	£12,000	

Black, White, Red and Yellow Capital Accounts

	Black £	White £	Red £	Yellow £		Black £	White £	Red £	Yellow £
Goodwill					Balance				
written off	6,000	3,000	6,000	3,000	b/d	18,000	12,500	13,500	11,500
Balance c/d	12,000	9,500	7,500	8,500					
	£18,000	£12,500	£13,500	£11,500		£18,000	£12,500	£13,500	£11,500
					Balance				
					b/d	12,000	9,500	7,500	8,500

The resulting, combined balance sheet shows:

Black, White, Red and Yellow
Balance Sheet as at 1 January 1995

		£
Fixed assets:	Land and buildings	23,000
	Plant and machinery	7,500
		30,500
Current assets		7,000
		£37,500
Capital accounts:	Black	12,000
	White	9,500
	Red	7,500
	Yellow	8,500
		£37,500

One point which often arises in examination questions is that an incoming partner may not simply make a straightforward introduction of one capital sum; the question may state that he introduces a certain amount as capital, perhaps a further sum as a 'premium' and another amount as a payment for goodwill, either to the firm as a whole or to one of the original partners privately. Wherever complications of this sort occur, the simplest way of dealing with them is to credit the incoming partner with the full cost to him of becoming a partner, and deal with the other half of the double entry as appropriate. For example, suppose C is being admitted to an existing partnership, A and B (who previously shared profits equally. The new profit sharing ratio is to be equal). He is to contribute £5,000 cash as capital, £2,000 as a premium and is to purchase a one-third share of goodwill valued at £12,000 from A, paying A privately for it. There is no distinction between capital and 'premium', for both the double entry is: credit 'C' debit cash. For the goodwill, C should be credited with cost to him – £4,000, while the debit is to the partner who receives the payment – A. It should be noted here that examiners do not always give the total value for goodwill – if you are told that a new partner pays, say, £6,000 for a one-fifth share of goodwill, you are expected to be able to work out that total goodwill must be worth 5 x £6,000 or £30,000.

The only time when it is impossible to put through the full entries is where the full value of goodwill is neither given nor can be worked out. For example, if the question stated that A and B who had been sharing profits equally admitted Z who paid in £20,000 of which £4,000 was for his share of goodwill but no indication was given of the future profit sharing ratio, it would not be possible to use the usual credit-at-new, debit-at-old rule. In this case all that is certain is that as A and B have been sharing profits equally, they must benefit equally from Z's payment. The double entry would be, therefore:

```
DR   Cash              20,000
CR    Z                              20,000
 – the introduction of the capital
DR    Z               4,000
CR    A                               2,000
      B                               2,000
```

Crediting his payment for goodwill to the existing partners.

Partnership dissolution

The final area of partnership accounting is the dissolution of partnerships.

Illustration 5:
James and John have been in business for many years, but have now decided to dissolve the partnership. They sell off the assets for the amounts stated, and in addition John took over one of the motor vehicles. There are now two objectives – one, to close off the books of the partnership, and two, to ascertain the profit or loss on the disposal of the business.

James and John
Balance Sheet as at 30 September 1994

		£	£
Fixed assets:	Land and buildings		10,000
	Plant and machinery		6,000
	Fixtures and fittings		3,000
	Motor vehicles		2,000
			21,000
Current assets:	Stock	5,000	
	Debtors	3,000	
	Cash	1,000	
		9,000	
Current liabilities:	Creditors	(4,000)	5,000
			£26,000
Capital accounts:			
	James	12,000	
	John	14,000	£26,000

James and John agree to dissolve the partnership as from 30.9.94.
They have share profits in the ratio 3:2.

The assets were sold at auction for cash as follows:

	£
Land and buildings	22,000
Plant and machinery	5,000
Fixtures and fittings	1,000
Motor vehicles	3,000
Stock	4,000

In addition one of the motor vehicles was taken over by John at a valuation of £1,000. The debtors realised £2,600 and the creditors were paid off for £3,800. There were expenses relating to the sale of the assets of £500.

The first step is to transfer all assets, with the exception of cash, to the debit of the realisation account. The realisation account records the transactions relating to the disposal of the assets, and is, in fact, effectively a profit and loss account on the sale of the business. So, for example, in order to close off the plant and machinery account, it is necessary to credit plant and machinery with the book value and debit realisation account. The realisation account will then show the total of the book values of all the assets. The assets are then sold, bringing in cash, so the double entry is: debit cash with the sales proceeds and credit realisation account.

The Partnership Act 1890 states that payments should be made in the following order:

a Outside creditors.

b Partners' advances in excess of agreed capitals.

c Partners' capitals.

d Any remaining amounts to be divided between the partners in their profit sharing ratio.

Given this legal position, the creditors should now be paid – debit creditors £3,800, credit cash £3,800. This leaves a balance on the creditors account of £200; this however, does not represent a liability but a discount received, or a sort of profit. The double entry to clear the creditors account, therefore, is: debit creditors £200, credit realisation account. We must also now pay the expenses incurred in selling the assets – credit cash £500, debit realisation account £500. You will note that both capital and revenue items are being dealt with through the realisation account; this is because the distinction between capital and revenue ceases to have any importance once the business is actually being sold and is no longer a going concern.

There is one asset which has not yet been sold – the motor vehicle taken over by John.

All that is happening is that he is taking part of his entitlement to repayment in the form of a fixed asset rather than in the form of cash. As far as the business is concerned, it is still a disposal, so the realisation account will be credited with £1,000; the debit entry being not to cash but to John's capital account. We can now calculate the balance on the realisation account, which is the profit or loss on the sale of the business. In this case, the profit is £9,300 which is split between the partners in their profit sharing ratio – James £5,580, John £3,720. There are now only two accounts left open – the cash book and the partners capital accounts. There are no partners' advances to repay, so the partners are now repaid their balances in cash. The balance on James' account is £17,580; on John's, after taking into account the motor vehicle he took over, £16,720. These total £34,300, which is the balance on the cash book. The partners are now paid their balances in cash, clearing their accounts and finally closing off the partnership books. You should note that, if you end up at the finish of a question with either a surplus or deficit of cash, you have made a mistake!

Solution:

DR	Partnership Realisation Account				CR
	£	£			£
Land and buildings		10,000	Cash: Auction		22,000
Plant and machinery		6,000	Cash		5,000
Fixtures and fittings		3,000	Cash		1,000
Motor vehicles		2,000	Cash		3,000
Stock		5,000	Cash		4,000
Debtors		3,000			35,000
Expenses: Cash		500	Cash: Debtors		2,600
Profit: James	5,580		Discount on creditors		200
John	3,720	9,300	Motor vehicle taken		
			over by John		1,000
		£38,800			£38,800

DR	Capital Accounts				CR	
	James	John		James	John
	£	£		£	£
Realisation a/c:			Balance b/d	12,000	14,000
Motor vehicle					
taken over		1,000	Profit on realisation	5,580	3,720
Cash	17,580	16,720			
	£17,580	£17,720		£17,580	£17,720

DR	Cash Book				CR
	£			£	£
Balance b/d	1,000	Creditors			3,800
Auction of assets	35,000	Expenses of realisation			500
Debtors	2,600	James:		17,580	
		John:		16,720	34,300
	£38,600				£38,600

DR	Creditors		CR
	£		£
Cash	3,800	Balance b/d	4,000
Realisation account: Discount	200		
	£4,000		£4,000

You should always have sufficient assets to pay off the partners exactly. There is one further question that students sometimes ask; why are debtors treated differently from creditors? Debtors are put through the realisation account with the other assets, and no attempt is made to distinguish the discount allowed, whereas creditors are kept completely separate. The reason for this is partly legal, partly common sense. Debtors can be assigned, or in other words the debts *can* be sold to third parties; but there is no way in which it can make sense to talk about 'selling' your liabilities. So debtors are treated the same as any other asset; creditors are kept separate and paid off, as is their legal entitlement.

It has just been stated that there should always be exactly enough cash, or other assets, to pay off the partners exactly. There is one case where, initially at any rate, this will not be so. Suppose in illustration 5 there had been a loss of £24,000 instead of a profit. Then James would have been debited with £14,400 and John with £9,600. This would have left James with a debit balance of £2,400 on his account and John with a credit balance of £3,400 on his, after taking into account the motor vehicle he took over. As capital must equal net assets, if the partners have a net capital of £1,000 between them there will only be £1,000 worth of assets, in the form of cash representing this. In other words, there is not enough cash to pay off John's credit balance.

The Partnership Act 1890 states that partners share profits and *losses* equally, or in their profit sharing ratios, and moreover the partners have unlimited liability as to recourse to their personal assets. Therefore, when on dissolution a partner ends up with a debit balance on his capital account, usually due to a substantial loss on realisation, he is required to bring in cash to reduce his debit balance to nil. James, therefore, will bring in £2,400 to cancel his debit balance leaving £3,400 now in cash with which to pay off John.

A different problem arises when a partner has a debit balance on dissolution, but is unable to pay in the cash because he is insolvent. The words to look for in an examination question are 'X was insolvent' or 'X had no private assets'. If you are not told that the partner is insolvent you should automatically assume that he brings in cash to cover his debit balance. You must not assume he is insolvent unless the question quite clearly says so. What, however, happens if the partner is insolvent? Where there are only two partners there is no room for argument, the remaining partner must stand the loss. So, in the example given, John would collect the £1,000 cash, but would have to write off the amount owing from James as a bad debt. Where there are more than two partners a problem arises.

Illustration 6:
Partner X is insolvent and has a debit balance on his capital account of £6,000. His two partners Y and Z have credit balances on their accounts of £5,400 and £8,600 respectively, and there is one asset remaining – cash at bank of £8,000. The partners share profits and losses in the ratio 3:2:1.

	X £	Y £	Z £		X £	Y £	Z £
Balance after realisation	6,000			Balance after realisation		5,400	8,600
X		3,600	2,400	Y and Z	6,000		
Cash		1,800	6,200				
	£6,000	£5,400	£8,600		£6,000	£5,400	£8,600

As X cannot bring in the cash, his loss must be split between the other two partners. But in what ratio? Logically, one would say in the ratio 2:1 as this is the ratio in which Y and Z share profits between themselves. This is not however the case, due to the decision in *Garner* v *Murray*, in which it was held that the loss should be split in the ratio of the partners' last agreed capitals, which for practical and examination purposes means their capital accounts on the last balance sheet date. So if Y had had a capital balance of £9,000 before the start of the partnership dissolution and Z a balance of £6,000 they would split X's debit balance in the ratio of 3:2, not in their profit sharing ratio of 2:1. The double entry would be, credit X £6,000 to clear his account and debit Y with £3,600 or $\frac{3}{5}$ of £6,000 and Z with £2,400 or $\frac{2}{5}$ of £6,000. There would then be sufficient cash to pay Y his balance of £1,800 and Z his balance of £6,200.

Sale of business as a going concern

Where the assets are not sold off piecemeal but to one buyer, an account with purchaser is needed.

Illustration 7:

A firm, Grocers Ltd, took over the business as a going concern, taking over the assets including cash and also took over the liabilities; and in exchange issued 40,000 £1 ordinary shares at par to the partners, and paid the expenses of realisation. John still took over the motor vehicle.

The purchaser is credited with the full cost to him of acquiring the business comprising shares issued at value, expenses paid and the *full* liability to pay the creditors. This forms the purchase consideration which is credited to the realisation account, the profit is again calculated and split between the partners who are then paid off by taking up shares.

Solution:

DR			Realisation Account		CR
	£	£			£
Sundry assets (including cash)		30,000	Purchase consideration		44,500
Expenses: Grocers		500	Motor vehicle		1,000
Profit: James	9,000				
John	6,000	15,000			
		£45,500			£45,500

Dr		Account with Grocer Ltd		CR
	£			£
Realisation account	44,500	Shares		40,000
		Creditors		4,000
		Expenses		500
	£44,500			£44,500

DR			Capital Accounts			CR
	James	John		James	John	
	£	£		£	£	
Motor vehicles		1,000	Balance	12,000	14,000	
Shares	21,000	19,000	Profit	9,000	6,000	
	£21,000	£20,000		£21,000	£20,000	

In this case the partners were paid entirely in shares, but frequently in examination questions they are paid partly in shares and partly in cash.

Illustration 8:

Black and Bird, who shared profits in the ratio 2:1, have sold their business to Robin Ltd. The purchase consideration consisted of £30,000 £1 ordinary shares at par and £20,000 cash. After realisation Black had a credit balance on his capital account of £40,000 and Bird £10,000.

How, then, should the purchase consideration be split, if the question does not give any guidance? One possibility would be to give Black all the shares and £10,000 cash, leaving the other £10,000 to clear Bird's account, but although this would have the merit of simplicity it has a major drawback – it leaves one of the partners with no interest in the new business.

The rule you should follow in examinations is to give the partners the shares in the new business in proportion to their profit sharing ratio and to make any adjustment on the cash.

DR			Capital Accounts			CR
	Black £	Bird £			Black £	Bird £
Shares in Robin Ltd (in ratio 2:1)	20,000	10,000	Balance after realisation		40,000	10,000
Cash	20,000					
	£40,000	£10,000			£40,000	£10,000

In this case the issue of shares exactly cleared Bird's balance, but in some examples it will be necessary for one partner to bring in cash if his allocation of shares (on the basis of his profit share) exceeds his capital balance.

Comprehensive examples

Illustration 9:

Johnson was in business as a sole trader and on 1 October 1994 he agreed to admit Brown as a partner. Brown was to bring £2,000 in cash and was to have a ⅖ interest in the profits and goodwill. Johnson's capital immediately before the admission of Brown was £5,600, the goodwill of the business was agreed to be worth £1,500 but no figure for goodwill is to appear in the business books.

On 1 October Johnson withdrew £1,000 from the business as part of the agreement to admit Brown as a partner.

Show journal and ledger entries recording the above matters in the books of the business:

Journal

		£	£
1 Oct	Cash	2,000	
	J Capital account		600
	B Capital account		1,400
	Being admission of Brown as a partner.		
	£2,000 cash introduced as follows:		
	Goodwill (⅖ x 1,500) 600		
	Balance being capital 1,400		
	J Capital account	1,000	
	Cash		1,000
	Being capital withdrawn in cash		

DR				Capital Accounts			CR
		J	B			J	B
		£	£			£	£
1 Oct	Capital			1 Oct Balance b/f	5,600		
	withdrawn			Cash purchase			
	in cash	1,000		of goodwill			
	Balances c/d	5,200	1,400	⅖ x £1,500	600		
				Cash balance			
				introduced			
				being capital			1,400
		£6,200	£1,400		£6,200		£1,400

When a partner retires it will be necessary to ascertain the amount due to him in respect of capital and profits, this usually means that a partner's retirement is accompanied by a revaluation of assets and goodwill. Any increases in assets and goodwill should therefore be credited rateably to the outgoing partner's capital account before he is 'paid off'.

Illustration 10:
Rook, Raven and Chough are in partnership sharing profits in the ratio 5:3:1 respectively. Raven is to retire on 30 September 1994 and is to be paid the amount due to him in cash.

The balance sheet drawn up immediately before Raven's retirement was as follows:

	£
Fixed assets	9,000
Current assets	2,000
Cash	6,000
	17,000
Creditors	(4,000)
	£13,000
Capital accounts:	
Rook	8,000
Raven	3,000
Chough	2,000
	£13,000

Goodwill is to be valued at £4,500 and fixed assets are to be revalued at £10,800 but no goodwill or revalued assets are to remain in the books after Raven's retirement.

Required: the partners' capital accounts and the balance sheet after Raven's departure from the business.

Dr				Capital Accounts				CR
	Rook	Raven	Chough			Rook	Raven	Chough
	£	£	£	£		£	£	£
Goodwill								
written off				Balances b/f		8,000	3,000	2,000
(⅚ : ⅙)	3,750		750	Goodwill				
Revaluation				(5/9:3/9:1/9)		2,500	1,500	500
written off	1,500		300					
Bank		5,100		Fixed asset				
Balances c/d	6,250		1,650	revaluation		1,000	600	200
	£11,500	£5,100	£2,700			£11,500	£5,100	£2,700
				Balances b/d		6,250		1,650

Balance Sheet		
	£	£
Capital accounts:		
Rook	6,250	
Chough	1,650	
		7,900
Represented by:		
Fixed assets		9,000
Current assets	2,000	
Bank	900	
	2,900	
Less: Current liabilities	4,000	
Net current liabilities		(1,100)
Net assets		£7,900

Illustration 11:

The following shows the position of Kaye and Jaye on the date on which they decide to dissolve the partnership. The partners' profit sharing ratio is Kaye 2: Jaye 1.

		£	£
Fixed assets:	Furniture		666
	Motor van		785
			1,451
Current assets:	Stock	2,064	
	Debtors	2,347	
	Cash	1,775	
		6,186	
Current liabilities:	Creditors	(1,887)	4,299
			5,750
Capital accounts:	Kaye	3,200	
	Jaye	2,550	
			£5,750

Kaye takes over the motor van at an agreed value of £650 and Jaye takes the office furniture at a value of £600. The sundry debtors produce £2,213 and the stock in hand is sold for £2,200. The expenses of realisation amount to £62.

Required: the journal entries necessary to record the dissolution of the partnership.

Journal

	£	£
Realisation account	5,862	
Office furniture		666
Motor vans		785
Stock in hand		2,064
Sundry debtors		2,347
	£5,862	£5,862
Being value of assets transferred		
Capital accounts: Kaye	650	
Jaye	600	
Realisation account		1,250
	£1,250	£1,250
Being assets taken over by partners at the value shown		
Bank	4,413	
Realisation account		4,413
Being sums realised from debtors £2,213 and from the sale of stock £2,200		
Realisation account	62	
Bank		62
Being expenses paid in connection with realisation		
Sundry creditors	1,887	
Bank		1,887
Being payment of sundry creditors		
Capital accounts: Kaye	174	
Jaye	87	
Realisation account		261
	£261	£261
Being loss on realisation charged to partners in their profit sharing ratio		
Capital accounts: Kaye	2,376	
Jaye	1,863	
Bank		4,239
	£4,239	£4,239
Being payment to partners in discharge of business capital		

Illustration 12:

The following is a summarised balance sheet of A, B, C and D who share profits and losses in the ratio of 4:3:2:1:

		£	£
Fixed assets:	Goodwill		1,000
	Plant		4,000
			5,000
Current assets:		1,200	
Current liabilities:	Creditors	(1,000)	200
			£5,200
Capital accounts:	A		3,000
	B		2,000
	C		300
	D		(100)
			£5,200

The partners decide to wind up the business and the following circumstances arise on disposal. Goodwill is worthless but fixed assets realise £3,000 and current assets £1,000. C can contribute only £50 from his own resources and D has no separate assets or liabilities. Costs of realisation amounted to £300.

Required: the partnership realisation, bank and capital accounts.

Dr		Realisation Account			CR
	£			£	£
Goodwill	1,000	Bank: Fixed assets			£3,000
Fixed assets	4,000	Current assets			1,000
Current assets	1,200	Loss on realisation			
Realisation expenses	300				
		A	$\frac{4}{10}$	1,000	
		B	$\frac{3}{10}$	750	
		C	$\frac{2}{10}$	500	
		D	$\frac{1}{10}$	250	
					2,500
	£6,500				£6,500

DR		Bank Account		CR
	£			£
Realisation account:		Sundry creditors		1,000
Fixed asset sale	3,000	Realisation account:		
Current asset sale	1,000	expenses		300
C: Capital account	50	A: Capital account		1,700
		B: Capital account		1,050
	£4,050			£4,050

DR					Capital Accounts				CR
	A	B	C	D		A	B	C	D
	£	£	£	£		£	£	£	£
Realisation					Balances				
account	1,000	750	500	250	b/f	3,000	2,000	300	(100)
					Bank			50	
					A: (Garner v				
C	90	60			Murray)			90	210
D	210	140			B: (Garner v				
Bank	1,700	1,050			Murray)			60	140
	£3,000	£2,000	£500	£250		£3,000	£2,000	£500	£250

Note: the solvent partners have made good the deficiency of the insolvent partners in the proportion A 3,000; B 2,000; this being the last agreed capital account balances of A and B.

Problems

Problem 11.1

Thick and Thin, who have traded in partnership for several years sharing profits and losses in the ratio 3:2 respectively, have decided to admit Stout as a partner on 1 June 1995.

The summarised balance sheet at 31 May 1995 of Thick and Thin is as follows:

	£	£
Land and buildings: Cost		7,000
Fixtures and fittings: Cost	11,000	
Depreciation	(3,000)	8,000
		15,000
Trading stock	5,000	
Trade debtors	6,000	
Balance at bank	2,000	
	13,000	
Trade creditors	(1,500)	11,500
		£26,500
Capital accounts: Thick	15,900	
Thin	10,600	
		£26,500

It has been agreed that on 1 June 1995, Thick should take from the partnership a number of items of antique office furniture at their current valuation of £1,500. In 1987, Thick had transferred the same furniture to the partnership at an agreed valuation of £600: aggregate depreciation to 31 May 1995 on this furniture amounted to £500.

The net assets including goodwill, and excluding only the antique furniture, have been valued at £30,000 at 1 June 1995 for the purpose of the transfer to the new partnership.

Upon being admitted as a partner, Stout transfers to the partnership his existing business assets and liabilities at the following valuations:

	£	£
Fixtures and fittings		4,000
Trading stock	1,000	
Trade debtors	500	
	1,500	
Less: Trade creditors	300	
		1,200
		£5,200

In the new partnership, Thick, Thin and Stout will share profits and losses in the ratio 2:2:1.

In the balance sheet of the new partnership, in addition to the capital accounts of the partners, the only accounts mentioned will be those included in the above balance sheet at 31 May 1995. The total of the balances of the partner's capital accounts at the commencement of the new partnership will be £31,600, the balances on the individual partners' capital accounts will be in proportion to their profit sharing ratios. Partners will introduce or withdraw cash where necessary to arrive at the correct balances: the partners have the private resources to do this.

Required:

a The capital accounts of Thick, Thin and Stout recording the above transactions.

b The balance sheet at 1 June 1995 of the new partnership, assuming no transactions have taken place other than those indicated above.

(25 marks)
Associated Examining Board – updated

Problem 11.2

Jack and Tom are partners in an old established business. Their partnership agreement provides that:

a Interest at the rate of 10 per cent per annum is paid on partners' fixed capital.

b Tom is credited with a salary of £3,000 per annum.

c The balance of the partnership's profits or losses is divided between Jack and Tom in the proportions three-fifths and two-fifths respectively.

The balances on the partners' capital and current accounts at 1 January 1994, were as follows:

	Capital accounts £	Current accounts £
Jack	12,000	1,000
Tom	8,000	700

Note: all balances are in credit.

During the year ended 31 December 1994, the partnership net profit, carried to the appropriation account, was £16,000 arising uniformly throughout the year. The partners' cash drawings during 1994 were as follows:

Jack   £5,000   Tom   £6,000

After reviewing the draft accounts for 1994, Jack and Tom decided to admit their senior clerk, Harry, as a partner with effect from 1 October 1994.

Harry has been with the business for many years and from the beginning of 1994 has received a salary of £4,000 per annum payable monthly.

For some years the partnership has used a house owned by Harry for offices and paid him a rent of £1,000 per annum. It has now been agreed that with effect from 1 October 1994, the property is transferred at its market valuation of £6,000 to the partnership as Harry's fixed capital; this change will mean that Harry is no longer to receive rent.

After stating that there will be no partners' salaries, the new partnership agreement provides that:

a interest at the rate of 10 per cent per annum is to be paid on partners' fixed capital;

b the balance of the partnership's profits or losses is to be shared between the partners in the proportions Jack a half, Tom three-tenths, Harry one-fifth.

Required:

a A statement showing the distribution of the partnership's net profit for 1994 between Jack, Tom and Harry.

b The capital and current accounts for the year ended 31 December 1994, of Jack, Tom and Harry.

(20 marks)
Associated Examining Board – updated

Problem 11.3

A, B and C have been in partnership for some years sharing profits and losses, one-half, one-third and one-sixth respectively. Their capitals at 1 April 1994 (no separate current accounts are maintained) were

A £95,000;   B £69,000;   C £38,000.

Their previous accountant retired on 31 March 1994 and a new one, Dennis Smart, was appointed from 1 April 1994. During the year to 31 March 1995 Dennis discovered certain errors previously made in the accounts, namely:

a Some years earlier A and B had made fixed loans to the partnership of £12,000 and £15,000 respectively, and the partnership deed provided that these loans carried interest at an annual rate of 10 per cent. Dennis discovered that in the year to 31 March 1993, the previous accountant had forgotten to provide for loan interest before dividing up the year's profit, and in the year to 31 March 1994, he had credited interest on A's loan account to B's capital account and vice versa.

b No entry had been made in respect of a partnership motor car taken over by C in January 1994. C had agreed to take over this car at £1,200, although its net book value at that date was £1,050.

Dennis prepared draft accounts for the year to 31 March 1995 which showed a profit of £70,000, before charging interest on partners' loans but after deducting Dennis's salary of £5,000. Dennis had so impressed the partners that they decided to admit him as a partner *retrospectively* from 1 April 1994. He was to bring in capital when he had sold some investments and was to be entitled to a one-tenth share of profits or losses, but was not to receive a salary. No other changes were made in the partnership agreement. Dennis agreed to pay into the business at 31 March 1995, £6,000 for his share of the unrecorded goodwill. The appropriate amounts were credited to the original partners' capital accounts.

Drawings during the year to 31 March 1995 were A £21,500; B £17,800 and C £7,400.

Required: the partners' capital accounts (preferably in columnar form) showing the balance due to each partner at 1 April 1995, after correcting the errors made in earlier years and after finalising the accounts for the year to 31 March 1995.

(18 marks)
Associated Examining Board – updated

Problem 11.4

Jim and Betty have traded as partners for many years. At 31 May 1995 their balance sheet showed the following position:

Balance Sheet			
	£		£
Capital accounts		Fixed assets	12,000
(no current accounts are kept)		Net current assets	6,000
Jim	10,000		
Betty	8,000		
	£18,000		£18,000

Jim and Betty propose to admit Junior to a one-quarter share in the partnership. Junior has £10,000 available which he is willing to pay into the firm's bank account as capital or for his share of goodwill. All parties agree that the fixed assets are worth £15,000 and that unrecorded goodwill is worth £5,000 and they also agree that no partner should benefit at the expense of another partner.

Required: draft balance sheets to reflect the following alternative situations, assuming in each case that the fixed assets are revalued and that Junior pays his £10,000 into the firm's bank account:

a Junior is admitted as a partner and all his £10,000 is credited to his capital account. Goodwill is to be recorded in the accounts.

(6 marks)

b Junior is admitted as a partner and pays for his share of the firm's goodwill, which asset is not to appear in the firm's accounts.

(9 marks)
Associated Examining Board – updated

Problem 11.5

X and Y have been in partnership for 31 years manufacturing printing inks and the following balances are taken from their books at 30 September 1994:

		£	£
Fixed assets, at cost		30,000	
Less: Aggregate depreciation to date		12,000	18,000
Stocks			9,000
Debtors			6,000
Creditors			19,500
Cash at bank			2,250
Capital	X		10,000
	Y		500
Current accounts	X	CR	1,250
	Y	DR	500

Profits are shares in proportion to the partners' fixed capital accounts. The partners are now considering retirement from the business which for the past few years has been managed by T, the young nephew of X. Profits available to the partners for the last two years have been £9,000 per annum after paying T a salary of £6,000, and these figures are thought to be typical and capable of being maintained in the future.

T has ambitious plans to expand the business and has secured additional orders, but these plans involve expenditure on new equipment of £60,000. The funds for this would have to be borrowed at 12 per cent interest per annum. Both the partners and T are agreed that the development should be undertaken and it is expected to increase maintainable profits, before loan interest charges, by £12,000 per annum.

After agreeing with T that the existing fixed assets should be revalued at £21,000, X and Y offer T the following alternatives, either:

a T will become a partner if he brings in cash of £10,500 of which £1,500 is to be a payment for goodwill and will be retained in the business. T will not receive a salary but, recognizing that he will be the only full time working partner, he will receive two-thirds of the profits, the remaining one-third being shared by X and Y in the same ratio as previously. Or

b T may purchase all the assets and assume all the liabilities of the business for £20,500.

Required: assuming that in either case the expansion plan goes ahead:

a Draft balance sheets to reflect the situation outlined in both 1 and 2 above as they would appear immediately after T accepts either offer.

(18 marks)

b Advise T, giving your reasons, which offer he should accept.

(7 marks)

Associated Examining Board – updated

Problem 11.6

The partnership of James, Charles and Harold was dissolved on 30 April 1995, at which date their balance sheet was as follows:

		£	£
Plant and equipment			32,000
Stock			19,000
Debtors			17,000
Creditors			(9,500)
Overdraft			(16,500)
			42,000
Capital:	James	12,000	
	Charles	8,000	
	Harold	7,000	
			27,000
Loan:	James		15,000
			£42,000

Notes:

a Profits have been shared: James one-half; Charles one-third and Harold one-sixth.

b James agreed to take over part of the business at the following agreed valuations, goodwill £5,000; half of the plant and equipment £18,000 and half of the stock £9,000.

c The balance of the plant and equipment was sold for £12,000 and of the stock for £7,000.

d The debtors realised £16,100 and the creditors were settled for £9,300.

e The costs of the dissolution came to £800.

Required: the following ledger accounts to record the dissolution:

a Realisation account. (10 marks)

b Bank account. (5 marks)

c The partners' capital accounts. (10 marks)

Associated Examining Board – updated

Problem 11.7

Brass and Smith have been partners for many years. They operate a foundry which produces a variety of metal goods which are sold from a shop attached to the foundry. The accounting year end is 31 December and profits and losses are shared between Brass and Smith in the ratio 2:1 respectively.

On 1 April 1994 they decided to admit Fender as an additional partner and from that date profits and losses would be shared between Brass, Smith and Fender in the ratio 4:2:1 respectively. On the same date goodwill was valued at £21,000. Goodwill has not appeared in the partnership accounts in the past and it was agreed that this policy should be continued. Fender paid £19,000 into the partnership to cover both his capital contribution and his share of goodwill. All adjustments relating to goodwill were to be processed through the partners' capital accounts.

It was further agreed that from 1 April 1994 interest of 5 per cent per annum would be allowed on the capital account balances at that date (after making the adjustments for goodwill), and that interest would be charged on drawings as follows – Brass £360, Smith £240 and Fender £150. It was also agreed that from 1 April 1994 Smith and Fender would be allowed salaries of £8,000 per annum and £12,000 per annum respectively.

The following is a list of balances as at 31 December 1994 after the preparation of the profit and loss account:

	£
Vehicles at cost	32,000
Foundry equipment at cost	69,000
Freehold land at cost	65,000
Provision for depreciation on vehicles	24,000
Provision for depreciation on foundry equipment	51,750
Capital accounts (before making the adjustment for goodwill)	
Brass	38,000
Smith	19,000
Fender	19,000
Bank overdraft	4,800
Cash in hand	1,250
Accrued expenses	1,050
Creditors	21,120
Debtors	25,950
Expenses pre-paid	600
Stock at cost	7,920
Drawings: Brass	12,000
Smith	8,000
Fender	5,000
Net profit for the year	48,000

Note: profits are deemed to have accrued evenly throughout the year.

Required:

a Prepare the profit and loss appropriation accounts of the partnerships covering the year ended 31 December 1994.

(15 marks)

b Compile, for the year ended 31 December 1994:

i   partners' capital accounts;   (6 marks)

ii   partners' current accounts.   (6 marks)

c Prepare the partnership balance sheet as at 31 December 1994.

(6 marks)

d Discuss *three* possible problems that are distinctive to the functioning of a partnership.

(9 marks)

Associated Examining Board – updated

Problem 11.8

Smith and Khan operate an international travel agency; their partnership agreement states that they share profits and losses in the ratio 4:3 respectively.

On 1 December 1994 Chow joined the partnership and paid into the partnership accounts £35,000 as his capital.

The terms relating to the distribution of profit of the new partnership which came into being on 1 December 1994 were:

Partners' annual salaries – Smith £9,000, Khan £6,600 and Chow £4,900:
Interest to be allowed on capital at 2 per cent per annum:
The balance of profits or losses to be shared between Smith. Khan and Chow in the ratio 4:3:2 respectively.

The trial balance of the partnership which relates to the year which ended at 31 May 1995 was:

	DR £	CR £
Bank		1,960
Commission on holiday bookings		70,420
Commission on holiday insurances sold		8,820
Loss on tours operated by the firm	22,600	
Debtors and creditors	16,400	28,800
Salaries (staff)	31,000	
Postage and telephone	3,850	
Printing and stationery	4,220	
Sundry expenses	2,100	
Freehold premises at cost	160,000	
Office furniture and equipment (cost £40,000) at 1 June 1994	18,000	
Cars (cost £30,000) at 1 June 1994	21,000	
Business rates	2,800	
Fixed capital accounts: Smith at I June 1994		100,000
Khan at 1 June 1994		55,000
Chow at 1 December 1994		35,000
Current accounts: Smith	8,000	
Khan	5,500	
Chow	3,700	
Bad debts written off	830	
	£300,000	£300,000

The following information is available at the year end 31 May 1995:

a Profits or losses are assumed to accrue evenly throughout the year.

b Business rates £600 and printing £520 were outstanding at 31 May 1995.

c The telephone rental of £150 was paid in advance on 25 May 1995 to cover the period 1 June to 31 August 1995.

d Depreciation is charged annually on cost at the following rates:

i office furniture and equipment 10 per cent;

ii cars 25 per cent.

Required:

a Prepare the profit and loss and appropriation accounts of the partnership for the year ended 31 May 1995.

(20 marks)

b Prepare a balance sheet as at 31 May 1995.

(14 marks)

c Prepare the partners' current accounts for the year ended 31 May 1995.

(8 marks)

Associated Examining Board – updated

Company accounts – background | 12

Limited companies

A company is a legal entity separate and distinct from its members. The capital of a company is divided into shares which are allotted to members in proportion to the money they put in.

The word 'limited' means that the liability of the members for the debts of the company is limited to the capital they have contributed or contracted to contribute. Except in rare instances members' private resources cannot be touched.

The majority of limited companies carrying on business in the UK may be divided into two categories:

a private companies

b public companies, whose shares *may* be quoted and dealt on a stock exchange.

Private and public companies

Private companies ('Limited' or 'Ltd' in name)

A private company is defined in the Companies Act 1985 as a company which by its articles:

a restricts the rights to transfer its shares;

b limits the number of its members to 50;

c prohibits any invitation to the public to subscribe for any shares or debentures of the company.

The private limited status is largely applicable to small- or medium-sized companies.

Public companies ('Public Limited Company' or 'plc' in name)

The main characteristics of a public company are:

a it must have a minimum of seven members;

b there is no maximum number of members;

c members' shares are freely transferable, eg by sale on the stock exchange;

d shares and debentures can be offered to the public for subscription;

e it must have an issued share capital of at least £50,000.

A large industrial or trading company requiring large amounts of capital would prefer public company status.

Private and public companies contrasted

Public company	Private company
Capital can be raised by subscription from the public	Shares cannot be offered for public subscription. No prospectus required for allotment of shares or debentures
Shares can be dealt with on the stock exchange	Articles of Association restrict the right to freely transfer shares
No limit to number of members	Number of members limited to 50 (except for employee shareholders)
Must have two directors	Need have only one director
Minimum capital £50,000	No minimum capital requirement

Company officials

Directors

The articles of association (or 'internal rules' of the company) may fix the minimum and maximum number of directors. A private company must have at least one director and a public company at least two. Directors are appointed to direct the affairs of the company, and as a body are known as the board of directors. They act in two capacities:

a trustees of company money and property;

b agents acting on behalf of the company.

Directors need not hold shares, but if a share qualification is required they must comply with this within two months of appointment.

In relation to directors the articles may contain references to:

a powers and duties;

b appointment and removal;

c remuneration.

Secretary

Every company must have a secretary, but a sole director of the company may not also be secretary. The secretary takes part in the authentication of documents issued on behalf of the company.

Auditors

A company is required to have auditors whose duty it is to examine and report on the company's accounts. The appointment, qualification, remuneration and removal of auditors is governed by the Acts.

Annual general meeting (AGM)

Every company is required to hold an annual general meeting of shareholders in each year.

Shareholders

The shareholders are the owners of a company. As shareholders, they take little part in its administration, although at the annual general meeting they have an opportunity to vote on election or re-election of the directors, in whose hands the control of the company lies.

To safeguard the shareholders, the Companies Act requires all companies to have auditors to report to the shareholders on the accounts presented to them by the directors. As we will see, the accounts must disclose a reasonable amount of information about the company's activities. This is extended by the directors' report which adds information on matters not normally covered by financial accounts.

The portion of a limited company's profits paid out to shareholders is referred to as a dividend. The distribution of profits by way of dividend is at the discretion of the directors. Normally a payment is made on account of the total distribution and this is termed an interim dividend. The final payment proposed by the directors is considered by the shareholders at the annual general meeting and invariably confirmed, the payment usually being made a few days after the AGM.

Classes of share capital

The share capital of a company may be divided into different classes:

a *Ordinary shares* are commonly referred to as 'equities'. The ordinary shareholders are the real owners of the company and are ultimately entitled to share the capital and revenue profits after any preferential rights have been dealt with. Dividends paid to the ordinary shareholders are normally determined by the directors. On a winding-up of the company the ordinary shareholders will receive any surplus after all prior claims by creditors or preference shareholders have been met.

b *Preference shares* carry preferential rights to dividend, usually at a fixed rate. They will carry preferential rights to repayment of capital in the event of a winding-up, provided the articles or the terms of issue so provide. Types of preference share are as follows:

i cumulative preference shares – these carry the right to receive arrears of preference dividend for earlier years before any dividend is paid to ordinary shareholders. Preference shares are deemed to be cumulative unless otherwise provided in the articles or terms of issue;

ii participating preference shares – these shares entitle the holder to receive a further dividend in addition to the fixed rate, usually pro rata to the ordinary dividend, eg a further 1 per cent for each 10 per cent of ordinary dividend;

iii redeemable preference shares can be issued if the company's articles so authorise. This type of shares will be redeemed (repaid) at a further date.

Classes of capital

Authorised capital

This is sometimes referred to as nominal capital. It is the amount up to which the company may issue shares.

Issued and unissued capital

Issued capital is the portion of authorised capital which has been issued. If the whole of the authorised capital has not been issued the balance is referred to as unissued capital.

Subscribed capital

This is the amount of issued capital which has been taken up or subscribed for by shareholders.

Called-up and paid-up capital

The distinction here is:

a called-up capital is the portion of subscribed capital which has been called-up for payment, whereas;

b paid-up capital is the part of called-up capital actually paid. The called-up capital not paid is referred to as 'calls in arrear'.

Working capital

This is an accounting term. A company's working capital is the excess of current assets over current liabilities. It is a guide to the solvency of the company.

Other capital terms

The word capital is frequently used for accountancy purposes in the following ways:

a capital expenditure referring to the purchase of fixed assets;

b capital receipts meaning cash received on the issue of shares and debentures or on the sale of capital assets

c capital profits and capital losses applying to the profits and losses arising on the sale of fixed assets.

The accounts of limited companies – form and content | 13

Introduction

The trading and profit and loss account for a company prepared for internal use is exactly the same as the ones you have been preparing for a sole trader or a partnership, with the following exceptions:

Profit and loss expenses

There are some new items of expenditure particular to companies, eg directors' remuneration, audit fees and debenture interest. These are charges in the profit and loss account in the same way as rent, rates etc. However there are often amounts outstanding at the year end in respect of both audit fee and debenture interest for which provision must be made.

Taxation

Corporation tax is levied on company profits at the rate prevailing for the accounting period. The amount payable is estimated at the year end and included in the accounts as a charge against the profit and shown as a current liability in the balance sheet. If the amount paid in the next accounting period differs from the estimate this is charged or credited in the profit and loss as part of the tax charge for the period in which the payment is made.

Dividend paid and proposed

A company may have many shareholders and they will receive a share of the profit at the discretion of the directors which is described as a dividend. This is expressed either as a number of pence per share or as a percentage of the nominal value of the shares issued. For example if the company has 40,000 authorised 50p shares of which 20,000 shares are issued, the dividend could be expressed as 10p per share, ie 20,000 @ 10p = £2,000, or as 20 per cent which is calculated as 20,000 @ 50p = £10,000 (nominal value) @ 20 per cent = £2,000.

The dividend is an appropriation of profit and will be shown as a debit in the profit and loss appropriation and as a current liability in the balance sheet.

The balance sheet is again very similar to that of a sole trader or a partnership with the exception of the share capital and reserves section of the balance sheet.

Share capital

The different classes of share capital are discussed in the previous chapter and simply replace the figure normally described as capital. Issued share capital is the nominal value of the shares issued to the shareholders who pay the required amount as requested.

It is a requirement of the companies act to show both the authorised and issued share capital on the balance sheet, or in the notes to the accounts (see later).

Reserves

The profits of a company are called reserves and these may be revenue or capital, realised or unrealised depending on how they have been generated. This may appear complicated but can be explained as follows:

Realised revenue reserves

This is the normal net profit of the year after taxation. The company directors may decide to transfer some of this profit to a general reserve or a reserve specifically designated for a purpose, eg plant, replacement reserve. This is to indicate to the shareholders that an equivalent amount of asset is being retained within the business and may be turned into cash and used in the future to provide for new plant etc. The indication is that they do not wish to pay out the assets as dividend and that they are being retained for future use. However these reserves are revenue reserves which are available for distribution and could be transferred back into the appropriation account if necessary.

Examples of this type of reserve are :

a general reserve;

b plant replacement reserve;

c capital reserve (non statutory).

Profit and loss reserve

After the amounts have been transferred to reserves as indicated above the remaining profit is available to the shareholders and a dividend will be agreed upon which represents the amount of cash that the company can 'afford ' to pay out of its liquid assets. A proportion of the dividend is usually paid during the accounting period as an interim dividend and the final balance proposed at the year end as an accrual. The amount of profit retained at the year end is added to past years accumulated profits and described on the balance sheet as profit and loss.

An appropriation account illustrating transfers to reserves is shown below:

		£
Profit on ordinary activities after tax		X
Dividends: Interim paid	(X)	
Final proposed	(X)	(X)
	X	
Transfer to general reserve		(X)
Retained for the year		X
Retained profit b/f		X
Retained profit c/f		X

Unrealised reserves/capital reserves

There are a variety of situations which give rise to the creation of certain types of reserves which may be classified as capital or statutory or unrealised or undistributable or a combination of several of these. The most common are described below and should be studied carefully.

Share premium

This is a statutory, capital, undistributable reserve. It is statutory because its creation is governed by the company's act which states that when shares are issued for an amount in excess of nominal value the excess must be credited to a share premium account.

It is non-distributable because the company's act restricts the uses to which the share premium account can be put. It cannot be used for the payment of dividends to the shareholders, but can be used to issue fully paid shares to existing shareholders as bonus shares (ie free of charge).

Capital redemption reserve

This is another statutory, capital reserve, which is non-distributable. If a company purchases or redeems shares out of profit available for distribution it is required by the company's act to make a transfer to a capital redemption reserve of an amount equal to the nominal value of the shares redeemed.

This section of the act is designed to protect creditors in the event of a company either purchasing or redeeming some of its share capital. They are allowed to redeem either out of a fresh issue of shares made for the purpose, or out of profit available for distribution, but in the second situation since no replacement capital is created a transfer must be made out of distributable profit to a non-distributable reserve.

The capital redemption reserve cannot be used for the payment of dividends, but can be used to issue shares to existing shareholders as bonus shares.

Revaluation reserve

This is also discussed at length in Chapter 3.

This reserve is created on the revaluation of assets. If an asset value is increased this will give rise to a credit to the revaluation reserve. Since the cash has not been received the balance on this reserve is an unrealised profit, and is not available for distribution as a dividend.

When the revalued asset is depreciated a proportionate part of the revaluation reserve becomes 'realised' and is therefore available for distribution. In addition when the asset is sold the balance of the revaluation reserve becomes 'realised' and is available for distribution.

If you refer to Chapter 3 you will be reminded that the revaluation surplus is disclosed in the new primary statement of total recognised gains and losses and will be taken into account when assessing the performance of the company. In addition to aid comparison with the results of other companies a note of historical cost profit and loss is prepared which adjusts the profit before and after tax as if the revaluation had not taken place.

Note how each of these items is disclosed in the balance sheet.

Loan stock and debentures

Another new item is the 'loan stock' category for the long-term loans and debentures. In the internal accounts this has been grouped into the same section as share capital and reserves but an alternative presentation as required by the companies act formats is to classify them as 'creditors: amounts falling due after more than one year'.

These are long-term loans on which the company must pay interest at the rate given in the question. Make sure that the correct amount of interest has been charged in the profit and loss account. Any outstanding amounts must be accrued for by charging profit and loss and including the accrual in the balance sheet under the heading of current liabilities. The alternative disclosure for this is creditors: amounts falling due within one year.

Specimen company accounts – internal

Study the specimen company accounts that follow very closely. There is no standard layout required but modern practice adopts the vertical approach (as shown) and as examiners encourage this form of layout you are advised to learn and use it whenever you are required to produce final accounts.

The accounts which follow are in a format frequently used for internal (or 'management') account. External or published accounts are dealt with later.

Curio Ltd
Manufacturing, Trading and Profit & Loss Account for the year ended
31 December 19XX

	£	£	£
Raw materials			
Opening stock	16,000		
Purchases	149,000		
Carriage inwards	3,000		
	168,000		
Closing stock	13,000	155,000	
Labour			
Factory wages		37,000	
Prime cost		192,000	
Overheads			
Detailed		20,000	
		212,000	
Work-in-progress			
Opening stock	4,000		
Closing stock	5,000		
		(1,000)	
Production cost of finished goods		£211,000	

Trading Account

Sales		299,000
Finished goods		
Opening stock	9,000	
Purchases (outside suppliers)	2,000	
Production cost of finished goods	211,000	
	222,000	
Closing stock	7,000	
Cost of goods sold		215,000
Gross profit		84,000

Profit & Loss Account

Administration and general expenses		
Detailed	XXX	
	XXX	
	XXX	
	XXX	
	18,000	
Selling and distribution expenses		
Detailed	XXX	
	XXX	
	XXX	
	XXX	
	8,000	
Financial expenses		
Detailed	XXX	
	XXX	
	XXX	
	XXX	
	3,000	
		29,000
Profit for the year before taxation		55,000
Corporation tax		28,000
Profit for the year after taxation		27,000

Profit & Loss Appropriation Account

Appropriations:		
Dividends: Interim paid	2,000	
Final proposed	4,000	6,000
Transfer to general reserve		(4,000)
Balance unappropriated for the year		17,000
Unappropriated profits b/f from		
previous years		83,000
Total unappropriated profits c/f		£100,000

Specimen balance sheet

Curio Ltd
Balance Sheet as at 31 December 19XX

	£ Authorised	£ Issued
Share capital		
10% Preference shares of £1	10,000	10,000
200,000 Ordinary shares of £1 fully paid	200,000	200,000
	£210,000	210,000
Reserves		
Share premium account		20,000
Profit & loss account	100,000	120,000
Capital employed		£330,000

Represented by:

	£ Cost	£ Depn.	£
Fixed assets			
Detailed	XXX	XXX	XXX
	XXX	XXX	XXX
	XXX	XXX	XXX
	XXX	XXX	200,000
Current assets			
Stock	210,000		
Debtors	330,000		
Cash	103,000		
		700,000	
Creditors: amounts falling due within 1 year			
Creditors	400,000		
Corporation tax	24,000		
Proposed dividend	4,000		
		525,000	
Net current assets			175,000
Total assets less current liabilities			375,000
Creditors: amounts falling due after more than 1 year			
7% Debentures			45,000
			£330,000

Company accounts for publication

The presentation and publication of the accounts of companies is governed by the Companies Act 1985 and 1989.

The prime requirement of the Act is that published accounts should give a 'true and fair view'. Whilst the Act does not specify how this is achieved, the following points need clarifying:

a   Accounts should be drawn up in accordance with commonly accepted accounting practice, consistently, and without ambiguity.

b   All information relevant to a proper understanding of the accounts should be disclosed, whilst maintaining a balance between completeness of disclosure and summarisation for clarity.

The student must appreciate that many factors need to be considered when examining disclosure requirements. It is not just the Company Acts, for example, that need to be followed, but also FRSs, SSAPs, accounting principles and conventions, and stock exchange requirements. However, a detailed knowledge of this area is not required for A-level purposes.

Account formats

The Associated Examining Board has issued a statement regarding the Companies Acts, and the following is a brief, relevant extract:

'i An *understanding* of the disclosure requirements of the Companies Acts 1985/89.
ii Candidates will not be asked to prepare accounts in a form required for publication. However, should some candidates in the examination wish to prepare accounts in accordance with the Act these will be equally valid, and no penalty will be incurred for so doing.
iii As before, questions may be set in which, for example, published profit and loss accounts are included as given data. In these cases, the information will be presented in a form required by the Act.

  Candidates may then be asked to comment. However, such questions will test some general accounting principles or methods from the syllabus rather than a knowledge of the presentation details required by the statute.
iv Questions may also be set, for example, of a structured essay type, involving an understanding of a company's position with respect to the purchase or redemption of its own shares or debentures.'

It therefore follows that an *understanding* of the form and content of published accounts is desirable.

It should be noted that there are two feasible profit and loss account formats, and two balance sheet formats.

The differences in the balance sheets are in presentation – one has a vertical format, the other a horizontal, whilst the profit and loss accounts have two different approaches, both of which can be presented either horizontally or vertically. Format 1 analyses by function, and 2 by nature. The text includes profit and loss accounts formats 1 and 2 and balance sheet format 1.

Profit & Loss Account
Format I

1. Turnover
2. Cost of sales
3. Gross profit or loss
4. Distribution costs
5. Administrative expenses
6. Other operating income
7. Income from shares in group companies
8. Income from shares in related companies
9. Income from other fixed asset investments
10. Other interest receivable and similar income
11. Amounts written off investments
12. Interest payable and similar charges

13. Tax on profit or loss on ordinary activities
14. Profit or loss on ordinary activities after taxation
15. Extraordinary income
16. Extraordinary charges
17. Extraordinary profit or loss
18. Tax on extraordinary profit or loss
19. Other taxes not shown under the above items
20. Profit or loss for the financial year.

Profit & Loss Account
Format 2

1. Turnover
2. Change in stocks of finished goods and in work-in-progress
3. Own work capitalised
4. Other operating income
5. a raw materials and consumables
   b other external charges
6. Staff costs:
   a wages
   b social security costs
   c other pension costs
7. a Depreciation and other amounts written off tangible and intangible fixed assets
   b Exceptional amounts written off current assets
8. Other operating charges
9. Income from shares in group companies
l0. Income from shares in related companies
11. Income from other fixed asset investments
12. Other interest receivable and similar income
13. Amounts written off investments
14. Interest payable and similar charges
15. Tax on profit or loss on ordinary activities
16. Profit or loss on ordinary activities after taxation
17. Extraordinary income
18. Extraordinary charges
19. Extraordinary profit or loss
20. Tax on extraordinary profit or loss
21. Other taxes not shown under the above items
22. Profit or loss for the financial year

Balance Sheet
Format 1

A   Called-up share capital not paid
B   Fixed assets
    I Intangible assets
        1. Development costs
        2. Concessions, patents, licences, trade marks and similar rights and assets
        3. Goodwill
        4. Payments on account
    II Tangible assets
        1. Land and buildings
        2. Plant and machinery
        3. Fixtures, fittings, tools and equipment
        4. Payments on account and assets in course of construction
    III Investments
        1. Shares in group companies

2. Loans in group companies
3. Shares in related companies
4. Loans to related companies
5. Other investments other than loans
6. Other loans
7. Own shares

C Current assets
  I Stocks
    1. Raw materials and consumables
    2. Work-in-progress
    3. Finished goods and goods for resale
    4. Payments on account
  II Debtors
    1. Trade debtors
    2. Amounts owed by group companies
    3. Amounts owed by related companies
    4. Other debtors
    5. Called up share capital not paid
    6. Prepayments and accrued income
  III Investments
    1. Shares in group companies
    2. Own shares
    3. Other investments
  IV Cash at bank and in hand

D Prepayments and accrued income
E Creditors: amounts falling due in less than one year
    1. Debenture loans
    2. Bank loan and overdrafts
    3. Payments received on account
    4. Trade creditors
    5. Bills of exchange payable
    6. Amounts owed to group companies
    7. Amounts owed to related companies
    8. Other creditors including taxation and social security
    9. Accruals and deferred income

F Net current assets (liabilities)
G Total assets less current liabilities
H Creditors: amounts falling due after more than one year
    1. Debenture loans
    2. Bank loans and overdrafts
    3. Payments received on account
    4. Trade creditors
    5. Bills of exchange payable
    6. Amounts owed by group companies
    7. Amounts owed by related companies
    8. Other creditors including taxation and social security
    9. Accruals and deferred income.

I Provision for liabilities and charges
    1. Pensions and similar obligations
    2. Taxation, including deferred taxation
    3. Other provisions

J Accruals and deferred income
K Capital and reserves
  I Called up share capital
  II Share premium account
  III Revaluation reserve

IV Other reserves
    1. Capital redemption reserve
    2. Reserve for own shares
    3. Reserves provided for by the articles of association
    4. Other reserves
V Profit and loss account

Accounting concepts and policies

The Companies Act specifies the following accounting principles which must be embodied in the statutory accounts:

a going concern;

b consistency;

c conservatism of prudence;

d accruals.

    The above points are adequately covered in Chapter 2.

    The accounting policies used in determining amounts to be included in respect of material amounts must be disclosed. Examples would include depreciation, valuation of stocks etc.

Accounting exemptions

All companies are required to submit to shares and debenture holders 'full accounts', containing all the required published material. There are, however, certain relaxations for small- and medium-sized non-public companies as regards submission of accounts for filing with the Registrar of Companies. Students should note that these provisions do not avoid the need to publish full accounts. Company size is determined by reference to turnover, balance sheet totals and employee number criterion, and so-called modified accounts may avoid the need to submit profit and loss accounts and directors' reports in the case of small companies, and less detailed information in the case of medium-sized companies.

The alternative accounting rules

Companies may now either continue to adopt the historical cost accounting rules, or they may elect instead to adopt the alternative accounting rules. It therefore follows that in order to comply with legislation, a company's accounts may take one of the following forms:

a historical accounts;

b historical accounts incorporating certain asset revaluations;

c current cost accounts (a method of accounting for inflation).

Illustration:

The Companies Act prescribes that companies shall disclose detailed accounting information in their annual accounts.

Required:

a Explain why companies are subject to detailed disclosure legislation, whereas other forms of organisation (such as partnerships) are not subject to such statutory requirements.

(6 marks)

b What other influences, apart from the statutory requirements of the Companies Acts, may be brought to bear on companies to disclose additional accounting information?

(3 marks)

Associated Examining Board
June 1979

Solution:

a Essentially companies are subjected to detailed disclosure legislation because the ownership of the assets is divorced from the control of those assets.

Partners and sole traders not only utilise the business's assets to produce profits but they also share them.

Shareholders own the shares of a company and the company owns the assets which work to produce the profits and hence the shareholders could be said to own the assets. However, it is not the shareholders who control the company's assets (dictate how they should be used) but the company's directors.

The disclosure requirements of the Companies Acts have evolved in an attempt to protect the owners (shareholders) against unscrupulous managers (the directors) and allow the shareholders some measure against which to assess the performance of the directors.

Also, potential creditors require the information (in order to assess the safety of their 'investment' in the company) as the shareholders have the protection of limited liability.

b The major influence is that of the professional accounting bodies, who issue accounting statements from time to time. These statements usually require some disclosure of information over and above that required by the Companies Act, eg SSAP 2: accounting policies.

A second major influence is that of the stock exchange. These requirements relate only to 'public' companies, eg the requirement for some firms to provide salient performance figures more often than annually.

Problems

Problem 13.1

The following trial balance was taken from the books of Hardnails Ltd at 30 June 1995:

	DR £000s	CR £000s
Land and buildings at cost	1,150	
Machinery at cost	250	
Aggregate depreciation on machinery 1 July 1994		65
Issued and fully paid ordinary shares of 50p each		200
Turnover		1,625
Materials purchased	730	
Wages	380	
Administration and selling costs	62	
Dividends received		4
Suspense account (see below)		611
Profit & loss account, 1 July 1994		48
Debtors and creditors	160	297
Quoted investments	48	
Stock, 1 July 1994	118	
Provision for doubtful debts		6
Cash in hand	2	
Bank (secured)		44
	2,900	2,900

Additional information:

a. The land and buildings have been revalued by a firm of surveyors at 30 June 1995 and their valuation reveals a surplus over book value of £150,000. The directors wish the revaluation to be included in the accounts.

b During the year no machinery has been bought. A machine was sold in April 1995 for £17,000 and the proceeds credited to suspense account. The machine had cost £39,000 and accumulated depreciation amounted to £24,000. Depreciation for the year ended 30 June 1995 has not yet been entered in the accounts. Machinery is depreciated at 20 per cent (reducing instalment method) calculated on machinery in use at the year end.

c £600,000 12 per cent loan stock was issued at a discount of 1 per cent on 1 April 1995, the proceeds being debited to the bank account and credited to suspense account. Provision is to be made at 30 June 1995 for interest payable on this loan.

d Quoted investments had a market value at 30 June 1995 of £59,000.

e Closing stocks have been costed at £185,000 (including £32,000 for factory overheads). The net realisable value of the stocks is £199,000.

f The directors propose a final dividend for the year at the rate of 8p per share. The authorised share capital is 500,000 ordinary shares of 50p each.

g Included in the item 'wages' were the following payments:

	£
Alan (managing director)	12,000
Bill (chairman)	8,000
Clive (sales manager)	9,000
Dennis (financial director)	10,000

h 'Administration and selling costs' includes the audit fee of £4,000.

i The doubtful debts provision is to be adjusted to 5 per cent of debtors' balances.

Required:

a Trading and profit and loss account of Hardnails Ltd for the year ended 30 June 1995.

(8 marks)

b Balance sheet as at 30 June 1995.

(12 marks)

c To what extent (if at all) would each of the following items mentioned in the additional information given above need to be disclosed in the Annual Report and accounts sent out to all the shareholders of the company:

  i   revaluation of land and buildings;
  ii   the quoted investments;
  iii the final dividend;
  iv   administration and selling costs;
  v   the doubtful debts provision.

(5 marks)

Associated Examining Board – updated

Problem 13.2

Companies which carry on substantially different classes of business activity are required to provide an analysis of their sales and profits between those different classes of business.

Required:

a Explain the purpose of such an analysis.

(9 marks)

b Critically consider the problems involved in providing such an analysis.

(16 marks)

Associated Examining Board
Summer 1994

Problem 13.3

Alice Tilbury had always invested her savings in a building society, but having read recently about the Government's drive for wider share ownership, she decided to buy some shares as an investment. She purchased 8,000 £1 ordinary shares in Boldventure plc on 1 November 1994 at £2.50 a share. (Ignore dealing costs.)

On 1 April 1995 she received an annual statement from the company as follows:

Revenue Statement for the year ended 31 December 1994

	£m	£m
Turnover	30.0	
Cost of sales	17.2	
Gross profit		12.8
Less: Distribution costs	2.3	
Administrative costs	3.1	5.4
Net profit		7.4
Retained earnings		
1 January 1994		9.1
		16.5
Less: Corporation tax	3.0	
Final ordinary dividend	2.5	
Preference dividend	1.0	6.5
Retained earnings 31 December 1994		£10.0

Balance Sheet as at 31 December 1994

	At cost £m	Aggregate deprecia- tion £m	Net £m		£m	£m
Fixed assets				Authorised & issued capital		
Freehold land				£1 ordinary shares:		
& buildings	20	–	20	fully paid		50
Other fixed				£1 10% preference		
assets	60	(19)	41	shares: fully paid		10
	80	(19)	61	Share premium		25
Current assets				General reserve		15
Stocks and work-				Retained earnings		10
in-progress		20				110
Trade debtors		21		Current liabilities		
Cash and bank				Trade creditors	10.0	
balances		25	66	Proposed dividends:		
				Ordinary	2.5	
				Preference	1.0	
				Corporation tax	3.5	17
			£127			£127

She received her dividend cheque for £400 on the same day, and she also noticed that the market value of her shares in Boldventure plc was now £3.50 a share. The preference share price had been constant at £1.20 per share since 1 November 1994. Despite being happy at having received her dividend she felt that she really did not understand the operations of public limited companies and she wrote down the following points to raise with her financial adviser.

a I understand that issued share capital is provided by shareholders. However, I do not understand the terms share premium, general reserve and retained earnings. Do they belong to ordinary shareholders?

b I have read in newspapers about company liquidity and profitability, but I do not really understand the terms.

c I remember that last year my interest from the building society, on the money I used to invest in these shares, was greater than the dividend I have now received. I am somewhat disappointed therefore in the amount of dividend I have received.

d I notice that Boldventure plc also issues preference shares and that they carry a dividend of 10 per cent. Would I have been better advised buying this type of share?

Required: as Alice Tilbury's adviser answer the following:

a Explain what is meant by:

   i   share premium account;

   ii   general reserve account;

   iii retained earnings account.

Explain to what use they may be put and who owns the funds represented by these accounts.

(16 marks)

b Define with respect to Boldventure plc:

   i   liquidity: (7 marks)

   ii   profitability.   (7 marks)

Use appropriate ratios to assist your explanation.

c For Alice Tilbury's investment calculate

   i   annual dividend yield based on the April 1995 dividend payment and the price of the shares on initial investment.

(3 marks)

   ii   the total return on her investment as at 1 April 1995. Express this as a percentage.

(3 marks)

   iii Advise her whether her investment has been satisfactory in the short run.

(4 marks)

d Explain the difference between ordinary shares and preference shares. Advise Alice Tilbury whether the preference shares would have been a better investment in the short run.

(10 marks)

Associated Examining Board
June 1993

Statements of standard accounting practice | 14

Introduction

The accountant must follow acceptable conventions when preparing accounts. This is to ensure that the financial statements have certain characteristics required by the ASB which are summarised very briefly below:

a Relevance. The information must provide the users with what they need to know. It must be relevant to the decisions they want to make about the future, and help them to evaluate the effects of past decisions.

b Reliability. The information must be free from error or bias. Freedom from bias implies that information is presented 'neutrally' so that no undue influence is exerted over the user as to his interpretation of the information. It must be 'complete' since to leave out information would be false and misleading. The concept of' substance over form' is applied which means that the economic reality of the transaction is recorded rather than the legal form. For example, hire purchase arrangements transfer all the rights and rewards of ownership to the lessee (the economic reality) whereas the asset legally belongs to the lessor until the option to purchase is paid (legal form). In this case the asset is treated as owned by the lessee. In addition 'prudence' must be exercised when making decisions about amounts to be included in the accounts.

c Comparability. This is a secondary characteristic of relevant information. The accounting treatment must be 'consistently' applied from one year to the next; must comply with accounting standards; and must be 'disclosed' according to those standards and the companies act. If these criteria are not followed, it may not be possible to make meaningful comparison between different period and for different companies. This would limit the usefulness, and relevance of the information being provided.

d Understanding. This is a secondary characteristic of reliable information. This is that the users can understand the information in the form in which it is presented and apply diligence when assessing the information. It is assumed that they have sufficient knowledge of the business and accounting and economic matters to be able to do this satisfactorily.

The characteristics described above act as an aid and guide in the standard setting process adopted by the ASB. Statements of Standard Accounting Practice (SSAPs) and Financial Reporting Standards (FRSs) describe the recommended procedures and practices to be adopted by professional accountants when dealing with the vast number of situations to be accounted for.

There are many standards and this text deals only with those that are examinable at A–level.

SSAP 1 Accounting for the results of associated companies

This topic is covered in the chapter on group accounts.

SSAP 2 Disclosure of accounting policies

Introduction

The objectives of SSAP 2 are to assist the user in the understanding and interpretation of financial accounts by improving the quality of information disclosed. To achieve this it requires the disclosure of all accounting policies followed in the preparation of the accounts, in so far as these are significant to give a true and fair view. However accounting policies are the application of accounting bases and these in turn are the developments of accounting concepts and so the standard describes and defines all three in an attempt to ensure its objectives are met.

Fundamental accounting concepts

The standard identifies and defines to users certain concepts which it is presumed underlie the preparation of financial statements. Fundamental accounting concepts are 'the broad basic assumptions which underlie the periodic financial accounts of business enterprises'. There are many concepts but the four defined in SSAP 2 are described below:

The 'going concern' concept
It is assumed that the business will continue in operation for the foreseeable future. This is an important assumption when deciding the value to be placed on assets. If the business is to continue then assets will be valued on the basis of their use in the business but, if the business is not going to continue, then it would be more appropriate to value assets on a break-up basis, which would be much lower.

The 'accruals/matching' concept
This requires revenue and expenses to be accounted for as they are earned or incurred, irrespective of when money is received or paid. Also that revenue and expenditure should be matched with one another in the accounting period to which both relate. For example sales of 100 items must be matched with the cost of the same 100 items. As you have already seen in previous exercises dealing with bookkeeping and accounts preparation this involves making an adjustment to carry forward that proportion of goods purchased that are still in stock at the year end. Adjusting the expenses to be charged in the accounts to include as an accrual any amounts outstanding at the year end, and adjusting expenses by transferring to the next period any payments which relate to services to be received in the next accounting period (prepayments), are further examples of the accruals and matching concept.

The 'consistency' concept
This requires the same accounting treatment to be applied from one accounting period to another, unless an estimate used in one calculation is incorrect, or an alternative and better method presents itself. If there is a change in accounting policy this will always require a note to the accounts and may require a prior year adjustment (see later).

The 'prudence' concept

This states that profits must not be anticipated and that revenue is recognised when there is reasonable certainty of its eventual receipt in cash (ie realised). All liabilities whether known or anticipated must be accounted for in full. This concept always takes precedence over any other.

The standard states 'In the absence of a clear statement to the contrary, there is a presumption that the four fundamental concepts have been observed.' If the accounts are prepared on the basis of assumptions that differ materially from those described above, the facts must be described.

Accounting bases

Provided the concepts described above are being observed, the next step is to apply these to the financial transactions. Accounting bases are 'the methods which have been developed for expressing or applying fundamental concepts to financial transactions'. You will have come across the procedure of charging depreciation on fixed assets, or the requirement to value stock and work in progress at the lower of cost and net realisable value. These are examples of accounting bases, providing a framework for determining the accounting period in which the costs or revenue should be recognised in the profit and loss account, and for determining the amounts at which material amounts should be stated in the balance sheet.

Accounting policies

Most SSAPs offered alternative ways of dealing with the transactions, to cater for their complexity or to offer alternatives to suit particular requirements of differing businesses, and therefore within each standard were a number of alternative accounting policies.

Accounting policies are 'the specific accounting bases judged by the business to be most appropriate to their circumstances and adopted by them for the purpose of preparing the financial accounts'.

In the case of depreciation the policy might be to use either the straight line method or the reducing balance method. In the case of stock valuations the policy might be to use 'first in first out' or a 'weighted average cost'.

The policy chosen can have a material effect on the results of the business. It is therefore essential that the policy followed be made explicit, and therefore accounting policies followed for dealing with items materially effecting the profit or loss for the year and the financial position of the business must be disclosed by way of a note to the accounts.

SSAP 3 Earnings per share

Introduction

A fundamental requirement of financial reporting is the disclosure of the salient features of the accounts in the clearest possible form. Outstanding among the matters of interest to shareholders in listed companies are earnings per share, dividends per share and the trend of these two figures over a number of years.

As new shares are issued, either for the purpose of acquisition or by way of a rights issue, a company may well show rising profits without reflecting a corresponding growth in earnings per share.

Earnings per share forms the basis for calculating the 'price earnings ratio' which is a standard stock market indicator. Price-earnings ratios relating to both past and prospective profits are widely used by investors in judging the relative worth of a share .

Calculation of earning per share

Earnings per share is calculated as the profit in pence attributable to each equity share based on the consolidated profit of the period (including the earnings of associated companies). This is calculated as: earnings, ie profit on ordinary activities after tax, after deducting minority interest and preference dividends, divided by the number of ordinary shares in issue and ranking for dividend.

Disclosure

The EPS figure expressed in pence is disclosed on the face of the published profit and loss account for both the period under review and for the corresponding period. The basis of the calculation should be explained either in the profit and loss account or in the notes to the accounts.

(Note that if there are changes in the number of shares because of new issues at full market price, rights issues, bonus issues etc this may require adjustment to the calculation of the number of shares to be included in the calculation. However the computational aspects of EPS, to the extent they are included in the syllabus, are covered in Chapter 17.)

SSAP 4 The accounting treatment of investment grants

Introduction

These are defined in SSAP 4 (revised) as 'assistance by government in the form of cash or transfer of assets to an enterprise in return for past or future compliance with certain conditions relating to the operating activities of the enterprise'.

Accounting requirements

Revenue grant

If a company receives a contribution towards paying an expense, eg rent or wages, this is a revenue grant and is credited against the expense in the same period.

Capital grant

If the contribution is towards a capital expense, eg purchase of plant and machinery, it must be credited to revenue over the expected useful life of the asset. To achieve this the standard offers two alternatives, although it should be noted that the first of these is not allowed for companies governed by Schedule 4 to the

Companies Act 1985, since grant aided assets would, as a result, not be shown at their purchase price or production cost. The two methods are:

a setting the grant against the cost of the asset in the balance sheet so that depreciation is charged on the net figure;

b carrying the grant in the balance sheet as a deferred credit, and transferring it to income over the life of the asset to offset the depreciation charge.

For example, assume asset cost £35,000, expected useful life five years and grant received of £10,000.

Under the first option the asset will appear as £25,000 (cost £35,000 less grant £10,000) and depreciation will be £5,000 per annum.

Under the second option the asset will remain at £35,000 and depreciation charged annually will be £7,000 per annum, but in addition a proportion of the grant, ie £2,000, will be credited against the depreciation charge. The balance of the grant ie £8,000 will appear on the balance sheet as 'deferred income'.

SSAP 5 Accounting for value added tax (VAT)

Introduction

VAT is a tax borne by the ultimate consumer and businesses not registered for VAT, but collected by businesses as part of the function of trading and paid over to Customs and Excise on a quarterly basis.

A registered trader will add VAT to his sales invoices at the appropriate rate and thus collect VAT from his customers. At the same time invoices for goods and services received will bear VAT which the trader must pay. The tax element of the invoice is recorded separately in an account for the Customs and Excise and periodically the balance will be settled. An excess of VAT on sales (output tax) over the VAT suffered on purchases (input tax) is paid over to the Customs and Excise, whereas an excess of input tax over output tax is recoverable. It can be seen that the trader should not suffer the penalty of VAT.

A trader who is not registered for VAT is unable to claim a repayment of input tax suffered and the cost will be added to the cost of goods and services received.

This standard does not deal with the accounting system necessary to maintain adequate VAT records, but deals only with disclosure and very simply requires that:
a turnover should be shown net of VAT on taxable outputs; and

b irrecoverable VAT should be included in the cost of fixed assets and expenses to which it relates.

SSAP 8 The imputation system of taxation

A detailed knowledge of taxation is not required for the A-level syllabus, it is sufficient to understand how a company will show taxation in their accounts. For this reason most of the matters covered by the standard will not be discussed here.

An estimated figure for the corporation tax charge for the year based on the taxable profit is shown as a charge in the profit and loss account after all income and expenditure has been dealt with. The corresponding liability is shown in the balance sheet as a creditor requiring payment within one year.

The nature of taxation is such that certain items of income and expenditure are accounted for in one period and become taxable in a later period, or sometimes not at all. To cater for this accountants assess the need to provide for deferred taxation on the timing differences in the anticipation that the tax will eventually become payable. A provision for deferred tax is created, and increased, by debiting the profit and loss account as part of the tax charge. The liability for deferred tax will appear under the heading of 'Provision for liability and charges' on the balance sheet.

If you refer to the published accounts format in Chapter 13 you will be able to locate both the profit and loss charge, the balance sheet creditor, and the provision for liability and charges.

SSAP 9 (Revised) stock and long-term contracts

Introduction

The principal objective of stock measurement is the proper determination of income through the process of matching costs with related revenues. 'Cost' of stock should comprise that expenditure which has been incurred in bringing the product to its present location and condition. In order to 'match' costs and revenue all costs incurred in respect of stock should be charged as costs of the accounting period, except for those that relate to the stock not sold in the period. These will be carried forward to be matched with the revenue that they will generate in the future. In other words stocks are being treated similarly to prepaid expenses.

However, carrying the goods forward to the next period implies that the asset will generate a future benefit at least equal to its cost. If it is anticipated that the future benefit will be less than cost, the prudence concept is applied and the carrying value of the stocks must be reduced to the new valuation, ie the net realisable value.

Valuation of stock and work-in-progress, other than long-term contract work in progress

The amount at which stock and work-in-progress, other than long-term contract work-in-progress, is stated in periodic financial statements should be at the lower of cost and net realisable value of the separate items of stock and work-in-progress or of groups of similar items.

Cost is defined as 'that expenditure that has been incurred in bringing the product or service to its present location and condition'.

Net realisable value is defined as ' the estimated proceeds from the sale of stock less all further costs to completion and less all costs to be incurred in marketing, selling and distribution'.

The appendix to SSAP 9 identifies the following situations where net realisable value might be less than cost:

a an increase in cost or a fall in selling price;

b physical deterioration of stocks;

c obsolescence of products;

d a decision as part of a company's marketing strategy to manufacture and sell products at a loss;

e errors in production or purchasing.

Determination of cost

Determining the actual cost of stock sold involves trying to match the item purchased with the one sold, which in practical terms will be very difficult. Imagine buying thousands of similar items over a period of time as prices are rising and then trying to discover the precise cost of the one sold. The standard states 'that the method used in allocating costs to stock needs to be selected with a view to providing the fairest possible approximation to the expenditure actually incurred'. Consequently, SSAP 9 sees the allocation of actual costs on the basis of physical flow as the ideal.

There are various pricing methods available for this purpose. In a situation where the actual cost can be identified this method will be adopted, eg stock of antiques, cars in the hands of dealers, jewellery. In other situations theoretical methods are used – FIFO (first in first out) and AVCO (average cost) are two of the possible choices. Remember that once a method has been chosen it must be applied consistently .

A more detailed explanation of the calculations involved is to be found in Chapter 3.

Long-term contract work-in-progress

A long-term contract is:

'one entered into for the design manufacture or construction of a single substantial asset where the time taken to complete the contract is such that the contract activity falls into different accounting periods. A contract that is required to be accounted for as long term by this standard will normally extend for a period exceeding one year. However a duration exceeding one year is not an essential feature of a long-term contract.'

Long-term contracts should be:

a assessed on a contract by contract basis;

b be reflected in the profit and loss account by recording turnover and related costs as contract activity progresses;

c turnover is to be ascertained in a manner appropriate to the stage of completion of the contract;

d an amount of attributable profit can be included in the profit and loss account as the difference between the reported turnover and related costs for the period. This is subject to the proviso that the eventual outcome of the contract can be determined with reasonable certainty;

e attributable profit is defined as 'that part of the profit'.

Disclosure requirements

The accounting policies which have been used in calculating cost, net realisable value, attributable profit and forseeable losses should be stated.

Stock and work-in-progress should be sub-classified in balance sheets or in notes to the financial statements in a manner which is appropriate to the business and so as to indicate the amounts held in each of the main categories.

For calculations and accounting requirements see Chapter 3.

SSAP 12 Accounting for depreciation

Definition

Depreciation is the measure of wearing out, consumption or other reduction in the economic life of a fixed asset whether arising from use, effluxion of time or obsolescence through technology and market changes (SSAP 12 – revised).

General

Provision for depreciation should be made by allocating the cost (or revalued amount) of the fixed assets less residual values, as fairly as possible to the periods expected to benefit from their use.

The allocation of depreciation to accounting periods involves the exercise of judgment by management, who have a duty to:

a allocate depreciation as fairly as possible; and

b select the method regarded as most appropriate to the type of asset and its use in the business.

An asset's useful life may be:

a pre-determined, as in leaseholds;

b directly governed by extraction or consumption (eg a mine);

c dependant on the extent of use (eg a machine);

d reduced by obsolescence or physical deterioration.

Accounting treatment

a *Fixed assets disposed of* – surplus or deficiency on book value should be reflected in the results of the year and disclosed separately if material.

b *Freehold land* – no provision for depreciation is normally required, unless the land is subject to depletion. If the value of freehold land is reduced it should be written down in the accounts.

c *Buildings* – should be depreciated having regard to the same criteria as in the case of other fixed assets – but see SSAP 19 on investment properties.

d *Useful life of an asset* – if revised, the unamortised cost of the asset should be charged over the remaining useful life.

e *Irrecoverable unamortised cost of asset* – write down the asset to its estimated recoverable amount and charge this new value over the remaining useful life.

f *Increase in market value of asset* – if account is taken of increased value by writing up the net book value then an increased charge for depreciation will become necessary.

g *Change of method of providing depreciation* – only permissible on the grounds that the new method will give a fairer presentation of the results and of the financial position. The unamortised cost should be written off over the remaining useful life commencing with the period in which the change is made.

Disclosures

The following should be disclosed for each major class of depreciable asset:

a the depreciation methods used;

b the useful lives or the depreciation rates used;

c total depreciation for the period;

d gross amount of depreciated assets and related accumulated depreciation.

In addition the effect, if material, of the following should also be disclosed:

a a change in the method of providing depreciation;

b a revaluation of assets in the financial statements.

Practical considerations

It is important that the concept of materiality is borne in mind when considering the company's accounting policy with regard to depreciation. If you follow in detail the criteria set out in SSAP 12 you will find that it is necessary to spend a very considerable amount of time deciding how any particular asset should be depreciated. It may be of interest to students to be aware that the vast majority of companies in the UK apparently depreciate their motor cars at 25 per cent per annum straight line which implies, if you follow the criteria set down in SSAP 12 that they believe that the car will be valueless at the end of four years, which obviously is not the case. In the case of machinery the vast majority of companies again will apply a policy of either using 15 or 20 per cent straight line. In general terms the companies will only attempt to allocate depreciation on a realistic basis where the cost of the asset involved is extremely high.

SSAP 13 Accounting for research and development

This is a difficult area, but it would be in the student's best interests to have a little knowledge of the accounting requirements. The Standard defines and differentiates between 'pure' and 'applied' research and 'development'. The provision of assets to provide research facilities may be capitalised, but otherwise all research expenditure is the use of technical knowledge gained from research to produce new or improved materials, services, etc, prior to commencing full commercial production. Development expenditure should be written off to revenue unless there is a clear indication that it is related to a feasible, viable project.

SSAP 15 Accounting for deferred taxation

Whilst a detailed appreciation of this topic is not required, it will be helpful for the student to understand the concept. Profit for taxation purposes is usually quite different from normal accounting profit. One cause of this is accelerated depreciation (capital allowances) for tax purposes. The object of deferred taxation is to smooth out timing differences caused by the differing rules. This is done by providing an extra taxation charge in the accounts when tax has been reduced by timing differences, and to release a taxation credit in years when the reverse effect happens.

Deferred taxation adjustments must be included in the taxation charge in the profit and loss appropriation account, and deferred taxation balances should be shown separately in the balance sheet, but not as part of the shareholders' funds.

SSAP 16 Accounting for inflation

Again, a detailed understanding of this topical, controversial Standard is not required, but the following is a brief summary of the main points:

The impact of inflation means that businesses need to earn higher profits, and to retain more funds in order to maintain existing operational levels. In other words, in inflationary conditions, businesses carry more value in stocks, and the other components or working capital are similarly affected. Also, if the intention of depreciation is to set aside funds for asset replacement, the current replacement cost is a more appropriate base for the depreciation charges than the historical cost. Inflation, of course, makes performance comparisons very difficult, not only from year to year, but also between different companies and industries.

Whilst the Standard is compulsory for all listed companies, you should remember that the 1981 Companies Act makes current cost accounts an acceptable alternative to traditional historical accounts.

The Standard attempts to adjust historical net profit by allowing for the impact of the items mentioned in the early portion of the above paragraph. To this end, working capital, cost of sales and depreciation adjustments are deducted from historical profit. One further adjustment is carried out, however, and this is known as the gearing adjustment. This is designed to recognise the fact that the way in which a company is financed can affect the impact of inflation on profits. For example, a company financed largely by contractual borrowing (eg 10 per cent fixed interest loan) benefits under inflationary conditions because the contracted repayments progressively lose their real value. This benefit is passed on to the shareholders in inflation adjusted accounts by way of the gearing adjustment, which is in fact a reduction of the previously mentioned adjustments, based on a fraction determined by the level of borrowing as compared to the total financing of the business.

The above explains how it is possible to examine retained profits and dividend policy in the light of inflationary conditions.

Fixed assets and stock will be valued in the inflation adjusted accounts at value to the business, and the net effect of all the inflation adjustments is represented in the balance sheet as a current cost reserve (normally a liability).

SSAP 16 ran into considerable difficulties on implementation and has, effectively, been withdrawn.

Example of Current Cost Profit & Loss Account for year ended 31 March 1995

	£000	£000
Historic profit before tax and interest	3,954	
Deduct: Current cost operating adjustments –		
Depreciation	262	
Cost of sales	64	
Monetary working capital	74	
		400
		3,554
Add: Gearing adjustment	94	
Deduct: Interest payable	274	
		180
Current cost profit before tax		3,374
Taxation		2,876
Current cost profit attributable to shareholders		498
Dividends		614
Reduction in reserves		£116

SSAP 17 Post-balance sheet events

Introduction

Post-balance sheet events are events, both favourable and unfavourable, which occur between the balance sheet date and the date of approval of the accounts by the board of directors. Certain of these events need to be reflected in the financial statements, either by changing the amounts included or by way of disclosure. These measures are considered necessary as a means of ensuring that the financial statements are not misleading.

The Standard defines two important types of event

a   Adjusting events are post balance sheet events which provide further evidence of conditions existing at the balance sheet date, and as such require alteration to amounts included in the financial statements. The following may be taken as examples of such events:

i   evidence that assumptions made concerning accrued profits on long-term contracts were materially inaccurate;

ii alteration to corporation tax rates;

iii discovery of error or fraud;

iv evidence of permanent diminuition in value of property.

Students should also be aware that if subsequent events indicate that the 'going concern' concept should not have been applied, then the accounts need to be adjusted accordingly.

b   Non-adjusting events relate to conditions that did not exist at balance sheet date. These events cannot therefore alter amounts included in the balance sheet, but disclosure, by way of a note is required if non-disclosure would adversely affect the ability of users to reach a proper understanding of the financial position of the business. Disclosure should include the nature of the event, and an estimate of the before taxation implications of the event where practicable. The following may be taken as examples of non-adjusting events:

i   mergers, reconstructions and acquisitions;

ii share and debenture issues;

iii fixed asset transactions;

iv alteration to trading activities;

v   foreign exchange rate movements;

vi government action, strikes, disputes, etc.

SSAP 18 Accounting for contingencies

The definition of a contingency is a little confusing, but leaves little doubt as to the nature of the subject matter. It is said to be a condition, existing at balance sheet date, where the outcome will be confirmed only on the occurrence or non-occurrence of one or more uncertain future events. A contingency could be a gain or a loss, and examples include unresolved legal disputes, insurance claims, etc.

The accounting Standard requires that, in addition to amounts accrued under normal prudence concepts, material contingent losses should be accrued where the loss can be reasonably accurately assessed at account approval date. Any loss not so accrued should be disclosed by way of a note. Contingent gains are not accrued, and only disclosed by a note if it is probable that the gain will be realised.

Disclosure, if required, should include the nature of the contingency, the uncertainties involved, and a prudent estimate of the financial implications before taxation. Where it is impracticable to ascertain the likely financial effect, this fact should be stated.

SSAP 19 Investment properties

The basic principle outlined by SSAP 12 (Depreciation) is that all fixed assets having a finite useful life (ie all fixed assets except freehold land) should be depreciated.

SSAP 19 embodies an exception to this rule in the form of investment properties. These are defined as an interest in land and/or buildings, on which construction and development work is complete, held as an investment to produce income which is determined on an 'arm's length' basis.

'Investment properties' must not be 'owner-occupied' properties ie they must be rented out on a commercial basis.

Under SSAP 19 such properties are not to be depreciated. They are, however, to be revalued annually with the revaluation surplus or deficit recorded in a separate 'investment' revaluation reserve.

SSAP 20 Foreign currency

(A detailed knowledge of this SSAP is not required.)

The standard outlines two different methods of translating foreign currency, their uses and how to account for the resulting gains or losses on translation.

An overview of the contents of SSAP 20 is given by the following diagram:

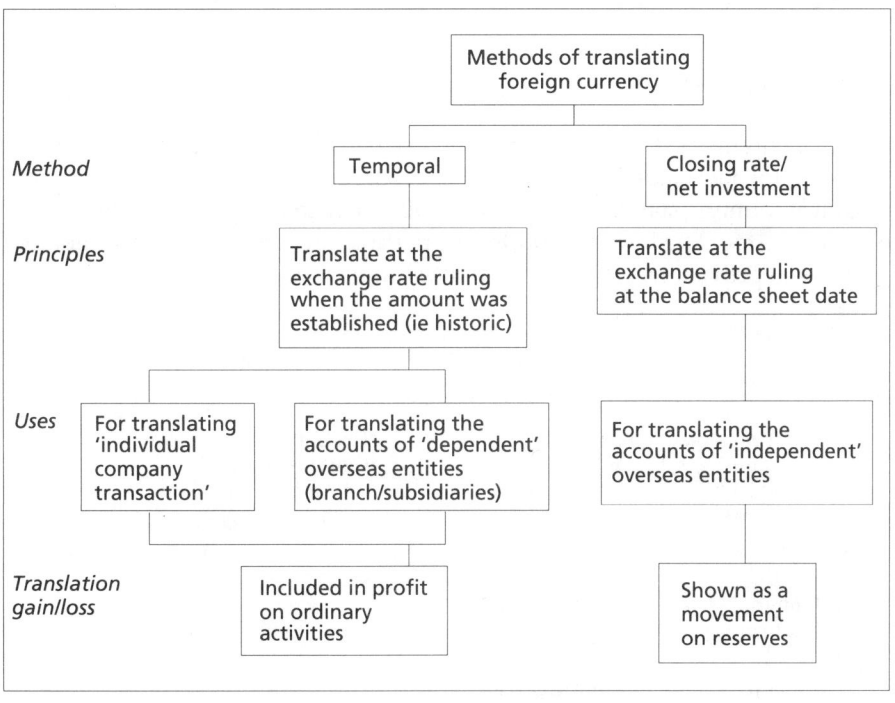

SSAP 21 Leases and hire purchase

This SSAP formalises the methods of accounting for hire purchase transactions outlined in Chapter 10.

In addition, 'new' rules are set out for accounting for 'lease' or 'rental' transactions which, as in the case of hire purchase, require accountants to record the commercial 'substance' of the lease transaction, not its strict legal form.

The position may be outlined as follows:

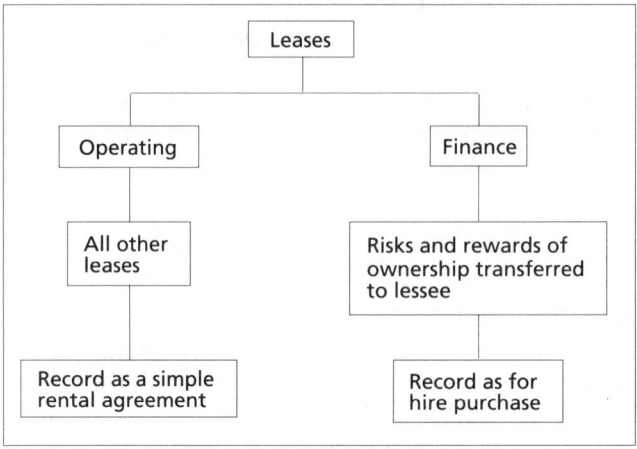

SSAP 22 Goodwill

SSAP 22 defines goodwill as the difference between the value of a business as a whole and the fair value of its separable net assets.

As an accounting standard, the SSAP applies only to company accounts and does not therefore regulate how sole traders or partnerships may account for goodwill.

The main provisions of SSAP 22 can be summarised as follows:

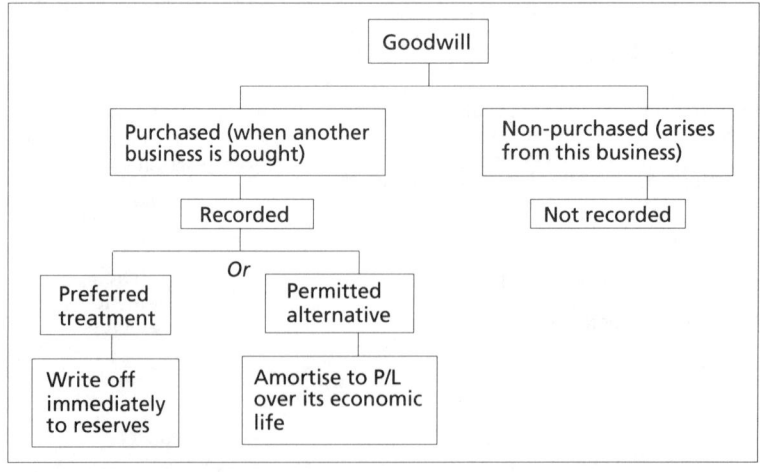

Problems

Problem 14.1

Given below are five unconnected transactions made by five different businesses together with the proposed treatment of each transaction in the final accounts of the business concerned.

a Perry Ltd commenced trading in the early 1980s. Since then company sales have increased by 400 per cent and the number of customers has doubled. The company has an extremely good name in the trade. As a result the directors propose to introduce £80,000 goodwill into the balance sheet as a fixed asset.

b Fishwick Ltd bought new premises in 1988. The market value of these premises fell between 1988 and 1992. Consequently the premises were depreciated until 1992. Since 1992 property prices have started to rise again so the directors are proposing to discontinue the practice of providing for depreciation on premises.

c Patel values all his business stock at cost. He is proposing to value his closing stock of clothing at £90,000. Included in this figure is a batch of damaged sweatshirts which cost £800. After undertaking repairs costing £100 they could be sold for £850. The cost of replacing the damaged sweatshirts would be £700.

d Glynn Ltd commenced business in January 1990. In the first two years losses were incurred. Since 1992 the company has started to make profits. For the year ended 31 December 1993 debenture interest paid amounted to £18,000. Bank overdraft interest was £1,500. The directors would like to declare a dividend of £20,000. They propose to show an entry in the profit and loss account interest and dividends £39,500.

e Nelson plc had written off a bad debt of £93,000 owed by Saunders & Co in the year ended 30 April 1991. In the current year Nelson plc has received a payment of £23,000 from the receivers of Saunders & Co. The directors are proposing to credit the £23,000 to retained earnings as the amount recovered refers to a previous year.

Required:

Explain, giving reasons, how each proposal should have been treated and explain which generally accepted accounting conventions and principles should have been applied.

(50 marks)
Associated Examining Board
Summer 1994

Problem 14.2

Alan and Brian are the sole shareholders of Convex Ltd a small private company which began to trade just one year ago. The accountant to the company has just drafted the accounts for the year ended 30 September 1994 which are as follows:

Profit & Loss Account for the year ended 30 September 1994

	£000's	£000's
Sales (6,000 units at £20)		120
Less: Direct materials	90	
Direct labour	40	
Cost of 10,000 units	130	
Less: Closing stock of 4,000 units	52	78
		42
Depreciation of plant and equipment	20	
Factory overheads	30	
General overheads and expenses	7	
Research and development expenditure	12	
Advertising	6	75
Net loss for the year		£33

Balance Sheet at 30 September 1994

	£000's		£000's
Ordinary share capital	80	Plant and equipment at cost	60
Trade creditors	62	*Less:* Depreciation	20
Bank overdraft	15		40
		Stock of finished goods	52
		Debtors	32
		Profit & loss a/c	33
	£157		£157

The company's accountant advised you that:

a He has provided depreciation on the reducing instalment method (at a rate of $33\frac{1}{3}$ per cent) so as to reduce substantially the book value of the plant and equipment by the end of its expected life of six years.

b Research and development expenditure consists of wages and the cost of materials in developing prototypes. These are thrown away after testing.

c Advertising represents the cost of the first six months – to the balance sheet date – of a 12-month advertising campaign.

d No stocks of raw materials are kept and there is no work in progress.

Alan and Brian tell you they do not understand why the accounts show a loss. They argue that sales in the first year were higher than planned and that future prospects for the product are very good. They suggest the situation would be improved by:

a providing depreciation on the straight line basis over six years (ignore scrap resale value);

b including factory overheads and depreciation in the stock valuation at 30 September; and

c treating all research and development expenditure and three-quarters of the advertising as a prepayment, the benefit of which extends over future years.

Required:

a Redraft the profit and loss account and the balance sheet in accordance with the suggestions made by Alan and Brian in (a), (b) and (c) above.

(15 marks)

b Comment on the issues and accounting principles raised by these suggestions.

(10 marks)

Associated Examining Board – updated

Problem 14.3

The main purpose of a company's annual published financial statements is to give information about the results of trading activities and also the financial position of the business.

Legal requirements influence the contents of such statements with companies frequently being faced with demands by a variety of users for greater and wider levels of disclosure.

Companies generally seek to improve the quality and effectiveness of the statements which they prepare to satisfy these requests.

Required:

a State clearly the purposes of published financial statements.

(8 marks)

b Describe the problems that public companies must consider when preparing annual financial statements for publication.

(8 marks)

c Outline what you consider are the basic characteristics (eg clarity) needed to produce effective financial statements.

(8 marks)

Associated Examining Board
Summer 1994

The cash flow statement | 15

Introduction

In addition to profit a business depends for its success on a positive cash flow. Unless the profits are ultimately realised it will be unable to pay its way. An inability to meet current financial obligations will often force a business to cease trading, so it is clear that a business must pay considerable attention to liquidity as well as profitability if it is to succeed.

It is possible to earn profits without generating an equivalent amount of cash and equally the reverse is true. Reported profit is an important indicator of company performance but so is its ability to generate corresponding cash flows.

With this in mind a variety of standards have been produced over the years in an attempt to explain and demonstrate the relationship between cash and profit, the most recent of these is FRS 1 'Cash flow statements' introduced in 1991, which replaced SSAP 10 'Source and application of funds statement'.

It requires reporting entities which fall within its scope to prepare a cash flow statement as part of their financial statements setting out on a standard basis the cash generated and absorbed within a period.

The decision to introduce cash flow reporting was a direct consequence of the shortcomings of funds flow reporting. These shortcomings are summarised below:

a The form and content of the statement were not prescribed which resulted in a wide variety of different styles of presentation, some more informative than others.

b This flexibility reduced the usefulness of statements because comparability from one statement to another was not meaningful.

c The statement simply listed changes in the balance sheet totals of assets, liabilities and capital, rather than showing how the various activities of the business have generated or absorbed funds.

d It did not demonstrate the company's ability to meet obligations or to pay dividends or about its need to arrange external financing.

e Numerous interpretations of the term 'fund' were used in practice although SSAP 10 had only defined them as net liquid funds. Some companies chose to represent them as working capital, others as net borrowings and some even as all financial resources of the company.

FRS 1 addresses the problems listed above in the following ways:

a The standard requires a uniform presentation of the statement and notes as prescribed by FRS 1, which will make such information more comparable among companies than the previous funds flow statement.

b The greater comparability will make the information more useful to users of the financial statements.

c It will give more information about a company's financial viability and liquidity showing how each activity of the business has generated or absorbed cash/cash equivalents.

d The term cash and cash equivalents are clearly defined in the standard and form the 'bottom line' of the statement so there is no doubt about the interpretation of the statement.

FRS 1 Standard format for the cash flow statement and notes

FRS 1 requires 'large' companies to prepare a cash flow statement as part of the statutory accounts. The purpose of the statement is to report the movements of cash and cash equivalents. Cash equivalents are defined as short-term, highly liquid investments which are readily convertible to known amounts of cash without notice and which are within three months of maturity when acquired.

FRS 1 sets out a prescribed format for the cash flow statement which highlights cash inflow and outflow from the main activities of the business. The classifications are:

	£
Operating activities	X
Return on investment and servicing of finance	X
Taxation	X
Investing activities	X
Financing	X

A total must be shown for each standard heading and for the net cash flow before financing.

The format also sets out the various sub-headings of cash inflow and outflow within each of the standard headings other than operating activities. Companies are required to follow this classification in the preparation of cash flow statements and since the FRS is prescriptive in this way it is advisable for students to learn the format thoroughly and not to deviate from it when answering questions.

Where cash flow relates to items that are reported as exceptional, or are derived from a discontinued activity, the cash flows are to be included under the appropriate standard heading according to the nature of the item and disclosed separately, to allow users to understand the effect on the cash flow of that particular category.

All cash flows should be reported net of VAT unless the tax is irrecoverable, in which case it is added to the cash flow.

Format

The format set out below is for a single company. The headings in the bold typeface are a requirement of the Standard and each category must be separately identified (unless there are no material cash flows to be reported under them) and in the order shown below.

ABC Ltd
Cash Flow Statement for the year ended 31 December 1994

	£000	£000
Net cash inflow from operating activities		6,889
Returns on investment and servicing of finance		
Interest received	3,011	
Interest paid	(12)	
Dividends paid	(2,417)	
Net cash inflows/(outflows) from returns on investment and servicing of finance		582
Taxation		
Corporation tax paid	(2,922)	
Tax paid		(2,922)
Investing activities		
Payment to acquire tangible fixed assets	(1,496)	
Payment to acquire intangible fixed assets	(71)	
Receipts from sales of tangible fixed assets	42	
Net cash inflow/(outflow) from investing activities		(1,525)
Net cash inflow before financing		3,024
Financing		
Issue of ordinary share capital	211	
Expenses paid on share issue	(5)	
Repayment of debenture loan	(149)	
Net cash inflow/(outflow) from financing		57
Increase/(decrease) in cash and cash equivalents		£3,081

Notes to the cash flow statement

1 Reconciliation of operating profit to net cash inflow from operating activities:

	£
Operating profit	6,022
Depreciation charges	893
Loss on sale of tangible fixed assets	6
(Increase)/decrease in stocks	(194)
(Increase)/decrease in debtors	(72)
Increase/(decrease) in creditors	234
Net cash inflow from operating activities	£6,889

2 Analysis of changes in cash and cash equivalents during the year:

	£
Balance at 1 April 1993	21,373
Net cash inflow	3,081
Balance at 31 March 1994	£24,454

3 Analysis of the balances of cash and cash equivalents as shown in the balance sheet:

	1994	1993	Change
Cash at bank and in hand	529	681	(152)
Short-term investments	23,936	20,700	3,236
Bank overdrafts	(11)	(8)	(3)
	£24,454	£21,373	£3,081

4 Analysis of changes in finance during the year:

	Share capital £	Debenture loan £
Balance at 1 April 1993	27,411	156
Cash inflow/(outflow) from financing	211	(149)
Profit on redemption of debenture loan for less than its book value		(7)
Balance at 31 March 1994	£27,622	£0

The cash flow statement format in detail

An explanation of each of the headings follows, showing the items to be disclosed and discussing some of the problems that may arise when calculating the figures.

Net cash inflow from operating activities

This represents the movement in cash and cash equivalents resulting from the transactions shown in the profit and loss account in arriving at operating profit, ie cash derived from sales less cash paid for purchases, services, wages and salaries and other operating expenses.

Operating cash flows may be reported on a direct or an indirect basis. However, whichever method is used, a reconciliation between the operating profit reported in the profit and loss account and the net cash flow from operating activities should be given in a note to the cash flow statement (see format note 1). Analysis of the net cash flow from operating activities on the direct method is encouraged but not required.

Both methods are discussed below with an example of the calculations and presentation required for each one. For examination purposes both must be studied very carefully.

Illustration:

Set out below is the trading and profit and loss account of Gamma Ltd for the year ended 31 December 1994, together with the balance sheets as at 31 December 1994 and 1993.

Gamma Ltd
Trading and Profit & Loss Account for year ended 31 December 1994

	£000	£000
Turnover		56,800
Opening stock	(12,450)	
Purchases	(38,260)	
	(50,710)	
Closing stock	16,260	
Cost of sales		(34,450)
Gross profit		22,350
Distribution costs	(2,470)	
Administration expenses (see note 1)	(3,620)	
		(6,090)
Operating profit		£16,260

Note 1: included in administration is the depreciation charge of £400 and a loss on sale of fixed assets of £120.

Balance Sheet as at 31 December 1994
(extract only)

	1993	1994
	£	£
Current assets		
Stock	12,450	16,260
Trade debtors	17,240	21,450
Cash at bank	2,165	4,239
	£31,855	£41,949
Current liabilities		
Trade creditors	11,900	9,235
Expense creditors (Admin)	3,265	4,362
	£15,165	£13,597

Direct method

This requires operating receipts and payments to be shown on the face of the cash flow statement as follows:

Cash Flow Statement

	£
Operating profit	
Cash receipts from customers (17,240 + 56,800 - 21,450)	52,590
Cash paid to suppliers (11,900 + 38,260 - 9,235)	(40,925)
Cash payments to and on behalf of employees	
Cash paid for other expenses (3,265 + 2,470 + 3,620 - 400 - 120 - 436)	(4,473)
Net cash inflow from operating activities	£7,192

In practice the cash flow information will be obtained from the accounting records but for exam purposes it will be necessary to use working schedules to calculate the figures from the question. These can be in the form of ledger accounts or simply a process of adding or subtracting the relevant figures, as shown above. Note carefully the adjustment to cash paid for other expense of -£400 and -£120 in respect of depreciation and loss on sale. As these are both non-cash items they have been deducted from expenses before calculating cash paid. The treatment of fixed assets, depreciation, and profit or loss on sale will be dealt with more fully in the section on investing activities.

The ASB encourages the use of the gross (direct) method of presentation but concurs with the view that the information presented does not, in all cases, provide benefits to users that outweigh the cost of providing the information. However, in keeping with the objective that a cash flow statement should only include items of pure cash flow it requires that the reconciliation of operating profit to net cash flows from operating activities is given in a supplementary note to the statement. This is the net (indirect) method described below.

Indirect method

This requires operating profit per the statutory accounts to be adjusted for non-cash items for movements in stock, debtors, and creditors and any other differences between cash flows and profit. This reconciliation must be disclosed as note 1 to the statement and is illustrated below.

Notes to the cash flow statement

Reconciliation of operating profit to net cash inflows/(outflows) from operating activities.

	£
Operating profit	16,260
Depreciation	400
Loss/(profit) on sale of fixed assets	120
Increase in stock	(3,810)
Increase in debtors	(4,210)
Decrease in creditors	(1,568)
Net cash inflow from operating activities	£7,192

As can be seen both methods give the same result but the information disclosed on the face of the statement only describes cash inflows and outflows whereas the disclosure in the notes refers additionally to non-cash items.

Return on investment and servicing of finance

These are the cash inflows resulting from the ownership of an investment and the outflows are payments to providers of finance.

a Cash inflows:

   i   interest received, including any related tax recovered;

   ii dividends received, net of any tax credit.

b Cash outflow:

   i   interest paid, including any tax deducted at source and paid over;

   ii dividends paid, excluding any advance corporation tax.

Illustration:

Gamma Ltd
Profit & Loss Account for the year ended 31 December 1994

	£000
Operating profit	16,260
Interest receivable	2,450
Interest payable	(1,200)
Profit before tax	17,510
Taxation	(6,250)
Profit after tax	11,260
Dividends	(6,600)
Retained for the year	£4,660

Balance Sheet (extract) as at 31 December 1994

	1993 £000	1994 £000
Current liabilities:		
Trade creditors	11,900	9,235
Expense creditors	3,265	4,362
Accrual (interest)	120	150
Corporation tax	4,900	5,930
Proposed dividend	3,500	4,400
	£23,685	£24,077

Workings:

Figures are calculated by adding and subtracting in brackets on the face of the statement, alternatively a ledger account could be opened, or a simple working schedule prepared.

DR	Dividends Payable		CR
	£		£
Missing figure = cash paid	5,700	B/f creditor	3,500
		P/l paid & proposed	6,600
C/F creditor	4,400		
	£10,100		£10,100

Calculation of Dividends Paid

	£
B/f creditor	3,500
P/l paid & proposed	6,600
	10,100
C/f creditor	(4,400)
Cash paid	£5,700

The figures are now inserted into the cash flow statement under the heading of return on investment and servicing of finance.

Cash Flow Statement

	£000	£000
Net cash inflow from operating activities		7,192
Return on investment and servicing of finance		
Interest received	2,450	
Interest paid (120 + 1,200 - 150)	(1,170)	
Dividends paid (3,500 + 6,600 - 4,400)	(5,700)	
Net cash outflow from return on investment and servicing of finance		(4,420)

Taxation

Taxation is to include the cash flows arising from revenue and capital profits. Cash flows in respect of other taxation, including VAT, employees income tax and income tax deducted at source from interest payments are dealt with elsewhere in the statement.

a Cash outflows:

    i   cash paid for corporation tax, including advance corporation tax;

    ii cash paid for certificates of tax deposit.

b Cash inflows:

    i   cash receipts from tax rebates, claims or overpayments.

Illustration:
In the previous illustration the profit and loss charge for taxation was £6,250 and the opening and closing creditors were £4,900 and £5,930 respectively. Using the same method as before, the cash paid for corporation tax can be calculated as £4,900 + £6,250 - £5,930 = £5,220. This is now inserted into the statement under the main heading of taxation.

Cash Flow Statement		
	£000	£000
Net cash inflow from operating activities		7,192
Return on investment and servicing of finance		
Interest received	2,450	
Interest paid (120 + 1200 - 150)	(1,170)	
Dividends paid (3500 + 6600 - 4400)	(5,700)	
Net cash outflow from return on investment		
and servicing of finance		(4,420)
Taxation		
Tax Paid		(5,220)

Investing activities

Investing activities generally include the cash effects of acquiring and selling fixed assets or current asset investments.

a Cash inflows:

    i   receipts from sale of fixed assets;

    ii receipts from sale of investment in subsidiary, net of any balance of cash or cash equivalent transferred as part of the sale;

    iii receipts from sale of other investments.

b Cash outflow:

    i   payment to acquire fixed asset;

    ii payment to acquire investment in subsidiary, net of balances of cash and cash equivalents acquired;

    iii payment to acquire investments.

Illustration:
Included in the profit and loss of Gamma Ltd under the heading of administration was the depreciation charge for the year in respect of fixed assets £400 and the loss on sale of assets £120. (These were adjusted in calculating net cash inflow from operating activities, if you remember! If not, refer back to the section on operating activities and review the adjustment.)

An extract of the balance sheet at 31 December 1994 shows the following details of fixed assets:

Balance Sheet as at 31 December 1994		
	1993	1994
	£	£
Fixed assets		
Tangible	8,500	12,600

Note on fixed assets: during the year tangible assets with a cost of £4,200 and accumulated depreciation of £1,400 were sold at a loss of £120.

Workings:
In the case of fixed assets it may be necessary to open ledger accounts, particularly if the transactions are complex. Most students are very familiar with these accounts from earlier sections of study and find this the most familiar way of dealing with the calculations. The objective is to calculate the cash paid for new assets and received in respect of those sold.

Fixed Asset A/C			
B/d @nbv	8,500	Disposal @nbv	2,800
Missing figure, ie		Depn	400
cash paid	7,300	C/d @nbv	12,600
	£15,800		£15,800

Disposal A/C			
Disposal	2,800	Loss	120
		Missing figure, ie cash paid	2,680
	£2,800		£2,800

The appropriate figures are inserted into the cash flow statement under the main heading of investing activities.

Cash Flow Statement

	£000	£000
Net cash inflow from operating activities		7,192
Return on investment and servicing of finance		
Interest received	2,450	
Interest paid (120 + 1200 - 150)	(1,170)	
Dividends paid (3500 + 6600 - 4400)	(5,700)	
Net cash outflow from return on investment and servicing of finance		(4,420)
Taxation		
Corporation tax paid	(5,220)	
Tax paid		(5,220)
Investing activities		
Payment to acquire tangible fixed assets	(7,300)	
Receipt from sale of tangible fixed assets	2,680	
Net cash outflow from investing activities		(4,620)
Net cash outflow before financing		(7,068)

Financing

Financing cash flows comprise receipts from or repayments to external providers of finance in respect of principal amounts of finance.

a Cash inflows:

   i   receipts from issuing shares;

   ii receipts from issuing debentures, loans, notes and bonds, and from other long-term and short-term borrowings (other than those included within cash equivalents).

b Cash outflows:

   i   repayment of amounts borrowed;

   ii the capital element of a finance lease;

   iii payments to reacquire or redeem the company's shares;

   iv payments of expenses or commissions on any issue of shares, debentures, loans, notes and bonds.

Illustration:
An extract of the balance sheet of Gamma Ltd at 31 December 1994 shows the following sources of finance:

Balance Sheet as at 31 December 1994		
	1993	1994
	£000	£000
Creditors: amounts falling due after more than one year		
Debentures	5,588	4,100
Capital and reserves		
Called up share capital	7,870	17,000
Share premium	1,200	2,700
Profit & loss a/c	2,012	6,672
	£16,670	£30,472

Workings:
Check the profit and loss balances to ensure that there have been no movements other than those through profit and loss, eg bonus issue of shares, which would effect the cash flow from issue of shares.

	£	£
B/F		2,012
retained profit (per profit & loss a/c)		4,660
C/F		£6,672
Debentures have gone down by		
(5,588 - 4,100), outflow		(1,488)
Share capital has gone up by (17,000 - 7,870)	9,130	
and share premium by (2,700 - 1200)	1,500	
Total cash inflow		10,630

Insert these figures into the cash flow statement under the main heading of financing. It is now possible to view the entire statement and see if it agrees to the movement in cash and cash equivalents.

XYZ Ltd Cash Flow Statement		
	£000	£000
Net cash inflow from operating activities		7,192
Return on investment and servicing of finance		
Interest received	2,450	
Interest paid (120 + 1,200 - 150)	(1,170)	
Dividends paid (3,500 + 6,600 - 4,400)	(5,700)	
Net cash outflow from return on investment and servicing of finance		(4,420)
Taxation		
Corporation tax paid	(5,220)	
Tax paid		(5,220)
Investing activities		
Payment to acquire tangible fixed assets	(7,300)	
Receipt from sale of tangible fixed assets	2,680	
Net cash outflow from investing activities		(4,620)
Net cash outflow before financing		(7,068)
Financing		
Payment to redeem debentures	(1,488)	
Issue of ordinary shares	10,630	
Net cash inflow from financing		9,142
Increase in cash and cash equivalents		£2,074

Notes to the cash flow statement:

1 Reconciliation of operating profit to net cash inflows/(outflows) from operating activities:

	£
Operating profit	16,260
Depreciation	400
Loss/(profit) on sale of fixed assets	120
Increase in stock	(3,810)
Increase in debtors	(4,210)
Decrease in creditors	(1,562)
Net cash inflow from operating activities	£7,192

2 Analysis of changes in cash and cash equivalents during the year:

	£
Balance at 1 January 1994	2,165
Net cash inflow	2,074
Balance at 31 December 1994	£4,239

3 Analysis of the balances of cash and cash equivalents as shown in the balance sheet:

	1993 £	1994 £	Change £
Cash at bank and in hand	2,165	4,239	2,074

4 Analysis of changes in financing during the year

	Share capital £	Debenture £
Balance at 1 January 1994	9,070	5,588
Cash inflow/outflow from financing	10,630	(1,488)
Balance at 31 December 1994	£19,700	£4,100

Preparation of a cash flow statement

a Set out the pro-forma cash flow statement with all the headings required by FRS 1. It would be logical to use one sheet of paper for the statement itself, another for the notes and a third for workings.

b Work through the question on a line by line basis building up the answer as you go. If possible put figures straight into the statement or notes (particularly note 1, the reconciliation of operating profit to net cash inflow) and in other circumstances open a working to calculate missing figures. You will find this particularly useful for calculating tax paid, dividends paid, purchase or sale of fixed assets, issue of shares, and profit or loss on sale of fixed assets.

c To complete the statement transfer the figures from the workings into the appropriate section of the cash flow statement.

This can be more fully understood by working carefully through the following illustration:

Illustration:

SEF Ltd
Balance Sheet as at 31 December

	1994 £	1993 £
Fixed assets	43,500	29,400
Current assets		
Stock	12,000	8,000
Debtors	8,200	9,500
Bank	1,200	1,000
Current liabilities		
Creditors	(5,700)	(3,500)
Taxation	(8,000)	(6,500)
Dividends	(8,000)	(4,000)
	£43,200	£33,900
Share capital	10,000	6,000
Share premium	2,000	
Profit & loss	31,200	27,900
	£43,200	£33,900

SEF Ltd
Summarised Profit & Loss Account for the year ended 31 December 1994

	£
Operating profit	23,000
(after charging depreciation of £7,000)	
Dividend received	1,200
Interest paid	(900)
P.O.O.A.B.T	23,300
Taxation	(8,000)
P.O.O.A.A.T.	15,300
Dividends paid and proposed	(12,000)
Retained for the year	3,300
Retained profit b/f	27,900
Retained profit c/f	£31,200

Prepare cash flow statement for the year ended 31 December 1994.

(20 marks)

Solution:
Set out pro-forma cash flow statement, notes and workings.

SEF Ltd
Cash Flow Statement as at 31 December 1994

Net cash inflow from operating activities
Return on investment and servicing of finance
Taxation
Investing activities
Financing
Increase in cash and cash equivalents

244 | Accounting

Notes to the cash flow statement:
1 Reconciliation of operating profit to net cash inflow:

Operating profit
Depreciation
(Profit)/loss on disposal of assets
(Increase)/decrease in stock
(Increase)/decrease in debtors
Increase/(decrease) in creditors

2 Analysis of changes in cash and cash equivalents during the year:

Balance at 1 January 1994
Net cash inflow/outflow
Balance at 31 December 1994

3 Analysis of the balances of cash and cash equivalents as shown in the balance sheet:

	1994	1993	change
Cash at bank and in hand			

4 Analysis of changes in finance during the year:

	Share capital	Debentures
As at 1 January 1994		
As at 31 December 1994		

Work through the question on a line by line basis, putting the figures into the statements notes or workings as appropriate.

Work through the question yourself and when you have finished refer to the completed statement, notes and workings.

To help you resolve any problems you may have experienced with either the technique or the accounting, a schedule follows which sets out the line by line approach that you should have adopted. Work through this with your own answer very carefully.

	Statement	Notes	Workings	Ref
Balance sheet:				
Fixed assets	Dr bal b/f & Cr bal c/f		FA a/c	W1
Stock	Insert increase £(4,000)	Note 1		
Debtors	Insert decrease £1,300	Note 1		
Bank	Insert bal b/f & bal c/f	Note 2		
Creditors	Insert increase £2,200	Note 1		
Taxation	Cr bal b/f & Dr bal c/f		Tax a/c	W2
Dividends	Cr bal b/f & Dr bal c/f		Dividends a/c	W3
Share capital	Cr bal b/f & Dr bal c/f		Share capital	W4
Share premium	Cr bal b/f & Dr bal c/f		S premium	W5
Profit & loss:				
Operating profit	Insert £23,000	Note 1		
Depreciation	Insert £7,000	Note 1	FA a/c – Cr	W1
Dividend rec'd	Insert £1,200 Return on			
Interest paid	Insert £900 Return on			
Taxation	Cr £8,000		Tax a/c	W2
Dividends	Cr £12,000		Dividends a/c	W3

Complete workings and transfer missing figures into statement and notes:

Working	Missing figures	Statement	Ref
Fixed assets	Balancing figure £21,100	Investing	W1
Taxation	Balancing figure £6,500	Tax paid	W2
Dividends	Balancing figure £8,000	Return on	W3
Share capital	Balancing figure £4,000	Financing	W4
Share premium	Balancing figure £2,000	Financing	W5

Now complete note 1 and finalise the cash flow statement.

Cash Flow Statement
for the year ended 31 December 1994

	£	£
Net cash inflow from operating activities		29,500
Return on investment and servicing of finance		
Dividend received	1,200	
Interest paid	(900)	
Dividend paid	(8,000)	
		(7,700)
Taxation		
Tax paid		(6,500)
Investing activities		
Payments for fixed assets		21,100
		(5,800)
Financing		
Issue of shares		6,000
Increase in cash and cash equivalents		£200

Notes to statement:

1 Reconciliation of operating profit to net cash inflow from operating activities:

	£
Operating profit	23,000
Depreciation	7,000
Increase in stock	(4,000)
Decrease in debtors	1,300
Increase in creditors	2,200
	£29,500

2 Analysis of changes in cash and cash equivalents during the year:

	£
Balance at 31 December 1993	1,000
Net cash inflow	200
Balance at 31 December 1994	£1,200

Workings 1:

Fixed Assets

	£		£
B/f	29,400	Depn	7,000
cfs	21,100	c/f	43,500
	£50,500		£50,500

Workings 2:

Taxation

	£		£
cfs	6,500	b/f	6,500
c/f	8,000	Profit & loss	8,000
	£14,500		£14,500

Workings 3:

Dividend Account

	£		£
cfs	8,000	b/f	4,000
c/f	8,000	Profit & loss	12,000
	£16,000		£16,000

Workings 4:

Share Capital

	£		£
		b/f	6,000
c/f	10,000	cfs	4,000
	£10,000		£10,000

Workings 5:

Share Premium

	£		£
		b/f	nil
c/f	2,000	cfs	2,000
	£2,000		£2,000

FRS 3 Reporting financial performance | 16

Introduction

This major new standard, introduced in 1992, made fundamental changes to an area of reporting that has been the subject of much criticism over the years. It replaces SSAP 6 'Extraordinary items and prior year adjustments' a standard whose provisions companies seemed easily able to avoid. SSAP 6 required that, in order to include all profits and losses in the profit and loss account, a distinction was to be made between those arising from ordinary and extraordinary activities and that extraordinary items be disclosed under a separate heading. The distinction between ordinary and extraordinary was important because one of the more widely used indicators of performance, earnings per share, included ordinary but excluded extraordinary items.

Despite all the attempts of the standard setters to give clear definitions and explanations of the differences between ordinary and extraordinary items the distinction between them was frequently blurred. In particular the area of reorganisations and restructuring costs was very susceptible to variations of accounting treatment, with companies adopting a subjective rather than an objective rationale.

A second problem arose concerning the reporting and assessment of items that are not included in the profit and loss account. Certain SSAP's and sections of the companies act permit items to be excluded from the profit and loss account and included only in the notes to the accounts. That 'movement on reserve note' or a cross reference to it was to follow the profit and loss account. This appeared to satisfy the need to give the items a degree of prominence but it was soon discovered that shareholders and other users of accounts did not regard the reserves note with the importance that it deserved.

The principal purpose of FRS 3 is to produce a set of rules for the presentation of information in financial statements that will be better than SSAP 6. To achieve this they have widened the range of information that must be given both in terms of detail and prominence, but at the same time removing the emphasis placed on individual measures of performance.

The new standard requires an 'information set' to be prepared which will now include:

a Profit and loss account – *layered*.

b Statement of total recognised gains and losses – *new*.

c Note of historical cost profit and loss – *new*.

d Balance sheet – *no change*.

e Notes to the accounts, including:

    reconciliation of movement in shareholders funds – *new*.

A more detailed explanation of the changes introduced by FRS 3 follows.

Extraordinary items

The new definition of extraordinary items is:

> 'material items possessing a high degree of abnormality which arise from events or transactions that fall outside the ordinary activities of the reporting entity and which are not expected to recur'.

In view of the extreme rarity of such items no examples are given and David Tweedie (Chairman of The Accounting Standards Board) likened them to Martians walking down the street .

Under SSAP 6 the definition was:

> 'material items which derive from events or transactions that fall outside the ordinary activities of the company and which are not expected to recur frequently or regularly'.

Profit and loss account

A layered format is to be used for the profit and loss account to highlight a number of important components of financial performance. These are:

a Results of continuing operations, showing separately results of new acquisitions.

b Results of discontinued operations.

c Certain exceptional items required to be shown on the face of the profit and loss account after operating profit, but before interest. These are:

   i   profit or loss on the sale or termination of an operation;

   ii   costs of a fundamental reorganisation or restructuring;

   iii   profit or loss on the disposal of fixed assets.

The analysis of trading results into continuing, new acquisitions and discontinued activities must be disclosed for all components up to operating profit. It is not considered appropriate to analyse interest and taxation since this would involve too much subjectivity.

Exceptional items other than those to be shown separately, as described above, must be included within the normal statutory headings to which they relate and disclosed in the notes if this is necessary for the accounts to show a true and fair view.

An illustration of layered profit and loss follows:

Profit & Loss Account

	Continuing operations	Acquisitions		Discontinued operations	Total	Total
	1994	1994	1994	1994	1993
	£	£	£	£	£
Turnover	550	50	175	775	690
Cost of sales	(415)	(40)	(165)	(620)	(555)
Gross profit	135	10	10	155	135
Net operating expenses	(85)	(4)	(25)	(114)	(83)
Less: 1993 provision			10	10	–
Operating profit	50	6	(5)	51	52
Profit on sale of properties	9			9	6
Provision for loss on operations to be discontinued					(30)
Loss on disposal of discontinued operations			(17)	(17)	–
Less: 1993 provision			20	20	–
Profit on ordinary activities before interest	59	6	(2)	63	28
Interest payable				(18)	(15)
Profit on ordinary activities before tax				45	13
Tax				(14)	(4)
Profit after tax				31	9
Minority interest				(2)	(2)
Profit for the financial year				29	7
Dividend				(8)	(1)
Retained profit for the financial year				£21	£6

Recalculation of EPS in line with new definitions

EPS is now calculated on the profit attributable to equity shareholders *after* minority interest, *extraordinary items* and preference dividends. Under SSAP 6 extraordinary items were excluded.

If an EPS figure is calculated on any other level of earnings, a reconciliation between the two figures must be given and the reasons for calculating the additional version should be explained. The EPS figure calculated in accordance with FRS 3 must be at least as prominent as any other version.

Statement of total recognised gains and losses

This new primary statement, which must be presented immediately after the profit and loss account, is a major innovation in financial reporting and is the cornerstone of the ASB's policy to highlight performance. In the introduction we referred to the intention of the ASB to encourage users and preparers of financial statements to move away from specific numbers and to make judgements about performance based on the information set of which this is a fundamental ingredient. It includes in one place all the gains and losses of the year, whether recognised in the profit and loss account or through reserves. Its purpose is to show the total financial performance of the company for the year. The information is presented as follows:

Statement of Recognised Gains and Losses		
	1994	1993 (as restated)
	£	£
Profit for the financial year	X	X
Unrealised surplus on revaluation of properties	X	X
Unrealised (loss)/gain on trade investments	(X)	X
	X	X
Currency translation differences on foreign currency net investments	X	X
Total recognised gains and losses relating to the year	XX	XX
Prior year adjustment	X	–
Total gains and losses recognised since last report	XX	XX

As can been seen from the above, transactions permitted to be dealt with by transfer directly through reserves, eg revaluation surpluses and exchange differences arising on the retranslation of the net investment in subsidiary, are now much more prominately displayed. SSAP 6 attempted to achieve the same degree of disclosure by requiring that the movement on reserves note should be disclosed immediately after the profit or loss account, or a cross reference to it should appear on the face of the profit and loss account. However, by selecting the second option, companies often placed the reserve note towards the end of the financial statements and a note number on the face of the profit and loss as a cross reference. In this way the information was not very prominent.

New notes to the accounts

Note of historical cost profit and loss

The note of historical cost profit is a memorandum and is designed to facilitate comparison between the results of companies which have revalued their fixed assets and those that have not. (It is only necessary where there is a material difference between the results disclosed in the profit and loss and those on an unmodified historic cost basis.)

To understand the requirement for the note of historical cost profit and loss it is necessary to understand the current accounting treatment of revalued assets. On revaluation the surplus is transferred to a revaluation reserve which is shown in the movement on reserves note, and now in accordance with FRS 3 *also* in the statement of recognised gains and losses.

The standard requires that the profit or loss on disposal of any asset should be accounted for in the profit and loss account as the difference between the net sale proceeds and the net carrying amount, whether at historic cost or at a valuation. The revaluation reserve is realised on the disposal of the asset and as such is available for distribution. A transfer can be made from the revaluation reserve to the profit and loss in the movement in reserves note, but the amount is not

the profit and loss in the movement in reserves note, but the amount is not included in the profit and loss account.

This requirement was clarified in FRS 3, until then there had been various alternate treatments. It was acceptable to calculate the profit/loss either by reference to the net book value (as above) or by reference to the asset's depreciated historic cost. The difference in the past was that under the first method the revaluation surplus does not go through the profit and loss, whereas under the latter the revaluation surplus is passed through the profit and loss.

It is important to the ASB that in accordance with their new approach the revaluation surplus is treated as a recognised gain in the period of revaluation and shown in the statement of recognised gains and losses as unrealised. When, as a result of sale, the gain is realised in future years it makes no sense to include it again in the profit and loss account. It has already been included as part of the 'performance' of earlier years. As discussed earlier 'performance' must be viewed by taking into account both the information presented in the profit and loss and the statement of recognised gains and losses.

The ASB, however, recognises that allowing companies the choice between the use of historic values or revaluations does create problems of comparability from one company to another and consequently the note of historical cost profit/loss is provided to show the adjustments necessary to convert the profit before and after tax back onto an unmodified historic cost basis. The adjustments are:

a Difference between historical cost depreciation charge and actual depreciation charge on revalued amount of fixed assets.

b Realisation of revaluation surpluses of previous years on assets sold in the year.

An illustration of the note of historical cost profit and loss follows:

Note of Historical Cost Profits and Losses

	1994 £	1993 £
Reported profit on ordinary activities before taxation	X	X
Realisation of property revaluation gains of previous years	X	X
Difference between a historical cost depreciation charge and the actual depreciation charge of the year calculated on the revalued amount	X	X
Historical cost profit on ordinary activities before taxation	XX	XX
Historical cost profit for the year retained after taxation, minority and dividends	X	X

A worked example

Two companies acquire identical assets cost £100 with an estimated useful life of five years and no residual value. Company two revalues the asset at the end of year two in the sum of £150. Both companies sell the asset at the end of year four for £50. No depreciation in year of sale.

	Company 1 £	Company 2 £
Profit & loss a/c		
Year 1 Depreciation	(20)	(20)
Year 2 Depreciation	(20)	(20)
Year 3 Depreciation	(20)	(50)
Year 4 Profit/(loss) on sale	10	(50)
Statement of recognised gains and losses		
Year 1 n/a	n/a	
Year 2 n/a	n/a	
Year 3 Unrealised surplus on revaluation of fixed asset	n/a	90
Year 4 n/a	n/a	
Note of historical cost profit and loss		
Year 1 n/a	n/a	
Year 2 n/a	n/a	
Year 3 Difference between historic depn and actual depn charged in the profit & loss a/c	n/a	30
Year 4 Realisation of revaluation surplus on sale	n/a	60 (balance)

As can be seen, the note of historical cost profit and loss enables a comparison to be made of the profits of both companies in the years after the revaluation which would otherwise have been distorted by the choice of accounting treatment relating to the fixed assets.

Reconciliation of movement in shareholders' funds

The second new note is designed to bring together into one statement all important movements in shareholders' funds. The profit and loss account and the statement of total recognised gains and losses reflect the performance of a reporting entity. There are however other important changes that can effect the shareholders' funds and these are highlighted in the reconciliation. The note will include the net results from the profit and loss account and the new statement of recognised gains and losses and in addition show the detail of capital contributed by or repaid to the shareholders.

The standard permits it to be included as a primary statement or as a note to the accounts, although it must be shown separately from the statement of recognised gains and losses.

An example of the reconciliation note follows:

Reconciliation of Movement in Shareholders' Funds

	1994 £	1993 £
Profit for the financial year	X	X
Dividends	(X)	(X)
	XX	X
Other recognised gains and losses relating to the year (net)	(X)	X
New share capital subscribed	X	X
Goodwill written off	(X)	–
Net addition to shareholders' funds	X	X
Opening shareholders funds	X	X
Closing shareholders' funds	X	X

Interpretation of accounts | 17

17.1 General principles

Definition

Interpretation of accounts is the analysis of financial statements in order to discover the strengths and weaknesses of a company and to reveal underlying trends in its activities.

Need for interpretation

There are three main reasons for interpretation of accounts.

Requirement	Management control	Investment decisions	Credit facilities
Undertaken by	Internal management	Existing and potential shareholders and investment analysts	Bank managers Large creditors

There are sometimes more specialised reasons for the interpretation of accounts.
Example: if it is intended to grant a long-term contract to a company it is desirable to examine the financial status of that company with particular reference to its ability to meet the contract.

Limitations of accounting ratios

It can be dangerous to apply accounting ratios slavishly without due regard for their limitations, ie:

a Accountancy is not an exact science, and different businesses may have different accounting policies which make a direct comparison of the accounts of those different businesses rather difficult. Accounting policies may differ with regard to depreciation, stock valuation, fixed asset valuation, etc.

b One business may own most or all of its fixed assets (in which case the assets will appear in the balance sheet and a depreciation charge will appear in the profit and loss account) whereas a business being compared may rent or lease most or all of its assets (in which case only a rental or hire charge will appear in the final accounts).

c The financial year end of a business often coincides with its period of lowest business activity and therefore some of the figures which appear in the annual accounts, particularly stocks and debtors, may not be representative of a true average.

d Accounts report on only those matters which are capable of being quantified in monetary terms.

e Different trades are likely to have appreciably different trading characteristics making direct comparison difficult. For example, business A may operate with a high sales volume, low gross profit margins and relatively low operating costs, whereas business B has a low sales volume, high gross profit margins and relatively high operating costs.

f   There is a tendency for some businesses to 'window dress' their accounts at the end of the financial year, ie make the balance sheet show a situation which is better than the real one.

Techniques

The principal technique used in the interpretation of accounts is the calculation of important ratios. These must then be subjected to comparisons:

a   internal comparison (intrafirm):

   i   with the company's own past;

   ii   with budgets and forecasts;

b   external comparison (interfirm):

   i   with the accounts of other companies;

   ii   industry statistics.

Projection of trends into the future

In some situations it is necessary to project trends into the future. For example, an analysis might reveal that a company has been steadily increasing sales over the past few years. A potential investor might deduce from this that the company will continue to increase sales in the future.

Great care must be taken when making such projections and any additional information available which is not actually contained in the accounts should be used. Examples:

a   general economic climate;

b   technical developments in the industry;

c   industrial relations;

d   possible takeover bids.

Importance of defining objectives

The purpose for which the interpretation is to be carried out will determine which aspects of any analysis are most important.

Example: an existing shareholder will wish to assess the efficiency of management which will be reflected by the profitability of the company. On the other hand a bank manager who contemplates lending money to a company will be primarily concerned with security which will be reflected in the financial strength of the company.

Interpretation check list and key ratios

Check list

All interpretations should be approached by considering the financial statements under each of the following headings:

a profitability;

b liquidity;

c growth;

d assets.

These headings provide a check list of points to be considered. The points which are most important will vary with the purposes for which the interpretation is being undertaken.

Key ratios

All ratios can be expressed in one of three ways:

a a ratio, eg 3:1;

b a percentage, eg 33⅓ per cent;

c the number of times one number can be divided by another, eg 9/3 = 3 times (often expressed as 3x).

The most important ratios to be considered are:

a *return on capital employed* – the profits of the company expressed as a percentage of the capital;

b *profit margins* – both the gross and net profits expressed as a percentage of sales;

c *current ratio* – current assets compared to current liabilities;

d *quick assets ratio* – very liquid assets compared to immediate liabilities;

e *stock ratio* – the number of days of sales held in stock;

f *gearing* – the ratio of fixed interest capital to equity capital.

These 'key' ratios are of value in almost all interpretation situations. Any one ratio may be relevant to several aspects of the same interpretation, for example, the stock ratio might be of value in discussing both the assets of a company and its liquidity situation.

There are many other ratios which may be used to illustrate and emphasise particular points. The use of many of these, including the 'key' ratios is illustrated by using the 'interpretation check list' and the following specimen accounts.

AB Ltd
Balance Sheet 30 June ...

	This year			Last year		
	£	£	£	£	£	£
Fixed assets						
Property			30,000			23,000
Machinery			21,000			7,000
Goodwill			5,000			5,000
Patents and trade marks			2,000			2,000
			58,000			37,000
Current assets						
Stocks and work-in-progress	25,000				34,000	
Debtors	28,000				22,000	
Cash and bank balances	2,000				1,000	
	55,000				57,000	
Deduct: Current liabilities						
Creditors	15,000			20,500		
Bank overdraft	10,000			6,000		
Corporation tax	6,000			5,500		
Proposed dividend	2,000	33,000		2,000	34,000	
			22,000			23,000
			£80,000			£60,000
			£			£
Share capital						
Ordinary shares of 25p each			30,000			25,000
5% preference shares of £1 each			20,000			20,000
			50,000			45,000
Share premium			5,000			2,000
Retained profits			15,000			13,000
			70,000			60,000
Long-term loan						
10% unsecured loan stock			10,000			–
			£80,000			£60,000

AB Ltd
Profit & Loss Account for the year ended 30 June ...

	This year		Last year	
	£	£	£	£
Sales		100,000		100,000
Deduct: Cost of sales				
Materials	25,000		28,000	
Other variable costs	20,000		22,000	
Fixed costs	15,000	60,000	15,000	65,000
Gross profit		40,000		35,000
Deduct: Other overheads				
Fixed costs	22,800		20,500	
Bank interest	1,200		500	
Loan interest	1,000		–	
		25,000		21,000
Profit before taxation		15,000		14,000
Deduct: Taxation		6,000		5,500
Profit after taxation		9,000		8,500
Deduct: Dividends				
5% Preference (paid)	1,000		1,000	
Ordinary – interim (paid)	4,000		3,000	
– final (proposed)	2,000	7,000	2,000	6,000
Added to reserves		£2,000		£2,500

Measures of profitability

Return on capital employed (ROCE)

This is one of the most fundamental measures of profitability. However, there are a number of definitions of both capital and profit and these must be considered.

Definition of 'capital employed'
The capital employed in a business may be regarded as any of the following:

a *total capital* – being total share capital, reserves, loan capital and current liabilities;

b long-term capital – being total share capital, reserves and loan capital;

c shareholders' capital – being total share capital and reserves;

d shareholders' equity – being ordinary share capital and reserves.

The definition to be used depends upon the objectives of the interpretation. Definitions (a) and (b) would indicate the overall profitability of the company. Definitions (c) and (d) would indicate the return for the shareholders.

Where a trading company holds investments outside the normal course of its business, it is usual to exclude these from the other capital employed and to calculate a separate figure of ROCE for the investment.

In AB Ltd the capital may be measured as:

a total capital (£80,000 + £33,000)   = £113,000

b long-term capital (£70,000 + £10,000)   = £80,000

c shareholders' capital (£50,000 + £20,000)   = £70,000

d shareholders' equity (£30,000 + £5,000 + £15,000)   = £50,000

Definition of 'return' or 'profits'

It is relevant to consider both pre-tax and post-tax profits. The former indicates the management's ability to trade profitably, the latter shows its ability to plan its tax position as well as its trading.

It is most important to 'match' correctly the profits against the relevant figure of capital employed. The profit figure to be used is as follows, for the appropriate definition of capital employed:

a *total capital employed* – profit before tax and before bank and loan interest;

b *long-term capital employed* – profit before tax and before loan interest;

c *shareholders' capital employed* – profit after tax;

d *shareholders' equity capital employed* – profit after tax and preference dividend.

Based on the profit and loss account of AB Ltd for this year, the relevant profit figures would be as follows:

a total capital employed (£40,000 – £22,800)   = £17,200

b long-term capital employed (£17,200 – £1,200)   = £16,000

c shareholders' capital employed (£16,000 – £1,000 – £6,000) =   £9,000

d shareholders' equity capital employed (£9,000 – £1,000)   =   £8,000

Return on capital employed

This is calculated as a percentage as follows:

$$\frac{\text{Return}}{\text{Capital}} \times 100$$

Based on the figures given above the various returns for this year can be calculated as follows (all to one place of decimals):

a return on total capital employed:

$$\frac{£17,200}{£113,000} \times 100 = 15.2\%$$

b return on long-term capital employed:

$$\frac{£16,000}{£80,000} \times 100 = 20.0\%$$

c return on shareholders' capital employed:

$$\frac{£9,000}{£70,000} \times 100 = 12.9\%$$

d return on shareholders' equity capital employed:

$$\frac{£8,000}{£50,000} \times 100 = 16.0\%$$

Changes in return on capital employed (ROCE)

Although the key ratio of ROCE is useful as an indicator of performance, it does not explain why profitability is improving or declining. To do this it is possible to subdivide the key ratio into a number of subsidiary ratios.

Example:
The ROCE for AB Ltd this year is 20 per cent.
   For last year ROCE is calculated as:

$$\frac{\text{Profit}}{\text{Capital}} \times 100 = \frac{£15,000}{£60,000} \times 100 = 25\%$$

Thus while the absolute profit figure has increased from £15,000 to £16,000 the capital invested has increased more than proportionately giving a decline in the ROCE from 25 per cent to 20 per cent. It is necessary to investigate the basic figures to determine the cause of this decline.

The basic figure of ROCE can be broken down as follows:

$$\frac{\text{Profit}}{\text{Capital}} = \frac{\text{Profit}}{\text{Sales}} \times \frac{\text{Sales}}{\text{Capital}}$$

The relevant figures from the accounts of AB Ltd are as follows:

	This year £	Last year £
Profit available for long-term capital	16,000	15,000
Long-term capital	80,000	60,000
Sales	100,000	100,000
	This year	Last year
Return on capital employed	20%	25%
Profit/sales	16%	15%
Sales: Capital employed	1.25:1	1.66:1

It can be seen that the reason for the decline in ROCE is the disproportionate increase in capital employed. Last year, £1 of assets produced £1.66 of sales whereas this year £1 of assets produced only £1.25 of sales. To ascertain the cause of this a series of subsidiary ratios can be produced as follows:

	This year	Last year
Sales: fixed assets	1.72:1	2.70:1
Sales: net current assets	4.54:1	4.35:1
Sales: current assets	1.82:1	1.75:1

It is apparent that the reduction in the return on capital employed is occasioned by a considerable increase in investment in fixed assets without a corresponding increase in sales or profit margins.

The pyramid of ratios

ROCE can be broken down into a whole pyramid of possible ratios. In calculating these ratios it is necessary to use the assets as the denominator in the ratio instead of capital. The total capital is naturally equal to the total assets.

In this way it is possible to isolate each type of asset as a factor in the profitability of the company.

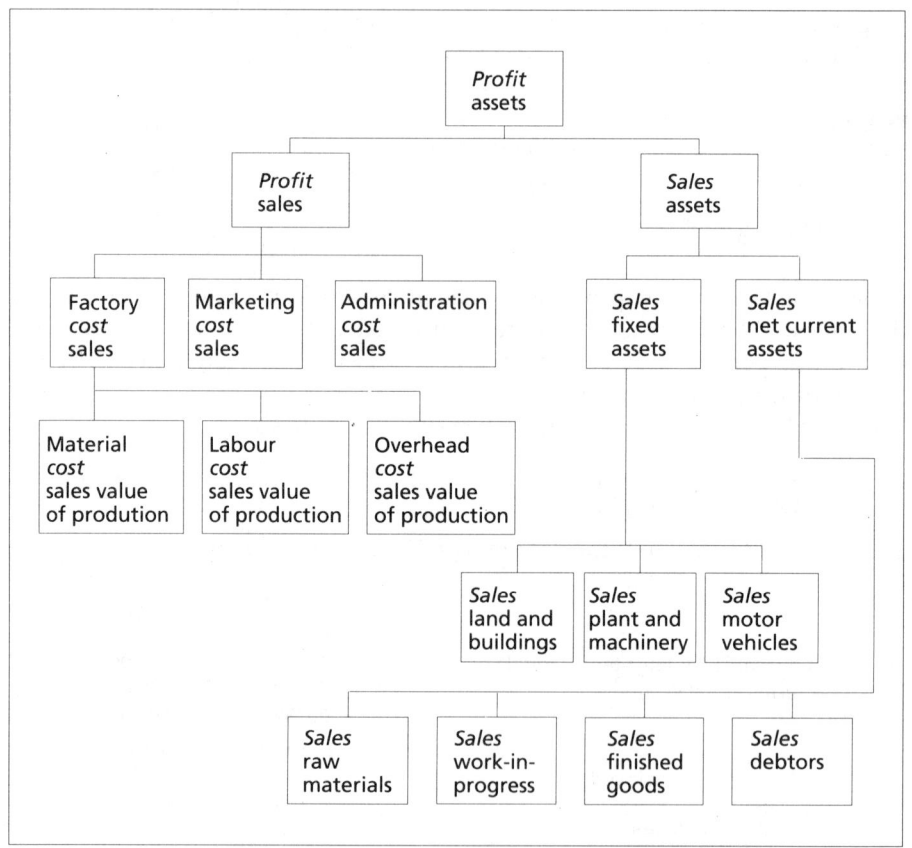

The process of interpretation must involve an assessment of the possible causes of important changes revealed by calculating any of the ratios.

Example:
An analysis of the profit and loss account of AB Ltd reveals the following changes:

Item	Change	Possible causes
Materials	Decrease from 28% of sales to 25%	a Reduction in prices b Errors in stock taking c Economies in production d Changes in product mix
Other variable costs	Decrease from 22% of sales to 20%	a Reduction in wage rates b Reduction in other costs c Greater efficiency d Greater use of capacity
Fixed costs of sales	No change	
Gross profit	Risen from 35% of sales to 40%	Reduction in variable costs brought about by any of the reasons stated above
Other overheads	Increase from £21,000 to £25,000	Analysis required to determine cause of increase
Profit before taxation	Increase from 14% of sales to 15%	Caused by improved gross profit margin offset by increase in general fixed overheads. If other overheads had been held to £21,000 net profit would have been 19% of sales

Profit margins

The calculation of both gross and net profit margins is usually very straightforward. They are usually calculated as a 'quick' comparison and as a prelude to a more detailed analysis.

Changes in profit margins can often indicate important areas for investigation.

Example:

AB Ltd	This year	Last year
Gross profit/sales	40%	35%
Net profit before tax/sales	15%	14%

The gross profit percentage has risen from 35 per cent to 40 per cent. This may have been caused by either an increase in sales price or a reduction in unit variable costs.

Despite this the net profit percentage has only risen 1 per cent. This indicates an increase in the level of overhead costs. ROCE is more important than profit margins as a measure of profitability and in situations where a more detailed analysis is required calculation of profit margins as a separate exercise is necessary.

Summary

Consideration of profitability may be summarised as follows:

a Calculate ROCE (if you are not sure which basis to use, a generally acceptable one is the return on long-term capital employed). Compare this with:

   i   last year;

   ii   other companies in the same industry;

   iii   other industries;

   iv the company's target figure.

b Investigate the profit/sales ratio and individual costs in the profit and loss account to isolate significant variations.

c Investigate the sales/capital employed and compute the ratios of sales/individual assets to determine significant variations.

d Where a basis for comparison is not available it may only be possible to calculate the various ratios without making comments thereon.

Measures of liquidity

Definition of 'liquidity'

In the context of interpretation of accounts, 'liquidity' is usually defined as the ability of a company to meet its liabilities as they fall due. It can be sub-divided as:

a *immediate liquidity* – eg paying the wages at the end of the week;

b *short-term liquidity* – eg paying the dividend and taxation in say four months' time;

c *medium and long-term liquidity* – eg repayment of debentures in seven years;

d *financial balance* – involving the company's long-term capital structure.

Need for liquidity

It is not enough for an enterprise to operate at a profit; it must also have an adequate cash flow to meet its liabilities as they fall due. An extremely profitable company may fail because of short-term liquidity problems whilst an unprofitable company has considerable cash balances which are largely unutilised.

Short-term liquidity

The company's short-term liquidity is indicated by its net current asset position. The current ratio compares current assets to current liabilities. The normally accepted ratio is in the region of 1.8:1 to 2:1.

Example:
The current ratio of AB Ltd for the two years is as follows:

	This year	Last year
Current assets:current liabilities	1.67:1	1.68:1

The ratio is almost unchanged but both years may be regarded as unsatisfactory with liabilities being higher in relation to available assets than is desirable.

The current ratio considers current assets and current liabilities which have approximately a nine-month life-cycle. It is important to consider the more immediate liquid position because a company could have a good current position but be unable to pay its immediate liabilities.

Immediate liquidity

Immediate liquidity is concerned with debts falling due for payment in the next six to eight weeks.

It is considered by use of the quick assets ratio which compares quick assets (usually cash and bank balances and debtors which can be liquidated within six to eight weeks) and immediate liabilities (usually trade creditors and, depending on the date of payment, current taxation and dividends). The normally accepted ratio is 1:1 or perhaps a little less (say 0.8:1).

The quick assets ratio of AB Ltd for the two years is as follows:

	This year	Last year
Quick assets:immediate liabilities	1.78:1	0.98:1

Quick assets have been arrived at as follows:

	£	£
Cash and bank	2,000	1,000
Debtors represent approximately ¼ of sales or 3 months debtors. Only ½ would therefore be realised in 6 weeks	14,000	11,000
	£16,000	£12,000

Immediate liabilities have been arrived at as follows:

	£	£
Creditors represent between 3 and 4 months' cost of sales and it is assumed that approximately ½ would fall due for payment in the next 6 weeks	7,500	10,250
Bank overdraft is assumed to be within limit and not immediately repayable	–	–
Proposed dividend is assumed to be immediately payable	2,000	2,000
	£9,500	£12,250

There has been a considerable improvement in the immediate position mainly due to a substantial reduction in creditors. Note that the assumption regarding the bank overdraft has a major effect. The legal situation is that an overdraft is repayable to the bank on demand, ie at any time. Hence it must be a current liability. However, banks rarely demand immediate payment and consequently the overdraft has something of the nature of a long-term liability. In addition, if the overdraft limit is £50,000 but the firm has used only £10,000 then the firm has an additional £40,000 available with which to pay its other current liabilities. The existence of a bank overdraft thus creates problems when using the quick asset ratio. In our example, we have excluded it entirely, which may be the best solution in an examination provided that you also include a note to the examiner explaining why you have done this.

Appraisal of stock and credit control

In consideration of the overall current position, attention must be paid to the adequacy of stock control and control over debtors and creditors. Ratios are useful here.

Stock ratio (stock turnover)

It is important to control the amount of capital tied up in stocks and the ratio shown is that of stocks to cost of sales.

There are several ways to compute this new ratio:

a 'Stock turnover' (favoured by the examiner) is cost of sales divided by average stocks. For AB we have:

Cost of sales	60,000
Opening stocks	34,000
Closing stocks	25,000

$$\text{Stock turnover} = \frac{60,000}{(34,000 + 25,000) \div 2} = 2.03 \text{ times}$$

b Days in stock: average stock divided by cost of sales x 365. This tells us how long the firm is holding its stocks. For AB Ltd:

$$\frac{(34,000 + 25,000) \div 2}{60,000} \times 365 = 179 \text{ days}$$

or in terms of months

$$\frac{(34,000 + 25,000) \div 2}{60,000} \times 12 = 5.9 \text{ months}$$

As the opening stock for last year is not available this ratio cannot be computed for last year.

Debtor ratio

Here the year end figures are taken:

a Debtor turnover $= \dfrac{\text{sales (on credit)}}{\text{closing debtors}}$

AB Ltd: this year $= \dfrac{100,000}{28,000} = 3.6 \text{ times}$

Last year $= \dfrac{100,000}{22,000} = 4.5 \text{ times}$

b No of days $= \dfrac{\text{closing debtors}}{\text{sales}} \times 365$ days (or 12 months)

AB Ltd this year $\dfrac{28,000}{100,000} \times 365 = 102$ days (3½ months)

Last year $\dfrac{22,000}{100,000} \times 365 = 80$ days (2½ months)

c Creditor ratio

Ideally this ratio would be the year's purchases on credit divided by closing creditors.

The longer-term position

The longer-term position requires an appraisal of the capital structure of a company. The principal sources of funds to a company are as follows:

Equity capital and retained profits	Members' capital	Residual return capital	Long-term capital
Preference capital		Fixed interest capital	
Loan capital	Non-members' capital		Short-term capital
Short-term loans		Interest free capital	
Trade credit			

a *Ratio of members' to non-members' capital* measures the extent to which the owners of the company have provided its finance. Too much reliance on finance from non-members may be a sign of weakness.

b *Gearing ratio* measures fixed interest capital to residual return capital:

  i low gearing = most of the capital is raised in the form of equity shares;

  ii high gearing = there is a considerable proportion of preference shares and loan capital;

  iii no gearing = all the capital is raised in the form of equity shares.

c *Ratio of long-term to short-term capital* indicates the extent to which the company relies on short-term borrowings, the forced repayment of which at short notice might cause serious difficulties.

The ratios for AB Ltd are as follows:

		This year	Last year
a	Ratio of members to non-members capital	£70,000 : £43,000	£60,000 : £34,000
		1.67 : 1	1.76 : 1
b	Gearing ratio	£30,000 : £50,000	£20,000 : £40,000
		1 : 1.67	1 : 2
c	Ratio of long-term to short-term capital	£80,000 : £33,000	£60,000 : £34,000
		2.42 : 1	1.76 : 1

The fall in ratio (a) is attributable to the loan capital issued in the current year.

The issue of the loan capital has also resulted in slightly higher gearing as shown in ratio (b). The improvement in ratio (c) is a result of the issue of loan capital and also a share issue at a premium.

Gearing may be regarded as a key ratio especially in an analysis required for investment purposes.

Measures of growth

A company's management will aim for growth in the following areas:

a *Growth in overall efficiency* as measured by the return on capital employed. A target may be 'an increase of 5 per cent in ROCE in the next five years'.

b *Growth in profit margins.* A company will endeavour to improve its profit margins by:

   i   selling price increases, with the hope that volume will not fall; or

   ii   selling price decreases, in the hope that volume will increase; or

   iii cost reduction, while holding the level of overall efficiency; or

   iv sales promotion, designed to increase sales volume.

c *Growth in turnover* – the management will seek to expand its share of the market and to diversify where appropriate. Growth in turnover is insufficient in itself. It must be of items having an adequate profit margin.

d *Growth in capital employed* – this may be achieved by retaining profits in the company or raising share or loan capital.

In a time of inflation, care must be taken to distinguish 'real growth' from growth in money amounts promoted by rising prices.

Asset position

Balance sheet

In interpreting financial statements, reference will inevitably be made to a company's balance sheet.

In particular, two items require careful consideration:

a fixed assets;

b stock valuation.

Fixed assets

In considering the fixed assets in a balance sheet, the following points should be considered:

a *Balance sheet figures:*

   i   Do the balance sheet figures for fixed assets represent cost or valuation, or a combination of the two?

   ii If the figures are at cost, what are the ages of the various items making up the total?

   iii If valuations are used how long ago were they made and how reliable are they?

b *Land and buildings:*

   i   What is the current value of freehold land and buildings, at its present use and for alternative uses?

   ii With regard to leasehold property, what is the unexpired term of the lease? What is the likelihood of renewal on acceptable terms?

c *Plant and machinery:*

   i   What age are the principal items of plant?

   ii Is there a regular maintenance programme in operation?

   iii What is the general state of repair of the plant?

   iv Is the most modern machinery in use or is some of the equipment out of date?

   v   Are detailed asset records maintained?

d *Depreciation provisions:*

   i   Is the provision for depreciation adequate?

   ii What is the basis of computation?

   iii Has any attempt been made to provide for the increase in replacement price of plant and machinery?

   iv Are sufficient funds available for capital expenditure as, and when, requried?

Stock valuation

A company should both establish and keep to a consistent and suitable basis of stock valuation. An incorrect stock valuation directly affects both the company's profit and its net worth.

Stock valuation may be based on either:

a actual cost, or

b valuations.

Where there are marked changes in the rates of gross profit from year to year the stock valuation should be investigated.

Difficulties in interpretation

There are two major difficulties when utilising ratios for analytical purposes.

Consistency

The analyst must ensure that the ratios are computed on a consistent basis. There is no point in comparing a ROCE based on total assets with one based on total *net* assets.

Comparability

In Chapter 1 it was stated that comparisons are necessary. The internal comparisons present little difficulty but there are many problems inherent in the use of external comparisons with either other companies or industry statistics.

a Each company will prepare its accounts differently and will have different accounting bases. This is especially important in the area of:

   i   depreciation methods;
   ii   stock valuation;
   iii fixed asset valuation;
   iv materiality.

In addition the firms being used in comparison will have different accounting periods (different year ends).

b Each firm will have different geographical locations which could well affect many items in the accounts including:

   i   delivery costs;
   ii   material costs;
   iii labour costs.

Inflation has different effects in different areas as well.

c The age of the fixed assets will differ from firm to firm and each firm will have different patterns of asset ownership. For example, two firms may operate from identical factories but one may own theirs whilst the other simply rents.

d Generally, analysts will have only the published accounts to help them. These have relatively little information shortage.

e Off balance sheet financing. This term is applied to the use of assets permanently (or semi-permanently) which are owned by people outside the firm and consequently no value appears in the balance sheet of the firm using the asset. It can arise where a firm hires or leases assets.

f Treatment of bank overdrafts. Is an overdraft short- or long-term financing? Do we know how much of the overdraft facility has been utilised?

g Window dressing. It is possible to dress up the accounts so that they appear to be better than they actually are.

Suppose that at the end of the last week before the year end the working capital position is as follows:

	£
Stocks	50,000
Debtors	100,000
Bank	150,000
	300,000
Creditors	100,000
Net current assets	£200,000

This could well be the 'normal' position, showing a current ratio of 3:1 and a quick asset ratio of 2½:1. Not too bad as it stands. But, if the firm pays off £50,000 of its creditors during the last week so that at the year end the position is:

	£
Stocks	50,000
Debtors	100,000
Bank	100,000
	250,000
Creditors	50,000
Net current assets	£200,000

We now have a current ratio of 5:1 and a quick asset ratio of 4:1. Much better! After the year end the firm could let the position drift back to 'normal' and the balance sheet would then be misleading.

Examination notes

Interpretation and ratio analysis can crop up in any question but there are also questions specifically in this area. They take one of three forms:

a essay questions;

b interpretation questions;

c utilising ratios.

Essay questions

Illustration:

You have been asked to compare by means of ratio analysis the final accounts of ten different companies. The major concern of the analysis is to assess the relative profitability and liquidity position of each of the companies. All the companies are in the same trade and are of roughly similar size.

Required:

a Select *five* ratios which you consider important to this project and explain how each is calculated and what you expect it to tell you.

(15 marks)

b Indicate some of the difficulties of applying such analysis across these ten companies.

(10 marks)

Associated Examining Board
November 1979

Solution:

On the assumption that 'final' accounts means published accounts five major ratios would include:

a *Profitability:*

   i *Return on capital employed*. This ratio is the pre-tax and interest profit as a percentage of capital employed. It illustrates how efficiently the firm is using its assets in terms of profitability and could be considered the 'yield' of the organisation as a whole.

   ii *Net profit percentage*. Calculated by showing net profits as a percentage of total sales. It illustrates the firm's efficiency in terms of its manufacturing and trading organisations.

   iii *Earnings per share*. Calculated by dividing net profits (after tax interest and preference dividends) by the total number of ordinary shares in issue. It shows the firm's capability in producing wealth for its ordinary shareholders. Other profitability ratios available from published accounts might include:

   sales to fixed assets;
   dividend per share;
   sales per employee;
   wages per employee;
   exports to house sales;
   return on equity.

b *Liquidity:*

   i *Current ratio*. The current ratio is the ratio of current assets to current liabilities. It illustrates how much of the firm's trading assets would be needed to repay its immediate (less than one year) liabilities.

ii *Quick ratio (acid test)*. Quick assets (debtors and bank) as a ratio of current liabilities. This ratio shows if the firm is able to pay its immediate liabilities without any additional trading. It is probably the most important liquidity ratio. Other liquidity ratios might include:

operating cycle;
debtors to sales;
stocks to sales (or preferably to cost of sales);
creditor turnover (preferably in terms of purchases).

Difficulties in applying analysis across different companies:

a The accounts will have different accounting bases, especially in relation to:

i depreciation;

ii stocks;

iii fixed asset valuation;

iv materiality.

b The firms will almost certainly have different accounting periods.

c Location: if the firms are not all in one geographical location the delivery costs might be higher for one; inflation effects will be different etc.

d Lack of information in published accounts.

e Age of underlying assets.

f Off balance sheet financing:
i hire of plant;
ii leasing.

g Treatment of bank overdrafts:

i long v short-term financing;

ii comparing one firm with cash in bank;

iii to one with an overdraft.

h Window dressing.

i Market conditions:

i seasonal trading;

ii degree of competition.

j Different patterns of asset ownership.

Interpretation questions

Illustration:
The following are the summarised final accounts for the years ended 31 March 1994 and 1995 of Meteor (Retail) Ltd.

Profit & Loss Accounts for year ended 31 March	1994	1995
	£	£
Turnover	600,000	950,000
Trading profit	58,000	65,000
Investment income	12,000	15,000
	70,000	80,000
Less: Dividends	15,000	30,000
Retained earnings	55,000	50,000

Balance Sheets at 31 March		1994		1995
		£		£
Fixed assets				
Freehold land and properties, at cost		60,000		20,000
at valuation		–		100,000
Other fixed assets, net of depreciation		90,000		105,000
		150,000		225,000
Investments		130,000		215,000
Current assets: Stocks	32,000		75,000	
Debtors	41,000		106,000	
Bank	–		54,000	
		73,000		235,000
		£353,000		£675,000
Ordinary share capital, shares of £1 each,				
issued and fully paid		80,000		180,000
Share premium account		30,000		140,000
Surplus arising on revaluation of properties		–		50,000
Retained earnings		210,000		260,000
		320,000		630,000
Current liabilities (creditors and				
proposed dividends)		29,000		45,000
Bank overdraft		4,000		–
		£353,000		£675,000

Required:

A critical consideration of the performance of the company over the year in relation to each of the following points which the chairman is planning to highlight in his speech at the company's annual general meeting.

a Turnover and profits substantially up on the year.

(5 marks)

b A doubling of the dividend to shareholders.

(5 marks)

c Substantial increase in fixed assets.

(5 marks)

d Greatly improved working capital ratio.

(5 marks)

e Successful rights issue of shares to finance further expansion.

(5 marks)

AEB – updated

Solution:

a Although turnover has increased by over 50 per cent trading profits are up by only 12 per cent (approximately).

Trading profits now represent only 7 per cent (9 per cent 1994).

Investment income represents only 11 per cent (14 per cent 1994) on cost.

Consequently one can say that turnover is up but profits have not risen proportionately due to higher total costs and a reduced investment income yield as a proportion of profits.

b The amount of dividend has doubled only in absolute terms. The dividend per share has fallen to $16\frac{2}{3}$ pence per share from 19 pence per share and it would be unwise for the chairman to highlight this fact.

c The substantial increase in fixed assets is made up of:

	£
Revaluation of freehold properties	50,000
Additions to freehold properties	10,000
Additions (net of year's depreciation and sales)	
to other fixed assets	15,000
	75,000
Cost of fixed assets 1994	150,000
Value of fixed assets 1995	£225,000

There is insufficient information to enable the analyst to determine the actual amounts invested in fixed assets but the increase is certainly not as large as the chairman implies. The reason for this is the large amount of the increase of value of existing properties, which has been reflected in the 1995 accounts.

d Both the stock and debtor turnovers have worsened in relation to sales with the increase in net liquid funds being provided largely by the rights issue.

In addition, as the firm is a retail organisation then the size of the debtor collection period is rather disturbing as it represents 40 days approximately (25 days, approximately 1994). There is nothing to explain why the proportion of credit sales has increased.

e The rights issue, which must have been five for four at £2.10/share, and the reinvestment of profits increased the capital employed by £260,000, reducing the return on capital employed from 22 per cent (1994) to 14 per cent (1995) approximately.

In addition, the money received has not necessarily been used in furthering the firm's expansion. To a large extent it has financed increases in working capital, and it can be argued that this is not true expansion.

Utilising ratios

Illustration:
Quickturn Ltd, a retail trading concern, is currently planning its operations for the year ending 31 May 1995.

The company's summarised final accounts for the year ended 31 May 1994, are as follows:

Trading and Profit & Loss Account for the year ended 31 May 1994

	£		£
Cost of sales	60,000	Sales	80,000
Gross profit c/d	20,000		
	£80,000		£80,000
Established expenses	7,000	Gross profit b/d	20,000
Administrative expenses	2,000		
Selling expenses	5,000		
	14,000		
Net profit	6,000		
	£20,000		£20,000

Balance Sheet at 31 May 1994

	£		£	£
Ordinary share capital	30,000	Fixed assets:		
Retained earnings	15,000	Freehold store premises		
Current liabilities		Fixtures and fittings at cost		45,000
Trade creditors	5,600	Less: Depreciation to date		20,250
				24,750
		Current assets:		
		Stock in trade	10,000	
		Trade debtors	8,000	
		Balance at bank	7,850	25,850
	£50,600			£50,600

The company's plans for the year ending 31 May 1995 are as follows:

a Sales volume to increase by 50 per cent compared with the previous year and no change in selling prices are envisaged.

b Overhead expenditure:

 i establishment: reduced by £2,000 compared with the previous year;

 ii administrative: 50 per cent increase over the previous year;

 iii selling: 100 per cent increase over the year.

c Some significant relationships:

 i $\frac{\text{Closing trade debtors}}{\text{Sales for year}}$ x 100 = 16⅔%

 ii $\frac{\text{Closing trade creditors}}{\text{Purchases for year}}$ x 100 percentage as in previous year

 iii $\frac{\text{Net profit for the year}}{\text{Sales for year}}$ x 100 = 5%

 iv $\frac{\text{Cost of sales for year}}{\text{Average of opening and closing stock}}$ 12 times*

 * The corresponding figure for the previous year was five.
 All purchases and sales are on credit.
 In April 1995, the company plans to purchase a piece of land for development purposes at a cost of £20,000.

In May 1995 it is planned to acquire new additional fixtures and fittings at a cost of £5,000.

There will be no creditors for fixed assets at 31 May 1995.

As customary, depreciation is to be provided on freehold store premises, fixtures and fittings at the rate of 5 per cent per annum on the cost at the end of the financial year. Depreciation is charged to establishment expenses.

Required:

The estimated trading and profit and loss account for the year ending 31 May 1995 and the estimated balance sheet at that date of Quickturn Ltd.

(25 marks)

Associated Examining Board – updated

Solution:

Quickturn Ltd
Estimated Trading and Profit & Loss Account for the year ended 31 May 1995

	£	£
Sales (1)		120,000
Opening stock	10,000	
Purchases (by balance)	92,000	
	102,000	
Closing stock (6)	6,000	96,000
Gross profit		24,000
Expenses: Establishment (2)	5,000	
Administration (2)	3,000	
Selling (2)	10,000	18,000
Net profit (4)		£6,000

Estimated Balance Sheet as at 31 May 1995

		£	£	£
Fixed assets:	Freehold property			20,000
	Fixtures (NBV) (8)			27,250
				47,250
Current assets:	Stock (6)		6,000	
	Debtors (3)		20,000	
			26,000	
Current liabilities: Creditors (7)		9,200		
	Bank (by balance)	13,050	22,250	3,250
				£51,000
Financed by:				
Ordinary share capital				30,000
Retained earnings (9)				21,000
				£51,000

Notes:

1. 80,000 x 50% of 80,000
2. Establishment = 7,000 – 2,000
   Administration = 2,000 x 50% of 2,000
   Selling = 5,000 x 100% of 5,000
3. $\frac{Debtors}{Sales}$ x 100 = 16⅔%

$$\frac{\text{Debtors}}{120,000} \times 100 = 16\tfrac{2}{3}\%$$

$$\text{Debtors} = \frac{16\tfrac{2}{3}}{100} \times 120,000$$

4. $\dfrac{\text{Net profit}}{\text{Sales}} \times 100 = 5\%$

$$\frac{\text{Net profit}}{120,000} \times 100 = 5\%$$

$$\text{Net profit} = \frac{5}{100} \times 120,000$$

5. GP – expenses = net profit
   GP – 18,000 = 6,000
   GP = 24,000
   Sales – cost of sales = GP
   120,000 – cost of sales = 24,000
   Cost of sales = 96,000

6. $\dfrac{\text{Cost of sales}}{\text{Average stock}} = 12$

$$\frac{\text{Cost of sales}}{(\text{Opening stock} + \text{closing stock}) \div 2} = 12$$

$$\frac{96,000}{(10,000 + \text{closing stock})} = 12$$

$$\text{Closing stock} = \frac{96,000 \times 2}{12} - 10,000$$

7. For 1981 $\dfrac{\text{Cost of sales}}{\text{Average stock}} = 5$

$$\frac{\text{Cost of sales}}{(\text{Opening stock} + \text{closing stock}) \div 2} = 5$$

$$\frac{60,000}{(\text{Opening stock} + 10,000 \div 2)} = 5$$

$$\text{Opening stock} = \frac{60,000 \times 2}{5} - 10,000$$

$$= 24,000 - 10,000$$

$$= 14,000$$

opening stock + purchases – closing stock = cost of sales
14,000 + purchases – 10,000 = 60,000
purchases = 56,000

$$\frac{\text{Creditors 1993}}{\text{Purchasers 1993}} \times 100 = \frac{\text{creditors 1986}}{\text{purchasers 1986}} \times 100$$

therefore $\dfrac{\text{Creditors 1993}}{92,000} = \dfrac{5,600}{56,000}$

$$\text{Creditors 1993} = \frac{5,600}{56,000} \times 92,000$$

8. Fixtures and fittings

Cost l.6.93	45,000	
Additions	5,000	
	50,000	
Depreciation 1.6.93	20,250	
Charge for year	2,500	22,750
		£27,250

9. 15,000 + 6,000

Problems

Problem 17.1

Your friend Stan Down has inherited 2,000 ordinary shares in a public quoted company which has interests in the hotel and catering trades and owns some 250 hotels all over the country. He has just received the annual accounts and he puts to you the following questions:

'a Can I calculate what my shares are worth from the balance sheet? If not, why not?

(7 marks)

b A press report I read said this company was "highly geared". What is gearing and is this a good or a bad thing from my point of view?

(6 marks)

c The company seems to have ample reserves as shown in the balance sheet. Should not these have been distributed to the earlier shareholders?

(6 marks)

d I have found a page headed "Statement of Accounting Policies" but it doesn't make a lot of sense to me. Please explain what I may expect to find here.'

(6 marks)

Associated Examining Board – updated

Required:

Answer each point raised by your friend.

Problem 17.2

Brian Bradshaw, a millionaire, is studying the accounts of two businesses in the same trade, one of which he intends to purchase. The final accounts of the two companies concerned for the year ended 31 March 1995 are summarised below:

Profit & Loss Accounts for the year ended 31 March 1995

	A Limited		B Limited	
	£	£	£	£
Sales		200,000		520,000
Less: Cost of sales		160,000		410,000
		40,000		110,000
Rent	8,000		–	
Loan interest (12%)	1,200		8,400	
Other expenses (including wages)	6,800		16,400	
Directors' salaries	9,000		18,000	
Depreciation	3,000	28,000	10,000	52,800
Net profit for the year		£12,000		£57,200

Balance Sheets as at 31 March 1995

	A Limited £	B Limited £
Freehold land and buildings	–	140,000
Plant and equipment, *less* depreciation	9,000	75,000
Stocks	12,000	22,000
Other net current assets	20,000	51,000
	£41,000	£288,000
Ordinary shares	5,000	50,000
Retained earnings	26,000	168,000
Loans (at 12% interest)	10,000	70,000
	£41,000	£288,000

Additional information:

a The results above are typical of those achieved in recent years.

b If Company B did not own its own property it would have to pay rent of £10,000 a year for equivalent premises.

c Company A has two directors and Company B has three directors. A director working in this type of trade can expect to earn £5,000 a year.

d Both companies depreciate their plant and equipment on the straight-line method but Company A uses a rate of 10 per cent per annum and Company B a rate of 20 per cent. Brian Bradshaw considers a rate of 15 per cent to be more appropriate in each case.

e Company A has expansion plans for the future which if carried out would double its sales and increase its gross profit/sales ratio to 25 per cent, but this would involve spending £80,000 on additional new plant and equipment. To finance the projected expansion the company would need to borrow £60,000 at 15 per cent interest per annum; wages would increase by £5,000 per annum but rent and other expenses would remain the same.

f Brian Bradshaw is willing to purchase either business but would wish to retain the existing management. He does not have the time himself to play a large part in the running of either business.

g Stocks are maintained at a constant level in both companies.

Required:

a A calculation for both companies for the year ended 31 March 1995 of:

i   the percentage net profit/sales ratio;

ii   the stock turnover ratio.

(5 marks)

b The redrafted profit and loss accounts for both companies to show the net expected profit if the accounts were produced on a comparable basis (ie taking account of the information given in notes b–d above).

(8 marks)

c Using the same comparable basis as in your answer to (b) above, prepare a statement to show by how much the annual net profits of Company A might be increased if the development envisaged in note (e) were carried out.

(8 marks)

d Any two additional items of information other than those which can be derived from the published accounts which would assist Brian Bradshaw in deciding which of the two businesses to buy.

(4 marks)

Associated Examining Board – updated

Problem 17.3

The following are the summarised balance sheets of Crow Ltd at 31 October 1994 and 1995:

	1994 £000s	1995 £000s
Equipment at cost	428	545
Less: Depreciation	105	161
	323	384
Trade investments at market value	162	185
Stock	196	311
Debtors	82	129
Bank	30	–
	£793	£1,009
Ordinary share capital	260	390
Share premium	30	92
Other reserves, including profit & loss	253	351
Loan stocks	150	–
Creditors	74	102
Proposed final dividend	26	39
Bank	–	35
	£793	£1,009

During the year ended 31 October 1995:

a Equipment which cost £80,000 (aggregate depreciation £59,000) was sold for £24,000.

b No trade investments were bought or sold.

c The loan stocks were redeemed at a premium of 2 per cent, this premium being provided out of the share premium account.

d An interim dividend of £16,000 was paid in June 1995.

Required:

a Calculate the working capital (ie current) ratio at 31 October 1994 and 1995.

(3 marks)

b What problems does the existence of a bank overdraft cause when interpreting the current ratio?

(3 marks)

Associated Examining Board – updated

Problem 17.4

The following information relates to the first year of Uthank Ltd which was formed on 1 May 1994:

a All the company's authorised capital of £20,000 was issued for cash on 1 May 1994; the total proceeds of this fully paid issue was £25,000.

b On 1 May 1994, the company issued 40 £100 10 per cent debentures at par.

c The net profit for the company's first year was 7½ per cent of the sales for the period.

d During the year under review, the company made the following capital expenditure payments:

April 1994	Freehold property	£7,000
June 1994	Plant and machinery	£8,000
November 1994	Motor vehicles	£3,000

e The company's depreciation policy is as follows:

Freehold property	Nil
Plant and machinery	10% on cost
Other fixed assets	25% on cost

f Payments for purchases £173,000.

g The only current liabilities at 30 April 1995 other than any mentioned below, were trade creditors £3,000.

h The stock turnover ratio was 20. The opening stock was nil; the closing stock was £16,000.

i Trade debtors at 30 April 1995 amounted to £4,000.

j The company always attains a gross profit at the rate of 20 per cent of sales revenue.

k The company's revenue expenditure, other than purchases and depreciation, can be summarised as follows:

Administration (inc directors' emoluments of £8,000)	£20,000
Establishment	2,550
Debenture interest	400
Audit fees	500

l It is proposed that there be a dividend of 25 per cent on the ordinary shares and £2,000 be transferred to general reserve.

m In April 1995, the company entered into a contract for the construction of a new warehouse at an estimated cost of £50,000.

Required:

The profit and loss account for the year ended 30 April 1995 and a balance sheet at that date.

Associated Examining Board – updated

Problem 17.5

Jacques Dennett, a sole proprietor, had always financed his business from his private wealth or with help from his family. In view of his ambitious plans to expand his business, he approached his bank for a large loan. In response to the bank's request for financial information he provided the following summarised data:

Summarised Revenue Statement for the year ended 30 September 1995

	£	£
Sales		950,000
Less: Cost of goods sold		485,000
Gross profit		465,000
Administrative expenses	120,800	
Selling and distribution expenses	81,700	
Financial charges	12,500	215,000
Net profit		£250,000

DR	Balance Sheet as at 30 September 1995		CR
	£		£
Fixed assets	426,000	Capital	504,000
Current assets	149,000	Current liabilities	71,000
	£575,000		£575,000

The bank now requires the above statements to be amended to take account of the following items.

a Sales included £27,000 of goods sold to members of Dennett's family. The goods were pro forma invoiced at the selling price, but Dennett later decided that the family members need not pay for the goods. If these goods had been sold they would have produced a gross profit of 10 per cent of the selling price.

b Dennett was advised by a friend that he could get a more accurate gross profit figure if he valued his stock of goods for re-sale at the market price. Thus he had valued the closing stock on 30 September 1995 at £91,000 instead of its cost valuation of £65,000.

c Dennett's main private pastime is rally-car driving. He spared no expense in ensuring that his cars were in tip-top condition and he made extensive use of his business workshops. It is estimated that servicing costs for the past year were £25,000 and they have been included in the administrative expenses above. On 1 January 1995 he bought a vintage car for £40,000 for his own private use. This amount has been included in the fixed assets above. He financed the purchase with £20,000 from his private wealth and the remainder was borrowed from his brother. The loan is included in the current liabilities above and it had been agreed that no interest would be payable. Depreciation has not been provided for on the vintage car.

d The bank had expressed concern that the value of the business premises bought several years ago for £20,000 and included in the balance sheet at that amount, had fallen; the current market value being £130,000. This fall in the market value had occurred owing to a prolonged economic recession.

e Dennett sub-let part of his premises for immediate occupancy to a friend for £5,000 per annum. A formal agreement had been signed on 1 October 1993 with rent due each 30 September. No rent had yet been received or accounted for.

f One of Dennett's suppliers provides him with six months' credit. During the last three months of the financial year ended 30 September 1995 invoices from this supplier amounting to £13,870 remained in Dennett's office unprocessed.

Required:

a A revised revenue statement for the year ended 30 September 1995 and a revised balance sheet as at that date, based on generally accepted accounting principles and conventions.

(22 marks)

b A report to the bank manager which should identify the accounting reasons for making any adjustments to the items (a) to (f) above. Note: answers should make reference to relevant accounting concepts.

(18 marks)

c An assessment of Dennett's liquidity and profitability based on the revised figures for the year ended 30 September 1995. Use ratios as appropriate.

(10 marks)

Associated Examining Board
November 1993 (updated)

Group accounts | 18

Introduction

A group of companies consists of a holding company (or parent company) and one or more subsidiary companies which are controlled by the holding company. In the simplest of situations one company invests in the shares of another, intending to hold the shares as a permanent investment, and because of the investment achieves control of its policies and decision-making functions. The cost of the investment appears in the balance sheet of the acquiring company as a fixed asset investment. However, the nature of group structures is complex, as one would expect in a sophisticated economy with complicated legal, taxation and accounting regulations, and in some circumstances a subsidiary may exist without any actual purchase of shares (see definition of 'subsidiary'). It can be seen that in order to provide more meaningful information relating to the group the results of the holding company and its subsidiaries must be combined, and both the Companies Act and FRS 2 require that the group accounts should be in the form of consolidated financial statements. These must comprise:

a a consolidated balance sheet dealing with the state of affairs of the parent and its subsidiaries;

b a consolidated profit and loss account dealing with the profit or loss of the parent and its subsidiaries;

c notes to the consolidated financial statements dealing with additional disclosure requirements;

d a consolidated cash flow statement and related notes.

The explanatory section of FRS 2 provides the following justification for the requirement for parent companies to prepare consolidated financial statements:

'For a variety of legal, tax and other reasons undertakings generally choose to conduct their activities not through a single legal entity but through several undertakings under the ultimate control of the parent undertaking of that group. For this reason the financial statements of a parent undertaking by itself do not present a full picture of its economic activities or financial position. Consolidated financial statements are required in order to reflect the extended business unit that conducts activities under the control of the parent undertaking.'

Definitions

There are now two definitions of a group in company law. The general definition refers to holding company and subsidiary company, but for accounting purposes the terms have been changed to include the word 'undertaking' instead of company, and these terms have been adopted by FRS 2. The reason for this is to ensure that all types of business enterprises, not just companies, that fall within the definitions of subsidiary, must now be consolidated. The term 'undertaking ' is to include not only incorporated businesses, but also unincorporated businesses like joint ventures, partnerships and even businesses carrying on a trade without a view to profit. This is to remedy the situation by which manipulation of information being reported could be achieved by omission of certain results.

A brief summary of the relevant definitions follows:

Parent company

This is one which:

a holds a majority of the voting rights in another undertaking; or

b is a member of the undertaking and has the right to appoint or remove directors holding a majority of the voting rights; or

c has the right to exercise a dominant influence over the undertaking (note that no shareholding is necessary); or

d is a member of the undertaking and controls alone, and by agreement, a majority of the voting rights in the undertaking;

e owns a participating interest in the undertaking and actually exercises dominant influence over it.

Most groups are very complex structures and FRS 2 provides a very comprehensive range of explanations of all the terms and definitions used to ensure that compliance with the standard can be achieved in even the most unusual of circumstances. However, one must recognise the practical difficulties involved, particularly in the area of dominant influence, and participating interest.

Dominant influence

The decision is judgmental and should take into account the following matters:

a the degree of board representation;

b the degree of day-to-day influence over the financial and operating policies;

c the extent of any power of veto held by the investor;

d evidence of intervention to ensure that investor's preferred policies are being implemented.

Participating interest

A participating interest is assumed to exist if the interest in shares is more than 20 per cent, unless the contrary is shown. It is defined as:

'an interest held in the shares of another undertaking, on a long term basis for the purpose of securing a contribution to its activities by the exercise of control or influence arising from its interest' (FRS 2 para 15).

Subsidiary undertaking

An undertaking is deemed to be a subsidiary, where the parent undertaking:

a holds a majority of voting rights;

b is a member of the undertaking and can appoint or remove directors having the majority of votes on the board;

c has a right to exercise dominant influence over the undertaking;

d is a member of the undertaking and operates control via an agreement with other shareholders;

e owns a participating interest in the undertaking and actually exercises a dominant influence or operates unified management.

It should be noted that all these situations now depend on the ability to control the undertaking, whereas in the past it was the legal ownership of equity shares in the undertaking which was used as the determining factor.

Associated undertaking

An 'associated undertaking' means an undertaking in which a member of the group has a participating interest and over whose operating and financial policy it exercises a significant influence, and which is not:

a a subsidiary undertaking of the parent company; or

b a joint venture. A parent company is required by law and by SSAP 1 to use 'equity accounting' to account for holdings in associated undertakings.

Exclusion from consolidation

In certain circumstances subsidiaries may be excluded from consolidation. It should be noted that where the company's act says that a company *may* be omitted, the requirements of FRS 2 are stricter in that they state the subsidiary *must* be omitted.

CA 1985 provides that a subsidiary *may* be omitted from the consolidated accounts of a group if:

a in the opinion of the directors, its inclusion is not material for the purpose of giving a true and fair view;

b there are severe long-term restrictions in exercising the parents company's rights; or

c the holding is exclusively for resale; or

d the information cannot be obtained without disproportionate expense or undue delay.

FRS 2 states that a subsidiary *must* be excluded from the consolidation in the following circumstances:

a if severe long-term restrictions are substantially hindering the exercise of the parent's rights over the subsidiary's assets;

b if the group's interest in the subsidiary undertaking is held exclusively with a view to subsequent resale and the subsidiary has not been consolidated previously;

c the subsidiary undertaking's activities are so different from those of other undertakings that its inclusion would be incompatible with the obligation to give a true and fair view.

FRS 2 sets out detailed disclosure requirements and accounting treatment for the undertakings excluded from the consolidation. However, these are not examinable under the A-level syllabus.

Provisions of FRS 2 regarding accounting procedures

FRS 2 does not set out the specific procedure for undertaking a consolidation, since this has been well documented in many text books over the years. It does, however, clarify the position regarding matters which in the past were dealt with in a variety of ways and also sets out criteria to ensure that the accounts are prepared in accordance with current recommendations. The consolidated financial statements provide information about the economic activities of the group as a whole, that is, as though the group were a *single entity*. Therefore when the combined position of all the group companies is prepared, certain adjustments need to be made. These include:

a Adjustments arising from the adoption of uniform accounting policies.

b Elimination of intra-group transactions.

c Elimination of pre-acquisition reserves.

d Fair value at acquisition adjustment.

e Treatment of goodwill on consolidation.

f Accounting for minority interest.

A range of the more usual types of adjustments follows with some simple examples of the calculations involved:

Inter-company indebtedness must be eliminated

Companies within the same group will trade, render management services, and pay dividends to one another. Additionally, loans may be made by the holding company to the subsidiary and vice versa. These inter-company transactions will generate internal debtors, creditors, and loan account balances. When consolidated accounts are prepared the assets and liabilities are combined and obviously it would be misleading for these to be overstated by internally generated transactions. The intra-group balances are agreed and then cancelled, so that the figures for debtors, creditors, and loans are for external transactions only. Similarly the income and expenditure relating to transactions between group companies is to be eliminated.

Inter-company 'sale' of fixed assets must be restored to original net book value

One company within the group may sell fixed assets to another as part of a perfectly normal arm's length transaction. However, this transaction will include a profit and for the consolidated accounts the profit must be eliminated and the asset restored to its original net book value. If this adjustment were not made, it would, in theory, be possible for companies within a group to manipulate the consolidated results by transferring assets around from one company to another.

Unrealised profit on transfer of stock must be eliminated

Similarly, one company in the group may sell goods to another at a profit. If at the year end some goods are still in stock then the 'profit' included in the cost price of such goods must be eliminated, and the stock restored to its original cost price. The reason for this adjustment is to avoid the overstatement of group profit by means of internal transactions. If the goods have not been sold outside the group then the profit has not been made. For example, H plc sells goods which cost £2,000 to S Ltd (its subsidiary) for £3,000, making a profit of £1,000 on the sale. S Ltd has sold all the goods for £4,000. Total combined group profit is £2,000 and as all the goods have been sold outside the group this is fine.

Now consider the same situation of H plc sells goods to S Ltd at a profit of £1,000, but this time they are all still in stock. Group profit (unadjusted) is £1,000 and closing stock (unadjusted) is £3,000. The reality of the situation is that since the goods have not been sold outside the group they have a real cost of £2,000 and no profit has been made. An adjustment is made for the consolidation which eliminates the profit (debit reserves £1,000) and restores the stock to original cost price (credit stock £1,000).

The share capital and reserves section of the balance sheet is slightly more complex to deal with in practice than the net assets section; however, since numerical questions are not set in the examination it is only necessary for you to be aware of the nature of the adjustments.

Elimination of pre-acquisition reserves

Profit earned by the subsidiary before acquisition is not consolidated as group revenue. It represents part of the net assets in existence at the date of purchase for which the holding company has paid. Pre-acquisition profits are not available for distribution to the holding company's shareholders, as it would be prejudicial to the creditors and other contributors of capital if part of the price paid for the subsidiary were to be used to pay dividends.

Reserves arising after acquisition, called 'post-acquisition' profits or losses, are consolidated by adding them to or deducting them from the holding company reserves on the consolidated balance sheet.

Fair value adjustment at acquisition

When a new subsidiary is acquired FRS 2 requires that its identifiable assets and liabilities are revalued at fair value at the date of acquisition for inclusion in the consolidated accounts. This rule applies even if the acquisition is made in stages. The excess over net book value is a pre-acquisition reserve. FRS 7 'Fair value at acquisition' deals with this subject in great detail but this is not examinable at A-level. It is sufficient to know that the net assets are subject to revaluation at the date of acquisition and that this will affect the calculation of goodwill.

Goodwill arising on consolidation

The cost of shares in the subsidiary (shown on the individual balance sheet as a fixed asset investment) must be cancelled against the share capital and reserves at the date of acquisition. Please note this is to include any revaluation reserve arising when the assets are revalued at the date of acquisition. The total of share capital and all reserves at the date of acquisition is equal to the net assets at acquisition at fair value. If the cost of shares is less than the net assets at fair value at acquisition the difference is positive goodwill. If however the cost of shares exceeds the fair value of the assets at acquisition the difference is negative goodwill. Goodwill must be dealt with in accordance with SSAP 22, which requires that purchased goodwill should normally be eliminated from the accounts immediately on acquisition against reserves. As an alternative, it may be amortised through the profit and loss account over its useful life.

Minority interest

Minority interest is the term used to describe outside interests in the share capital and reserves of subsidiaries.

It must be noted that the term was originally introduced into company law at a time when consolidation was based on equity ownership rather than control. Under the current provisions of the Act, where consolidation is based on control, there is no reason why the minority might not exceed 50 per cent.

FRS 2 requires that the consolidated balance sheet should show the total of share capital and reserves attributable to minority interest at the end of the period under the heading 'minority interest'. The Act formats for the balance sheet permit two alternative positions, after capital and reserves or after accruals and deferred income. Profit and loss formats require the minority to be shown after 'profit on ordinary activities after taxation'.

Associated companies – SSAP I

An associated company is one in which the interest of the parent is long term, is substantial, and having regard to the disposition of the other shareholdings, the investing company is in a position to exercise a significant influence over the company.

A significant influence is presumed to exist when the investing company holds more than 20 per cent of the equity voting rights.

Disclosure requirements for the results of an associate are:

a In the individual accounts of the investing company dividends received and receivable are credited in the profit and loss under the heading of 'Income from participating interests'.

b The cost of the investment in shares less any amounts written off will be disclosed in the balance sheet under the heading of 'Fixed assets - investment in participating interest'.

In the consolidated accounts the form of accounting prescribed by SSAP 1 is known as the equity method:

a In the consolidated profit and loss account, the investing group's share of the profit/loss before tax must be shown. This is disclosed under the heading of 'Income from interests in associated undertakings'. Also, disclose the share of taxation and the retained profit.

b The investing group's share of the net assets of the associated company is included under the heading of 'Fixed assets – investment in associated undertaking'.

c It is required that the investment in net assets at fair value at acquisition be shown separately from the share of goodwill, either original or arising on acquisition, less any amounts written off.

FRS 6 Acquisitions and mergers (previously FRED 6)

a Merger accounting can only be used if the business combination meets all the criteria set out below:

  i Role of the parties: no party to the combination is portrayed as being either the acquirer or the acquired.

  ii Dominance of management: all parties to the combination (as represented by the boards of directors etc) must participate in establishing the management structure of the combined entity and in selecting the management personnel. The decisions must be by consensus between parties.

  iii Relative size of the parties: no one party is able to dominate the combination by virtue of size.

  iv Non-equity consideration: the purchase consideration must comprise primarily equity shares in the combined entity and any non-equity consideration (eg cash) must be an immaterial proportion of the fair value of the total purchase consideration.

  v Minorities etc: no equity shareholders of the combining entities retain any material interest in the future performance of only part of the combined entity.

b Merger accounting requirements:

   i   The carrying value of assets and liabilities are not required to be adjusted to fair value on consolidation, although appropriate adjustments should be made to achieve uniformity of accounting policies in the combined entity.

   ii The results and cash flows of all combining entities should be bought into the financial statements of the combined entity from the beginning of the financial year. The comparative figures should also be restated by including the results for the combining entities for the previous period and their balance sheets for the previous balance sheet date.

   iii The difference between the nominal value of the shares issued plus the fair value of any other consideration given, and the nominal value of the shares received in exchange, should be shown as a movement in reserves in the consolidated accounts. These should also be shown in 'the reconciliation of shareholders' funds'.

   iv Merger expenses should be charged to the profit and loss account as reorganisation or restructuring expenses per FRS 3.

c Acquisition accounting: business combinations not accounted for by merger accounting should be accounted for using acquisition accounting. In this method:

   i   The identifiable assets and liabilities of the companies acquired should be included in the consolidated balance sheet at fair value at the date of acquisition.

   ii The results and cash flows should be brought into the group accounts only from the date of acquisition. The figures for the previous periods are not adjusted.

   iii The difference between the fair value of the identifiable net assets acquired and the fair value of the purchase consideration is goodwill, positive or negative.

d Disclosure requirements:

   i   For both acquisitions and mergers:
- the names of combining companies;
- whether the combination is an acquisition or a merger;
- the date of the combination.

   ii For mergers:
- an analysis of the current year's profit and loss and statement of recognised gains and losses into:

     a amounts for the period after the merger, combined;

     b for each party the amounts for the period up to the merger;

- an analysis of the results for the previous year for each party separately;
- the composition and fair value of the consideration given;

- the aggregate book value of the net assets of each party at the date of the merger;
- the nature and amount of significant accounting adjustments made to the net assets either to achieve uniformity of accounting policies or as a result of the merger;
- a statement of the adjustments to consolidated reserves resulting from the merger.

iii For acquisitions:

- the composition and fair value of the consideration given by the acquiring company is to be disclosed. Any deferred or contingent consideration must be described along with the range of possible outcomes and the principle factors that effect the outcome.
- A table should be provided showing for each class of asset and liability:

    a   the book value before any adjustment;

    b   the fair value adjustments analysed as:

        revaluations

        to achieve consistent accounting policy

        other

    c   the fair values at the date of acquisition;

    d   a statement of the amount of goodwill arising on the acquisition.

- As required by FRS 3, in the period of acquisition the post-acquisition results of the acquired company should be shown as a component of the continuing operations and, if material, described as newly acquired.

Sources of finance | 19

Short-term and long-term capital

The relative requirements for short-term and long-term capital in a business will be determined by:

a the need for fixed assets in relation to labour intensity;

b the length of the manufacturing period;

c the variation in levels of jobs, particularly seasonal variation;

d the variation in trade credit advanced to customers and taken from suppliers;

e the timing of tax payments.

Sources of short-term capital

Short-term credit may be obtained in the following ways:

a trade credit;

b bank overdrafts and loans;

c bill discounting;

d hire purchase;

e leasing;

f factoring of debtors.

Trade credit is the most important of these sources but its utilisation is dependent on the nature of the industry, the extent to which it is offset by the need to finance sales to customers, and the danger of damaging the company's own credit standing by excessive delay in payment.

Factoring, or the discounting of trade debts, is an increasingly popular source of short-term finance primarily amongst small companies; but it has the disadvantage of introducing a third party who comes between the supplier and his customer and who is not concerned with maintaining good relations between them. The other methods should only be used if the interest charged will be more than covered by the increased profit earned.

Sources of long-term capital

The type of long-term capital employed will differ with the size and nature of the business. Types of long term-capital are:

Ordinary shares

These shares make the holder a member of the company, and usually give him (a) the right to vote at shareholders' meetings and (b) an expectation of dividends.

Normally, members have one vote per share and the ordinary shareholders collectively own the 'equity' of the company. This means that they are entitled to all rights and benefits after the claims of debenture-holders and preference shareholders have been satisfied. The articles frequently reflect this principle by giving the ordinary shareholders the sole right to receive any surplus assets on a winding up. Dividends are paid solely at the discretion of the directors, and no class of shareholders has an absolute right to dividends.

Changes in company taxation have tended to reduce share capital issues in favour of fixed interest borrowing, due to the lower net cost of such borrowing against equity dividends.

Preference shares

These shares have the right to a fixed maximum rate of dividend which must be paid in full before any dividend is paid to the ordinary shareholders. If they are cumulative preference shares any unpaid dividends will be carried forward to be paid in a future year before the ordinary shareholders receive anything. Preference shares may also be participating, ie they have a right to a part of the surplus profits. The details of these rights will be specified in the articles of the company.

A preference share may be redeemable, if this is permitted by the articles. In this case, the company can raise capital on a temporary basis without a formal reduction of capital on redemption. However, the Companies Act 1985 regulates the redemption of these shares in such a way as to prevent an actual reduction of the capital invested.

Preference capital is of declining importance in company finance because:

a since 1965 it has a substantial tax disadvantage, because the dividends cannot be offset against the corporation tax liability;

b the investor to whom it appealed is no longer an important source of savings, ie the private individual prefers the inflation 'hedge' of equities whilst the institutions prefer straight equity or fixed interest.

Deferred shares

Deferred or founders shares are not common. They are sometimes issued to promoters or managers of a newly floated company. Dividends are not usually paid until a certain percentage has been paid on the ordinary shares; but they are then entitled to the whole, or a substantial part of the remaining profits. They may thus be very valuable in the case of a prosperous company.

Debentures

These are not a part of the company's share capital. A debenture is a written acknowledgement of a debt by the company, and the debenture-holder is a creditor, and not a member of the company, who therefore has no voting rights. The income of the debenture-holders is a fixed amount of interest which is payable before any dividends; and in the event of liquidation of the company, the secured debenture-holder is entitled to repayment before any shareholders. It is common for a debenture to be secured on the assets of the company by a fixed or floating charge, in which case the debenture-holder will, if the charge is properly registered, rank before the other creditors (but a floating charge ranks after the statutory preferential creditors).

Debentures may be a cheap way of raising capital; the debenture-holder has greater security and so does not require such a high income. He will not be able to interfere in the management of the company unless it is doing badly and the debenture deed allows him to appoint a receiver and manager. The main disadvantage to the company of this type of capital is that the interest must be paid regardless of the profits.

Securing debentures by a fixed charge may be inconvenient to industrial companies because of the need to change location with growth, with a resulting need to refinance the change. The floating charge overcomes this problem as it permits the inter-change of assets. Certain companies, however, do make use of fixed charges, such as hotel and cinema companies, where the basic asset is a building with little likelihood of fundamental change.

a *Usecured loan stocks* – these are relatively uncommon in company finance, except where the company has an asset/liability ratio which provides considerable security or where the poor security is compensated by some form of equity conversion right (see below).

b *Convertible debentures* – these carry a right for the holder to convert the debentures to ordinary shares at a given date and price. This adversely affects the position of the ordinary shareholders but protects the debenture-holder against inflation if share prices rise. Until recently convertible loan stocks were growing in popularity, but the movement away from equity issues has checked this trend.

c *Note issue* – this is a short dated unsecured loan stock. These notes can be placed directly with institutions and the cost of a public debenture issue may be avoided.

d *Direct borrowing* – it may be possible to borrow directly from individuals without security or by means of a mortgage on the company's property.

Gearing

The ratio of fixed interest and preference capital to equity capital is referred to as the 'capital gearing'. The ratio is measured in terms of cost of servicing the respective types of capital rather than the amount of capital issued. UK industry has for long been low geared in comparison with other countries, particularly Germany. The incidence of corporation tax, however, has reversed this situation and UK industry is increasingly moving towards high gearing. In industries where there is little likelihood of sharp profit variation, high gearing is acceptable. It becomes dangerous, however, when applied to industries with erratic levels of profitability.

Example:

	A Ltd £	B Ltd £	C Ltd £
Ordinary shares	100,000	50,000	10,000
10% Debentures	nil	50,000	90,000
	100,000	100,000	100,000
30% Return on capital employed	30,000	30,000	30,000
Debenture interest	nil	5,000	9,000
Net profit	30,000	25,000	21,000
Corporation tax @ 50% (say)	15,000	12,500	10,500
Ordinary dividends @ 15% (on capital)	15,000	7,500	1,500
Retained profits	nil	5,000	9,000
Maximum ordinary dividend	15%	25%	105%
Earnings per share	15p	25p	£1.05
Maximum commitment to rewards	nil	£5,000	£9,000
Cost of capital	15%	12½%	10½%

At a first glance it appears that the highly-geared structure of C Ltd is much to be preferred because:

a C Ltd could pay a much higher rate of ordinary dividend, and has higher earnings per share.

b C Ltd has the lowest cost of capital. But the C Ltd type capital structure is not likely to be practicable because:

i C Ltd is committed to the payment of £9,000 of rewards (ie the debenture interest) whereas A Ltd could, if necessary, totally avoid payments of rewards to contributors of capital. In difficult trading years the high commitments to interest payments could cause considerable difficulty for C Ltd.

ii C Ltd would normally have to offer suitable security for the debenture holders. It is unusual for a company's fixed assets to be structured in such a way as to provide suitable security for a 90 per cent debenture issue (exception – property investment companies).

iii The stock market in general, and the large institutional investors in particular, are seeking to invest mainly in high yielding ordinary shares, not in low yielding debentures.

Bonus issue

There is no actual inflow of capital into the company on a bonus issue (or capitalisation issue): it is simply a correction of the divergence between issued capital and the retained profits. As the earnings and dividend are related to the issued capital and not the total capital employed, a large divergence between the two values will possibly give an exaggeration of the earnings and dividend percentages. A capitalisation of the reserves overcomes this problem. Shares are allotted, fully paid up, to the existing shareholders on a pro rata basis.

The new issue market

The institutions engaged in raising long-term capital are collectively referred to as the new issue market. These institutions are:

a *Issuing houses* – merchant banks and finance companies which specialise in providing means of raising capital. They tend to cater for a particular field or area, eg local authority loans and small industrial companies.

b *Underwriters* – a few 'market makers' organise issues themselves, but their priority role is acting as liaison between the stock exchange council and the issuing houses.

c *Investing institutions* – investment trusts, insurance companies, unit trusts and other corporate bodies, such as pension funds, which have large funds to invest.

d *Specialist capital-providing organisations* – such as the Industrial and Commercial Finance Corporation and the Finance Corporation for Industry.

Methods of launching a new issue

The methods available depend on the size of the capital to be raised. The new issue market becomes relevant for issues over £25,000, although for issues of publicly quoted stock the issue would have to be at least £250,000. The following types of issues can be defined:

Direct offer by company

The company must comply with the prospectus requirements of the Companies Acts. It is usual to employ underwriters who, for a commission, guarantee to take up any shares for which the public do not subscribe. The other costs involved include stamp duties, brokerage, advertising, printing and other administrative costs. This method is rarely used.

Offer for sale

In this case the offer is made by an issuing house or other body that has bought the shares from the company. The offer is subject to the prospectus requirements of the Companies Acts. Its advantage is that it guarantees the success of the issue for the company. The issuing house makes its profit on the margin between the price it pays and the price at which it offers to sell which must be stated in the offer. If the issue is very big and there is any risk of under-subscription, it will be underwritten.

The offer can be made on a fixed price basis or on a tender price basis. In the case of an offer for sale by tender, the minimum price is fixed and the public are invited to subscribe at any price above this minimum. An 'average' price is then chosen at which the shares will be fully subscribed for by those people who have offered over the 'average' price: all successful subscribers pay the same 'average' price.

The attraction of a tender offer to the issuing house is that it obtains a higher price for the capital. A straight offer for sale at a fixed price usually results in fixing a low price to attract subscribers and a resulting over-subscription. Investors on the other hand prefer fixed price issues because they are certain of their commitment. Where an over-subscription does occur, it is usually met with a ballot or rationing solution.

Rights issue

This is a method by which a company raises money from its existing shareholders. The members are offered the right to purchase new shares in the company proportional to their existing holdings at a price which is usually below the market price. The advantage to the company is that this is a cheap way of raising capital.

Placing

This is usually effected through the company's 'stockbroker' who approaches various institutions and 'places' the shares with them. Stock exchange rules require that details of the securities must be advertised in the press before the placing. Permission to deal will be granted in the usual way. This method has been criticised as favouring certain investors, and the stock exchange usually requires that a fair proportion of these securities should be made available to the public through stock-jobbers before dealings are allowed to start.

It may be possible to place a block of shares with an institution privately without going through the market at all. A high yield security will be necessary in this case to persuade the institution to forego easy marketability.

Introduction

Strictly this is not an 'issue' of new shares at all, but a method of obtaining a stock exchange quotation for existing shares. A proportion of the company's shares must be made available to stock-jobbers for sale to the investing public. Details of the securities must be advertised under stock exchange rules, but the prospectus rules under the Companies Acts do not apply.

The recognition of revenue

In the section on basic accounting concepts the accruals concept was introduced. In this section we will look rather more closely at the problem of when to recognise (ie record) income and profit.

The accountant does not wish to show a profit unless he is 'certain' that the profit has been made, and that events which may happen later will not reduce that profit.

The earning of revenue is a gradual process, often called a cycle. Raw materials become finished goods which are then sold. The asset stock becomes the asset debtor and the difference between the values of the two is the profit. The asset debtor becomes asset cash on payment. The problem of recognition of revenue concerns deciding at which point in the cycle the profit will be considered to have been made, and therefore available for distribution. The basic conditions for the recognition of revenue are:

a Has the revenue been *earned*? That is, has the value generated by the transaction been added to the assets of the business?

b Can that revenue be *measured* objectively? That is, has it undergone the test of the market or of an 'arms length' transaction?

c Has the *'critical event'* occurred?

For most transactions these three conditions can be said to exist at the point when the sale is made and this is the general rule which accountants follow when recognising revenue.

There are, however, the following different approaches which take account of the differing circumstances of transactions:

The critical event approach

Under this basis the recognition of revenues triggered by a crucial event in the operating cycle. This event could be:

a the point of sale;

b the completion of production;

c receipt of payment.

The sales basis is justified because:

a the price of the product is known with certainty;

b the exchange has been finalised by the delivery of goods, leading to an objective knowledge of the total costs incurred;

c in terms of realisation, a sale constitutes a crucial event.

The completion of production basis may be justified when a stable market and a stable price exist for a standard commodity, eg when there is a government backed intervention scheme. In this case the production process constitutes the crucial event rather than the sale, which is effectively guaranteed and the selling price is also guaranteed.

The cash basis is justified when the sale has been made, but an accurate valuation of the transfer cannot be made. This might occur when a sale has been made to a politically unstable country whose remittances cannot be guaranteed, or to an individual on an instalment payment basis. In this case the actual receipt of cash is the crucial event.

The accrual approach

This basis implies that revenue should be reported *during* production. This normally occurs in the following situations:

a Rent, interest and commission are recognised as earned, provided there is a contract in existence.

b Long-term contracts. Revenue from long-term contracts, particularly in the building and civil engineering industries, is recognised on a percentage of completion, or progress or construction basis. If this were not the case, a company which started several contracts in year one, but completed them all in year three would show substantial losses in years one and two and massive profits in year three, whereas in fact the profit would have been accruing throughout (see SSAP 9 in Chapter 14)

c Accretion, where the value of work in progress increases gradually through natural growth or an ageing process. Examples of this would be timber, animals and maturing wines and spirits. It is possible to value the stocks of such items at the beginning and end of an accounting period and to gauge the increase in value achieved during the year. This increase is an income, even though it has not arisen from transaction and has not been realised. It should not, however, on the principle of prudence, be considered as available for distribution.

The measurement of earnings

The problem of recognition of revenue concerned the question 'When?' in relation to earnings; the problem of measurement is concerned with answering the question 'How much?'.

There are three distinct views on measuring earnings:

a the asset/liability view;

b the revenue/expense view;

c the non-articulated view.

The asset/liability view

Also called the balance sheet or capital maintenance view, this holds that revenue and expenses result purely from changes in assets and liabilities – revenues are increases in assets (or reductions in liabilities) and on the other hand costs are increases in liabilities (or reductions in assets). In measuring the changes certain items have to be excluded, namely capital contributions and withdrawals, corrections of errors in previous periods and holding gains and losses.

The revenue/expense view

Also called the income statement or matching view, this holds that earnings are the difference between the revenues of a period and the expenses of earning those revenues.

This comprises two steps – revenue recognition and expense recognition. Revenue recognition was discussed in the previous section; expense recognition can be in three possible ways – associating cause and effect, as the cost of sales, systematic allocation as for depreciation, and immediate recognition, as for selling and administration costs.

The main distinction between this and the asset/liability view is that this method emphasises the measurement of the earnings of the firm, whereas the asset/liability model emphasises the increase or decrease in net capital.

The non-articulated view

Both the asset/liability and the revenue/expense view hold that the income statement 'articulates' with the balance sheet in the sense that they are both part of the same measurement process. The non-articulated view holds that this leads to a redundancy of information, as all events in the income statement are also reflected in the balance sheet, though from a different perspective, and what should happen is that the definition of assets and liabilities should be of most importance in the balance sheet, whereas revenues and costs should dominate the income statement. As the two statements are independent, different measurement schemes may be used for them; eg in the valuation of stock LIFO could be used in the income statement, FIFO on the balance sheet. This view has been gaining ground recently, at least in the US where the American Accounting Association said: 'We find no logical reason why external financial reports should be expected to "balance" or articulate with one another. In fact, we find that forced balancing and articulation have frequently restricted the presentation of relevant information.'

If articulation is regarded as essential, the choice of method then lies between the asset/liability and revenue/expense models. Current thinking tends to favour the revenue/expense model, as it, unlike the asset/liability model, can deal with such deferred charges and credits as deferred tax liabilities and also reserves and provisions.

Criticisms of financial accounting

Criticisms of accounting concepts

The basic accounting concepts described earlier set a framework for accounting, but any framework by definition sets its own limitations. Some criticisms which have been levelled at the basic concepts are:

a The historic cost principle – of all the principles this is perhaps the most vulnerable. The rapid inflation of the past 20 years has made the practice of showing fixed assets at original cost less depreciation increasingly untenable, and this has been recognized and in part rectified by the introduction of various systems of inflation accounting – although many would hold that these are even more suspect and confusing than the evil they were designed to cure.

b Even before inflation accounting became an issue the realisation concept was being eroded. It has been common practice for many years for permanent increases in fixed asset values, particularly land and buildings, to be reflected in the balance sheet.

c The going concern principle might be thought of more as a matter of common sense; or at least stating the obvious. The major problem is not so much the accounting treatment of assets in a going concern but the far more pertinent question of how to decide when a company is not a going concern. At present there is an element of the self-fulfilling prophecy in that if an accountant expresses any doubt as to whether a business is a going concern or not, it will almost certainly cease to be one as suppliers withdraw credit and press for immediate payment.

d Materiality causes many differences of opinions. Obviously, in a multimillion pound enterprise a difference of a few pounds on the petty cash is not material, but the sums involved can run into millions and still be dismissed as immaterial. Frequently, this seems to be used as an excuse for not presenting facts explicitly.

Criticisms of the income statement

Some authorities take the view that the income statement falls short of its real purpose because although it shows the profit or loss that has been made, it takes no account of any risks that have been taken or any potential but unrealised profits in the period. It summarises the past year's trading but makes no comment on the maximisation of profit, and gives no forecast of the future to assist in decision making. The choice of one year as an accounting period can also set limitations in that it is not necessarily a suitable time span for a project with a life span of say, ten or 15 years.

The profit calculation itself is affected by the accounting policies followed, so accountants using different bases could produce different profit figures for the same period and the same business.

The major weaknesses of the profit as shown by the income statement are caused by the multiplicity of acceptable policies, a false reliance on the stability of the monetary unit and a failure to incorporate current values into the statement. In the past prudence helped prevent over-optimistic claims but now this tends to obscure the true profit. What is being shown as the profit for the year is the part of the gain which has been realised, plus gains from previous periods now realised, less unrealised losses which the accountant thinks may be experienced in the future, and this is accepted as being the best estimate. Many, particularly economists, would not agree.

Criticisms of the balance sheet

A long-standing criticism of the balance sheet arises from its essential nature – a 'snapshot' of the business at a particular point in time, showing a picture of the company which could be very different from that shown even a few days before or after, to the extent that 'window-dressing' a balance sheet at the year end to show a healthier position is a common practice.

The balance sheet gives no information about the past or future, it does not tell the reader how the current position was reached, and unless previous years' figures are provided gives little information from which to deduce any trends. The fixed assets are frequently at historic cost less depreciation, which confuses many readers into thinking they are at their current market value – in other words, it may be a conventional document consistent with accepted principles, but as far as the lay reader is concerned it is effectively in a form of code to which he does not have the key.

The assets on the balance sheet are unlikely to be at their 'true' value. A further point is that not all the assets are shown on the balance sheet. The money measurement principle dictates that those assets which cannot be quantified should not be included in the accounts, so good labour relations, know-how, management calibre etc are all excluded. Some liabilities may also be excluded, eg if an asset is leased then there may be heavy penalty clauses for early termination which would not be disclosed.

Problems

Problem 19.1

Explain the limitations of financial accounting.

Problem 19.2

Explain the concept of accounting profit. What difficulties and problems arise in the determination of accounting profit?

(20 marks)

Associated Examining Board

Problem 19.3

Kankan Ltd wishes to buy a new factory for £500,000 and is currently considering two alternative ways of raising the finance.

Alternative A. To issue £300,000 in 12 per cent debentures at a discount of 5 per cent. The discount is to be written off against profits over the ten-year term of the debentures. A loan from Westland Bank at 10 per cent interest would provide the balance of finance. This loan would be repaid in five equal annual instalments. Both the debentures and the bank loan would be secured on the factory.

Alternative B. To raise the cost of the factory through a rights issue to existing shareholders of 800,000 new ordinary shares of 50p each at 62½p each. The new shares would have a dividend yield to an investor of 11 per cent per annum.

Required: in respect of the first year only:

a Calculate the cost of each alternative source of funds to be charged in the profit and loss account.

(6 marks)

b Show for each alternative, how the factory and its associated method of finance would appear in the balance sheet of Kankan Ltd at the end of the year.

(9 marks)

Issue and redemption of shares and debentures | 20

Issue of shares

Block diagram of issue and forfeiture of shares

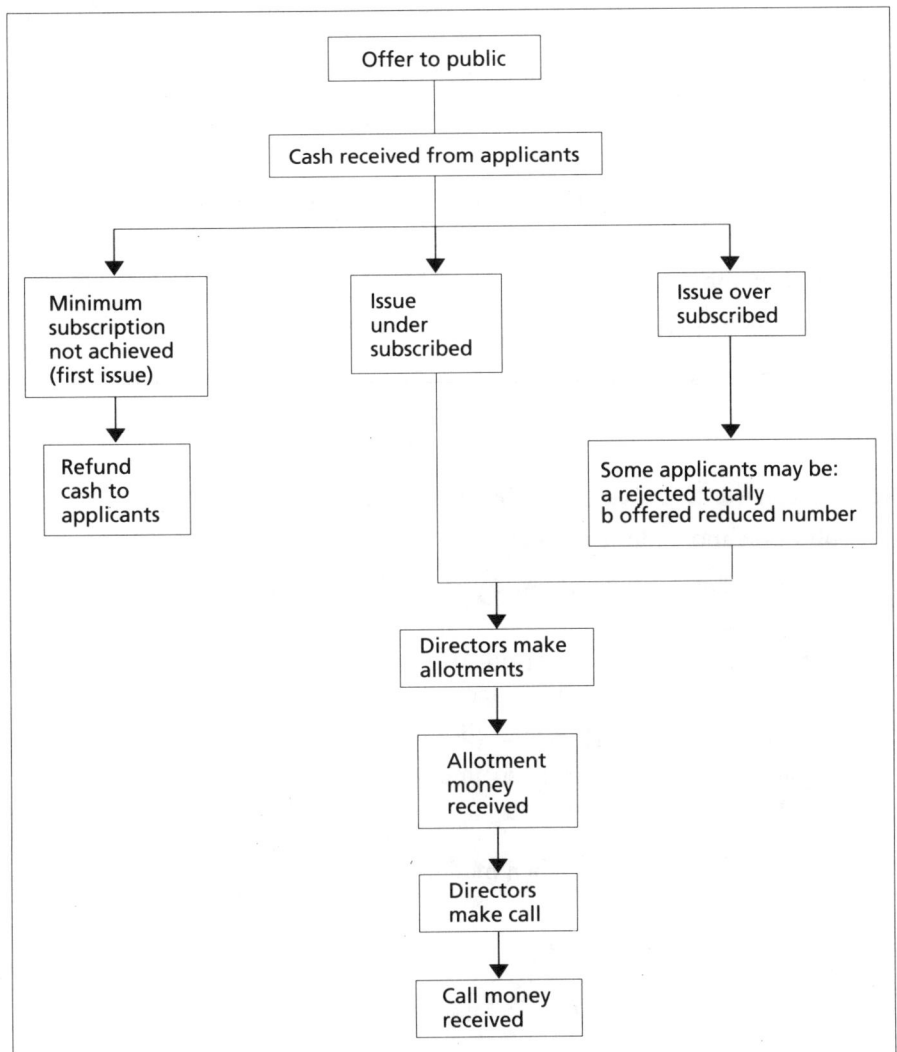

Legal aspects

All shares in UK companies must have a 'face' value – the nominal or par value. If shares are issued at a price in excess of this, they are issued at a 'premium'.

a   there is no restriction on issuing shares at par or premium. The share premium account may only be applied in:

i   paying up unissued shares to be issued as fully paid bonus shares;

ii   writing off preliminary expenses;

  iii writing off:
  - expenses of issue of,
  - commission paid on, or
  - discount allowed on issue of shares or debentures.

b to issue shares at a discount, court permission must be obtained;

c any application form for shares offered to the public must be accompanied by a prospectus;

d first allotment by a public company may not proceed until minimum subscription is achieved;

e application money may not be less than 5 per cent of nominal value of shares;

f calls on shares may be made in accordance with:

  i terms of share issue, or
  ii the company's articles.

Accounts required and their purpose

a Application and allotment account:

  i records cash received on application and allotment and refunds to applicants;
  ii shows amounts due on application and allotment, both on share capital account and share premium account (if appropriate);
  iii the balance, if any, represents allotment money due.

b Share capital account: records the amount of called up capital.

c Call accounts:

  i records amount of call when made;
  ii the balance, if any, represents:
    - calls in arrears (debit),
    - calls in advance (credit).

Sundry matters

a Under subscription – if shares applied for are fewer than those offered for sale, entries in the accounts will obviously be made only for those applied for.

b Over subscription – if share applications exceed the number available for issue some applications may:

  i be totally rejected and application money returned, or
  ii allotment made for smaller number of shares than those applied for and excess application money utilised for reducing amounts due on allotment.

c Application and allotment account and call accounts are in fact total or control accounts on share issues. The detailed entries will be made in the memorandum accounts of individual shareholders and total amounts only entered in the above mentioned accounts.

Double entry

	Transactions	Debit	Credit
a	Application money received	Cash account	Application and allotment account
b	Application money refunded	Application and allotment account	Cash account
c	Allotment by directors whentotal due on application and allotment is due	Application and allotment account	Share capital account
d	Share premium included in amounts due on application	Application and allotment account	Share premium account
e	Allotment money received	Cash account	Application and allotment account
f	Call made by directors	Call account	Share capital account
g	Call money received	Cash account	Call account

Account outlines

Application and Allotment Account

	£		£
Cash account – refunded in respect of applications not accepted	60	Cash account – amounts received from applicants for shares	3,060
Share capital account – capital amount due on application and allotment	6,000 A	Cash account – amounts received on allotment	4,000
Share premium account – premium due on application and allotment	1,000 B		
	£7,060		£7,060

Call Account

	£		£
Share capital account – amount of call	4,000 C	Cash account – call money received	3,960
		Balance c/d – calls in arrear	40
	£4,000		£4,000

Share Capital Account

	£		£
Balance c/d – called up value of issue of shares capital	10,000	Applicaton and allotment account – capital amount due on application and allotment	6,000 A
		Call account – amount of call	4,000 C
	£10,000		£10,000

Share Premium Account

	£		£
		Application and allotment account – premium due on	1,000 B
Balance c/d	1,000	application and allotment	
	£1,000		£1,000

Redemption of preference shares

Block diagram illustrating redemption of preference shares

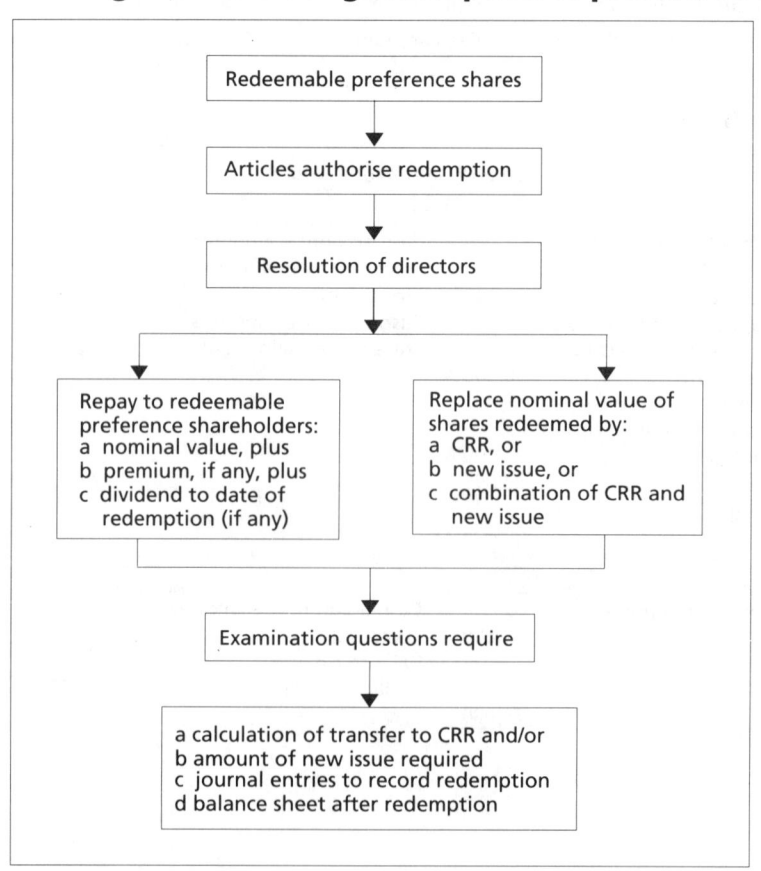

Legal aspects

Redemption of preference shares
These may be summarised as follows:

a an issue of redeemable preference shares must be authorised by the articles;

b redeemable preference shares are capable of redemption only when fully paid;

c a 'redemption fund' must be provided out of either:

   i   profits available for dividend, or

   ii process of new issue of shares for that purpose (but see below);

d when 'redemption fund' is provided out of profits available for dividend, a sum equal to the nominal amount redeemed must be transferred to capital redemption reserve;

e any premium on redemption must be provided for out of either:

   i   profits, or

   ii share premium account (but see below);

f the capital redemption reserve can only be reduced in the same way as the share capital account and court permission must be obtained;

g the capital redemption reserve may, however, be used in issuing fully paid bonus shares to members.

Balance sheet disclosure requirements
The company must state:

a the earliest and latest date of redemption;

b whether the shares must be redeemed in any event or are liable to be redeemed at the option of the company;

c the amount of premium, if any, payable on redemption.

Accounts required and their purposes

Preference share redemption account
Transfer to the credit of this account:

a the nominal value of shares to be redeemed;

b any premium due on redemption;

c any dividend accrued to the date of redemption;

This account 'collects' the total amount due to the preference shareholders on redemption and is closed off by the cash payment.

Sundry matters

You must clearly understand that a redemption of preference shares is not a capital reduction. The nominal value of the redeemed preference shares must be replaced by capital redemption reserve, or new issue or by a combination of the two.

Premium on redemption or on the new issue in no way affects the amount of capital to be replaced by capital redemption reserve or the new issue, it is only the nominal value that is to be considered.

Examination questions on this topic frequently:

a give the information with which to work out the maximum transfer to CRR leaving you to deal with the new issue required for the purpose of the redemption, or

b state the amount of the new issue leaving you to work-out the transfer to CRR.

You are almost always required to prepare a balance sheet showing the position after the redemption has taken place.

Under 'new' rules in the Companies Act 1985, a redemption premium must primarily be provided for out of profits and may only be charged to share premium account up to a maximum of whichever is the *lowest* of three figures:

a the proceeds of any fresh issue to 'fund' the redemption;

b the issue premium on shares being redeemed;

c the balance on share premium account after any fresh issue.

Finally, Companies Act 1985 permits a *private* company to redeem shares out of 'capital'. This means that a private company is not obliged to fully replace the nominal value redeemed with the proceeds of a fresh issue and/or a transfer to CRR.

In the case of a private company, there can be a 'gap' between nominal value redeemed and the total of the proceeds of a fresh issue plus CRR. This gap must not exceed the 'permissible capital payment', calculated as:

The redemption price	£X
Less: Proceeds of fresh issue	(X)
Less: Distributable profits	(X)
Permissible capital payment	£X

The same Act also extends the provisions dealt with in this chapter on redemption of (redeemable) shares to the purchase by a company of its own shares which may originally have been issued as non-redeemable. Any such shares purchased must be cancelled by the company.

Account outlines

Preference Share Redemption Account

	£		£
Cash a/c – payment to shareholders to be redeemed	5,600	Redeemable preference shares a/c – nominal value of shares redeemed	5,000
		Share premium a/c or profit & loss a/c – premium, if any, payable on redemption	200 A
		Profit & loss a/c – dividend, if any, to date of redemption	400 B
	£5,600		£5,600

Share Premium Account

	£		£
Preference share redemption a/c – premium payable on redemption	200 A	Balance b/d	1,000
		Application and allotment a/c – premium on new issue for purposes of redemption	500
Balance c/d	1,300		
	£1,500		£1,500
		Balance b/d	1,300

Profit & Loss Account Appropriations

	£		£
Preference share redemption a/c – dividend payable on shares to be redeemed	400 B	Balance b/d	7,000
Capital redemption reserve fund – nominal value of shares redeemed out of profits (£1,000 out of new issue)	4,000		
Balance c/d	2,600		
	£7,000		£7,000
		Balance b/d	2,600

Issue and redemption of debentures

Block diagram illustrating principles of debentures

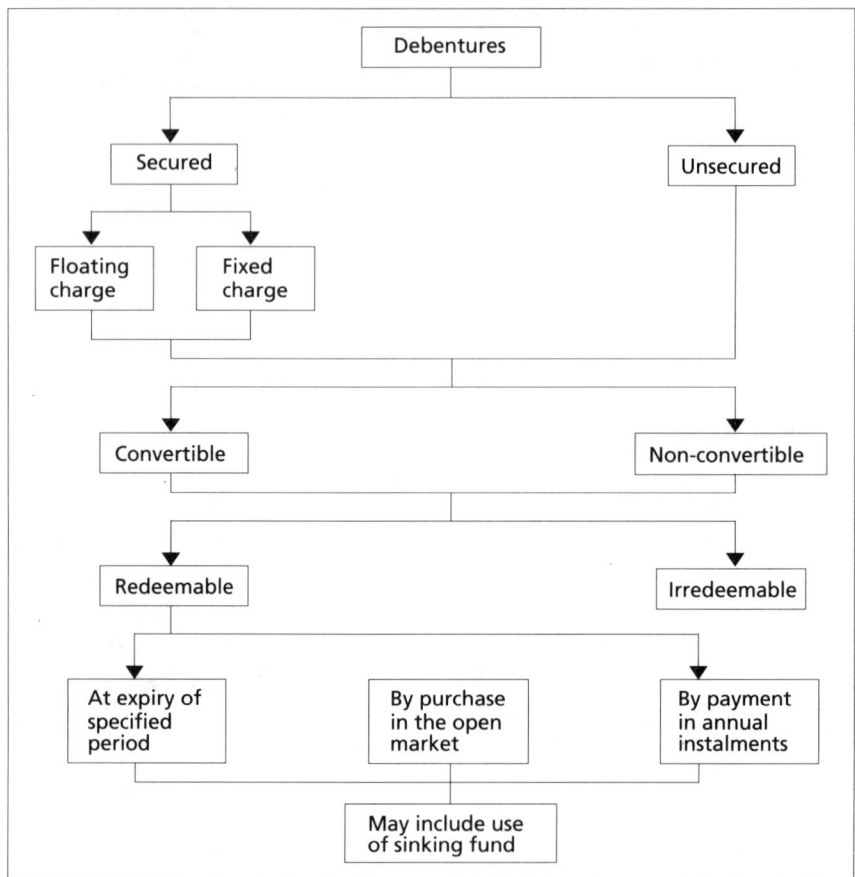

Legal aspects

Definition
A written acknowledgement of a debt by a company.

Security
Debentures may be:

a naked (unsecured) debentures, giving no form of security;

b fully or partly secured by:

    i fixed charge, giving a mortgage of specific assets;

    ii floating charge, giving a charge over the general assets of the company, present and future.

Priority
A company may issue several series of debentures which rank either in order of priority (first debentures, second debentures, etc), usually by reference to the date of issue, or pari passu (equally).

Convertible debentures
A debenture issue may carry the right to convert into equity share capital on or after a specific date, possibly at a specified price.

Permanence
Debentures may be:

a irredeemable;

b redeemable, either:

  i   at expiry of specified period;

  ii   by purchase in the open market;

  iii by repayment of part of the issue by annual drawings.

Trustees for debenture holders
Where there are a number of debenture holders, it is usual for the security to be charged in favour of trustees who will act on behalf of all the debenture holders.

The debenture trust deed will specify the various terms as to payment of interest, repayment of capital, the establishment of a sinking fund to finance redemption and other provisions to safeguard the rights of the debenture holders.

Disclosure provisions
The disclosure provisions relating to loan capital are covered in the note on Companies Acts 1948 and 1967, para 2.2.

Accounts required and their purpose

Debenture account
Records the nominal value of debentures issued by a company. Debenture holders are, of course, creditors – not shareholders.

Debenture premium account
Records the premium (if any) on issue of debentures. Note that this is not transferred to the share premium account, and whilst the Companies Acts do not prohibit the payment of a dividend out of a premium on issue of debentures this is not normally done.

Debenture discount account
Records the discount (if any) on issue of debentures. This would generally be written off to share premium account or profit and loss account or alternatively carried forward as a separate item in the balance sheet and deducted from the aggregate of share capital and reserves.

Debenture redemption account

Shows the nominal value of debentures to be redeemed, plus any premium on redemption, plus interest due to date of redemption.

Sinking fund account

Credited with amounts available for investment to provide funds for redemption of debentures. Sources of credit:

a annual transfer from profit and loss account;

b profits on sale of sinking fund investments (losses debited);

c income from sinking fund investments;

d profits on purchase of own debentures in open market (losses debited).

The balance on the sinking fund account should equal the balance on the sinking fund investment account plus any balance on sinking fund cash account.

Sinking fund investment account

This shows the investments held to provide the funds for the debenture redemption.

Sinking fund cash account

It may be convenient to maintain a separate cash account for funds pending investment.

Sundry matters

It is absolutely vital to appreciate that debenture holders are merely creditors of the company, unlike preference shareholders who are members.

Whilst it is not mandatory, it is accepted as good financial practice to transfer to a general reserve an amount equivalent to the nominal value of the debentures redeemed, in order to preserve the company's capital structure.

Where debentures are redeemable at a premium, and a sinking fund is to be employed, this should be sufficient to pay the premium as well as the nominal value of the debentures. Where there is no sinking fund, the premium may be debited to share premium account or, if there is none, must be written off to profit and loss account or against a reserve.

The interest due on the debentures will be credited to the sinking fund account (debit debenture interest account) and included in the transfer to profit and loss account.

Issue of debentures

Issue at par, premium or discount

Debentures, like shares, may be issued at par or at a premium or at a discount. The Companies Act is silent as to what may be done with a premium on issue although normal commercial prudence would require it to be classified as a non-distributable reserve. A discount on issue may be written off to share premium account.

Double entry
Issue at par

Transaction	Debit	Credit
Cash received on issue of debentures at par	Cash a/c	Debenture a/c

Issue at premium

Transaction	Debit	Credit
Par value of debentures issued	Cash a/c	Debentures a/c
Premium on issue of debentures	Cash a/c	Debenture premium a/c

Issue at discount

Transaction	Debit	Credit
Cash received on issue of debentures at discount	Cash a/c	Debentures a/c
Discount on issue of debentures	Debenture discount a/c	Debentures a/c

Redemption without a sinking fund
Double entry

Transaction	Debit	Credit
Nominal value of debentures to be redeemed	Debentures a/c	Debenture redemption a/c
Premium on redemption of debentures	Share premium a/c	Debenture redemption a/c

Transaction	Debit	Credit
Interest accrued to date of redemption	Profit & loss a/c	Debenture redemption a/c
Total amount paid to debenture holders	Debenture redemption a/c	Cash a/c

Account outline

Debenture Redemption Account

	£		£
Cash a/c – total amount due to debenture holders	12,300	Debentures a/c– nominal value of debentures redeemed	10,000
		Share premium a/c– or profit & loss a/c – premium payable on redemption	2,000
		Profit & loss a/c – debenture interest due to date of redemption	300
	£12,300		£12,300

Redemption with sinking fund

Introduction

The objective of using a sinking fund is simply to try to ensure that the company has sufficient cash available to redeem the debentures when redemption date comes.

It is easiest to consider the accounting entries for redemption with a sinking fund in the following four stages:

a annual entries for appropriation, receipt of income on investments and investment of available cash;

b entries relating to a sale of investments;

c entries for a partial redemption of debentures by purchase in the open market;

d entries for a final redemption of all outstanding debentures.

The system involves the company establishing a separate reserve or 'fund' which is held in the form of investments which are sold to realise cash when redemption of the debentures falls due.

Double entry

Annual entries for appropriation, receipt of income on investments and investment of available cash:

Transaction	Debit	Credit
Annual appropriation out of profits	Profit & loss a/c	Sinking fund a/c
Transfer of cash to special bank a/c	Sinking fund cash a/c	General cash a/c
Receipt of interest on sinking fund investments (in all but the first year)	Sinking fund cash a/c	Sinking fund a/c
Investment of cash	Sinking fund investments account	Sinking fund cash a/c

These entries are simply repeated every year.

Entries relating to a sale of investments:

Transaction	Debit	Credit
Sale proceeds of investment of sinking fund	Sinking fund cash a/c	Sinking fund investment a/c
Profit on sale of investments (reverse entries for a loss)	Sinking fund investments a/c	Sinking fund a/c

Entries for a partial redemption of debentures by purchase in the open market:

Transaction	Debit	Credit
Cost of debentures purchased	Debenture redemption a/c	Sinking fund cash a/c
Accrued interest included in purchase price (assuming 'cum div' price)	Debenture interest a/c	Debenture redemption a/c
Accrued interest re-imbursed out of general cash	Sinking fund cash a/c	General cash a/c
Nominal value of debentures redeemed	Debentures a/c	Debenture redemption a/c
Sinking fund no longer required being amount equivalent to nominal value of debentures redeemed	Sinking fund a/c	General reserve a/c

Entries for a final redemption of all outstanding debentures:

Transaction	Debit	Credit
Nominal value of debentures to be redeemed	Debenture redemption a/c	Debentures a/c
Premium payable on redemption	Sinking fund a/c	Debenture redemption a/c
Cash payment to debenture holders	Debenture redemption a/c	Sinking fund cash a/c
Balance on sinking fund a/c no longer required	Sinking fund a/c	General reserve a/c
Any cash remaining in the sinking fund bank a/c	General cash a/c	Sinking fund cash a/c

Account outlines

On 1 January 1994 a company had in issue £90,000 6 per cent debentures. The debenture trust deed provided that:

a interest was payable on 30 June and 31 December;

b a sinking fund for redemption of debentures was to be built up by an annual appropriation of £1,500 which together with any interest received on the investments of the sinking fund were to be invested on 31 December in each year; and

c sinking fund investment could be realised at any time to purchase debentures in the open market at or below par for immediate cancellation.

You ascertain that:

a The sinking fund balance at 1 January 1994 was £8,000.

b Sinking fund investments were realised on 1 March for £950 (cost £925) and the proceeds were used to purchase debentures of a nominal value of £1,000.

c Interest on sinking fund investments for the year ended 31 December amounted to £450 on which date the available funds were duly invested.

Write up the relevant ledger accounts for the year ended 31 December 1994. Assume taxation at 50p in the £.

Six per cent Debentures Account

	£		£
Debenture redemption a/c – nominal value of debentures redeemed	1,000A	Balance b/d	90,000
Balance c/d	89,000		
	£90,000		£90,000
		Balance b/d	89,000

Sinking Fund Account

	£		£
General reserve a/c – nominal value of debentures redeemed	1,000	Balance b/d – amount of sinking fund at commencement of period – should equal balance on investment a/c	8,000
Balance c/d	9,035	Sinking fund investment a/c – profit on realisation of investments	25C
		Debenture redemption a/c – profit on purchase of debentures	60F
		Interest received	450G
		Profit & loss appropriation a/c – annual appropriation	1,500H
	£10,035		£10,035
		Balance b/d	9,035

Sinking Fund Investment Account

	£		£
Balance b/d – amount of sinking fund investments at commencement of period	8,000	Sinking fund cash a/c – proceeds of realisation of investments	950C
Sinking fund a/c – profit on realisation of investments	25E	Balance c/d	9,035
Sinking fund cash a/c – purchase of investments made up of:	1,960I		
Annual appropriation 1,500			
Interest received 450			
Accrued interest on redeemed debentures reimbursed from general cash 10			
	£1,960		
	£9,985		£9,985
Balance b/d	9,035		

Debenture Redemption Account

	£		£
Sinking fund cash a/c – purchase of debentures on open market	950D	Debenture a/c – nominal value of debentures redeemed	1,000A
Sinking fund a/c – profit on debentures redeemed	60F	Debenture interest a/c – accrued interest included in purchase price of debentures	10B
	£1,010		£1,010

Debenture Interest Account

	£		£
Debenture redemption a/c – accrued interest included in purchase price of debentures	10B	Profit & loss a/c	5,350
Cash a/c – interest on remaining debentures, less tax	2,670		
Taxation a/c – tax deducted on debenture interest paid	2,670		
	£5,350		£5,350

Sinking Fund Cash Account

	£		£
Sinking fund investment a/c – proceeds of realisation of investment	950C	Debenture redemption a/c – purchase of debentures on open market	950D
Sinking fund a/c– interest on investments	450G	Sinking fund investment a/c – purchase of investments at end of period	1,960I
General cash a/c – reimbursementof interest on debentures redeemed	10		
General cash a/c – annual instalment	1,500H		
	£2,910		£2,910

Note: it will very often be found in practice that a sinking fund cash account is not maintained and that payments and receipts are dealt with in the general cash account.

Examination questions do not normally require a debenture interest account which is shown in order to clarify the position.

Bonus and rights issue

Firms can issue shares in many ways, two of the most popular being bonus and rights issues.

Bonus issue

A bonus issue (or scrip issue, or capitalisation issue as it is sometimes known) is the issuing additional share capital to existing shareholders. In the case of a bonus issue the shareholders do not have to pay the firm at all. It is effectively a gift to the existing shareholders and they represent reserves which are already part of the shareholders existing equity.

This is sometimes referred to as capitalisation of reserves because the reserves are turned into paid up capital.

Example:
The balance sheet of Bost Ltd at 31 December 1994 was as follows:

	£	£		£
Share capital:				
Ordinary £1 shares		100,000		
Share premium	20,000		Fixed assets	350,000
CRR	75,000			
Revaluation	55,000		Net current assets	50,000
Profits	150,000	300,000		
		£400,000		£400,000

The directors propose that a two for one bonus issue be made. The resulting balance sheet will be as follows:

	£		£
Share capital			
Ordinary £1 shares	300,000	Fixed assets	350,000
Reserves		Net current asserts	50,000
Profits	100,000		
	£400,000		£400,000

and the journal would have been:

	£ DR	£ CR
Share premium	20,000	
Capital redemption reserve	75,000	
Revaluation reserve	55,000	
Retained profits	50,000	
Ordinary £1 shares		200,000

The phrase 'two for one' refers to the number of new shares to be issued in relation to the number already held, eg if a shareholder in the above example held ten shares he would have received 20 new ones.

The order for utilising the reserves is as follows:

a Capital reserves:

    i   share premium;

    ii   capital redemption reserve;

    iii revaluation reserves.

b Revenue reserves:

    i   general reserve;

    ii   retained profits.

If the capitalisation needs more than exists in the share premium account then the CRR is also utilised. If both of these are not sufficient then the revaluation reserve is utilised. If these three are not sufficient, etc.

Why should a firm bother to capitalise its reserves when it has no effect on the economic realities of the firm's operations? Basically, there are three reasons:

a to bring the shareholding into line with the fixed assets;

b to provide a type of dividend for the shareholder;

c to increase the marketability of each share.

Rights issue

A rights issue is again an issue to existing shareholders, but this time they must pay for the share they receive.

In fact, the shareholders do not have to buy the shares offered, it is simply that they have the 'right' to do so because the shares are offered first to the existing shareholder. Only if the shareholders refuse the 'right' can the shares be sold to someone else.

Revaluation

Examination questions on the issue and redemption of shares often require knowledge of:

a journals;

b revaluation of properties.

Journals

As you have already seen, journals are simple – a written record of double entry and should pose no problems.

Revaluation of properties

Where a firm has some land, for example, which it has owned for many years the balance sheet value may differ drastically from its market value.

Firms often wish to reflect a more accurate value of these fixed assets and to reflect this entries must be made in the ledgers.

The entries are:

a debit the fixed asset account;

b credit a revaluation reserve.

Example:
A firm has the following balance sheet:

	£		£
Share capital	40,000	Fixed assets	20,000
Retained profits	10,000	Net current assets	30,000
	£50,000		£50,000

Suppose the fixed assets are actually worth £50,000 and the firm wishes to reflect this, the entry is:

Fixed Assets

	£		£
Balance b/d	20,000		
Revaluation reserve	30,000	Balance c/d	50,000
	£50,000		£50,000

Revaluation Reserve

	£		£
Balance c/d	£30,000	Fixed assets	£30,000

and the balance sheet would be as follows:

	£	£		£
Share capital	40,000		Fixed assets	50,000
Reserves				
Retained profits	10,000			
Revaluation	30,000	40,000	Net current assets	30,000
		£80,000		£80,000

Revaluation reserve

This reserve, although not a 'capital' reserve by statute, cannot be distributed by way of dividend.

There are two reasons for this

a statute – only 'realised' profits can be distributed;

b prudence.

It can, however, be utilised in creating a CRR or in paying up a bonus issue to shareholders.

Problems

Problem 20.1

The summarised balance sheet of Pear Ltd as at 1 January 1995 was as follows:

	£	£
Fixed assets		
Property at cost	150,000	
Less: Depreciation	30,000	120,000
Plant at cost	160,000	
Less: Depreciation	75,000	85,000
		205,000
Goodwill		15,000
		220,000
Current assets		
Stock	109,000	
Debtors	41,000	
	150,000	
Current liabilities		
Creditors	(32,000)	
Overdraft	(34,000)	84,000
		£304,000
Capital and reserves		
Ordinary shares (£1)		160,000
Share premium		16,000
Retained profits		28,000
		204,000
Long-term liabilities		
8% loan stock		100,000
		£304,000

During the three months to 31 March 1995:

a On 2 January, the directors decided to revalue the freehold properties at £200,000. *Properties now £200000   50000 revaluation*

b On 5 January, the company made a public issue of 200,000 additional ordinary shares at a price of 80p each; 50p (including the premium) being payable immediately and the balance of 30p on 25 March. The issue was oversubscribed and applications were received for 400,000 shares. Applicants for 100,000 shares were unsuccessful and their monies were refunded on 30 January. Each of the other applicants were allotted two-thirds of the number of shares applied for, and the overpayment was carried forward to be set against the sums due on 25 March. On 25 March the balance due was received.

c On 29 March the 8 per cent loan stock was repaid at a premium of 2 per cent and the goodwill of £15,000 was written off.

Required:

a Journal entries, including those for cash, to record the above changes. (*Note*: narratives are not required.)

(15 marks)

b) The balance sheet of Pear Ltd at 31 March 1995 after completion of the above transactions.

(10 marks)

Associated Examining Board – updated

Problem 20.2

The summarised balance sheet of Putty Ltd at 1 May 1995 was as follows:

	£			£	£
Capital and reserves		Fixed assets			
Ordinary shares of £1		Freehold property at cost	80,000		
each authorised	75,000	*Less:* Depreciation	20,000		
					60,000
Issued fully paid	25,000	Plant & machinery at cost	50,000		
Share premium a/c	5,000	*Less:* Depreciation	31,000		
Retained earnings	18,000				
	48,000	Current assets			19,000
		Stock			17,000
9% Debentures 1995	15,000	Debtors			14,000
Current liabilities					
Bank overdraft	35,000				
Creditors, accruals and					
provisionals	12,000				
	£110,000				£110,000

During May 1995 the following transactions took place:

a The freehold property was revalued at £95,000.

b On 6 May 30,000 new ordinary shares were issued for cash at £3 each, payable in full on application. Application monies received by 10 May totalled £330,000 and on 12 May the unsuccessful applicants were repaid.

c On 15 May a further 15,000 new ordinary shares were issued at an agreed value of £3 per share in exchange for the net assets of another company. Putty Ltd included the tangible assets acquired in its own books at £36,000.

d The 9 per cent debentures 1995 were redeemed on 20 May at a premium of 1 per cent.

e It was decided that a provision for repairs of £1,400 which had been made some years earlier was no longer necessary.

Required:

Journal entries, including those for cash, to record the above transactions. Narratives are not required.

Associated Examining Board – updated

Problem 20.3

The summarised balance sheet of Pantile Ltd at 30 April 1995 was as follows:

	£		£
90,000 Ordinary shares of		Fixed assets, less	
50p each	45,000	depreciation	85,000
40,000 8% redeemable		Stock	34,000
preferenceshares of £1 each	40,000	Debtors	41,000
Share premium a/c	17,000	Bank	3,000
Profit & loss a/c	26,000	Goodwill	4,000
Current liabilities	39,000		
	£167,000		£167,000

During the week to 7 May 1995 the following transactions took place:

a Sales on credit totalled   £10,500
Cash sales totalled   £13,200
Credit sales are made at cost plus 25 per cent and cash sales are made at cost plus 20 per cent.

b No goods were purchased, but suppliers were paid £14,000 owing to them. £7,000 was received from debtors.

c Goodwill was written off.

d On 7 May all the 8 per cent redeemable preference shares were redeemed at a premium of 2 per cent, partly out of profits which were used to the maximum extent possible, and partly out of the proceeds of a new issue of 10 per cent preference shares. On 7 May the company issued for cash at par the minimum number of 10 per cent preference shares necessary to provide for the redemption of those preference shares in issue which could not otherwise be redeemed.

e Assume any necessary bank overdraft facilities are available if required.

Required:

a The profit and loss account of Pantile Ltd for the seven-day period.

(9 marks)

b The summarised balance sheet of the company at 7 May 1995 after completion of the above transactions.

(16 marks)

Associated Examining Board – updated

Capital investment appraisal | 21

The importance of the correct investment decision

All businesses need capital in order to finance their operations. That finance may be raised from a variety of sources; the way in which the sources of capital are structured is of great importance, and this topic is considered in another part of this textbook.

Businesses need capital in order to invest it in various types of assets, with the objective of making a profit. The way in which a business invests its capital is of considerable importance for several reasons:

a the choice of capital investment projects will affect the future prosperity of the company and its shareholders;

b the choice of capital investment projects by businesses will affect the future prosperity of the nation;

c investment in fixed assets is likely to tie-up capital for a considerable period of time, and the choice of a wrong investment project could not only yield an unsatisfactory rate of return on the invested capital but could also be difficult and costly to escape from;

d a wrong investment decision restricts the supply of finance for other investment opportunities;

e an investment in fixed assets may also necessitate additional investment in working capital, eg higher levels of stocks and debtors;

f the investment project must earn a rate of return which is greater than the cost of the capital invested, eg it would not make good financial sense to borrow finance at a cost of 15 per cent per annum to invest in an asset which produces a rate of return of 14 per cent per annum.

Clearly the choice of correct investment projects is of great importance, and reliable techniques for selecting the 'best buy' are necessary.

Types of capital expenditure

Capital investment techniques can be used to assess any expenditure project which is of a capital nature, eg the purchase of:

a land and buildings;

b plant, machinery and equipment;

c motor vehicles;

d other businesses;

e investments in businesses or other securities;

f working capital.

Traditional techniques

Two techniques which have been used by business for many years are:

a the average annual rate of return method;

b the payback period method.

These two methods are rather primitive in their operation and can produce a wrong answer.

The average annual rate of return method

The procedure, which is applied to each of several competing investment projects, is as follows:

a the annual cash flows which are expected to arise as a consequence of the investment are budgeted over the expected life of the project;

b these annual cash flows are aggregated;

c from the total budgeted cash flow is deducted the budgeted capital cost;

d the remaining amount represents the budgeted total surplus; this is divided by the number of years of expected life to produce an average annual surplus;

e the average annual surplus is expressed as a percentage of the budgeted capital cost;

f the competing projects are ranked in order of their respective percentage average annual rate of return.

Example:

		Project A £	Project B £
Capital cost		10,000	10,000
Cash flow	Year 1	1,000	5,000
Cash flow	Year 2	2,000	4,000
Cash flow	Year 3	3,000	3,000
Cash flow	Year 4	4,000	2,000
Cash flow	Year 5	5,000	1,000
	Total	£15,000	£15,000
Total surplus		5,000	5,000
Average annual surplus		1,000	1,000
Average annual surplus %		10%	10%

According to the average annual rate of return method Projects A and B are equally viable, both producing an average rate of return of 10 per cent per annum. But Project B is clearly preferable because it produces larger returns in the earlier years, and these extra returns can be re-invested by the business in other projects to earn further returns. Clearly, therefore, the timing of cash flows is of fundamental importance.

The payback period method

This method calculates, for each competing project, the time during which the budgeted cash flows will pay back the capital cost.

Example:

		Project C £	Project D £
Capital cost		12,000	12,000
Cash flow	Year 1	5,000	2,000
Cash flow	Year 2	4,000	3,000
Cash flow	Year 3	3,000	3,000
Cash flow	Year 4	3,000	4,000
Cash flow	Year 5	3,000	8,000
		£18,000	£20,000
Payback period (years)		3	4
Ranking		1st	2nd

(The brackets indicate the payback period.)

Project C clearly pays back in three-quarters of the time required by Project D, and pays back during the first three years £4,000 more than Project D which would be available for re-investment with financial benefit. But Project D produces an extra £2,000 of total cash flows during its estimated lifetime.

The payback period method concentrates on the period required to pay back the original capital investment, and by so doing could eliminate a project which is relatively slow to gather momentum but which produces significantly larger returns in later years.

Requirements of a reliable investment appraisal technique

It must take into consideration the following factors:

a the timings of the cash flows;

b varying lengths of life of competing projects;

c the cost of the capital to be invested in the project;

d rates of interest;

e residual asset values;

f the effects of taxation and tax allowances.

Compound interest

Compound interest arises in situations where the interest earned during a period by a project is added at the end of the period to the principal sum invested, so that thereafter the reinvested interest will also earn interest.

For example:

Year	Principal b/f £	Compound interest @ 10% £	Principal c/f £
1	1,000	100.00	1,100.00
2	1,100	110.00	1,210.00
3	1,210	121.00	1,331.00
4	1,331	133.10	1,464.10

This can be expressed in a mathematical formula:

$$A = P (1 + R)^n$$

where A = compounded value of the investment at the end of n years
P = principal sum invested
R = annual rate of interest, as a decimal
n = number of years of investment

The maturity value of an investment can also be calculated with the aid of compound interest tables, for example:

	Compound sum of £1		
Rate of interest per annum Year	8%	9%	10%
1	1.080	1.090	1.100
2	1.166	1.188	1.210
3	1.260	1.295	1.331
4	1.360	1.412	1.464
5	1.469	1.539	1.611

Thus the maturity value of an amount (say, £4,500) at the end of five years with a compound rate of interest of 10 per cent can be calculated by multiplying £4,500 by a factor of 1.611, ie £7,249.50.

Discounting

The compound interest formula and tables enable the future value of a present amount of investment to be calculated for a stated rate of interest and for a stated period of years. But we may wish to turn the problem around, and ask 'how much is it necessary to invest now to achieve a stated amount at the end of a specified period of years with a stated rate of compound interest?' The technique required to solve this problem is called discounting, and discounting is the reverse of compounding. What we need to be able to do is to discount a future value to its equivalent present value.

If £100 is invested now at a compound rate of interest of 10 per cent per annum then its value at the end of one year will be £100 + (10 per cent of 100) ie £110. The present value of the future value after one year is therefore the future value x 100/110. With an interest rate of 15 per cent per annum the present value of any future sum in one year's time can be calculated by multiplying that future sum by 100/115. For investment periods of one year it is therefore possible to compile a table of discounting (present value) factors, as follows:

Rate of interest per annum	Fraction	Present value factor
5%	100/105	0.952
8%	100/108	0.926
10%	100/110	0.909
12%	100/112	0.893
15%	100/115	0.870

That is, the present value of £1,000 receivable at the end of one year with a rate of interest of 10 per cent per annum is £1,000 x 0.909 = £909. If £909 is invested now at a compound rate of interest of 10 per cent per annum then at the end of one year its value will be £909 + (10 per cent of £909, ie £91) = £1,000.

For periods in excess of one year the calculation by formula is more complicated, the required formula being:

$$P = \frac{f}{(1 + R)^n}$$

where P = present value
       F = future amount
       R = rate of interest per annum, as a decimal
       n = number of years

Fortunately, calculation by formula is unnecessary because tables of discounting factors are available, for example:

Present Value of £1

Rate of interest per annum Year	8%	9%	10%
1	0.926	0.917	0.909
2	0.857	0.842	0.826
3	0.794	0.772	0.751
4	0.735	0.708	0.683
5	0.681	0.650	0.621

Therefore the present value of a stated amount to be received in five years time at a rate of interest of 10 per cent per annum can be calculated using a discount factor of 0.621. If the amount required at the end of five years is £3,500 then the amount to be invested at the commencement of year one (ie the present value) is:

£3,500 x 0.621 = £2,173.50

The accuracy of this figure can be proved by compounding over five years, as follows:

Year	Investment at year commencement £	Compound interest @ 10% per annum £	Investment at year end £
1	2,173.50	217.35	2,390.85
2	2,390.85	239.08	2,629.93
3	2,629.93	262.99	2,892.92
4	2,892.92	289.29	3,182.21
5	3,182.21	318.22	3,500.43

The excess amount of 43p is due to the fact that the discount factors have been rounded to three decimal places; discount factors rounded to four or more decimal places would give a higher degree of accuracy.

Calculation of the present value of a future stream of cash flows

Suppose that a person requires to invest a sum of money now which will provide stated amounts of income at the end of each of five years, with a prevailing rate of interest of 10 per cent per annum. The stated amounts of income are:

Year 1	Year 2	Year 3	Year 4	Year 5
£3,000	£5,000	£7,000	£6,000	£4,000

The calculations are as follows:

Year	Income required £	Discount factor 10% per annum	Present value £s
1	3,000	0.909	2,727
2	5,000	0.826	4,130
3	7,000	0.751	5,257
4	6,000	0.683	4,098
5	4,000	0.621	2,484
		Total present value	£18,696

The accuracy of this calculation can be proved as follows:

Year	Balance of investment	Interest @ 10% per annum	Investment plus interest	Income withdrawn
1	18,696	1870	20,566	3,000
2	17,566	1757	19,323	5,000
3	14,323	1432	15,755	7,000
4	8,755	876	9,631	6,000
5	3,631	363	3,994	4,000
			Difference	£6

The difference of £6 is due to the fact that:

a calculations have been expressed in round pounds; and

b discount factors to only three decimal places have been used.

Discounted cash flow techniques

The arguments in the last two sections can now be used to develop a capital investment appraisal technique – discounted cash flow.

Suppose that the five annual incomes stated in the last section (ie £3,000, £5,000, £7,000, £6,000, £4,000) could be generated by the purchase of a machine, that the machine would cost £15,000, and that the capital invested in the machine would cost 10 per cent per annum. Which is the cheapest method of producing the required stream of incomes? By purchase of the machine, or by purchase of the imaginary investment illustrated in the last section? The imaginary investment would cost £18,696 compared with the machine's cost of £15,000, so clearly the purchase of the machine is preferable. If the cost of the machine were, say, £20,000 then its purchase would not be justified on financial grounds because the stream of incomes could be provided at a reduced capital cost of £1,304 by purchase of the imaginary investment.

In effect, the discounted cash flow method compares each investment project with an imaginary conventional investment which produces a rate of interest which is the same as the investment project's cost of capital. Consider the following example:

Year		PV factor 10%		Machine A		Machine B		Machine C	
					Present value		Present value		Present value
			£	£	£	£	£	£	£
Capital cost	0	1.000	18,000	18,000	15,000	15,000	20,000	20,000	
Cash flows	1	0.909	2,000	1,818	4,000	6,636	4,000	3,636	
	2	0.826	5,000	4,130	8,000	6,608	5,000	4,130	
	3	0.751	6,000	4,506	7,000	5,257	9,000	6,759	
	4	0.683	6,000	4,098	3,000	2,049	8,000	5,464	
	5	0.621	5,000	3,105	2,000	1,242	4,000	2,484	
			£24,000		£24,000		£30,000		
Present value				17,657		18,792		22,473	
Net present value				(343)		3,792		2,473	
				17,657		18,792		22,473	
				£18,000		£15,000		£20,000	
Performance index				0.981		1.253		1.124	
Ranking				3rd		1st		2nd	

The net present value is the difference between the present value of the cash flows and the amount of the capital investment. The fact that Machine A has a negative present value indicates that this project is not acceptable on financial grounds because its true rate of return is less than the cost of capital (10 per cent). Machines B and C, having positive net present values, are acceptable on financial grounds.

Machines B and C cannot be reliably ranked solely according to the size of their net present values because the capital costs are different. The total present values must be related to the amounts of capital and this is done by means of a performance index which is calculated by dividing the total present value by the capital cost. The performance indices rank Machine B first (1.253), Machine C second (1.124) and Machine A third (0.981).

The three investment projects can also be ranked by calculating the internal rate of return for each project. A project which produces a positive net present value must be earning a true rate of return which is greater than the cost of capital (ie 10 per cent) and conversely a project with a negative net present value must be earning a true rate of return of less than 10 per cent. The true rate of return is determined largely by trial and error, by finding the interest rate which discounts the cash flows to an amount equal to the capital cost. This is calculated for Machine B as follows:

Machine B

Year	Cash flows	12% Factor	PV	15% Factor	PV	20% Factor	PV	22% Factor	PV
0	15,000	1.000	15,000	1.000	15,000	1.000	15,000	1.000	15,000
1	4,000	0.893	3,572	0.870	3,480	0.833	3,332	0.820	3,280
2	8,000	0.797	6,376	0.756	6,048	0.694	5,552	0.672	5,376
3	7,000	0.712	4,984	0.658	4,606	0.579	4,053	0.552	3,864
4	3,000	0.636	1,908	0.572	1,716	0.482	1,446	0.452	1,356
5	2,000	0.567	1,134	0.497	994	0.402	804	0.372	744
	£24,000		£17,974		£16,844		£15,187		£14,620

Clearly the true rate of return lies between 20 and 22 per cent. An approximation of the true rate can be calculated by interpolation, using the formula:

$$\text{Lowest of the two interest rates} + \text{Difference between the two interest rates} \times \left(\frac{\text{Difference between total present value and capital cost of the lowest interest rate}}{\text{Difference between total present values of the lower and the higher interest rates}} \right)$$

ie   20% + (2% x 187/567) = 20.66%

Returning to the conventional investment idea of the last section, a repayment statement can be prepared for Machine B as follows:

Year	Balance of investment b/f £	Interest @ 20.66% £	Required cash flow £	£
1	15,000	3,099	18,099	4,000
2	14,099	2,913	17,012	8,000
3	9,102	1,862	10,874	7,000
4	3,874	800	4,674	3,000
5	1,674	346	2,020	2,000
6				
20 (rounding error)		£9,020		£24,000

Discounting Tables
Present value of £1

Year	1%	2%	3%	4%	5%	6%	7%	8%	9%	10%	12%	14%	15%
1	0.990	0.980	0.971	0.961	0.952	0.943	0.935	0.926	0.917	0.909	0.893	0.877	0.870
2	0.980	0.961	0.943	0.925	0.907	0.890	0.873	0.857	0.842	0.826	0.797	0.769	0.756
3	0.971	0.942	0.915	0.889	0.864	0.840	0.816	0.794	0.772	0.751	0.712	0.675	0.658
4	0.961	0.924	0.889	0.855	0.823	0.792	0.763	0.735	0.708	0.683	0.636	0.592	0.572
5	0.951	0.906	0.863	0.822	0.784	0.747	0.713	0.681	0.650	0.621	0.567	0.519	0.497
6	0.942	0.888	0.838	0.790	0.746	0.705	0.666	0.630	0.596	0.564	0.507	0.456	0.432
7	0.933	0.871	0.813	0.760	0.711	0.665	0.623	0.583	0.547	0.513	0.452	0.400	0.376
8	0.923	0.853	0.789	0.731	0.677	0.627	0.582	0.540	0.502	0.467	0.404	0.351	0.327
9	0.914	0.837	0.766	0.703	0.645	0.592	0.544	0.500	0.460	0.424	0.361	0.308	0.284
10	0.905	0.820	0.744	0.676	0.614	0.558	0.508	0.463	0.422	0.386	0.322	0.270	0.247
11	0.896	0.804	0.722	0.650	0.585	0.527	0.475	0.429	0.388	0.350	0.287	0.237	0.215
12	0.887	0.788	0.701	0.625	0.557	0.497	0.444	0.397	0.356	0.319	0.257	0.208	0.187
13	0.879	0.773	0.681	0.601	0.530	0.469	0.415	0.368	0.326	0.290	0.229	0.182	0.163
14	0.870	0.758	0.661	0.577	0.505	0.442	0.388	0.340	0.299	0.263	0.205	0.160	0.141
15	0.861	0.743	0.642	0.555	0.481	0.417	0.362	0.315	0.275	0.239	0.183	0.140	0.123
16	0.853	0.728	0.623	0.534	0.458	0.394	0.339	0.292	0.252	0.218	0.163	0.123	0.107
17	0.844	0.714	0.605	0.513	0.436	0.371	0.317	0.270	0.231	0.198	0.146	0.108	0.093
18	0.836	0.700	0.587	0.494	0.416	0.350	0.296	0.250	0.212	0.180	0.130	0.095	0.081
19	0.828	0.686	0.570	0.475	0.396	0.331	0.276	0.232	0.194	0.164	0.116	0.083	0.070
20	0.820	0.673	0.554	0.456	0.377	0.319	0.258	0.215	0.178	0.149	0.104	0.073	0.061
25	0.780	0.610	0.478	0.375	0.295	0.233	0.184	0.146	0.116	0.092	0.059	0.038	0.030
30	0.742	0.552	0.412	0.308	0.231	0.174	0.131	0.099	0.075	0.057	0.033	0.020	0.015

Discounting Tables
Present value of £1

Year	16%	18%	20%	24%	28%	32%	36%	40%	50%	60%	70%	80%	90%
1	0.862	0.847	0.833	0.806	0.781	0.758	0.735	0.714	0.667	0.625	0.588	0.556	0.526
2	0.743	0.718	0.694	0.650	0.610	0.574	0.541	0.510	0.444	0.391	0.346	0.309	0.277
3	0.641	0.609	0.579	0.524	0.477	0.435	0.398	0.364	0.296	0.244	0.204	0.171	0.146
4	0.552	0.516	0.482	0.423	0.373	0.329	0.292	0.260	0.198	0.153	0.120	0.095	0.077
5	0.476	0.437	0.402	0.341	0.291	0.250	0.215	0.186	0.132	0.095	0.070	0.053	0.040
6	0.410	0.370	0.335	0.275	0.227	0.189	0.158	0.133	0.088	0.060	0.041	0.029	0.021
7	0.354	0.314	0.279	0.222	0.178	0.143	0.116	0.095	0.059	0.037	0.024	0.016	0.011
8	0.305	0.266	0.233	0.179	0.139	0.108	0.085	0.068	0.039	0.023	0.014	0.009	0.006
9	0.263	0.226	0.194	0.144	0.108	0.082	0.063	0.048	0.026	0.015	0.008	0.005	0.003
10	0.227	0.191	0.162	0.116	0.085	0.062	0.046	0.035	0.017	0.009	0.005	0.003	0.002
11	0.195	0.162	0.135	0.094	0.066	0.047	0.034	0.025	0.012	0.006	0.003	0.002	0.001
12	0.168	0.137	0.112	0.076	0.052	0.936	0.025	0.018	0.008	0.004	0.002	0.001	0.001
13	0.145	0.116	0.093	0.061	0.040	0.027	0.018	0.013	0.005	0.002	0.001	0.001	0.000
14	0.125	0.099	0.078	0.049	0.032	0.021	0.041	0.009	0.003	0.001	0.001	0.000	0.000
15	0.108	0.084	0.065	0.040	0.025	0.016	0.010	0.006	0.002	0.001	0.000	0.000	0.000
16	0.093	0.071	0.054	0.032	0.019	0.012	0.007	0.005	0.002	0.001	0.000	0.000	
17	0.080	0.060	0.045	0.026	0.015	0.009	0.005	0.003	0.001	0.000	0.000		
18	0.069	0.051	0.038	0.021	0.012	0.007	0.004	0.002	0.001	0.000	0.000		
19	0.060	0.043	0.031	0.017	0.009	0.005	0.003	0.002	0.000	0.000			
20	0.051	0.037	0.026	0.014	0.007	0.004	0.002	0.001	0.000	0.000			
25	0.024	0.016	0.010	0.005	0.002	0.001	0.000	0.000					
30	0.012	0.007	0.004	0.002	0.001	0.000	0.000						

Cost accounting – introduction | 22

Need for cost accounting

a In order to determine the total cost of a manufactured product or a service. Without a knowledge of such costs it will be difficult to reliably determine selling prices, to decide upon acceptance of orders, etc.

b For purposes of planning and control, eg budgetary control and standard costing.

c To provide a reliable basis of information for decision making.

Comparison with financial accounting systems

Financial accounting systems and cost accounting systems operate from the same information base. This common information is processed and used in different ways.

a Cost accounts are produced for the needs of internal management and, unlike financial accounts, there is no legal requirement to distribute cost accounting information to parties outside the business.

b Unlike financial accounts, the form and content of cost accounts is not prescribed by law.

c There is no legal requirement that cost accounts must be audited.

d Cost accounting information is generally concerned with short periods of time, whereas financial information tends to relate to longer time periods.

e Cost accounting information deals with individual aspects of a business whereas financial accounts tend to treat the business as a whole.

Cost units

A cost unit is a unit of production or of service to which costs can be readily related. In some instances the output of a business can be measured in natural units (eg cars, tables, shoes) whereas in other businesses it is necessary to use artificial units of measurement (eg gallons of beer, tons of chemical, kilowatts of electricity).

Costing methods

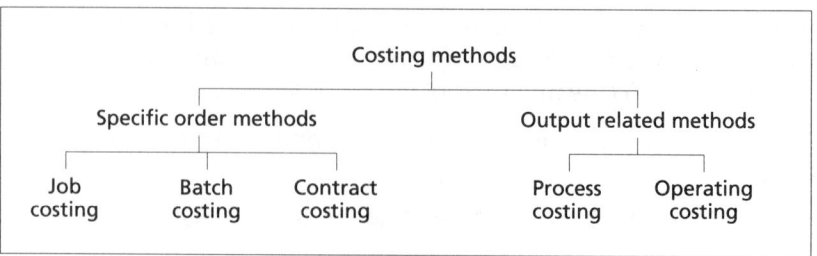

Specific order methods are used in businesses where there are natural and discrete units of output; output related methods are used in businesses where the output is virtually a continual flow and there are no natural and discrete units of output.

Batch costing may be described as job costing on a small scale, and contract costing as job costing on a large scale.

The choice of a costing method is likely to be governed by the type and nature of the industry.

Costing techniques

There are a range of techniques which may be employed in order to implement any of the costing methods indicated above. The choice of technique will be governed by the attitudes and policy of the management with regard to the provision of accounting information.

a Cost accounts may be prepared on (a) a historical cost, or (b) a standard cost basis. Historical cost systems are compiled from actual costs after such costs have been incurred. Standard cost systems are based upon what the costs should be under reasonably efficient operating conditions. In many ways standard costs operate as a 'target' or a 'yardstick', and actual costs may be compared with standard costs in order to calculate variances.

b Cost accounts may also be prepared on (a) a total cost (absorption cost) basis, or (b) a marginal cost (direct cost) basis. Absorption costing systems attempt to charge each cost unit with a portion of all costs, whereas marginal costing systems charge each cost unit only with those costs which are directly related.

Direct and indirect costs

Direct costs are those costs which are directly contained in, or directly associated with, a particular cost unit. For example, in the manufacture of furniture the wood required to make a table top is a direct cost because the wood forms an integral part of the product. Direct costs, because of their direct association with the product, can usually be fairly readily quantified.

Indirect costs are those which are necessarily incurred in order to operate the business but which have no direct or natural connection with the individual cost units of the business. For example, a furniture manufacturer may pay a rent for the use of his factory premises but there is no direct relationship between the total rent paid and the individual products manufactured. Because of the lack of a direct relationship between indirect costs and individual cost units it is difficult to accurately calculate unit costs.

Elements of cost

The costs which a business incurs can be classified into three elements:

a materials

b labour

c expense.

Each of these elements can be subdivided into direct costs and indirect costs, ie:

Direct materials
Direct labour } prime cost
Direct expenses

Indirect materials
Indirect labour } overheads
Indirect expenses

The total of all indirect costs is called overheads. Overheads can, in turn, be subdivided according to function, ie:

a production overheads;

b administration overheads;

c Selling and distribution overheads.

This classification of costs is recognised in the manner in which a product cost is compiled, ie:

	£	£
Direct materials	X	
Direct labour	X	
Direct expenses	X	
Prime cost		X
Production overheads		X
Factory cost		X
Administration overheads		X
Selling and distribution overheads		X
Total cost		X

Allocation, apportionment, and absorption of overheads

If a business is to operate at a profit then all of the costs of the business must be passed on to its customers via the products or services which are sold to them. The main purpose of preparing a product cost is to attempt to ensure that each product carries a fair portion of all the costs, and that the total volume of production thereby conveys all of the costs of the business, plus a profit margin, to the customers.

When a product cost is being prepared it is not particularly difficult to calculate the costs of direct materials, direct labour, and direct expenses, because, of course, there is a direct relationship between direct costs and products. It is the treatment of overheads which causes problems because there is no direct relationship between items of overhead cost and products.

At this point the term 'cost centre' should be introduced. A cost centre is simply a point within a business organisation at which costs can be recorded and used for purposes of cost control. A cost centre could be a particular location, a person, a machine or item of equipment, or any combination of these things. Managements will use their own judgments in deciding which points are to be cost centres bearing in mind the characteristics of their particular business and their own needs for cost control information. A cost centre can be a productive cost centre (eg in an engineering factory the drilling, lathes, welding, milling departments etc could each be a cost centre) or it can be a non-productive cost centre (eg canteen, maintenance, stores).

Some overhead costs will have a definite relationship with individual cost centres, though not, of course, with the products which pass through those cost centres. For example, the wages of a departmental supervisor is an overhead cost but it relates with certainty to the department which he supervises. Such overhead costs can be allocated with precision to relative cost centres.

Most overhead costs will not be capable of being allocated to cost centres. These overheads must be apportioned to cost centres by the selection of a sensible basis of apportionment for each item of overhead cost.

Methods of apportionment

a In proportion to floor area (eg rent, rates, lighting and heating).

b In proportion to cubic capacity (eg heating, interior decoration).

c In proportion to numbers of employees (eg canteen expenses, supervision).

d In proportion to capital values (eg fire insurance, depreciation, general maintenance).

e In proportion to direct labour hours (eg indirect labour, indirect materials).

f In proportion to direct wages cost.

g In proportion to a technical estimate (eg electric power, lighting).

Overheads absorption

The overheads which are loaded on to cost centres by allocation and apportionment must be off-loaded on to the production which passes through each cost centre. The technique by which this is accomplished is known as absorption.

Overhead absorption rates need to be calculated in advance, ie as part of the budgeting process. Basically, the formula for this is:

$$\frac{\text{budgeted fixed overheads}}{\text{budgeted activity}}$$

Budgeted activity can be measured in several ways:

a in terms of the number of units of budgeted production;

b in terms of the material content of the budgeted production;

c in terms of the labour content of the budgeted production;

d in terms of the prime cost of the budgeted production;

e in terms of the number of labour hours needed to make the budgeted production;

f in terms of the number of machine hours needed to make the budgeted production.

Example:
Suppose that a business has budgeted its production for the following financial year as follows:

Number of units of production	£3,000
Material cost	£16,000
Labour cost	£8,000
Prime cost	£24,000
Labour hours	£10,000
Machine hours	£20,000
Fixed overheads	£12,000

The following alternative bases of overhead absorption are possible:

a Cost per unit of product:

$$\frac{\text{fixed overheads}}{\text{number of units}}$$

ie $\dfrac{£12,000}{3,000 \text{ units}} = £4.00 \text{ per unit}$

b Percentage on cost of direct materials:

$$\frac{\text{fixed overheads}}{\text{material cost}} \times \frac{100}{1}$$

ie $\dfrac{£12,000}{£16,000} \times \dfrac{100}{1} = 75\% \text{ on direct materials}$

c   Percentage on cost of direct labour:

$$\frac{\text{fixed overheads}}{\text{direct labour cost}} \times \frac{100}{1}$$

ie $\dfrac{£12,000}{£8,000} \times \dfrac{100}{1}$ = 150% on direct labour

d   Percentage on prime cost:

$$\frac{\text{fixed overheads}}{\text{prime cost}} \times \frac{100}{1}$$

ie $\dfrac{£12,000}{£24,000} \times \dfrac{100}{1}$ = 50% on prime cost

e   Direct labour hour rate:

$$\frac{\text{fixed overheads}}{\text{direct labour hours}}$$

ie $\dfrac{£12,000}{10,000 \text{ hours}}$ = £1.20 per direct labour hour

e   Machine hour rate:

$$\frac{\text{fixed overheads}}{\text{machine hours}}$$

ie $\dfrac{£12,000}{20,000 \text{ hours}}$ = £0.60 per machine hour

The student should realise that there are no rules which determine the choice of methods of (a) overhead apportionment and (b) overhead absorption. The accountant must select the methods of apportionment/absorption which he considers to be most suitable bearing in mind the characteristics of his particular business in its particular trade/industry. Different methods will produce different results and have different effects upon product costs.

On the next page is a diagram illustrating the flow of costs in a simple manufacturing business.

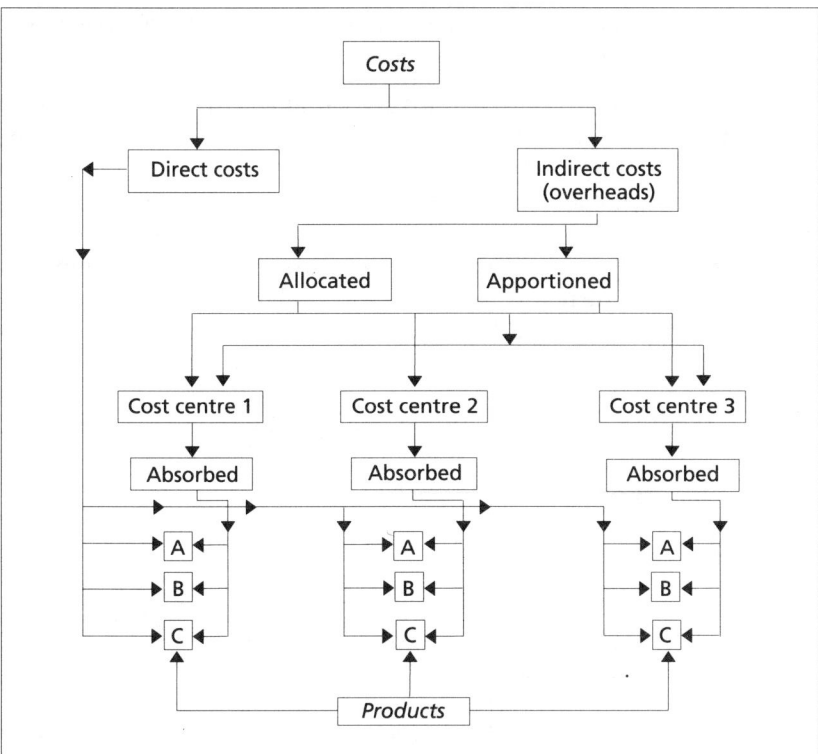

Cost behaviour

The whole range of costs which a business incurs can be classified in another way, ie according to behavioural characteristics. Cost behaviour means the way in which the total cost of an item responds to changes in the level of activity.

a A *fixed* cost is one which, in total, is unaffected by changes in the level of activity. For example, if a manufacturer agrees to pay a rent of £4,000 per year for use of his factory premises then the total rent payable will not be affected by changes in levels of output; he will pay £4,000 per year regardless of whether his output is 100 units or 100,000 units.

b A *variable* cost is one which, in total, increases or decreases in proportion to increases or decreases in activity. For example, if the wood required to make one table costs £20 then the total cost of wood to make 100, 200, 300 tables will be £2,000, £4,000 and £6,000 respectively.
   In the case of a fixed cost, the *unit* cost of production decreases as production increases, total cost being constant. In the case of a variable cost, the *total* cost of production increases as production increases, the unit cost being constant.

c A *semi-variable* cost is one which in total tends to increase or decrease in response to increases or decreases in activity, but the change in total cost is not directly proportional to the change in activity. Semi-variable costs are capable of further

proportional to the change in activity. Semi-variable costs are capable of further classification (eg fixed plus variable, step semi-variable).

Costs are unlikely to be truly fixed or truly variable. For example, as activity increases a manufacturer may be able to purchase his direct materials more efficiently, thereby gaining a reduction in unit variable cost. If the manufacturer pays a fixed rent of £4,000 per annum for the use of his factory premises then that rent is fixed only within his present manufacturing capacity; when the capacity is fully utilised he can only increase production further by renting further factory space, ie in the long run the rent is really a semi-variable cost.

If these different types of cost behaviour are plotted on graphs they will appear as follows:

a Fixed cost:

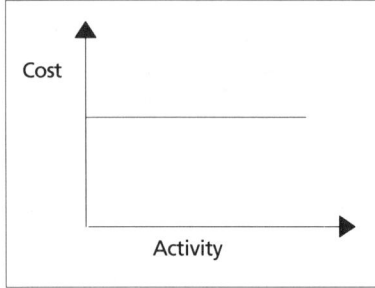

b Variable cost:

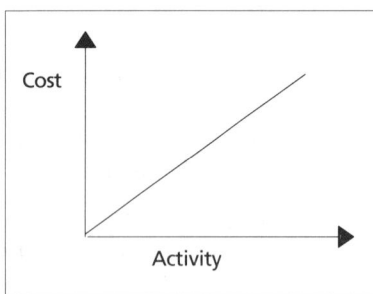

c Semi-variable ('fixed and variable' type):

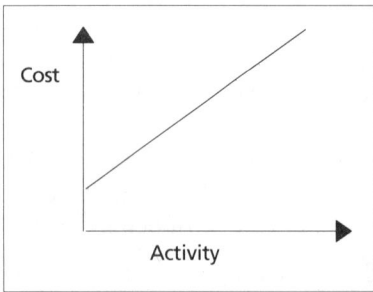

d Semi-variable ('step' type):

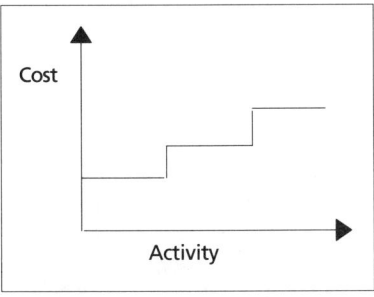

Segregation of fixed and variable costs

Questions sometimes require a calculation of total fixed costs and unit variable costs when only total costs are given. For example, consider the following situation:

Activity (units)	Total costs (£s)
9,500	58,500
12,500	67,500

The total fixed costs and the unit variable costs can be calculated by determining the effects of the change in activity level. An increase of 3,000 units of activity has caused an increase in total costs of £9,000. Fixed costs are by definition fixed, therefore, the £9,000 increase must be caused by variable costs. The unit variable cost is, therefore:

$$\frac{£9,000}{3,000 \text{ units}} \text{ ie £3 per unit}$$

The fixed cost can now be calculated:

a At 9,500 units:

Total costs	=	£58,500
Variable costs = 9,500 x £3	=	£28,500
Fixed costs, therefore	=	£30,000

b At 12,500 units:

Total costs	=	£67,500
Variable costs = 12,500 x £3	=	£37,500
Fixed costs, therefore	=	£30,000

Relationships between costs/volume/profit

An understanding of the behavioural characteristics of costs and revenues is most important for decision making purposes. Many business decisions are concerned with determining the financial consequences of different levels of activity. If fixed costs and variable costs can be separately identified then the results of various

costs and variable costs can be separately identified then the results of various levels of activity can be tabulated. For example, suppose that:

Fixed costs	=	£30,000
Variable costs	=	£3 per unit
Selling price	=	£8 per unit

Activity (1,000 units)	Sales	Variable costs	Fixed costs	Total costs	Profit (loss)	Cost per unit
	£	£	£	£	£	£
1	8,000	3,000	30,000	33,000	(25,000)	33.00
2	16,000	6,000	30,000	36,000	(20,000)	18.00
3	24,000	9,000	30,000	39,000	(15,000)	13.00
4	32,000	12,000	30,000	42,000	(10,000)	10.50
5	40,000	15,000	30,000	45,000	(5,000)	9.00
6	48,000	18,000	30,000	48,000	Nil	8.00
7	56,000	21,000	30,000	51,000	5,000	7.29
8	64,000	24,000	30,000	54,000	10,000	6.75
9	72,000	27,000	30,000	57,000	15,000	6.33
10	80,000	30,000	30,000	60,000	20,000	6.00
11	88,000	33,000	30,000	63,000	25,000	5.73
12	96,000	36,000	30,000	66,000	30,000	5.50
13	104,000	39,000	30,000	69,000	35,000	5.31
14	112,000	42,000	30,000	72,000	40,000	5.14
15	120,000	45,000	30,000	75,000	45,000	5.00

The final column shows the cost per unit, arrived at by dividing the total cost by the number of units of activity. This shows that as activity increases the cost per unit of activity decreases; this arises because as activity increases the same amount of fixed costs (ie £30,000) is shared by an increased number of units.

Break-even analysis

The break-even point is the level of activity at which sales revenue equals total costs, ie there is neither profit nor loss. The tabulation above shows that the break-even point is 6,000 units.

The break-even point can also be calculated by formula, as follows:

$$\frac{\text{total fixed costs}}{\text{unit selling price} - \text{unit variable cost (or contribution per unit)}}$$

Using the basic data in the tables:

$$\text{break-even point} = \frac{£30,000}{£8 - £3} = 6,000 \text{ units}$$

This formula calculates the break-even point in terms of units of activity. It can also be calculated in terms of total sales revenue as follows:

$$\text{fixed costs} \times \frac{\text{unit selling price}}{\text{unit selling price} - \text{unit variable cost)}}$$

$$= £30,000 \times \frac{£8}{£5} = £48,000$$

Break-even chart

A third method of calculating the break-even point, and of demonstrating costs/volume/profit relationships, is by use of a break-even graph.

The procedure is as follows:

a mark the horizontal (x) axis with units of activity;

b mark the vertical (y) axis with units of costs/sales revenue;

c draw the fixed cost line, which will be parallel to the x axis;

d draw the variable costs line;

e draw the total costs line (effectively this is the sum of (c) and (d));

f draw the sales line;

g the point where the total costs line and the sales line intersect is the break-even point;

h the area between the sales line and the total costs line, to the left of the break-even point, is the loss angle; the corresponding angle to the right of the break-even point is the profit angle. The profit or loss at any chosen level of activity is calculated by measuring the perpendicular distance between the sales line and the total costs line.

The margin of safety is the distance between the chosen level of activity and the break-even point. It indicates the amount by which activity would have to fall before losses start to occur.

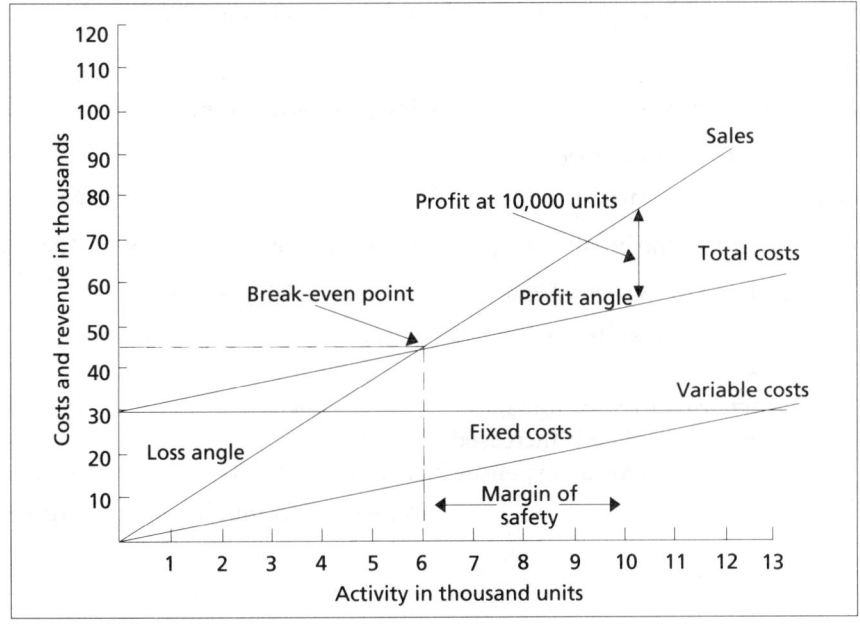

Now try the following illustration, which is A-level standard.

Illustration:

The summarised manufacturing, trading and profit and loss account for the year ended 30 June 1995, of Spectacular Ltd, which commenced business on 1 July 1994, is as follows:

	£	£
Sales		60,000
Less: Cost of goods sold:		
Cost of goods manufactured:		
Direct materials	25,000	
Direct labour	15,000	
Overheads: variable	10,000	
fixed	7,000	
	57,000	
Less: Stock of finished goods at		
30 June 1995	12,500	
		44,500
Gross profit		15,500
Less: Administrative expenses	4,000	
Selling and distribution expenses	3,500	
Financial expenses	500	
		8,000
Net profit		£7,500

Additional information:

a Spectacular Ltd manufacture and sell only a single product.

b During the year under review 3,000 units at £20 per unit were sold, whilst 4,000 units were produced.

c There was no work-in-progress at 30 June 1994, or 30 June 1995.

Required:

a A distinction between each of the following groups of costs:

   i   direct costs and indirect costs;

   ii fixed costs and variable costs. (6 marks)

b) A computation of the break-even point and margin of safety of Spectacular Ltd:

   i   on the basis of the actual results for the year to 30 June 1995;

   ii assuming the results for the year ended 30 June 1995 were amended as follows:

   sales increased to 3,500 units;
   fixed factory overheads increased to £8,000;
   selling and distribution expenses increased to £4,000. (5 marks)

Associated Examining Board – updated

Solution:

a   Direct costs – those which can be allocated 'directly' to a product.

Indirect costs – those which must be apportioned.
Fixed costs – costs which do not change regardless of the level of production.
Variable costs – those which vary proportionately with production levels.

b i   Contribution:

	£	£
Sales price		20.00
Direct materials	6.25	
Direct labour	3.75	
Variable overheads	2.50	12.50
Contribution		£7.50
Fixed costs:		
Overheads		7,000
Administrative expenses		4,000
Selling expenses		3,500
Financial expenses		500
		£15,000

B-E pt	= FC ÷ contribution
	= 15,000 ÷ 7.50
	= 2,000 products

Margin of safety	= 3,000 – 2,000
	= 1,000 products

ii   Contribution remains at £7.50

Fixed costs:	
Overheads	8,000
Administration	4,000
Selling	4,000
Financial	500
	16,500

B-E pt	= FC ÷ contribution
	= 16,500 ÷ 7.50
	= 2,200 units

Margin of safety	= 3,500 – 2,200
	= 1,300 units

The examiner sometimes takes another approach to break-even analysis. Information has been given in the form of:

Quarter ended	31 March	30 June	30 September
	£	£	£
Sales	30,000	40,000	35,000
Profits	5,000	10,000	7,500

From this information it is possible to work out the sales level necessary to reach the break-even. The above can be expanded as follows:

	31 March £	30 June £	30 September £
Sales	30,000	40,000	35,000
Less: profits	5,000	10,000	7,500
Total cost (by balance)	£25,000	£30,000	£27,500

As we know, total cost = fixed cost plus variable cost.

Fixed costs do not change from quarter to quarter and as the increase of £10,000 in sales between quarter one and two brought an associated total cost increase of £5,000, we know that this cost increase is all variable.

Therefore we can tell that variable costs are:

$$\frac{5,000}{10,000} \text{ x 100\% (50\%) of sales revenue}$$

'Contribution' is also, therefore, 50 per cent of sales revenue. This can be tested:

	£	£	£
Total cost	25,000	30,000	27,500
Variable cost	15,000 (30,000 x 50%)	20,000 (40,000 x 50%)	17,500 (35,000 x 50%)
Fixed cost (by balance)	£10,000	£10,000	£10,000

To find the break-even point all one needs to do is consider the definition of the break-even point, which is:

B-E pt = total fixed cost ÷ contribution/unit
B-E pt = 10,000 50%
= £20,000

Marginal costing | 23

Marginal cost

The marginal cost is the amount, at any given level of activity, by which aggregate costs are changed if the volume of activity is increased or decreased by one unit.

Fixed costs are, by definition, fixed in relation to output, and therefore an increase in activity of one unit will cause only the variable costs to change. The marginal cost of one unit is therefore the sum of all the unit variable costs, ie usually prime cost plus variable production overheads plus variable administration overheads plus variable selling and distribution costs.

Contribution towards fixed costs and profits

The excess of sales revenue over marginal cost is defined as the contribution. Strictly speaking, the full term is 'contribution towards fixed costs and profits', because this excess must firstly recover the fixed costs and any amount then remaining will produce a net profit.

Product cost

A product cost, prepared on an absorption cost basis, might be produced in the following format:

Product Cost
Product Type – XYZ
Level of Output – 8,000 units

			£ Per unit
Direct material			2.00
Direct labour			1.50
Direct expenses			0.50
	Prime cost		4.00
Production overheads:			
Fixed		0.70	
Variable		0.30	1.00
	Factory cost		5.00
Administration overheads:			
Fixed		1.25	
Variable		0.25	1.50
Fixed		0.55	
Variable		0.45	1.00
Total cost			7.50
Profit			1.50
Selling price			£9.00

If re-stated in a marginal cost format it would appear as:

		£ Per unit
Direct material		2.00
Direct labour		1.50
Direct expenses		0.50
Prime cost		4.00
Variable overheads:		
Production	0.30	
Administration	0.25	
Selling & distribution	0.45	1.00
Marginal cost		5.00
Selling price		9.00
Contribution		£4.00

Contribution

If one more unit of XYZ is produced then sales revenue will be increased by £9 and total costs will be increased by the marginal cost of £5, ie contributing an additional £4 towards fixed costs and profit.

Composition of marginal cost

Marginal costing makes a clear distinction between those costs which are influenced by changes in activity levels (ie the variable costs) and those which are not (ie the fixed costs). Marginal costing makes no attempt to distribute fixed costs to units of activity.

Limitations of absorption costing

Absorption costing has several in-built weaknesses, including the following:

a In order to produce absorption costs, overheads of a fixed nature must be apportioned to cost centres by one of several bases, which are arbitrary in their effects.

b In order to produce absorption costs the overheads which are loaded on to cost centres must be absorbed by products by one of several methods, all of which are arbitrary in their effects.

c An absorption cost is only true at the level of activity at which it has been calculated. The tabulation in page 360 shows, in the extreme right column, the absorption cost per unit.

At an activity level of 8,000 units the total unit cost is £6.75, but this unit cost will not be true at any other level of activity. Many problems which confront management are concerned with predicting the probable outcome of operating at different activity levels, and absorption costs will be useless in this context. For example, at 8,000 units of activity the product cost would show a unit cost of £6.75 and therefore a unit net profit of (£8.00 – £6.75) ie £1.25. There is a danger that the ignorant businessman might assume that if activity were increased to 10,000 units then the resultant net profit would be 10,000 units x £1.25, ie £12,500; the correct profit figure would be £20,000.

Calculation of profit

If the basic data used in the example on page 360 (ie selling price = £8 per unit, variable cost = £3 per unit, total fixed costs = £30,000) is viewed with a marginal costing attitude, then it will be realised that each unit of production makes a contribution of £5 (ie £8 – £3). The profit (loss) at any level of activity can be easily and accurately calculated as follows:

a multiply the chosen activity by the unit contribution to ascertain the total contribution;

b deduct from the total contribution the total fixed costs;

c the resultant figure is net profit (or net loss).

For example:

	£	£	£	£
Level of activity (units)	8,000	9,000	10,000	5,678
Unit contribution	5	5	5	5
Total contribution	40,000	45,000	50,000	28,390
Fixed costs	30,000	30,000	30,000	30,000
Net profit (loss)	10,000	15,000	20,000	(£1,610)

Break-even formula

The following break-even formula is given of page 360:

$$\frac{\text{total fixed costs}}{\text{unit selling price - unit variable cost}}$$

The denominator in this equation can now be amended to read:

'unit contribution' ie number of units to break-even

$$= \frac{\text{total fixed costs}}{\text{unit contribution}}$$

Marginal costing and decision making – accepting business on a 'marginal cost' basis

In 'Contribution' (above), a product cost for product XYZ is shown. Suppose that, in this situation, business is poor and that the only additional business available is an order for 500 units at a selling price of £6 per unit. Should the order be accepted, an initial reaction might be:

	£
Selling price offered per unit	6.00
Total cost per unit	7.50
Net loss per unit	1.50
Total apparent loss x 500 units =	£750

This calculation is incorrect, because each additional unit will cost only its marginal cost. The correct calculation is:

	£
Selling price offered per unit	6.00
Marginal cost per unit	5.00
Contribution per unit	1.00
Total contribution, ie additional profit	
= 500 units x £1 =	£500

The key point here is that fixed costs are incurred at a given level whether the order is taken on or not – they are therefore not relevant to the decision and can be ignored.

Under normal circumstances the business should insist upon its normal selling price of £9 per unit. But under exceptional circumstances, as for instance during a severe trade recession, total profits might be increased by accepting business at well below normal selling prices, provided that such business makes a positive contribution.

This policy does have several dangers:

a The business could, by accepting business below normal selling price, be creating a dangerous precedent in that customers might expect a continuance of supplies at similar reduced prices when business conditions have returned to normal.

b Competitors might retaliate with similar price reductions and such collective action could damage the market, ie in future customers might not be prepared to pay the higher prices.

c If when a business accepts an order it informs its customer that the order is being accepted on a marginal cost basis then the business is also informing the customer that 'all is not well' and the customer may try to reduce the offered price even further.

d Business should be accepted on a 'marginal cost' basis only if no better business exists and there is idle production capacity. There is a danger that 'marginal cost' business might in fact displace normal business.

Marginal costing and decision making – multiple activity situations

Most businesses have several activities. Those activities could be several products, several product groups, several production lines, several departments, several factories, several sales areas, several shops, etc.

A multiple activity situation can be viewed diagrammatically as follows:

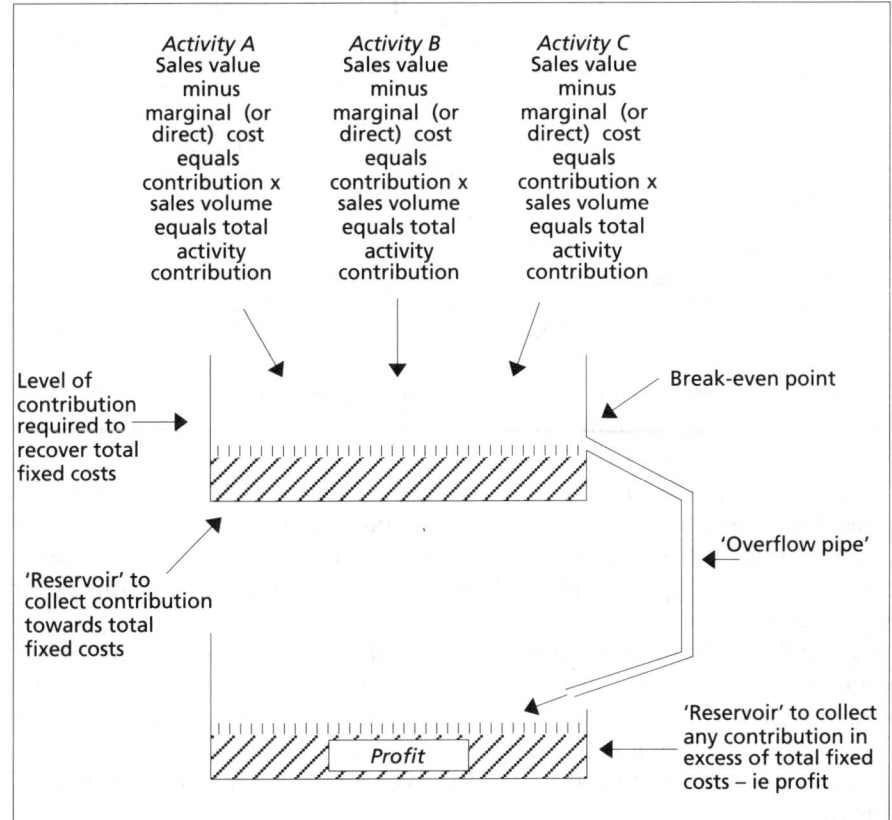

There will be a 'flow' of contribution from each activity. These contribution flows are required firstly to provide wholly for the recovery of fixed costs. When fixed costs have been fully recovered (ie the break-even point has been reached) any further contribution will then go wholly towards profit.

It follows that if any one activity were to cease then its contribution would cease, and total net profit would be reduced by the amount of the contribution lost.

Illustration:

RE Taylor Ltd operates a chain of five shops. Branch profit and loss accounts are produced for the last financial year, as follows:

	Total £	Bedford £	Luton £	Reading £	St Albans £	Watford £
Sales	200,000	40,000	30,000	60,000	20,000	50,000
Cost of sales	120,000	29,000	18,500	32,500	11,500	28,500
Gross margin	80,000	11,000	11,500	27,500	8,500	21,500
% of sales	40.00	27.5	38.3	45.8	42.5	43.0
Shop wages	26,000	6,000	5,000	7,200	2,600	5,200
Shop rents	12,500	3,500	3,000	2,800	900	2,300
Shop rates	5,500	1,500	1,000	1,600	500	900
Shop light, heat telephones, etc	6,000	1,400	1,000	1,600	700	1,300
General overheads	20,000	4,000	3,000	6,000	2,000	5,000
Total expenses	70,000	16,400	13,000	19,200	6,800	14,700
Net profit (loss)	£10,000	£(5,400)	£(1,500)	£8,300	£1,800	£6,800

The general overheads are fixed in nature and represented the cost of head office administration, warehousing, transportation, etc, and are apportioned to the branches in proportion to sales.

Management is concerned about the two loss-making branches (Bedford and Luton). An investigation has revealed that nothing can be done to improve branch performances by increasing selling prices, increasing sales volume, reducing cost, etc. Can the total company profit be increased by the closure of any branches, and if so, which branches?

An initial (and incorrect) reaction might be that the two loss-making branches, Bedford and Luton, should be closed thereby eliminating losses of £6,900 and also improving total company profit to £16,900. But the general overheads are of a fixed nature, so the closure of these two branches would mean that their combined overhead apportionment (£7,000) would have to be borne by the remaining three branches.

The key piece of information – branch contributions – is missing, and this information is vital to the solution.

	Total £	Bedford £	Luton £	Reading £	St Albans £	Watford £
Gross margin	80,000	11,000	11,500	27,500	8,500	21,500
Direct shop costs						
Shop wages	26,000	6,000	5,000	7,200	2,600	5,200
Shop rent	12,500	3,500	3,000	2,800	900	2,300
Shop rates	5,500	1,500	1,000	1,600	500	900
Shop light, heat telephone etc.	6,000	1,400	1,000	1,600	700	1,300
	£50,000	£12,400	£10,000	£13,200	£4,700	£9,700
Contribution	30,000	(1,400)	1,500	14,300	3,800	11,800
General overheads	20,000					
Net profit	£10,000					

This re-organised branch profit and loss account shows that Bedford has a contribution deficit of £1,400 and that Luton has a positive contribution of £1,500. The closure of Bedford only would eliminate a contribution deficit of £1,400 thereby improving total net profit to £11,400; the closure of Luton only would

thereby improving total net profit to £11,400; the closure of Luton only would surrender its contribution of £1,500 and thereby reduce total net profit to £8,500.

Closure of both branches would reduce total contribution by £100 and reduce total net profit to £9,900. The correct decision is therefore to close Bedford branch only.

After the closure of Bedford branch the profit and loss accounts, with re-apportioned general overheads, would appear as follows:

	Total £	Bedford £	Luton £	Reading £	St Albans £	Watford £
Sales	170,000	40,000	–	60,000	20,000	50,000
Cost of sales	101,500	29,000	–	32,500	11,500	28,500
Gross margin	68,500	11,000	–	27,500	8,500	21,500
Shop wages	21,000	6,000	–	7,200	2,600	5,200
Shop rents	9,500	3,500	–	2,800	900	2,300
Shop rates	4,500	1,500	–	1,600	500	900
Shop light, heat telephone etc	5,000	1,400	–	1,600	700	1,300
General overheads	20,000	4,706	–	7,059	2,353	5,882
Total expenses	60,000	17,106	–	20,259	7,053	15,582
Net profit (loss)	£8,500	£(6,106)	–	£7,241	£1,447	£5,918

It should be noticed that the net profits (losses) of the four remaining branches are different from the original situation – and yet nothing has changed at any of these branches. This emphasises the weakness of trying to judge the results of multiple activity situations on an absorption cost basis.

Marginal costing and limiting factors

Businesses need a supply of various resources in order to operate profitably, eg labour, machines, materials, working capital. If activity is to be increased then the demand for these resources will also be increased. A progressive increase in activity will, sooner or later, use up the existing supply of one of these scarce resources, and further increases in activity cannot be achieved until an additional supply of the scarce resource is obtained. These scarce resources are called 'limiting factors' and the scarcest of the limiting factors is called the 'key' or 'principal' limiting factor.

If the supply of a limiting factor is insufficient to enable the business to fulfil the demand for its products then production and sales should be concentrated on those products which use the limiting factor most profitably.

Example:

Products	A	B	C	D
Selling price	£35	£30	£45	£60
Marginal cost	£25	£13	£30	£36
Contribution	£10	£17	£15	£24
Ranking by size of contribution	4th	2nd	3rd	Ist
Labour hours	5	10	15	20
Contribution per labour hour	£2.00	£1.70	£1.00	£1.20
Ranking by size of contribution per labour hour	1st	2nd	4th	3rd
Forecast sales (units)	5,000	4,000	4,000	2,000

Fixed costs are assumed to be £144,000.

Suppose that the supply of labour hours is restricted to 120,000 hours. The number of labour hours needed to meet the sales forecast will be:

Product	Forecast sales (units)	Labour hours per unit	Total hours
A	5,000	5	25,000
B	4,000	10	40,000
C	4,000	15	60,000
D	2,000	20	40,000
			165,000

It will not be possible to produce all of the sales forecast because of a shortfall of labour hours amounting to 45,000 hours. The 120,000 hours available should be allocated to those products which show the *highest contribution per labour hour*, as follows:

Products	A	B	C	D
Ranking	1	2	3	3
Allocated sales (units)	5,000	4,000	1,000	2,000
Labour hours required	25,000	40,000	15,000	40,000
Contribution per unit	£10	£17	£15	£24
Product contributions	£50,000	£68,000	£15,000	£48,000
Total contribution		£181,000		
Less: Fixed costs		£144,000		
Optimum net profit		£37,000		

The labour hours have been allocated firstly to product A, secondly to product B, thirdly to product D, and the remaining 15,000 hours to product C. It will not be possible to produce 3,000 units of the 4,000 units forecast for product C.

The procedure for solving this type of problem is as follows:

a identify the limiting factor (here, labour hours);

b quantify the limiting factor (here, 120,000 hours);

c calculate, for each product, the contribution per limiting factor;

d rank the products in order of profitability based on (c);

e allocate the supply of limiting factor in the order of this ranking to determine the optimum product mix;

f multiply the optimum quantities of each product by the unit contributions to arrive at total contributions;

g deduct total fixed costs from total contribution to determine optimum net profit.

Profit/volume (P/V) ratio

This is really a poor name for the ratio. It expresses as a percentage the relationship between the contribution and the selling price of a product, and is, therefore, better described as the contribution/sales ratio. Management should be seeking to increase the contribution/sales ratio for each product.

Referring to the example above, the P/V ratios of the four products are:

Product	A	B	C	D
Ranking	1	2	3	4
Selling price	£35	£30	£45	£60
Contribution	£10	£17	£15	£24
PV ratio %	28.57	56.66	33.33	40.00

Profit graph

This is an alternative form of displaying costs/volume/profit relationships. It plots profit/loss on the vertical (y) axis against volume on the horizontal (x) axis. At nil volume there will be a net loss equivalent to the total amount of fixed costs.

Using the basic data from page 360, a profit graph would be constructed as follows: the profit arising from £80,000 of sales is shown to be £20,000. The horizontal scale could be alternatively/additionally graduated to record sales volume in units.

Illustration:
Bubonic Ltd produces cosmetics. The company has three factories, each factory concentrating on a different type of cosmetic. Budgets are prepared annually on a factory basis and the budgets for the year to 30 September 1995 are given below:

Factories		A	B	C	Total
		(all figures are given in £000s)			
Turnover		700	400	300	1,400
Less: Costs:	Materials	150	100	120	370
	Labour	250	120	80	450
	General expenses	50	30	20	100
	Depreciation of equipment	100	40	20	160
	Research expenses	60	60	60	180
	Head office admin	35	20	15	70
	Net profit (loss)	55	30	(15)	70
		£700	£400	£300	£1,400

The above results are considered typical of operations for a number of years to come. Because of the loss forecast for Factory C and since this factory is rented and the lease expires on 30 September 1995, the managing director has proposed that Factory C should be closed down as soon as possible and certainly before a new lease is signed.

You are given the following further information:

a If the lease of Factory C were to be renewed, this would involve an increased annual rental of £2,000. The present rent is included under general expenses.

b Closure of Factory C would not affect activity at the remaining two factories.

c The equipment at Factory C is highly specialised and its estimated resale value is only £10,000. This equipment, although it is nearly fully depreciated, is still sound and will be efficient for several years to come.

d All research is carried out centrally in London and the cost apportioned equally to each factory. If Factory C were to close, research expenses would in total fall by not more than £20,000 per annum.

e The head office is situated in London and its expenses are apportioned to the factories on the basis of sales. Closing Factory C would reduce head office administration expenses by £10,000 per annum.

Required:

A report, supported by figures, which show the effect on company profits of closing down Factory C, addressed to the managing director of Bubonic Ltd on the decision whether or not this factory should be closed.

(25 marks)

Associated Examining Board – updated

Solution:
Bubonic Ltd
Report on closure of Factory C

	Closure £	Continuation £
Sales	1,100	1,400
Materials	250	370
Labour	370	450
General expenses	80	102
Depreciation	140	140
Research	160	180
Head office admin	60	70
	1,060	1,312
	40	88
Profit on sale of FA	10	–
Net profit	50	88

It can be seen from the above that continuing with Factory C would enhance profits by £18,000.

The additional reduction in profits of £20,000 if the factory were closed down is made up of:

	£	£
Loss in sales		(300)
Reduction in costs of:		
Materials	120	
Labour	80	
General expenses	20	
Research	20	
Head office admin	10	250
		(50)
Add: Depreciation	20	
Profit on sale of FA	10	30
		20

The examiner often requires decisions between two or more alternatives. Try this illustration.

Illustration:
Optimist Ltd are manufacturers of three products ADOS, BIGOS and CEDOS. The company has prepared the following budget for the quarter ending 31 March 1995.

	ADOS	BIGOS	CEDOS
Based on maximum capacity production	4,000	3,000	2,000
	£	£	£
Materials	24,800	10,500	16,500
Labour	38,400	18,300	5,600
Overheads: Variable	20,800	19,200	15,600
Fixed	36,000	12,000	12,000
Turnover	148,000	84,000	60,000

In preparing the above budget it has been assumed that the selling price for each of the three products will not change throughout the first quarter of 1995.

It is company policy that each product must be financially beneficial to the company in each quarter.

The company's marketing advisers have reported that estimated sales in the quarter ending 31 March 1995, based on budgeted sales prices are expected to be:

ADOS	3,000
BIGOS	2,400
CEDOS	1,600

However, the company is considering the following additional proposals for the quarter ending 31 March 1995:

a Accept an order for 500 ADOS at a unit price of £24. This order is from a foreign customer and would not affect other sales volumes or prices for ADOS.

b Revise the sale price of CEDOS. A market survey indicates the following possibilities: If the price per unit of CEDOS is as budgeted, sales volume is expected to be 1,600 per quarter. If the price per unit is 25 per cent below that budgeted, sales volume would increase by 20 per cent above original

budgeted, sales volume would increase by 20 per cent above original expectations. If the price per unit is 33⅓ per cent below that budgeted, sales volume would increase by 50 per cent above original expectations.

Required:

a A statement showing clearly the budgeted detailed manufacturing costs and profits for each product for the quarter ending 31 March 1995, if the company's marketing advisers' estimated sales are achieved.

(14 marks)

b A report, incorporating appropriate computations, advising the company as to which, if any, of the proposals it should accept for the quarter ending 31 March 1995.

(7 marks)

Note: state any essential assumptions made.

Associated Examining Board – updated

Solution:
Optimist Ltd

a Manufacturing costs/profits quarter ended 31 March 1995:

	A £	B £	C £
Materials	18,600	8,400	13,200
Labour	28,800	14,640	4,480
Overheads: Variable	15,600	15,360	12,480
Fixed	36,000	12,000	12,000
	99,000	50,400	42,160
Sales revenue	111,000	67,200	48,000
Profits	£12,000	£16,800	£5,840

b To the management of Optimist Ltd. This report is in two sections. The first is the financial considerations of the proposals and the second deals with non-financial factors.

Section 1: financial factors

a

Special order	£	£
Selling price		24.00
Variable costs (note l):		
Materials	6.20	
Labour	9.60	
Overheads	5.20	21.00
Contribution/unit		£3.00

It can be seen from the above table that acceptance of the special order would increase profits by £3 per ADOS or £1,500 in total.

b Price reductions:

	Reduction	
	20%	33⅓%
Selling price	24.00	20.00
Variable costs:		
Materials	8.25	
Labour	2.80	
Overheads	7.80	
	18.85	18.85
Contribution	5.15	1.15
Volume (in units)	1,920	2,000*
Total contribution	9,888	2,300
Fixed overheads	12,000	12,000
Loss	£2,112	£9,700

* maximum capacity

Section 2: non-financial considerations

a It would probably be possible to extend the maximum capacity for production of CEDOS by, say, paying overtime to the labour force. As the benefit would only be 400 more units sold and as the contribution would be reduced it is apparently not worthwhile.

b If the firm's budget shows expected sales of 3,000 ADOS it seems likely that they would have sufficient labour for that capacity. If this is the case there may be problems in providing enough labour to fulfil the special order without damaging production of the other products.

c The figures themselves may be unreliable due to such factors as those costs taken as variable costs being semi-variable in actual fact.

Notes: these costs have been assumed to be variable in direct proportion to production (NB this is highly unlikely in real life).

Another illustration shows the choice of installing new machinery. Before attempting this you should consider the following points:

a The fixed costs are stated as amounts per unit, eg fixed factory costs £2.40/unit. As fixed costs do not change with the level of production this £2.40/unit is true only at a production level of 15,000. Total fixed factory costs are 15,000 x £2.40 or £36,000 and consequently fixed factory costs would be:

$\dfrac{36,000}{20,000}$ or £1.80/unit at the 20,000 motor production level.

b An alternative (c) involves the installation of new machinery. You must consider what would happen if demand dropped so that the firm could not sell all it could make.

Illustration:
Periwinkle Ltd manufactures a small motor used in electric drills. The factory has the necessary capacity to produce 20,000 motors per annum, but has been operating in recent years at only 75 per cent capacity.

Unit costs etc based on an output of 15,000 motors per annum, are:

		£
Direct materials		7.00
Direct labour		4.00
Factory costs:	Variable	1.00
	Fixed	2.40
Delivery costs:	Variable	1.20
	Fixed	0.60
Administrative costs :	Fixed	0.80
		17.00
Profit		3.00
Selling price		£20.00

The directors are concerned to improve profitability and are considering the following mutually exclusive proposals for the next year.

a Reducing selling prices by 5 per cent would increase sales and enable the factory to operate at full capacity.

b Accepting a special order from Bogoland to supply 8,000 units at a special price of £22 each. In this case other sales would be reduced to 14,000 units per annum. If this overseas order were to be accepted, additional delivery costs of 80p per unit would arise because of the extra distance. The necessary production in excess of 100 per cent capacity would involve overtime working. In overtime conditions direct labour costs would rise by 50 per cent and variable factory costs by 20 per cent.

c Installing new machinery would speed up production and enable 30,000 motors to be produced and sold each year. New machinery would increase fixed factory costs by £25,000 per annum and selling price would need to be reduced by 10 per cent to sell the increased production.

Required: A detailed calculation of:

a The profit currently made, based on an output of 15,000 motors per annum.

(5 marks)

b The profit Periwinkle Ltd may expect to make under each of the proposals given in (a), (b) and (c) above.

(16 marks)

c A short report to the directors indicating your recommendations as to which proposals they should select.

(4 marks)

Associated Examining Board

Solution:

a

Periwinkle Ltd

Profit on 15,000 output	Total		Per unit	
	£	£	£	£
Sales		300,000		20.00
Variable costs:				
Materials	105,000		7.00	
Labour	60,000		4.00	
Factory	15,000		1.00	
Delivery	18,000		1.20	
		98,000		13.20
Contribution		102,000		£6.80
Fixed costs:				
Factory	36,000			
Delivery	9,000			
Administration	12,000			
		57,000		
Profit on 15,000 units		£45,000		

b Proposal (a)

	£	£
Reduced sales price		19.00
Variable cost		13.20
Contribution/unit		£5.80
Sales, full capacity 20,000		
Contribution from sales		
(20,000 x 5.80)	116,000	
Fixed costs	57,000	
Profit	£59,000	

Proposal (b)

		£	£
Domestic sales			280,000
Special order			176,000
			456,000
Materials (22,000 x 7.00)		154,000	
Labour normal (20,000 x 4.00)		80,000	
o/t 2,000 x 6.00		12,000	
Factory variable normal			
20,000 x 1.00		20,000	
o/t 2,000 x 1.20		2,400	
Delivery: Normal	14,000 x 1.20	16,800	
Special	8,000 x 2.00	16,000	301,200
Contribution			154,800
Fixed costs			57,000
Profits			£97,800

Proposal (c)

	£		£
Sales	30,000 @ 18.00		540,000
Materials	30,000 @ 7.00	210,000	
Labour	30,000 @ 4.00	120,000	
Factory	30,000 @ 1.00	30,000	
Delivery	30,000 @ 1.20	36,000	396,000
			144,000
Fixed costs (57,000 + 25,000)			82,000
			£62,000

c On the assumption of profit maximisation the proposal to adopt would be (b); accepting the special order.

However, there are many problems to consider in addition to profit maximisation.

a If the firm can sell 15,000 at the current price and the special order forces production of only 14,000, which customers will they now reject and what effect will this have on the firm?

b Can the firm find sufficient labour to enable it to operate at 110 per cent capacity?

c Labour has been treated as a variable cost, yet in reality it is simply semi-variable. Other factors to consider are:

i training costs;

ii redundancy costs.

d There is no guarantee that the special order would be repeated in later years.

Selling at below total cost

Management may adopt a policy of deliberately selling below total cost for any of the following reasons:

a to make use of idle production facilities;

b to stimulate sales;

c to 'unload' surplus stocks;

d to promote a new product;

e to act as a 'loss leader'.

Such a policy may be very dangerous in the long term.

Contribution per unit of limiting factor

In every business, there is always a limiting factor which prevents the enterprise expanding to infinity.

Management will aim at earning the largest profit possible and this will be achieved by maximising the contribution per unit of limiting factor.

Where a limiting factor is operating, management will choose the work which yields the highest contribution per unit of limiting factor.

Illustration:
A company manufactures three products, as follows:

		Product	
	P	Q	R
	£	£	£
Materials	6	4	2
Labour	4	8	10
Variable overhead	2	4	5
	12	16	17
Selling price	20	24	22
Contribution	£8	£8	£5
Material used	12 lbs	8 lbs	4 lbs
Direct labour hours	4	8	10

The following table sets out the various limiting factors which might exist, the contribution per unit of limiting factor, and the product to be chosen for manufacture in each case:

	Contribution per unit of limiting factor			
Limiting Factor	P	Q	R	Product to be
	£	£	£	manufactured
a Number of units that can be sold	8.00	8.00	5.00	P or Q
b Total amount of turnover	0.40	0.33	0.23	P
c Raw materials	0.67	1.00	1.25	R
d Direct labour	2.00	1.00	0.50	P

Make or buy decisions

Management is frequently faced with the choice between buying in a component from a supplier or producing it internally.

Where there is a *spare productive capacity* it is only worth buying out a component if the marginal cost of production exceeds the buying-out cost.

Where there is *no spare productive capacity* other work will be displaced if the component is to be manufactured. The comparison in this case should be between the buying-out price and the marginal cost of production plus the contribution lost because of the work displaced.

Illustration:
The cost accountant has computed the cost of manufacturing a component as follows:

	£
Direct material	10
Direct labour (4 hours)	5
Variable overhead	2
Fixed overhead	6
	£23

The component can be purchased from an outside supplier for £18. Should the company make or buy, assuming:

a there is spare productive capacity,

b there is no spare productive capacity?

If there is spare productive capacity, it is better to manufacture because the marginal cost of £17 is less than the buying-out price.

If there is no spare productive capacity, it is necessary to know the contribution which could otherwise be earned per hour of production. For example, standard production might be as follows:

	£	£
Selling price		10.00
Direct materials	2.50	
Direct labour (2 hours)	2.50	
Variable overhead	1.00	6.00
Contribution		£4.00

From this it will be seen that the contribution earned per hour on standard production is

$$\frac{£4}{2} = £2$$

The cost of displacing sufficient production to manufacture one component is therefore 4 x £2 = £8. The total cost of manufacturing a component is, therefore, the marginal cost plus the lost contribution which is £17 + 8 = £25. It is, therefore, better to buy the component from a supplier.

Alternative production methods

The most usual decision under this heading is the choice between *hand labour* and *mechanised production*.

The method to be chosen is that with the largest contribution after deducting any additional fixed costs incurred by the process.

Illustration:

A company can manufacture a product by hand or by machine. The use of the machine involves additional fixed costs of £2,000. The costs are as follows:

	Hand £	Machine £
Selling price	20	20
Variable cost	16	12
Contribution	£4	£8

Advise the management.

Alternative break-even pont $=\dfrac{\text{aditional fixed costs}}{\text{additional contribution}}$

$=\dfrac{£2{,}000}{£4}$

$=500$ units

For up to 500 units it is better to manufacture by hand. For 500 units or more it is better to manufacture by machine.

Whether to continue or to suspend operations

Other factors beside cost will influence this decision but from the viewpoint of costs, it is always profitable to continue operations if the contribution from operations is greater than the difference between existing fixed overheads and those remaining on closure.

Costs/volume/profit analysis

Management has to review its selling price from time to time. Some executives may consider that prices should be reduced to stimulate sales while others may consider price increases to be more beneficial. The management accountant will calculate the effect of these alternative proposals on profit.

Short-term and long-term decisions

It should be emphasised that many of these marginal costing techniques relate to short-term decisions. In the long term other matters must be taken into consideration.

Standard costing | 24

Problems with 'actual cost'

The preparation of an actual cost for each job of work completed by a business can be very time consuming. There are other problems associated with actual costs:

a The actual costs calculated by identical jobs, completed at different times and possibly done by different workers, can vary quite considerably because of differences in operating efficiency.

b Having calculated a total actual cost for a particular job the business man may not really know whether that resultant cost is satisfactory or not. It may be satisfactory when compared with previous costs relating to the same type of work, but those previous costs may not reflect efficient working conditions and therefore are not suitable for use as a basis for comparison.

c Actual costs are historical in nature and therefore may not be suitable as a basis for predicting future costs and performances.

Standard cost

A standard cost is a pre-determined cost for the manufacture of a unit of product during a specified future period of time, calculated on the assumption that reasonably efficient operating conditions will be achieved. A standard cost should be prepared by carefully and scientifically determining the quantities and prices of labour and materials etc which should be used under reasonably efficient operating conditions. The assistance of work study technicians, designers, production engineers etc can be very valuable in this respect.

Advantages

Standard costing systems offer many advantages including:

a Actual performance is capable of being compared with pre-determined standards, and thereby showing the deviations (variances) from standard cost, these variances being either favourable or adverse.

b The variances can be analysed in detail thereby enabling management to investigate causes and take corrective action.

c Management by exception is facilitated, ie management can concentrate their attention on important matters which are not proceeding according to plan.

d A stable pricing policy is facilitated.

e Can be used as the basis for an incentive payment scheme.

f Permits stocks to be valued on a realistic and consistent basis.

g Is of assistance in the preparation of budgets.

The purpose of variances

A set of accounts which compare, for each item, the actual amount against the budgeted amount will give a good indication of where and by how much the business is 'off course'. But they do not necessarily indicate fully why the business is off course. For example, the budgeted profit for a period might be £50,000 and the actual profit £40,000, ie there is a £10,000 shortfall in net profit. Management should be keen to correct the adverse factors which have caused the £10,000 shortfall in profit, but they cannot do so unless they know what those contributory factors are and the amounts attributable to each factor. Variance analysis can do just this. But how does the accountant identify and quantify the contributory causes when all that he knows is that there is an adverse variance of net profit?

Cost and sales variances

A first line of reasoning will show that profit can vary primarily for two reasons, singly or in combination, ie:

a   a variation in the cost of the product; and

b   a variation in the sales margin of the product.

Suppose that the standard cost for a product is:

Selling price	£10
Total cost	£7
Profit	£3

and that 80 units are produced and sold giving an actual net profit of £160. The possible explanations for the adverse profit variance of (80 @ £3, ie £240 – £160) ie £80 can be shown as follows:

	Standard cost of 80 units	Actual cost of 80 units Explanation (a)	Explanation (b)
Selling price	80 @ £10 = £800	80 @ 9 = £720	80 @ £10 = £800
Total cost	80 @ £7 = £560	80 @ £7 = £560	80 @ £8 = £640
Profit	80 @ £3 = £240	80 @ £2 = £160	80 @ £2 = £160

Explanation (a) shows that the actual selling price per unit was £1 less than the budgeted selling price, causing profit to be reduced by £1 per unit, whereas explanation (b) is different, showing that the only variation was in the cost per unit which was £1 greater than the budgeted cost per unit, also causing profit to be reduced by £1 per unit. In explanation (a) the adverse profit variance was caused by an adverse variation of selling price, ie a *sales margin variance*, whereas in explanation (b) the adverse profit variance was attributable to an adverse variation of total cost, ie a *total cost variance*.

In practice it is likely that the profit variance will be caused by a combination of both a sales margin variance and a total cost variance, each either favourable or adverse, as is illustrated by the following possible explanations:

	Actual cost of 80 units		
	Explanation (c)	Explanation (d)	Explanation (e)
Selling price	80 @ £9.5 = £760	80 @ £11 = £880	80 @ £8.5 = £680
Total cost	80 @ £7.5 = £600	80 @ £9 = £720	80 @ £6.5 = £520
Profit	80 @ £2 = £160	80 @ £2 = £160	80 @ £2 = £160

Explanation (c) shows an adverse sales margin variance coupled with an adverse total cost variance; explanation (d) shows a favourable sales margin variance coupled with an adverse total cost variance; explanation (e) shows an adverse sales margin variance coupled with a favourable total cost variance.

Further sales margin variances are too complex to warrant treatment in a textbook of this nature, so they are ignored. But what factors may cause a total cost variance? Since total cost is the sum of direct labour, direct materials, direct expenses, and overheads, then a total cost variance can be caused by a variance, adverse or favourable, in any or all of these factors.

The analysis of variances so far considered can be represented diagrammatically as follows:

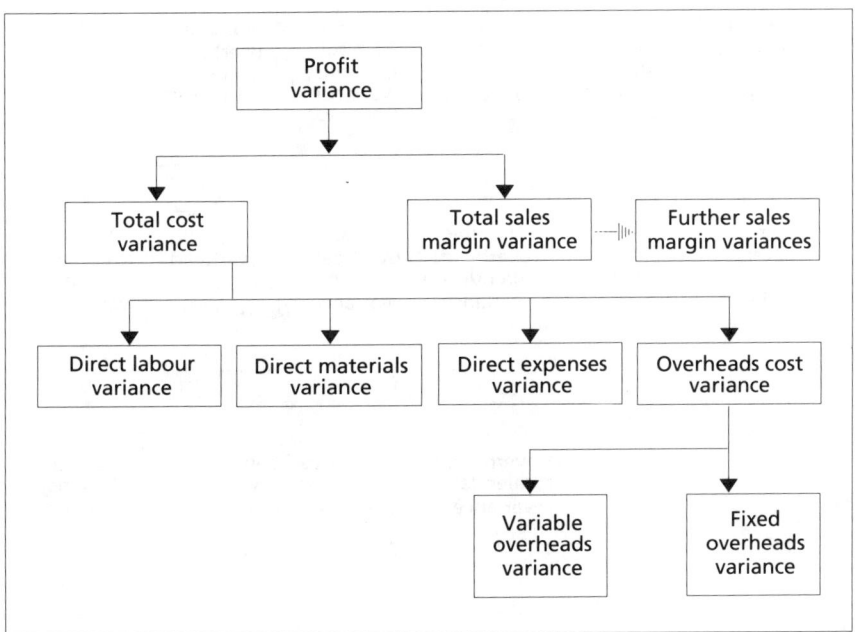

Notice that the diagram shows that the overheads cost variance can be sub-divided into a variable overheads variance and a fixed overheads variance.

A diagram which shows a complete 'family tree' of all the variances and their relationships follows:

Cost variance relationships

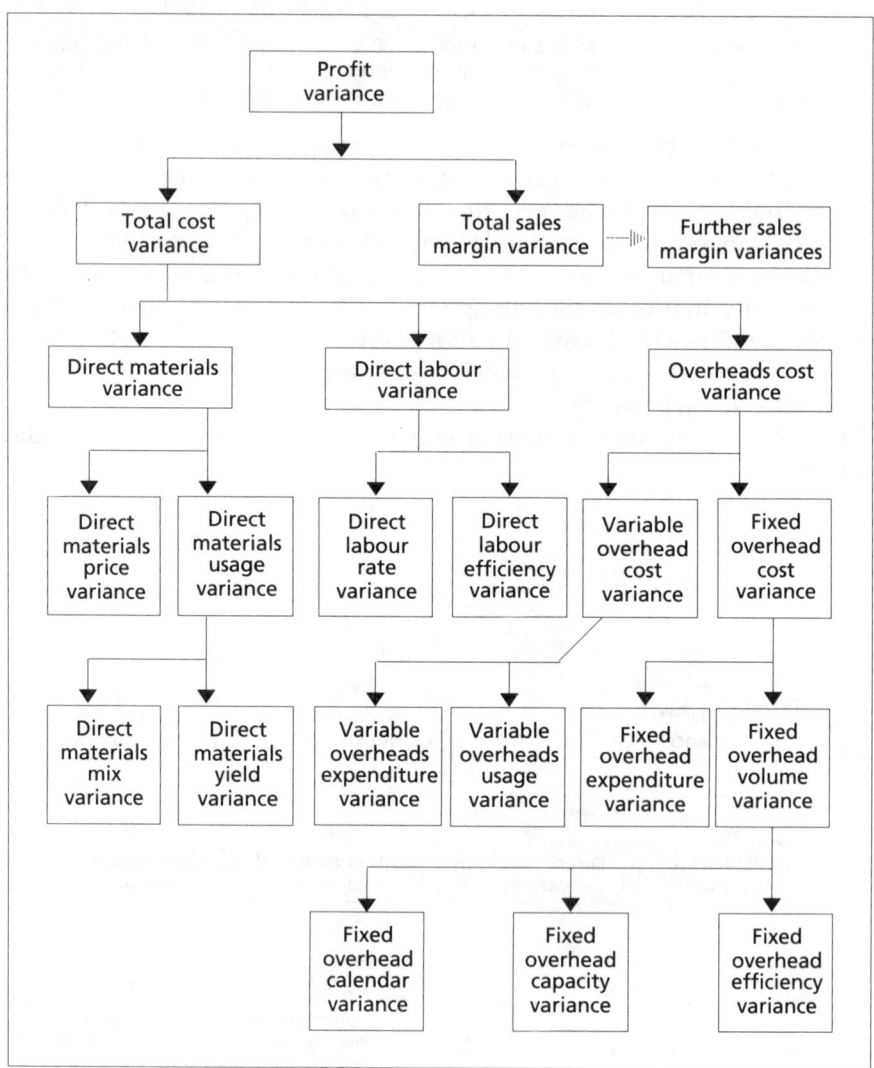

Price and usage variances

To understand further sub-divisions of variances it is firstly necessary to consider a standard product cost form and the part which it has to play:

Standard Product Cost

	£	£	£
Product description: XXX			
Direct materials:			
5 units @ £8.00 per unit =	40		
2 units @ £4.00 per unit =	8		
10 units @ £2.00 per unit =	20		
		68	
Direct labour:			
8 hours @ £1.50 per hour =	12		
12 hours @ £1.25 per hour =	15		
4 hours @ £1.75 per hour =	7		
24		34	
Direct expenses:			
8 units @ £0.50 per unit =		4	
Prime cost			106
Overheads:			
a Variable 24 hours @ £1.00 = 24			
b Fixed 24 hours @ £1.25 = 30			
			54
Total cost			160
Profit @ 10% on cost			16
Selling price			£176

The standard product cost shows that the manufacturer intends to sell the product for £176 – or another way of looking at it, which is helpful as an understanding of variance analysis, is that he intends to resell the materials embodied in the product for £68, the labour for £34, the direct expenses for £4, the overheads for £54, etc.

It will be observed that the total cost of each of the elements shown in the standard product cost is the product of a quantity multiplied by a rate or cost per unit. A total cost variance for any of the elements therefore has two contributory causes, ie:

a a price or rate variance, and

b a usage or efficiency variance.

Example:

Suppose that the standard product cost of product KLM567 specifies 20 units of material at a standard cost of £5.00 per unit of material. The actual manufacture of product KLM567 causes 27 units of material to be used which have an actual cost of £4.00 per unit. This can be summarised as follows:

Standard cost of I unit of product KLM567
  = 20 units of material @ £5.00 per unit = £100
Actual cost of I unit of product KLM567
  = 27 units of material @ £4.00 per unit = £108

This means that the manufacturer is selling the material content of product KLM567, embodied in the product standard cost, for £100, but the actual cost of material incurred in manufacturing the product was £108, ie the manufacturer has incurred a loss of £8.00.

The loss, or more correctly the material cost variance, has arisen because (a) the actual price per unit of material differed from the standard price per unit, ie there was a materials price variance, and (b) the actual quantity and the standard quantity of material were different.

The variances are calculated as follows:

a Materials price variance:

> Formula: (standard price per unit *minus* actual price per unit) x actual quantity used
> = £5.00 – £4.00 ie £1.00 per unit (F) x 27 units = £27.00 (favourable)

b Materials usage variance:

> Formula: (standard quantity specified *minus* actual quantity used) x standard price per unit
> = 20 units – 27 units, ie 7 units (A) x £5.00 per unit = £35.00 (adverse)

The difference between these two sub-variances (ie £35 (A) and £27 (F)) explains the total materials cost variance of (£100 – £108) ie £8.00 (adverse).

Note that favourable variances are indicated by (F) and adverse variances by (A). It should also be appreciated that subsidiary variances always account exactly for the superior variance from which they are derived; but the individual variances must always be separately calculated, and not determined by taking the sum or difference of other variances.

The variances just illustrated may alternatively be calculated as follows:

> Actual usage at actual cost = 27 units @ £4.00 = £108

now convert to standard cost, ie:

> = 27 units @ £5.00 = £135
> Difference = material price variance £27 (F)

now convert to standard usage, ie:

> = 20 units @ £5.00 = £100
> Difference = material usage variance £35 (A)

In the example which we have just considered materials were used by way of an illustration, but the same logic would equally apply to any of the other variable elements of cost, ie to direct labour, to direct expenses, or to variable overheads. For example, suppose that product KLM567 requires the same quantities and costs of labour as it does for materials:

> Standard cost of I unit of product KLM567
> 20 hours of labour @ £5.00 per hour = £100

> Actual cost of I unit of product KLM567
> 27 hours of labour @ £4.00 per hour = £108

a Labour rate variance

> Formula: (standard rate per hour *minus* actual rate per hour) x actual hours worked
> = £5.00 – £4.00, ie £1.00 per hour (F) x 27 hours = £27.00 (F)

b Labour efficiency variance:

>Formula: (standard hours specified *minus* actual hours worked) x standard rate per hour
>= 20 hours – 27 hours, ie 7 hours (A) x £5.00 = £35.00 (A)

The following example combines price and usage variances for both materials and labour.

The standard product cost of product QR234 is as follows:

Labour	20 hours @ £1.50 per hour	=	£30,000
Material	15 units @ £3.00 per unit	=	£45,000
			£75,000

The actual cost of manufacturing the product was:

Labour	16 hours @ £1.75 per hour	=	£28.00
Material	20 units @ £2.80 per hour	=	£56.00
			£84.00

The variances are analysed as follows:

a Total cost variance:

>Total standard cost – total actual cost
>ie £75.00 – £84.00   =   £9.00 (A)

b Labour cost variance:

>Standard labour cost – actual labour cost
>ie £30.00 – £28.00   =   £2.00 (F)

c Materials cost variance:

>Standard materials cost – actual materials cost
>ie £45.00 – £56.00   =   £11.00 (A)

d Labour rate variance:

>ie £1.50 – £1.75 = £0.25 (A) x 16 hours =   £4.00 (A)

e Labour efficiency variance:

>ie 20 hours – 16 hours – 4 hours (F) x £1.50 = £6.00 (F)

f Materials price variance:

>ie £3.00 – £2.80 = £0.20 (F) x 20 units   =   £4.00 (F)

g Materials usage variance:

>ie 15 units – 20 units = 5 units (A) x £3.00 = £15.00 (A)

The relationships between these variances may be illustrated in diagrammatic form:

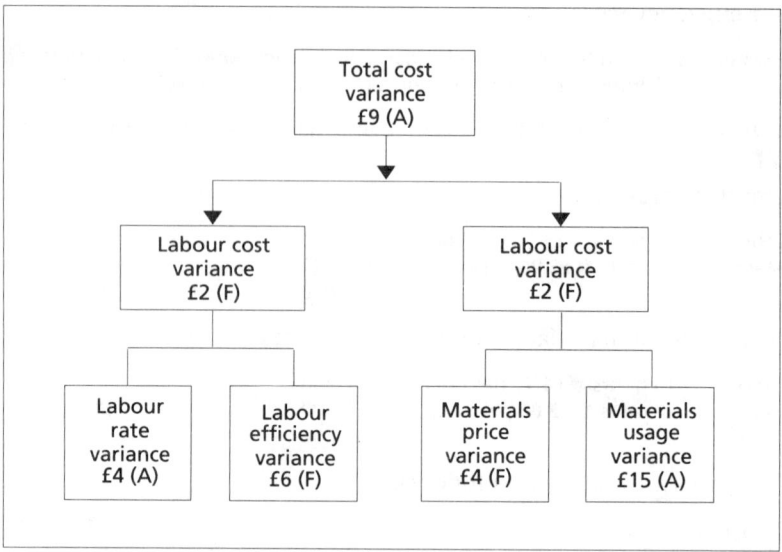

Fixed overhead variances

The fixed overhead cost variance has its own unique characteristics, and it has two sub-variances, ie:

a the fixed overhead expenditure variance; and

b the fixed overhead volume variance.

To understand these two variances it is necessary to understand the principle of fixed overhead absorption. A fixed overhead absorption rate will be determined in advance as part of the budgeting process. For example, if budgeted fixed overheads for a year are £40,000 and the budgeted production for that year, expressed in standard labour hours, is 100,000 then the absorption rate will be £40,000/100,000 standard hours = £0.40 per standard hour. It is extremely unlikely that the actual overhead cost and the actual production volume will equal the corresponding budget figures, and in practice both are likely to differ. If the actual expenditure is different from the budgeted expenditure, but the actual production and the budgeted production are the same, then a fixed overhead cost variance will arise solely because of variation in the expenditure, ie there will be a *fixed overhead expenditure variance*. If the actual and the budgeted expenditure are the same but the actual production varies from the budgeted production then a fixed overhead cost variance will arise solely because of a variation in the production volume, ie there will be a *fixed overhead volume variance*.

Examples:

Using the budgeted data just mentioned and assuming:

a That actual expenditure on fixed overheads is £40,250, and the actual volume of production is as budgeted, then there will be an adverse fixed overhead cost variance of £250 due solely to adverse fixed overhead expenditure of £250.

b That actual expenditure on fixed overheads is £39,600, and that the actual volume of production is as budgeted, then there will be a favourable fixed overhead cost variance of £400 due solely to favourable fixed overhead expenditure of £400.

c That the actual volume of production was 98,000 standard hours and expenditure was as budgeted then there will be an adverse fixed overhead cost variance of 2,000 standard hours at £0.40, ie £800, due solely to an adverse volume of production.

d That the actual volume of production was 101,500 standard hours and expenditure was as budgeted then there will be a favourable fixed overhead cost variance of 1,500 standard hours at £0.40, ie £600, due solely to a favourable volume of production.

In practice both actual expenditure on fixed overheads and the actual volume of production will differ from budget. The variances are calculated as follows:

a The *fixed overhead expenditure variance* = budgeted fixed overheads for the period *minus* the actual fixed overheads for the period.

b The *fixed overhead volume variance* = fixed overheads absorbed by the actual production achieved *minus* the budgeted fixed overheads.

Example:

a Budgeted fixed overheads for the year = £120,000.

b Working days in the year = 240.

c Budgeted hours per working day = 1,000.

d Budgeted annual production in standard hours (b x c) = 240,000.

e Budgeted annual production in units (d/g) = 12,000 units.

f Overhead absorption rate (a/d) = £0.50 per standard hour.

g Standard hours per unit (d/e) = 20 standard hours.

h Budgeted fixed overheads for the month (a/12) = £10,000.

j Actual production in the month = 1,050 units.

k Actual fixed overheads in the month = £10,200.

Solution:

a Fixed overhead cost variance:

> Absorbed overheads = 1,050 units x 20 standard hours per unit,
> ie 21,000 standard hours @ £0.50 = £10,500
>
> Actual overheads incurred = £10,200
> Variance = £10,500 – £10,200 = £300 (F)

b Fixed overhead expenditure variance:

> Budgeted overheads for the month = £10,000 minus actual overheads incurred
> £10,200 = £200 (A)

c Fixed overhead volume variance

> Absorbed overheads £10,500 minus budgeted overheads for the month
> £10,000 = £500 (F)

The student should notice the inter-relationships of the initial data (a) to (h). Sometimes in questions not all of this data is given, but the missing pieces can be calculated from the data which is given, eg if (f) is not given then it can be calculated from (a) and (d), and if (d) is not given then it can be calculated from (b) and (c).

Fixed overhead volume variances

The fixed overhead volume variance can be further divided into:

a fixed overhead efficiency variance;

b fixed overhead capacity variance;

c fixed overhead calendar variance.

At this level it is necessary only to understand the reasons for the fixed overhead efficiency variance and the fixed overhead capacity variance. Calculations of these variances are not required.

The volume of production can be affected, favourable or adversely, by two separate influences. The budgeted level of activity, on which the fixed overhead absorption rate has been based, assumes:

a that a certain number of hours will be worked during the budget period (ie the budgeted capacity); and

b that this number of hours will be worked at an expected level of efficiency (ie the budgeted level of labour efficiency).

In practice, of course, both the actual number of hours worked and the efficiency with which they were worked will vary from the budgeted expectations. The combinations of variations which are possible can be summarised as follows:

Number of hours worked efficiency	Level of working	Effect on volume
Greater than budget	As budget	Increased – due solely to increased capacity
Less than budget	As budget	Reduced – due solely to reduced capacity
As budget	Higher than budget	Increased – due solely to increased labour efficiency
As budget	Lower than budget	Reduced – due solely to reduced labour efficiency
Greater than budget	Greater than budget	Increased – due to both increased capacity and increased labour efficiency
Less than budget	Less than budget	Reduced – due to both reduced capacity and reduced labour efficiency
Greater than budget	Less than budget	Could be increased or reduced dependent upon which of the opposing variances is the greater
Less than budget	Greater than budget	

Example of calculations

(Calculation questions on overhead variances will not be set in the A-level examination. This section could be read to aid understanding.)

This example is based on the information used in the example in 'Fixed overhead variances', ie:

Production in month	1,050 units
Standard hours per unit	20 std hours
Absorption rate	£0.50 per std hr
Budgeted fixed overheads for year	£120,000
Actual overheads for month	£10,200
Actual hours worked	19,000

The fixed overhead volume variance (previously calculated) showed:

a Overheads budgeted for the month:

$\frac{1}{12}$ of £120,000 = £10,000
(which is also $\frac{1}{12}$ of 240,000 std hrs @ £0.50)

b Overheads absorbed by production during the month:

1,050 units @ 20 std hrs @ £0.50 = £10,500
ie volume variance = £500 (F)

Overall, the volume of production during the month was favourable, but how was this influenced by (a) capacity and (b) labour efficiency?

a *Capacity*:

The capacity available during the month was 20,000 std hrs ($\frac{1}{12}$ x 240,000 std hrs). The actual hours worked were 19,000 – ie 1,000 hours were lost. If the

1,000 hours had been worked then overhead absorption could have been improved by 1,000 std hrs @ £0.50 ie £500. The fixed overhead capacity variance is therefore £500 (A).

b *Efficiency*:

The actual hours worked were 19,000 and during this time work was produced having a standard hour content of 21,000 std hrs (ie 1,050 units @ 20 std hrs each). This produced a saving of 2,000 hours, which at £0.50 per hour produces a fixed overhead efficiency variance of £1,000 (F).

The capacity variance (£500 (A)) and the efficiency variance (£1,000 (F)) together explain the volume variance of £500 (F).

Illustration

Weston Ltd have budgeted for the financial period as follows:

Budgeted production 1,500 units
Budgeted fixed overheads £36,000

The product cost is as follows:

	(£ per unit)
Direct materials 72 lbs @ £0.50	36
Direct labour 10 hours @ £3.00	30
	66
Fixed overheads 10 hours @ £2.40	24
Total cost	£90

The actual results for the financial period were:

Fixed overheads	£37,000
Actual production	1,600 units
Actual materials	103,000 lbs @ £0.60
Actual labour	15,400 hours @ £3.10

The variances are calculated as follows:

Standard cost of actual output (1,600 units)		£
Direct materials	1,600 x 72 lbs = 115,200 lbs @ £0.50	57,600
Direct labour	1,600 x 10 hrs = 16,000 hrs @ £3.00	48,000
		105,600
Fixed overheads 16,000 hrs @ £2.40		38,400
		£144,000
Actual cost of actual production:		
Direct materials	103,000 lbs @ £0.60	61,800
Direct labour	15,400 hrs @ £3.10	47,740
		109,540
Fixed overheads		37,000
		£146,540

a Total cost variance:

    £144,000 – £146,540 =   £2,540 (A)

b Material cost variance:

    £57,600 – £61,800 =   £4,200 (A)

c Labour cost variance:

    £48,000 – £47,740 =   £260 (F)

d Fixed overhead cost variance:

    £38,400 – £37,000 =   £1,400 (F)

e Material price variance:

    £0.50 – £0.60, ie £0.10 (A) x 103,000 lbs =   £10,300 (A)

f Material usage variance:

    115,200 lbs – 103,000 lbs, ie 12,200 lbs (F) x £0.50 =   £6,100 (F)

g Labour rate variance:

    £3.00 – £3.10, ie £0.10 (A) x 15,400 hrs =   £1,540 (A)

h Labour efficiency variance:

    16,000 hrs – 15,400 hrs, ie 600 hrs (F) x £3.00 =   £1,800 (F)

i Fixed overhead expenditure variance:

    £36,000 – £37,000 =   £1,000 (A)

j Fixed overhead volume variance:

    £36,000 – £38,400   £2,400 (F)

Budgets and profit forecasts | 25

Introduction

Budgetary control is most probably the most important of all business control techniques. Budgets are financial plans, prepared in advance, which deal with all aspects of the business, and are intended to guide the business during the forthcoming period in achieving its stated objectives.

Budgets are intended to assist the business in optimising the use of its existing resources.

The budgets should be prepared by a budget committee which represents all the main functional areas of the business, eg sales, production, finance, research and development, distribution etc. Budgets will usually be prepared for sales, production, materials, labour, purchasing, stocks, debtors, creditors, capital expenditure, finance, bank, production expenses, administration expenses, selling and distribution expenses.

The advantages of budgetary control are many, including:

a the activities of a business are planned, co-ordinated and controlled;

b they create a forward thinking mentality;

c actual performance can be compared with carefully prepared budgets, and deviations from planned performance (variances can be investigated to provide explanations, leading to appropriate corrective action);

d the preparation of budgets enables problems to be foreseen, and plans for dealing with the problems can be prepared well in advance ready for when those problems arise;

e they facilitate the introduction of standard costing systems.

Cash budgets

Introduction

A cash budget is concerned with liquidity, rather than profitability. A business needs not only to earn profits, but also to be able to pay debts as they fall due. A budget, or forecast of cash requirements is therefore advisable in the ordinary course of trading and essential where expansion or capital expenditure is contemplated.

A budget is concerned with cash inflows and outflows; therefore no account is taken of sales until the debtor pays, nor of purchases or other expenditure until the business pays the creditor. As the budget deals with future events an estimate has to be made as to average periods of credit to be given and taken. A decision also has to be made as to the time-span of the budget and the intervals; a company which practised overnight lending, for example, might want a daily cash budget; whereas for many businesses a monthly one would be adequate.

Cash inflows and outflows are netted off against each other to show the net cash requirement or surplus at a given point in time. This is especially useful for indicating the maximum bank overdraft a firm will require during a period of expansion, and pinpointing when this will occur.

Method

The method to be used is to take the information available and convert it onto a cash basis. These cash transactions are then listed and totalled for the shortest time bases being used. These totals are then summarised in the format shown below.

Example:

A Brown opens up a business on 1 January with a business cash balance of £2,000. From the following information prepare a monthly cash budget for six months to 30 June which indicates the maximum overdraft required and when it will occur:

Purchases:	£4,000 in month 1, £2,000 per month thereafter
	1 month's credit allowed
Sales:	£3,000 per month. Credit given – two months
Expenses:	£200 per month payable mid-month on average

	January £	February £	March £	April £	May £	June £
Income						
Sales	–	–	3,000	3,000	3,000	3,000
Total	–	–	3,000	3,000	3,000	3,000
Expenditure						
Purchases	–	4,000	2,000	2,000	2,000	2,000
Expenses	200	200	200	2,000	200	200
Total	200	4,200	2,200	2,200	2,000	2,200
Net inflow/(outflow)	(200)	(4,200)	800	800	800	800
Opening balance b/f	2,000	1,800	(2,400)	(1,600)	(800)	–
Closing balance c/f	1,800	(2,400)	(1,600)	(800)	–	800

The maximum overdraft required will be in the region of £2,400 and it will occur in February.

Note carefully that neither sales nor purchases appear on the budget until the cash changes hands at the expiry of the credit period, eg sales made in January will not produce cash until March.

Other sources of information for cash budgets

a Opening balance sheets. When the business has just commenced it will probably be necessary for information to be taken from an opening balance sheet. The items required will be:

i   cash balance;

ii   bank balance;

iii debtors;

iv   creditors.

This will lead to further questions which must be answered for the purposes of the cash budget namely:

   i   how much of the debtors' balances will be received and when?

   ii   how much of the creditors' balances will be paid and when?

b Profit forecasts. It is often advisable for companies to forecast what their profit is likely to be in a future period. When we have this information it is highly desirable for us to use this information, which is considered by management to be fairly important and therefore will be reasonably accurate.

With only a minimum of other information a cash budget can be created.

Extension of use of cash budgets

It is possible to construct a trading and profit and loss account and balance sheet from the information given, provided the figure for closing stock, or alternatively the percentage mark-up, is known.

Assuming in this case the mark-up is 50 per cent on cost:

A Brown
Trading and Profit & Loss Account for six months ended 30 June

	£	£
Sales (6 x £3,000)		18,000
Deduct: Cost of sales:		
Purchases (£4,000 + (5 x £2,000))	14,000	
(1) *Deduct:* Closing stock	2,000	12,000
Gross profit (33⅓ x £18,000)		6,000
Expenses (6 x £200)		1,200
Net profit		£4,800

Balance Sheet as at 30 June

	£	£
Capital at 1 January		2,000
Add: Profit for period		4,800
		£6,800
Fixed assets		
Current assets:		
Stock	2,000	
(2) Debtors	6,000	
Cash	800	
	8,800	
Deduct:		
Current liabilities		
(3) Creditors	2,000	
Net current assets		£6,800

Notes:

1 The closing stock is a balancing figure.

2 Two months' sales are outstanding.

3 One month's purchases are outstanding.

Examination questions often include references to depreciation. Whilst depreciation is an expense, and is therefore included in the profit and loss account, it is not expenditure, and must *never* be included in a cash budget.

Try this illustration.

Illustration:

A new formed company, Danum Ltd, is planning its first six months' trading operations covering the period 1 January to 30 June 1995. The company makes a single product which sells at £80 per unit and budgeted production/sales for the first six months are:

1995	Budgeted production units	Budgeted sales units
January	6,000	8,000
February	7,000	8,000
March	7,500	9,000
April	9,000	9,000
May	9,000	8,500
June	9,000	8,500

To cope with expected demand in the early part of the year before production gets fully under way, the company plans to buy for cash in January from another supplier 6,500 units at a cost of £60 each.

Further information is as follows:

a One-half of the sales will be for cash and one-half will be made on one months' credit terms.

b Raw material cost per unit is £30 and each month the company will purchase enough material to meet the following month's production requirement, except that in January, enough materials will be purchased to meet the production demand of both January and February. Suppliers of material give one month's credit.

c Labour costs of £14 per unit will be incurred and monthly fixed costs (excluding depreciation) are budgeted at £200,000. Both these expenses will have to be met as incurred.

d Equipment costing £3 million will be purchased on 1 January 1995 and paid for in March, and is to be depreciated at a rate of 20 per cent per annum on cost (straight line method).

e Stocks of finished goods are to be valued on the basis of prime cost. No work-in-progress is maintained.

Required:

a Assume that the above plans are to be financed by a bank overdraft (ignore interest thereon) and prepare a monthly cash budget for the six months to 30 June 1995, showing the amount overdrawn at the end of each month.

(15 marks)

b Prepare a budgeted profit and loss account for the first six months' operations to 30 June 1995.

(10 marks)

Associated Examining Board – updated

Solution:

a

Danum Ltd
Cash Budget
6 months to June 1995

£000

		J	F	M	A	M	J
Income:	Cash sales	320	320	360	360	340	340
	Credit sales	–	320	320	360	360	340
	Sub total	£320	£640	£680	£720	£700	£680
Payments:							
Purchases:	Units	390					
	Materials	–	390	225	270	270	270
	Labour	84	98	105	26	126	126
	Fixed	200	200	200	200	200	200
	Equipment	–	–	3,000	–	–	–
	Sub total	£674	£688	£3,530	£596	£596	£596
Surplus/(deficit)		(354)	(48)	(2,850)	124	104	84
Balance b/fwd		–	(354)	(402)	(3,252)	(3,128)	(3,024)
Balance c/fwd		£(354)	£(402)	£(3,252)	£(3,128)	£(3,024)	£(2,940)

b

Danum Ltd
Budged Profit & Loss Account for 6 months ended 30 June 1995

		£000	£000
Sales			4,080
Purchases:	Units (note 1)	390	
	Materials	1,425	
Direct wages		665	
		2,480	
Closing stock 3,000 units @ (£30 + £14) (note I)		132	
Cost of sales			2,348
Gross profit			1,732
Fixed costs		1,200	
Depreciation		300	
Net profit			1,500
			£232

Note 1: the raw material purchases should include the production for July (which the question does not give). However, the cost of sales is unaffected because the closing stock should also include raw materials for the next month's production.

Problem

Problem 25.1

The balance sheet of Sandforth Ltd at 31 May 1994 was as follows:

	£		£	£
Ordinary shares of £1 each	6,000	*Fixed assets*		
Retained earnings	2,200	Plant at cost	5,000	
		Less: Depreciation	1,800	3,200
	8,200			
Current liabilities		*Current assets*		
		Stock	4,400	
		Trade debtors	5,600	
Trade creditors & accruals	9,300	Bank	5,300	
Proposed dividend	1,000			15,300
	£18,500			£18,500

The company is developing a system of budgetary control and on 1 June 1994 provides the following information:

a

Month	Credit sales £	Cash sales £	Credit purchases £
May 1994 (actual)	5,600	2,800	9,000
June 1994 (budgeted)	6,700	4,000	9,500
July 1994 (budgeted)	8,200	4,500	10,000
August 1994 (budgeted)	8,000	4,500	10,400

b All trade creditors will be paid in the month following receipt of the goods and all trade debtors will be allowed (and take) one month's credit.

c On 1 June 1994 plant which cost £2,000 (accumulated depreciation to date £800) was replaced by new plant costing £6,000. A trade in allowance of £1,400 was given on the old plant and the balance due will be paid on 1 July 1994. Depreciation is to be provided on plant at 12 per cent per annum on cost (calculated monthly).

d The following expenses, to be paid monthly in cash, are estimated to arise:

Wages £900 per month
General expenses £350 per month

e Rent is £1,800 per year, payable in full in June 1994, for the year to 31 March 1995.

f The proposed dividend will be paid in July 1994.

g The gross profit/sales ratio is estimated at 20 per cent.

Required:

a A cash budget for each of the three months June, July and August 1994, showing clearly the bank balance (debit or credit) at the end of each month.

(13 marks)

b A budgeted trading and profit and loss account for the three months to 31 August 1994.

(12 marks)

Associated Examining Board – updated

Profit and loss budgets

Introduction

The general format of questions in this area is to give the examinee the latest profit and loss account and balance sheet with information as to how things will change. Often one figure, such as the budgeted closing bank balance, is missing and hence must be found by balance (after preparation of everything else).

Note in the following illustration that it is the debenture issue figure which is not given.

Illustration:

The summarised accounts of Greenday Ltd for the year ended 31 December 1993 are as follows:

Trading and Profit & Loss Account for the year ended 31 December 1993

		£000s	£000s
Sales			600
Cost of sales: Stock at 1 January 1993		17	
Purchases		356	
		373	
Stock at 31 December 1993		13	360
Gross profit			240
Establishment expenses			25
Administrative expenses			54
Depreciation – fixed assets		27	106
Net profit carried forward			£144

Balance Sheet as at 31 December 1993

		£000s	£000s
Ordinary shares of £1 each fully paid			100
Retained earnings			95
			£195
Fixed assets:	At cost	270	
	Less: Aggregate depreciation	108	162
Current assets:	Stock in trade	13	
	Trade debtors	50	
	Balance at bank	14	
		£77	
Less:	Current liabilities:		
	Trade creditors	34	
	Expense creditors	10	
		£44	33
			£195

Illustration:

The company's budget for the year ending 31 December 1994, is based on the following assumptions:

a All sales will continue to be on a credit basis, however the credit period allowed to customers will be extended to two months.

b Unit selling prices will be reduced by 10 per cent, but the volume of sales will increase by 20 per cent as compared with 1993.

c The average rate of stock turnover will be the same as for 1993.

d The cost of all sales will be at the same unit prices as in 1993.

e Additions to fixed assets will be purchased at a cost of £100,000; there will be no dispoosals of fixed assets.

f Establishment expenses will be increased by £20,000.

g Administrative expenses will be increased by 50 per cent compared with 1993.

h Provision for depreciation of fixed assets will continue to be on the straight line basis on the assets held at the relevant accounting year end.

i Current liabilities at 31 December 1994 will be:

Trade creditors   £43,000
Expense creditors   £15,000

j The balance at bank at 31 December 1994 will be the same as a year earlier.

k There will be no dividends paid or proposed for 1994.

l It is proposed to make an issue of 8 per cent debentures, at par, in December 1994 sufficient to permit these budget plans to be achieved.

Note: ignore interest on the debentures in the budgeted accounts for the year ending 31 December 1994.

Required:

a The budgeted trading and profit and loss account for the year ending 31 December 1994.

(13 marks)

b The budgeted balance sheet at 31 December 1994.

(12 marks)

Associated Examining Board – updated

Solution:

Greenday Ltd
Budgeted Trading, Profit & Loss Account
for the year ended 31 December 1994

			£000		£000
Sales		(1)			648
Stock 1.1.94			13		
Purchases			442		
			455		
Stock 31.12.94		(4)	23		
Cost of sales		(3)			432
Gross profit			216		
Expenses:	Establishment		45		
	Administrative		81		
	Depreciation	(5)	37		163
Net profit					£53

Balance Sheet as at 31 December 1994

		£000	£000	£000
Ordinary £1 shares, fully paid				100
Retained earnings 1.1.94			95	
Profit for year			53	
Retained earnings 31.12.94				148
				248
8% Debentures (by balance)				64
				£312
Represented by:				
Fixed assets:	At cost			370
	Depreciation			145
				225
Current assets:	Stock		23	
	Debtors (2)		108	
	Bank		14	
			145	
Current liabilities:	Trade creditors	43		
	Expense creditors	15	58	87
Net current assets				312

Notes:

1 $600 - 10\% \times 600 = 540$

$540 + 20\% \times 540 = 648$

2 Two months' credit $= 648/6 = 108$

3 Volume increased by 20% but same unit price therefore cost of sales $= 360 + 20\% \times 360 = 432$

4 Av. stock at 31.12.93 $= \dfrac{17 + 13}{2} = 15$

Av. stock t/o at 31.12.93 $= \dfrac{3\ 60}{15} = 24$

As stock t/o at 31.12.94 is the same (ie 24) then closing stock = $\frac{432 \times 2 - 13}{24} = 23$

5 Depreciation = $\frac{27}{270}$ or 10%

Years depreciation = 10% x 370 = 37

Problems

Problem 25.2

The accounts of Abba Ltd for the year ended 31 December 1993 were as follows:

Trading and Profit & Loss Account for the year ended 31 December 1993

	£000s	£000s
Sales (all on credit terms)		300
Cost of sales Stock, 1 January 1994	45	
Purchases	210	
	255	
Stock, 31 December 1994	55	200
Gross profit		100
Wages	23	
Overhead expenses	12	
Depreciation	30	65
Net profit for the year carried forward		£35

Balance Sheet as at 31 December 1993

	£000s	£000s
Ordinary shares of £1 each, fully paid		200
Profit & loss a/c	102	
Current liabilities: Trade creditors	35	
Expense creditors	2	37
		£339
Fixed assets at cost	300	
Less: Aggregate depreciation	(90)	210
Current assets: Stock	55	
Debtors	50	
Bank	24	129
		£339

The directors propose, for 1994, that:

a Selling price per unit shall be reduced by one-ninth. Consequent on this price reduction, sales revenue will double to £600,000 but the purchase price per unit will remain the same as in 1993.

b The average rate of stock turnover will increase by 50 per cent.

c Wages will increase by 100% and other expenses by 50 per cent.

d Additional fixed assets will be acquired at a cost of £80,000. Depreciation will be provided (as in 1993) at the rate of 10 per cent per annum on the cost of fixed assets held at the year end. No fixed assets will be sold.

e One month's additional credit will be allowed on average to debtors, but all creditors will allow the same period of credit as in 1993.

f The ratio of quick assets (current assets excluding stock) to current liabilities will be the same at the end of 1994 as at the end of 1993. The budgeted amount of cash at bank is to be ascertained by application of this ratio.

g Any additional finance required to meet these plans will be provided by long-term interest free loans from the directors. The directors propose to invest £82,000 by way of such loans.

h No dividends were paid or were to be proposed in either year.

Required:

a Prepare, from the forecasts above, a budgeted trading and profit and loss account for the year ended 31 December 1994.

(11 marks)

b A budgeted balance sheet at 31 December 1994.

(14 marks)

Note: all calculations should be to the nearest thousand pounds.

Associated Examining Board – updated

Problem 25.3

The summarised balance sheet at 31 October 1993, of Keensuppliers Ltd is as follows:

	£		£	£
Ordinary share capital	30,000	Freehold premises		
		at cost		20,000
Share premium account	4,700	Fixtures and fittings:		
	34,700	At cost	6,000	
		Less: Depreciation		
		to date	1,800	4,200
Less: Profit & loss a/c	5,700			
	29,000	Trading stock	7,800	
Bank overdraft	5,000	Trade debtors	7,200	
Trade creditors	5,200			15,000
	£39,200			£39,200

The company is now reviewing its activities with a view to improving performance as far as profit is concerned.

The following budgeted information relates to the forthcoming financial year ending 31 October 1994:

a The cost of goods sold will be 80 per cent of sales revenue throughout the year.

b Fixed overheads will be:

Rates, heat and light	£4,000
Basic salaries	£10,000
General administration	£6,100

c   Staff bonuses will be 5 per cent of gross profit.

d   Cash sales will be £50,000, the remainder will be paid at the end of the month following the month of sale.

e   Depreciation policies:

> Freehold premises – nil.
> Fixtures and fittings – 10 per cent on the cost of assets held at the accounting year end.

f   It is considered it will be necessary to obtain some additional shelving (fixtures and fittings) in January 1994 at an estimated cost of £2,000.

g   Trade suppliers give two months' credit; it can be assumed that all overheads, staff bonuses and the additional shelving will be the subject of cash transactions.

h   All trading transactions will take place at an even rate throughout the year.

i   Trading stock at 31 October 1994, will be 5 per cent of cost of goods sold during the year. It is assumed that all trade debtors and trade creditors at 31 October 1994, will be settled in November 1994.

It is not planned to declare any dividends for the forthcoming year. Ignore bank overdraft interest and taxation.

The directors, who still see very difficult times ahead, are considering two alternative plans for the year to 31 October 1994:

Plan A: To increase sales so that after taking all costs and expenses into account, they will just break even (ie the net profit will be nil).

Plan B: To increase sales so that, after taking all costs and expenses into account, they will make enough profit to extinguish the present debit balance on the profit and loss account.

Note: assume the financial year consists of 12 months of equal duration.

Required:

a   The estimated trading and profit and loss account for the year ending 31 October 1994, and the estimated balance sheet at that date if Plan A is followed.

b   A computation of the sales for the year ending 31 October 1994, and trade creditors at that date if Plan B is followed.

(25 marks)
Associated Examining Board – updated

Flexible budgets

Flexible budgets are similar to ordinary budgets but are a more useful control medium.

For example, the following is a budget for a firm at the 100 per cent activity level (theoretically maximum production).

		£000
Costs:	Direct materials	40
	Direct labour	100
	Production overheads	60
	Admin overheads	100
	Selling overheads	100
		£500

Suppose you are told that the firm actually produced at the 75 per cent activity level and achieved the following actual costs:

		£000
Costs:	Direct materials	120
	Direct labour	60
	Production overhead	55
	Admin overheads	110
	Selling overheads	95
		£440

It would appear that the firm had done well in the direct materials, labour, production overhead and selling overheads, but badly in admin overheads and that overall £60,000 had been saved over the budgeted total.

Very good but totally untrue!

If you were to be told that the following costs were variable:

direct material
direct labour
$\frac{2}{3}$ of production overhead at 100 per cent activity level
$\frac{1}{3}$ of selling overhead at 100 per cent activity level

you would be able to compile a budget for the 75 per cent activity level as follows:

		£000	£000
Direct materials			105
Direct labour			75
Production overhead:	Fixed	20	
	Variable	30	50
Admin overhead:	Fixed	100	
Selling overhead:	Fixed	80	
	Variable	15	195
			£425

Now let us compare the two:

	Actual £	Budget £
Direct material	120	105
Direct labour	60	75
Production overheads	55	50
Admin overheads	110	100
Selling overheads	95	95
	£440	£425

It can now be seen that direct materials, production overheads and admin costs have overspent whereas selling overheads is exactly as it should be. The only saving has been in labour and the firm has overspent by £15,000 in total.

Try this illustration.

Illustration:

The annual flexible budget for Boot Ltd, is as follows:

Level of activity	40%	60%	75%	100%
Costs:	£000s	£000s	£000s	£000s
Direct labour	208	312	390	520
Direct material	128	192	240	320
Production overhead	92	108	120	140
Administration, selling and				
distribution overheads	56	64	70	80
	£484	£676	£820	£1,060

Depressed trading conditions have caused management to consider whether the factory should be closed down temporarily and re-opened to coincide with the anticipated upsurge in demand expected sometime in the following year. Current production output is only 50 per cent of capacity with a forecast annual sales revenue of £500,000 at that level of production. Informed sources forecast that in the 12 months following the re-opening date, sales could run at 80 per cent of capacity.

Required: a financial statement showing the variable costs, contribution, fixed costs, and profit and loss at 50 per cent and 80 per cent levels of activity.

(16 marks)

Solution:

Boot Ltd

Variable costs, contribution, fixed costs, profits and losses

	Activity			
	50%		80%	
	£000	£000	£000	£000
Sales revenue		500		800
Variable costs:				
Labour	260		416	
Material	160		256	
Product overhead (1)	40		64	
Admin selling etc (2) overhead	20	480	32	768
Contribution		20		32
Fixed costs:				
Production overhead (1)	60		60	
Admin, etc overhead (2)	40	100	40	100
		£(80)		£(68)

Notes:

		Activity		Difference
		75%	100%	
1	Production overhead	120	140	20
2	Admin, etc overhead	70	80	10

The difference must represent entirely variable costs as fixed costs are constant. Thus an increase in 25 per cent activity increases variable costs by £20,000 and £10,000 respectively.

Therefore, at the 100 per cent activity level, variable costs must be £80,000 and £40,000 respectively, leaving fixed costs of £60,000 (150,000 – 80,000) and £40,000 (80,000 – 40,000) respectively.

Introduction to inflation accounting | 26

Introduction

As can be seen by everyone, prices for goods and services have been rising in recent years. These price rises can have dramatic effects on businesses in several ways.

Effects of inflation

On 1.1.94 a man buys 50 shirts at £2 each and during the year to 31.12.90 he sells them at £5 each. On 1.1.95 he purchases 50 more shirts but this time they cost him £3 each.

Compare the situations

	No. of shirts	Cash
1.1.94	50	Nil
1.1.95	50	£100

It can be seen that at the end of 1.1.95 the increase in the man's wealth was £100 (sales of £250 less £150 to buy the new shirts).

Now consider his profit and loss account.

	£
Sales (50 @ £5)	250
Cost of sales (50 @ £2)	100
Profit	£150

His profit and loss account tells him he has made £150 but in real terms he has increased his wealth by only £100.

Consequently, inflation affects the cost of sales of items in that it tends to cause their understatement (in real terms) and hence overstates profits.

Consider now a man who buys a lorry for £8,000 on 1.1.91. His profits before depreciation in the years to 31.12.91, 92, 93 and 94 were £5,000 each year. The lorry has no value and on 1.1.95 he scraps it and buys another identical to the first, for £12,000.

Compare his situation at the beginning and end of the four years.

	No. of lorries	Cash
1.1.91	One	Nil
1.1.95	One	£8,000

Now look at his profit and loss for those four years:

	91 £	92 £	93 £	94 £
Profits	5,000	5,000	5,000	5,000
Depreciation	2,000	2,000	2,000	2,000
	£3,000	£3,000	£3,000	£3,000

His profit and loss tells him he earned £12,000 but his wealth has increased by only £8,000 in real terms.

Consequently, inflation tends to overstate profits because the depreciation charge is insufficient to cover the replacement cost of the lorry.

Problem

Problem 26.1

A and B are keen rival traders in Megs, a consumer good; A's business is long established whilst B commenced trading on 1 January 1994.

The activities of A and B for the year ended 31 December 1994 are compared in the following summarised results:

A			**B**	
£	£		£	£
	40,000	Sales (1,000 Megs)		40,000
		Less: Cost of sales		
20,000		Opening stock	nil	
nil		Purchases	20,000	
10,000	10,000	*Less:* Closing stock	nil	20,000
	30,000	Gross profit		20,000
5,000		*Less:* General overheads	5,000	
1,000	6,000	Depreciation	2,000	7,000
	£24,000	Net profit		£13,000
	£48,000	Net capital employed		£104,000

Both A and B use similar premises and equipment. However, B is not at all pleased with his results especially as he considers that he has worked equally as hard as A. Relations between A and B are not helped when the experienced A announces that his net profit of £24,000 justifies cash drawings of £20,000 for the purchase of a country cottage.

Required:

a The two main reasons for the apparent difference between the results of A and B for 1994.

b To what extent is A justified in his decision to have cash drawings of £20,000?

(25 marks)

Associated Examining Board – updated

Contract costing | 27

Introduction

Contract costing is a form of 'specific order costing' – it is in effect job costing on a large scale.

Applications

Contract costing methods may be used in the following industries:

a building and contracting;

b civil engineering;

c shipbuilding;

d aircraft manufacture.

Special features

The special features of contract costing are:

a The contractor carries out a small number of large contracts in the course of a year.

b The contracts may continue over more than one accounting period or financial year.

c The contracts are carried out away from the contractor's main premises, with perhaps some assemblies prepared at the premises, eg window and door frames, pre-cast concrete frames, roof trusses, steelwork.

d Since the contracts are physically separate (ie one contract may be for the construction of a hospital, another for a length of motorway, another for a housing estate, etc) it is usually possible to identify a greater proportion of costs as direct costs.

e Materials may be purchased and delivered direct to the contract site and/or drawn from the central stores at the contractor's premises.

f Specialist sub-contractors may be employed, eg ventilation engineers, lift manufacturers, electricians, plasterers, flooring and ceiling specialists.

g Plant and equipment may be purchased, or hired for the duration of the contract from another business or from a central plant department.

h In the case of long-term contracts (ie exceeding one year in duration) the contract may be broken down into separate stages, each of which is payable separately.

i Penalties may be incurred by the contractor for failing to complete the work in the agreed time.

j The contract price is normally estimated in advance. Additional work found necessary may be charged on a cost plus basis. In addition clauses may be inserted into the contract to permit the contractor to pass on to the client additional costs incurred as a result of wage awards, etc.

k The payroll may be prepared at either the site or at a central administrative office.

Cost units

Although the contract itself can be regarded as a cost unit, sub-units will normally be required for purposes of cost analysis and progress payments. These will form natural divisions of the work, eg in a contract for the building of factory premises the work might be sub-divided into the following stages:

Stage 1 Foundations and drainage.
     2 Steelworks.
     3 Walls.
     4 Roof.
     5 Electrical installations.
     6 Plumbing and glazing.
     7 Floors and ceilings.
     8 Carpentry, painting and decorating.

Certification of work completed

a If a contractor who is engaged on long-term contracts did not receive payment until completion of the whole contract then his financial resources are likely to be severely strained. This is one of the reasons why long-term contracts are broken down into the stages as illustrated above.

b On completion of each stage of the contract the architects acting for the contractee will issue a certificate to the contractor which certifies the value of the work performed so far. This certificate in effect acts as an invoice from the contractor to the contractee.

c The certified value (in effect the resale value) will be debited to an account in the name of the client and credited to the contract account.

d Contracts frequently provide that a percentage of the total value of the certificate may be withheld from payment by the contractee until shortly after completion of the contract. The purpose of this deduction, called retention money, is to place the contractee in a favourable position should faulty work be discovered or penalties become payable by reason of late completion of the contract.

e At the end of the retention period the contractee's architect will ensure that any faults or defects which have come to light have been remedied before he authorises the release of the retention monies.

f The amounts of retention monies may be carried forward on the contractee's account *or* transferred to a separate retentions account.

g The main contractor may withhold retention monies when paying sub-contractors.

Sub-contract work

a It is common practice for a contractor to sub-contract certain types of specialist work, eg electrical installations, the installation of floors, ceilings and lifts.

b If the work of the sub-contractor extends over an appreciable period of time then he too may require progress payments from the main contractor. The sub-contract may permit the main contractor to deduct retentions.

c The contractor must ensure that the full value of sub-contracted work is charged to the contract account.

d Provisions must be made in the contract account for items not charged by the sub-contractor, otherwise the main contractor's profit may be overstated. Main contractors do sometimes have difficulty in getting accurate and up-to-date information from sub-contractors.

Issue of materials

Materials may be issued to a contract in any of several ways:

a Purchased specifically for a contract and delivered direct to the contract.

b Delivered to a central stores, and from there issued to various contracts or to a fabrication department.

c Issued from a fabrication department, eg doors and window frames.

d Transferred from other contracts.

Extras

a In many contracts modifications, additional work or variations from the original specifications may be required by the client. This work will be the subject of a separate charge.

b It is important to separate the expenditure on extras from that of the main contract so that it can be charged to the client separately.

Plant

a Where plant is purchased careful records must be maintained to ensure that none is lost or improperly disposed of, and that the contract is duly charged for the use of plant.

b A plant register should be kept and careful records maintained of all movements between individual sites and also between the central yard and sites.

c A complete physical inventory of all plant should be made at suitable intervals, all discrepancies being investigated.

d The following methods are in use for charging contracts for the use of plant:

   i The cost of the plant issued to the site (or the written down value) may be charged direct to the contract account.

   ii A charge for the hire of the plant may be made to each contract, based upon the time the plant is in use.

e The advantages of method (ii) above are:

   i Full deployment of the plant is encouraged as the site foreman will not want to be charged for plant standing idle.

   ii It will be possible to compare the economics of purchase against hire.

   iii If the rate issued is the market rate then the efficiency of the plant department can be established.

f The rate used may include all charges for plant, ie driver, fuel, lubricants, insurance, maintenance and repairs, plant, office costs, depreciation. The rate may be divided between standing costs charged on a weekly basis, and running costs charged on an hourly basis.

g Plant operating costs will be debited to a plant operating account, which will be credited with the hiring charges made to individual contracts.

h It will be necessary to set up a provision account for unrealised profit, ie in respect of plant charges included in work-in-progress, as any profit on the plant account is internal to the contractor's business.

i The contractor may hire out some of his own plant where surplus capacity exists.

Calculation of profit on uncompleted contracts

a A distinction needs to be made between (i) short period contracts, ie of one year's duration or less, and (ii) long period contracts, ie of more than one year's duration.

b It may be relatively easy to determine the total cost, and hence the total profit of a short period contract, but in the case of a long-term contract it may be extremely difficult to predict total costs accurately until the contract is completed. Furthermore, the contracting industry is a hazardous one – extra unanticipated costs may be incurred by the contractor because, for example, of unknown geological faults, adverse weather conditions, constructional delays, faulty materials or faulty workmanship, unreliable sub-contractors, increased costs. The longer the period of the contract then the more likely is the contract to be affected by such adverse factors. (Note: every year there are more bankruptcies and liquidations in the building and contracting industry than in any other.)

c Because of the hazardous nature of the industry there has been an accepted principle that a prudent and conservative attitude should be taken in the calculation of profits earned at an intermediate stage during a complicated long-term constructional contract. The attitudes of individual firms have varied:

   i   some firms have not taken account of any profit until the contract has been completed;

   ii   some firms have not taken any profit until the contract is nearing completion and the remaining costs and the financial outcomes can be foreseen with reasonable accuracy;

   iii   some firms have calculated a notional profit at the end of each accounting period which has then been reduced by a pre-determined percentage to allow for unseen hazards and contingencies.

d An attempt has been made to standardise the valuation of work-in-progress on long-term constructional contracts (and thereby to standardise the computation of intermediate profits) by the publication by the Accounting Standards Committee of a Statement of Standard Accounting Practice (SSAP 9) effective from 1 January 1976.

e The accounting standard mentioned above needs to be read fully in order to fully appreciate its requirements. But briefly what it requires is that where a contract (a) is a long-term contract, and (b) the outcome of that contract can be assessed with reasonable certainty before its conclusion, then the profit attributable to the period of the contract which has elapsed should be reported in the accounts for that period – but the judgment involved should be exercised with prudence.

f Many constructional firms have, since 1976, disregarded this accounting standard by refusing to take credit for profits earned before completion, with the consequence that their accounts have been qualified by their auditors.

g The way in which profits earned to date are calculated varies in practice according to the nature of the contract. But a method which is commonly demonstrated in textbooks, and which the student should use, is as follows:

   i   the total costs expended on, or attributable to, the contract to date are calculated;

ii   the contract is credited with the value of unused material stocks;

iii the balance represents the cost of all work done to date;

iv   from this cost is deducted the cost of work which has been done but *not* certified by the architect;

v   the balance represents therefore the cost of work done which *has* been certified;

vi   this cost is deducted from the total value of work which has been certified by the architects;

vii the difference represents the total notional profit earned to date;

viii this notional profit is then reduced to $\frac{2}{3}$ of its amount to allow for unforeseen costs and contingencies;

ix   the remaining $\frac{2}{3}$ notional profit is further reduced by a fraction which is:

$$\frac{\text{amounts paid by contracts to date}}{\text{total value of work certified}}$$

eg if the contractee's retentions are at the rate of 10 per cent then this fraction will be $\frac{9}{10}$, and overall the notional profit would be reduced to $\frac{9}{10} \times \frac{2}{3} = \frac{3}{5}$.

Example:

A contractor has undertaken a long-term contract worth £400,000. At the end of his current accounting period the total costs of all work done amounts to £140,000, of which £20,000 relates to work which has not been certified. The client's architects have issued certificates to the value of £150,000 against which the client has paid 90 per cent.

Value of certificates issued		£150,000
Total costs incurred	£140,000	
Less work done not certified	£20,000	
Cost of work certified		£120,000

£30,000 x $\frac{2}{3}$ = £20,000

£20,000 x $\dfrac{£135,000}{£150,000}$ = £18,000

or

£30,000 x $\dfrac{2}{3}$ x $\dfrac{£135,000}{£150,000}$ = £18,000

h Where a loss arises on a long-term contract then the whole of the loss should be written off against profit and loss account as soon as the loss is known together with adequate provision for any other anticipated losses.

i When a contract is nearing completion and the expenditure required to complete can be estimated with reasonable accuracy then the anticipated total profit can be calculated as follows:

i   ascertain the total expenditure to date;

ii   add to this the anticipated expenditure required to complete;

iii add any adequate provision for contingencies

iv deduct this figure (ie total estimated expenditure) from the total contract price to arrive at the estimated total profit on completion.

j Only a proportion of the profit so ascertained should be taken to profit and loss account. This may be computed in one of two ways:

i by dividing the total estimated profit in the proportion which the total of the certificates issued to date bears to the total contract price (ie in accordance with 'sales values');

ii by dividing the total estimated profit in the proportion which the cost of the work so far peformed bears to the estimated total cost.

(See the example below which is taken from *Cost Accounts*, 9th edn, by Walter W. Bigg.)

Illustration

The contractor must show in his balance sheet the value of the work carried out to date, which will be shown as work-in-progress.

Example:
At 31 December, £97,000 has been expended upon a contract and certificates have been received to date to the value of £110,000. The cost of work performed, but not yet certified, is £3,000. Up to the end of the previous year profit of £6,000 had been taken on the contract. It is estimated that the contract will take a further three months to complete and that it will necessitate the additional expenditure of £20,000. The total estimated expenditure upon the contract is to include a provision of 2½ per cent for contingencies. The contract price is £140,000, and £100,000 has been received in cash to date.

The proportion of profit to be taken to the credit of profit and loss account at 31 December is ascertained as follows:

	£
Total expenditure to date	£97,000
Estimated additional expenditure	20,000
	117,000
Provision for contingencies (2½%on total estimated expenditure)	
= $\frac{2.5}{97.5}$ of £117,000)	3,000
	£120,000
Contract price	140,000
Estimated total expenditure	120,000
Estimated total profit	£20,000

The cumulative profit taken to the profit and loss account to 31 December would be:

First method:

$$\frac{\text{Value of work certified}}{\text{Contract price}} \quad = \quad \frac{£110,000}{£140,000} \times £20,000 = £15,714$$

Second method:

$$\frac{\text{Cost of work to date}}{\text{Estimated total cost}} \quad = \quad \frac{£97,000}{£120,000} \times £20,000 = £16,167$$

The profit credited to the profit and loss account for the year would be either of these figures less £6,000 which has already been credited for previous years. If required the above profits could be reduced as follows:

First method:

$$\frac{\text{Cash received}}{\text{Work certified}} \quad = \quad \frac{£100,000 \times £15,714 = £14,286}{£110,000}$$

or

Second method:

$$\frac{\text{Cash received}}{\text{Work certified}} \quad = \quad \frac{£100,000 \times £16,167 = £14,698}{£110,000}$$

b This will be made up of the total cost of work done less cash received on account plus any profit taken.

c Using the data in the previous section this would appear:

	£
Total costs incurred to date	140,000
Less: Payments received from client	135,000
	5,000
Plus: Portion of notional profit	18,000
Value of work-in-progress	£23,000

This could alternatively be calculated:

	£
Work not certified	20,000
Add: Amount owing by client	15,000
	35,000
Less: Provision for profits c/f	12,000
Value of work-in-progress	£23,000

Specimen question and answer

A contractor is building swimming baths for the Westchester Corporation. The following data relates to the financial period just ended:

	£
Materials stock b/f	4,000
Materials issued from stores	6,500
Materials delivered direct by suppliers	7,400
Materials returned from contract to stores	750
Direct labour costs paid	3,800
Direct labour costs accrued	650
Indirect labour costs paid	1,450
Indirect labour costs accrued	300
Plant issued to site, at cost	17,000
Plant on site at period end, at valuation	16,600
Overhead costs incurred	5,150
Materials on site at period end, c/f	4,900
Cost of work completed not certified	6,000
Value of certificates issued by the client's architects for work completed	21,600

The client has paid the amount due less retentions of 10 per cent.
The profit earned to date should be reduced:

a to ⅔ of its amount, and further reduced;

b by a fraction which the amounts paid to date by the client bear to the total value of the work completed and certified to date.

Prepare:

a contract account;

b client's account;

c balance sheet (extracts).

Solution:

Contract Account

DR			Swimming Baths for Westchester Corporation	CR
	£	£		£
Direct materials			Cost of work completed to	
Comm. stock	4,000		date c/f	24,000
Ex stores	6,500			
Return to store	(750)			
Ex suppliers	7,400			
	17,150			
Closing stock	4,900	12,250		
Direct labour	3,800			
Accrual	650	4,450		
Indirect labour	1,450			
Accrual	300	1,750		
Overheads		5,150		
Plant issued to site:				
At cost	17,000			
At valuation c/f	16,600	400		
		£24,000		£24,000
Cost of work completed b/f		24,000	Cost of work completed but	
			not certified c/f	6,000
Profit to date:			Client's a/c – valuation of	
Transfer to profit &			work certified to date	21,600
loss a/c	2,160			
Carried forward	1,440	3,600		
		£27,600		£27,600
Materials stock b/f		4,900	Accruals b/f	
Cost of work not certified b/f		6,000	Direct labour	650
Plant, at valuation, b/f		16,600	Indirect labour	300	950
			Profit provision b/f	1,440

Westchester Corporation

	£			£
Contract account:			Bank	19,440
Value of work certified	21,600		Retentions c/f	2,160
	£21,600			£21,600
Retentions b/f	2,160			

Balance Sheet (Extract)

	£		£	£	£
		Fixed assets			
		Plant at cost		17,000	
		Less: Cumulative			
		depreciation		400	
					16,600
Current liabilities		*Current assets*			
Accruals	950	Raw materials		4,900	
		Work-in-progress			
		not certified	6,000		
		Less: Profits			
		provision	1,440		
			4,560		
		Retentions	2,160		
			6,720		
				6,720	
					11,620

Calculation of profits

	£	£
Value of work certified		£21,600
Cost of work completed	£24,000	
Cost of work not certified	£6,000	
Cost of work certified		£18,000
Total profit to date		£3,600
Profit taken (x ⅔ x £19,440)		£2,160
£21,600		
Profit carried forward		£1,440

Specimen question and answer

Timberplan Ltd commenced business on 1 January 1992, as sole erectors of the Timbercraft 'factory built' bungalow which is assembled on customers' sites at a price of £30,000 each.

The cost of manufacturing and erecting a Timbercraft bungalow is £24,000 approximately although this is subject to variation according to individual site locations and conditions.

The marketing of the Timbercraft bungalow is through local agents who are paid a commission of £400 for each bungalow sold; the commission is paid immediately a firm order is received.

Timberplan Ltd's customers are required to pay for their bungalow on the following basis:

Per bungalow	£
On placing order	3,000
When site work commences	4,000
On completion of erection	21,000
Six months after erection is completed	2,000

The company's work-in-progress is valued at each accounting year end (31 December) according to the proportion of the total work done on each bungalow under construction. The work in progress valuation is determined by applying that proportion to the sale price of the bungalow, eg:

Bungalow being built for Mr Smith – sale price £30,000
Bungalow estimated to be 75% complete

Therefore work-in-progress valuation = $\frac{75}{100}$ x £30,000 = £22,500

The company's activities during the three years ended 31 December 1994, are summarised as follows:

a Number of bungalows

	Orders received	Orders commenced	Orders completed
1992	4	3	3
1993	3	3	2
1994	2	3	4

b

Year	Bungalow number	Percentage work done in year	Month of completion	Building costs incurred in year
1992	1	100	June	23,000
	2	100	August	24,500
	3	100	September	24,100
	4	–	–	
1993	4	100	March	23,900
	5	100	April	24,300
	6	40	–	9,400
	7	20	–	4,700
1994	6	60	February	14,300
	7	80	May	18,900
	8	100	September	24,300
	9	100	December	24,200

c The company's administrative expenses incurred and paid in each financial year amounted to £7,000.

d All cash transactions occurred on the due dates.

Required:

a Alternative revenue accounts for each of the years 1992, 1993 and 1994:

  i on the basis of the company's work-in-progress valuation policy;

  ii on the basis of valuing the company's work-in-progress valuation on actual building costs.

(16 marks)

b A concise report commenting on the relative success of the company in each of the years under review.

(9 marks)

Associated Examining Board – updated

Solution:

Timberplan Ltd

DR		Bank Account		CR
	£			£
1992				
Orders received (4 x £3,000)	12,000	Building costs		71,600
Orders commenced (3 x £4,000)	12,000	Administration expenses		7,000
Orders completed (3 x £21,000)	63,000	Commission (4 x £400)		1,600
Final payments (1 x £2,000)	2,000	Balance c/d		8,800
	£89,000			£89,000
1993				
Balance b/d	8,800	Building costs		62,300
Orders received (3 x £3,000)	9,000	Administration expenses		7,000
Orders commenced (3 x £4,000)	12,000	Commissions (3 x £400)		1,200
Orders completed (2 x £21,000)	42,000	Balance c/d		9,300
Final payments (4 x £2,000)	8,000			
	£79,800			£79,800
1994				
Balance b/d	9,300	Building costs		81,700
Orders received (2 x £3,000)	6,000	Administration expenses		7,000
Orders commenced (3 x £4,000)	12,000	Commissions (2 x £400)		800
Orders completed (4 x £21,000)	84,000	Balance c/d		25,800
Final payments (2 x £2,000)	4,000			
	£115,300			£115,300
1995				
Balance b/d	25,800			

DR		Customers Account		CR
	£			£
1992				
Contract account	90,000	Bank		89,000
Advance payments c/f	3,000	Payments due c/f		4,000
	£93,000			£93,000
1993				
Payments due b/f	4,000	Advance payments b/f		3,000
Contract account	60,000	Bank		71,000
Advance payments c/f	10,000			
	£74,000			£74,000
1994				
Contract account	120,000	Advance payments b/f		10,000
		Bank		106,000
		Payments due c/f		4,000
	£120,000			£120,000
1995				
Payments due b/f	4,000			

Contract Account
Basis (1)

DR	£		CR	£
1992				
Building costs bungalow 1	23,000	Customers		90,000
Building costs bungalow 2	24,500	Work-in-progress c/d		nil
Building costs bungalow 3	24,100			
Administration expenses	7,000			
Commissions	1,600			
Profit & loss a/c	9,800			
	£90,000			£90,000
1993				
Work-in-progress b/d	nil	Customers		60,000
Building costs bungalow 4	23,900	Work-in-progress c/d		18,000
Building costs bungalow 5	24,300			
Building costs bungalow 6	9,400			
Building costs bungalow 7	4,700			
Administration expenses	7,000			
Commissions	1,200			
Profit & loss a/c	7,500			
	£78,000			£78,000
1994				
Work-in-progress b/d	18,000	Customers		120,000
Building costs bungalow 6	14,300	Work-in-progress c/d		nil
Building costs bungalow 7	18,900			
Building costs bungalow 8	24,300			
Building costs bungalow 9	24,200			
Administration expenses	7,000			
Commissions	800			
Profit & loss a/c	12,500			
	£120,000			£120,000

Balance Sheets
Basis (1)

DR	£		CR	£
1992				
Creditors	3,000	Work-in-progress		nil
Profit & loss a/c	9,800	Debtors		4,000
		Bank		8,800
	£12,800			£12,800
1993				
Creditors	10,000	Work-in-progress		18,000
Profit & loss a/c	17,300	Debtors		nil
		Bank		9,300
	£27,300			£27,300
1994				
Creditors	nil	Work-in-progress		nil
Profit & loss a/c	29,800	Debtors		4,000
		Bank		25,800
	£29,800			£29,800

Contract Account

DR		Basis (2)		CR
	£			£

1992 — Same as *Basis (1)*

1993

	£		£
Work-in-progress b/d	nil	Customers	60,000
Building costs	2,300	Work-in-progress c/d	14,100
Administration expenses	7,000		
Commissions	1,200		
Profit & loss a/c	3,600		
	£74,100		£74,100

1994

	£		£
Work-in-progress b/d	14,100	Customers	120,000
Building costs	81,700	Work-in-progress	nil
Administration expenses	7,000		
Commissions	800		
Profit & loss a/c	16,400		
	£120,000		£120,000

Balance Sheets

DR		Basis (2)		CR
	£			£

1992 — Same as *Basis (1)*

1993

	£		£
Creditors	10,000	Work-in-progress	14,100
Profit & loss a/c	13,400	Debtors	nil
		Bank	9,300
	£23,400		£23,400

1994

	£		£
Creditors	nil	Work-in-progress	nil
Profit & loss a/c	29,800	Debtors	4,000
		Bank	25,800
	£29,800		£29,800

Social accounting | 28

An evaluating concept

This is not some new method of book-keeping, but a concept based on evaluating the economic function and performance of the business entity in relation to society and the national interest, together with any social costs or benefits generated by it.

This concept was given publicity by the Corporate Report, published in 1975 by the Accounting Standard Committee. This report concerned itself with the users and usefulness of periodic financial statements of reporting business entities.

Statements of corporate objectives

Currently there is no obligation for companies to comment on such matters, but it has been suggested that statements of corporate objectives should include reference to such matters as consumer, environmental, and other social issues. Examples of such information may well include the following – it is the intention of the company, wherever possible:

a to benefit the local community and to preserve the quality of life and the environment;

b to avoid premature redundancy of employees by careful planning and recognising the need for change at the earliest possible time, and to develop and train employees accordingly;

c to protect the health and safety of employees, customers and members of the community;

d and to respect the need to preserve scarce resources.

A clash of interests?

It can be seen from the above that there may well be a clash of interests between the company and members of the workforce and the community. This will be particularly so if the company sees its main priority or objective to be a maximisation of profits on behalf of the shareholders. In this case the company may well attempt to economise on less productive aspects, such as health, safety, pollution control, training. There are also contentious items relating to trading with customers that may have moral or political implications. It would not be difficult to find arguments against such policies, but comments and discussion can easily become too political for examination purposes. The student, therefore, must be prepared to recognise and discuss the strengths and weaknesses of the profit objective, and to balance these sensibly with the benefits and costs accruing to the community as a result of the existence of the business, particularly where he or she has strong pesonal views on these matters. This is also an area where trade unions have an increasing interest, and students may wish to consider the position of these bodies and other pressure groups, and the way in which they can bring pressure on companies. Also of relevance is the growing volume of legislation, particularly in recent years, relating to employment, health and safety, and pollution.

One-off projects

The student may also wish to consider occasions when a business may adopt a marginal approach to business decisions for certain one-off projects where there is spare capacity. In this case, profit may be foregone in order to gain an order which would protect the workforce from temporary layoff during slack periods. It is this kind of argument that the student may well have to put forward in written questions based on social accounting, but the relevant portion of the syllabus also mentions such areas as the effect on labour of advanced technology, closure of unprofitable branches in rural areas (inferring depriving the community of facilities), advertising ethics and psychological factors relating to premature retirement.

Cost benefit analysis

The concept of cost benefit analysis may also have some relevance in this subject area as it is a topic that recognises and quantifies the discounted costs and benefits of both the financial and the non-financial aspects of projects. The usual example quoted is that of the Victoria Underground line which, although originally seemed not to be financially viable, could be justified on other grounds – particularly in relation to the comfort and convenience of all commuters, road users and the community.

Social accounting is obviously a wide area which requires analysis of topics beyond the range of mere accounting theory, but it serves to remind us that accounting has to be considered in conjunction with all the other requirements and constraints of life in today's society.

The application of computers to accounting | 29

Introduction

Some accountants are reluctant to involve themselves in computers because of a mistaken belief that they must be able to write programs for computers. Some knowledge of computer programming can be an advantage for the accountant and can enhance his understanding of computers and computing, but it is certainly *not* essential. Most people can quite successfully drive a car without knowing or understanding what goes on 'under the bonnet' of a car – similarly the businessman can quite successfully operate a computer without understanding what is going on within its case. Indeed, it is unlikely that most businessmen would be able to afford the time to learn how to program computers or to actually write the programs, and in many cases the attempt to do so could be a waste of time because there is a wide range of general purpose accountancy programs ('software') which meet most accounting requirements.

Today the computer has become an indispensable tool for the accountant. It has completely replaced the 'books of accounts' and ledgers of the past, except in the smallest operations. The advantages of speed, accessibility, security, analysis and control enable accounting for the largest organisations to be carried out by the minimum number of people. The advances in modern technology even over a period as short as 15 years have revolutionised office and accounting systems and with the advent of the international linking of computers through the internet and other networks, new concepts and methods are continually being created. The two principal constituents of any computer system are: 'hardware' and 'software'.

Hardware

Hardware comprises the following components:

a the central processing unit (CPU);

b an input device; and

c an output device.

These components will be found in all computer systems irrespective of size, from the largest mainframe to the smallest personal computer.

a The CPU is a microprocessor made up of linked silicon 'chips' and the power of even a comparatively small microprocessor today is many times the power of very much larger processors some years ago. The CPU includes 'memory' chips. A modern personal computer is likely to have at least eight megabytes of Random Access Memory and 80 megabytes of Storage Memory on its hard disc drive.

b The commonest types of input devices include:

i a keyboard;

ii a disc drive;

    iii a tape drive;

    iv a CD ROM drive.

c The commonest types of output devices include:

    i   a visual display unit (VDU) (also called a monitor);

    ii   printers;

    iii the various input drives referred to in (b) above may also be used as output devices.

Software

Software is the term used to describe the computer programs which determine the use to which a computer is put. Computer software may be either *bespoke* in which case it is written to a unique specification as part of a specialist designed system, or a *package* which is written for general use and tailored by the users for their own particular needs. Software packages include accounting systems, payroll systems, and spreadsheets which have been designed to cater for the needs of all types of businesses.

Accounting Packages

Most accounting systems generate input from journal entries. All transactions are thus monitored by the computer from point of entry and some journal entries will be automatically generated by other connected systems, eg invoicing systems, stock control systems, etc.

    Other standard facilities which are to be found in many accounting software packages include:

a sales and purchase ledgers;

b fixed asset registers;

c payroll;

d order processing;

e invoice generation;

f credit control;

g trial balance;

h stock control;

i credit control – aged analysis of debtors.

    In addition, special facilities may be incorporated depending on the nature of the business and the environment within which it operates. These include:

a *Budgetary control* – this enables a budget to be prepared at the beginning of an accounting period during which expenditure and profitability are automatically measured against the predetermined budget, with variances shown separately. This provides management with a valuable tool to monitor the progress of the business.

b *Designing financial reports* – financial reports may be tailor made to meet the needs of an individual business and automatically distributed to all appropriate levels within an organisation. This may also assist regulatory reporting for the purposes of taxation and reporting to various government bodies for statistical analysis.

c *Multi-currency accounting* – if a business operates in other countries with different currencies, there may well be a requirement to use a standard accounting package when reporting in the various currencies which would translate and consolidate financial information into the main base currency.

Spreadsheets

In addition to accounting packages, wide use is made of spreadsheets such as Lotus 1–2–3 or Excel which facilitate analysis of all business information and statistics and when combined with word processing enable the production of complex financial reports including, for instance, annual accounts. The spreadsheets also have significant graphs capabilities and may thus be used to present information using diagrams, charts and graphs.

Solutions | 30

Suggested solution 2.1

a Consistency: there is consistency of accounting treatment of like items within each accounting period and from one period to the next (SSAP 2), eg depreciation, changing methods of computation from straight line in one year to reducing balance in the next for the same asset is an example of inconsistency.

b Prudence: revenue and profits are not anticipated, but are recognised by the inclusion in the profit and loss account only when realised in the form of either cash or other assets, the ultimate cash realisation of which can be assessed with reasonable certainty. Provision is made for all known liabilities (expenses and losses) whether the amount of these is known with certainty or is a best estimate in the light of the information available (SSAP 2), eg quoted investments:

    10,000 shares purchased 31.12.92 at £2/share
    value 31.12.93 £3/share
    value 31.12.94 £1.50/share

Balance sheet extract

	31.12.92	31.12.93	31.12.94
Quoted investments	£20,000	£20,000	£15,000

Note that in 1993 the 'gain' of £10,000 has been ignored as it has not been realised but the 'loss' in 1994, also unrealised, has been debited against the profits and the balance sheet value reduced.

c Going concern: the enterprise will continue in operational existence for the foreseeable future. This means in particular that the profit and loss account and balance sheet assume no intention or necessity to liquidate or curtail significantly the scale of operation (SSAP 2), eg:

    Plant and machinery:
    Net book value 31.12.93   £240,000
    Net realisable value 31.12.93   £150,000

Under the going concern concept the value in the balance sheet would be £240,000 (the net book value) but if the firm cannot be considered a going concern the net realisable value of £150,000 must be taken into account.

d Materiality: accounting does not serve a useful purpose if the effort of recording a transaction in a certain way is not worthwhile. The main distinction is in deciding whether an asset should be shown as an expense of a period, and if so, how much of it should be shown.

For example, a manufacturing firm buys 'loose' tools during a year costing £1,000. It is possible to show these loose either as an asset or as a reduction in profits (an expense). The treatment will depend on the materiality of the item to the firm. If the firm has sales of only £20,000 then the £1,000 will be material but if it has £20,000 million sales it will not.

Note: it can be seen that materiality is decided on the individual facts relating to each organisation.

Suggested solution 2.2

a Both the prudence and consistency conventions are being breached by reducing the depreciation charge for the year.

b Obviously, it is not consistent to change the basis for charging depreciation from year to year and it is imprudent to do so simply because profits have slumped.

Unless there is a better reason for changing the basis the old rate should be used ie 20 per cent on cost.

If it can be shown that the benefit, in terms of reserves, from the advertising will be received over the five years under consideration then this course of action is not incorrect.

Where this cannot be shown the proposed course of action breaches the accruals concept/principle (matching the revenues with their associated expenses).

As it would be extremely difficult to show that the revenues would be received in the manner suggested (or implied) it would be best to charge the full amount to the first period's income statement, which would also comply fully with the principle of prudence.

c This proposal breaches the going concern convention. The going concern convention forces the assumption that a business entity will continue to trade unless knowledge to the contrary is available.

In these circumstances it would be best to depreciate the asset using one of the available methods over its estimated useful life. It also breaches the accruals principle – several years revenues will benefit.

d Trading profit is that derived from the firm's manufacturing and selling operations. If the firm is not in the property trade then the profit on this sale cannot be considered 'trading' profit.

It is normal to credit/debit the profit and loss account with any small gains/losses on sales of fixed assets, but this is true only where the items are not 'material'. Hence this transaction breaches the convention of materiality.

It would be reasonable to strike a trading profit before including this gain in the profit and loss account.

Suggested solution 3.1

a An accrual is an expense/revenue incurred (receivable) in the current accounting period but which is not paid/received until the next or later accounting period.

A prepayment is an expense/revenue of the next or later accounting periods which has been paid/received in the current accounting period.

Profits are stated to be the difference between *revenues* and *expenses*, not necessarily receipts and expenditures.

The most obvious example of this is the using up of a fixed asset, which is often the *expense* of many accounting periods but the *expenditure* of only one. Adjustment is therefore necessary and in this case is known as depreciation.

This is known as the matching concept and takes several forms, eg:

opening stock + purchases – closing stock = cost of sales

but in terms of expense accounts the adjustments to match expense (as opposed to expenditure) against revenue are called accruals and prepayments.

b

Rent and Rates Account

		£			£
1994	Bank: Rents	2,500	1.1.94	Rent accrual b/d	750
1994	Bank: Rates to 31.3.87	600	1.1.94	Rates accrual b/d	300
1.4.94	Bank: Rates to 30.9.87	600	31.12.94	P&l a/c Rent and rates	4,200
1.10.94	Bank: Rates to 31.3.87	600	31.12.94	Rates prepayment c/d	300
31.12.94	Rent accrual c/d	1,250			
		£5,550			£5,550
1.1.95	Rates prepaid b/d	300	1.1.95	Rent accrued b/d	1,250

Workings:

Reconciliation:

Rates for year	600 x 2	£1,200
Rent for year	250 x 12	£3,000
Profit & loss a/c		£4,200

Suggested solution 3.2

Tom Thumb

	To 30.9.93				To 31.12.93				To 31.3.94			
	FIFO		LIFO		FIFO		LIFO		FIFO		LIFO	
	£	£	£	£	£	£	£	£	£	£	£	£
Sales		900		900		2,400		2,400		2,100		2,100
Opening stock	–		–		170		150		595		575	
Purchases	320		320		945		945		640		640	
	320		320		1,115		1,095		1,235		1,215	
Closing stock												
(see notes)	170		150		595		575		715		655	
Cost of sales		150		170		520		520		520		560
Gross profit		750		730		1,880		1,880		1,580		1,540
Overheads		300		300		300		300		300		300
Net profit		£450		£430		£1,580		£1,580		£1,280		£1,240
Total net profit	(FIFO)	3,310										
	(LIFO)	3,250										

Notes:

1 Stock valuations – FIFO

	Purchases	Sales	Stock 30.9.93	Sales	Stock 31.12.93	Sales	Stock 31.3.94
July	20	(15)	5 (£10)	(5)			
August	10		10 (£12)	(10)			
October	30			(25)	5 (£14)	(5)	
December	35				35 (£15)	(30)	5 (£15)
January	40						40 (£16)
			15 £170		40 £595		45 £715

2 Stock valuation – LIFO

	Purchases	Sales	Stock 30.9.93	Sales	Stock 31.12.93	Sales	Stock 31.3.94
July	20	(5)	15 (£10)	(10)	5 (£10)		5 (£10)
August	10	(10)	–		–		–
October	30			(30)	–		–
December	35				35 (£15)		35 (£15)
January	40					(35)	5 (£16)
			15 £150		40 £575		45 £655

Suggested solution 3.3

Ben Bow

a Trading, Profit & Loss Account for years ended 31.12.92 and 31.12.93

	31.12.93				31.12.94			
	FIFO		LIFO		FIFO		LIFO	
	£	£	£	£	£	£	£	£
Sales		16,000		16,000		46,300		46,300
Opening stock	–		–		18,300		17,100	
Purchases	26,300		26,300		7,000		7,000	
	26,300		26,300		25,300		24,100	
Closing stock	18,300		17,100		–		–	
Cost of sales		8,000		9,200		25,300		24,100
Gross profit		8,000		6,800		21,000		22,200
Expenses	2,000		2,000		2,000		2,000	
Commission:								
Plow	2,000		1,700		–		–	
Roe	–		–		2,100		2,220	
		4,000		3,700		4,100		4,220
Net profit		£4,000		£3,100		£16,900		£17,980

Total	FIFO	20,900
	LIFO	21,080

Workings:

Stocks 31 December 1994

	Purchases	Sales	Stock	£
FIFO				
January	100	(80)	20 @ £100	2,000
May	60	–	60 @ £120	7,200
November	70	–	70 @ £130	9,100
				£18,300
LIFO				
January	100	(20)	80 @ £100	8,000
May	60	(60)	–	
November	70		70 @ £130	9,100
				£17,100

b Cost of decision

	£
Increase in price	5,000
Loss of earnings	18,000
	23,000
Total profits	21,080
'Cost' of decision	£1,920

The report should explain the basis of the above calculations.

Suggested solution 3.4

Jack Jackson
Statement Showing Stock Value as at 31 September 1994

	£	£
Stocks as at 10.9.94		9,870
Less: Goods received 1.9.94 to 10.9.94	360	
Returns from customers at cost	125	
Transposition error	180	
Casting errors (net)	60	
Stocks written down to NRV	70	
Stocks written off: age	120	
		(915)
Add: Sales 1.9.94 to 10.9.94 (at cost)	1,250	
Goods on sale or return (at cost)	375	
Purchase returns	760	
		2,385
Value of stock to be included in the accounts at 31.8.94		£11,340

Suggested solution 3.5

a

Silas Tapp
Calculation of the Provision for Doubtful Debts

	30 September 1992			30 Spetember 1993	
	£	£		£	£
T Barnes		264	Paid		Nil
A Camache Ltd		45	Bad		Nil
H Singh Ltd		72	Paid	54	
			Bad	18	Nil
M Grimmett		96	Paid	56	
			Due	40	Nil
F Ming		60	c/f		60
K O'Reilly		184	Paid		Nil
'Specific'		721			
			R Viljoen		94
			U McDuff Ltd		176
			'Specific'		330
General based on			General based on		
total debtors	39,321		total debtors		
Less specific	(721)		Less specific	36,400	
			Less bad from		
	38,600		1992 (18 + 45)	(63)	
@ 4%		1,544		36,337	
		£2,265	@ 4%		1,453
					£1,783

b

Bad Debts Account

	£		£
K Smit Ltd	70	E Pancho	52
Q Toni	98	Profit & loss a/c	116
	£168		£168

Note (1):

The bad debts of A Camache and H Singh had been specifically provided for in 1992 and therefore the amounts are debited against the provision and credited to debtors.

c

Silas Tapp
Provision for Doubtful Debts Account

	£		£
Debtors (see note 2)	63	1 Oct 93	
Profit & loss a/c (see note 2)	419	Balance b/d:	
Balance c/d:		Specific	721
Specific	330	General	1,544
General	1,453		
	£2,265		£2,265

Note (2):
Once the closing provision for specific and general has been calculated in schedule (a) the transfer to profit and loss to reduce the overall provision is simply the balancing figure. However, it is interesting to consider the treatment for each individual specific debtor – as follows:

(Credit in bracket)			Profit & loss	Provision	Debtors
(1) T Barnes	£264	Paid	(264)	264	
(2) H Singh Ltd	£54	Paid	(54)	54	
	£18	Bad		18	(18)
(3) M Grimmett	£56	Paid	(56)	56	
	£40	Due	(40)	40	
(4) A Camache Ltd	£45	Bad		45	(45)
(5) K O'Reilly	£184	Paid	(184)	184	
(6) F Ming	£60	c/f			
(7) R Viljoen	£94	New	94	(94)	
(8) U McDuff	£176	New	176	(176)	
Decrease in general					
provision from 1,544 to 1,453			(91)	91	
As above:			£419		£63

For customers who paid – the provision is no longer required and is written back to profit and loss (Dr provision, CR profit and loss).

For customers who are now bad – the debt must be written off and the provision is no longer required (Dr provision, Cr debtors)

d The features of good credit control are:

i   check and assess customers credit-worthiness before allowing credit;

ii   submit invoices and statements regularly and promptly;

iii accounting must be kept up to date and should be controlled;

iv debtors' balances must be reviewed and an age analysis prepared;

v   offer customers cash discounts to encourage prompt payment;

e The adverse consequences if creditors are paid slowly:

i   cash discounts will not be available;

ii   supplier may withdraw credit facilities altogether and may eventually refuse to supply goods;

iii business may get a bad reputation and suppliers will ask for cash on delivery. This will have an adverse effect upon cash flow;

iv serious delays in payment may lead to legal actions, a decline in credit rating and ultimately to compulsory liquidation or bankruptcy.

Suggested solution 4.1

Bennie Ltd

a

	£
Original depreciation charge for 1994:	
Plant 160,000/10	16,000
Vehicles 70,000/5	14,000
	£30,000
Revised charge for 1994:	
Buildings 200,000 x 2%	4,000
Plant 160,000/10	16,000
Vehicles (70,000 – 28,000) 30%	12,600
	£32,600

The charge in accounting for depreciation would be dealt with under the 'Accounting Policies' note in the published accounts.

Under the section for depreciation information regarding both the old and new policies would be given. In addition, it is possible that the comparative figures for 1993 should be adjusted so as to make them comparable with 1994. If this is done, however, the revised charge for 1994 would be different as the accumulated depreciation on vehicles would have been computed using a reducing balance method for 1.1.93 (not 1.1.94 as in the above example).

b

Increase in working capital	1992 £	1993 £	1994 £
Profits for year	60,000	75,000	70,000
Items not involving movement in			
funds: depreciation (note 1)	30,000	30,000	30,000
	90,000	105,000	100,000
Applications			
Dividends	60,000	60,000	60,000
Movement in working capital and			
Net liquid funds (note 2)	£30,000	£45,000	£40,000

Notes:

1   As the straight line method for depreciation has been used the depreciation for both 1992 and 1993 must be the same as the original charge in 1994 draft accounts.

2   There may well have been other sources and applications of which we have no knowledge. Common examples would be:

source – issue of debentures,
application – tax paid.

c i   reduction in reported profits;

   ii   reduction in earnings per share;

   iii   movement in ratio of return on capital employed;

iv   more/less accurate reflection of actual depreciation suffered;

v   difficulty in interpreting trends in profits.

Suggested solution 4.2

a Year   1   2   3   4

i   Reducing balance:

63,000 x 40% (63,000 – 25,200) 40% (63,000 – 40,320) 40% (63,000 – 49,392) 40%

25,200   15,120   9,072   5,443

ii Usage: Total usage = 40,000 running hours

$\therefore$ depn = $\frac{9.5}{40}$ (63,000 – 3,000) $\frac{12}{40}$ x 60 $\frac{8}{40}$ x 60 $\frac{105}{40}$ x 60

14,250   18,000   12,000   15,750

iii Revaluation:

Cost	63,000	63,000	63,000	63,000
Accumulated				
depn	–	23,000	38,000	51,000
	63,000	40,000	25,000	12,000
MV	40,000	25,000	12,000	3,000
Charge for				
year	£23,000	£15,000	£13,000	£9,000

iv Sinking fund:

Cost	63,000	63,000	63,000	63,000
Depreciation				
Sinking b/f		12,928	27,149	42,793
Fund: P&L	12,928	12,928	12,928	12,928
Interest	–	1,293	2,716	4,279
C/f	12,928	27,149	42,793	60,000

Note: normally only the £12,928 would be entered on the profit and loss account; the interest element would be omitted both from the debit and the credit sides.

b No 'right' method:

'Depreciation is the measure of the wearing out, consumption or other loss of value of a fixed asset whether arising from use, effluxion of time or obsolescence through technology or market changes.' (SSAP 12)

Two points:

i   Choice of method involves a decision regarding the speed, nature of depreciation and cause. All these will be unclear at the time of choice and thus how accurately the method chosen reflects actual depreciation will depend on the experience and expertise of the decision maker.

ii All methods of calculation involve two estimates: that of useful life and that of residual value. Obviously, these two factors cannot be known in advance for the majority of assets and thus there can be no accurate method of depreciation.

In addition to the above, there are other factors which means that depreciation set aside is rarely adequate to provide for the replacement of fixed assets. The most common of these is inflation which causes the replacement cost of the assets to continually increase.

Another factor is technological advance. It is unlikely that any asset can be replaced with an exact replica because the models will have been improved over time through technological advance and the price of the asset will reflect this (in real terms).

Suggested solution 4.3

a

Chefs & Co

DR		£	Vehicles	CR	£
1.3.90 (G11 ABC)		12,000	Disposal		12,000
1.3.92 J22 CBC		21,200			
1.3.92 J33 CBC		9,500	C/d		30,700
		£30,700			£30,700
1.3.93 B/d		30,700			

DR		Depreciation Provision		CR
	£			£
		31.2.93		
		Depn @ 25%		5,300
C/d	7,675	Depn @ 25%		2,375
	£7,675			£7,675

DR		Depreciation Provision		CR
	£			£
Disposal	5,250	31.2.91 Depn		3,000
		31.2.92 Depn		2,250
	£5,250			£5,250

DR		Disposals Account		CR
	£			£
1.3.92 (G11 ABC)	12,000	1.3.92 Acc Depn		5,250
		1.3.92 Trade-in		6,200
		Profit & loss		550
	12,000			12,000

b

Profit & Loss Account for year ended 28 February 1993

	£
Depreciation	(7,675)
Loss on sale	(550)
Motor running expenses (238 + 26 + 200 + 110 + 120)	(694)

c

Balance Sheet as at 28 February 1993

	£
Motor vehicles at cost	30,700
Less accumulated depreciation	(7,675)
	£23,025

d Depreciation is the measure of wearing out due to obsolescence, passing of time, use within the period of ownership, etc. It must be provided for in order to charge a proportion of the cost of the asset to each accounting period that derived benefit from its use.

Suggested solution 5.1

a *Either:*

DR		Debtors' Ledger Control			CR
Date		£	Date		£
1.4.95	Balances b/d	65,200	1.4.95	Balances b/d	900
	Sales	213,500		Cash received	179,800
				Returns	2,300
				Bad debts	700
				Discounts allowed	3,400
				Contras	1,200
30.4.95	Balances c/d	700	30.4.95	Balances c/d	91,100
		£279,400			£279,400
1.5.95	Balances b/d	91,100	1.5.95	Balances b/d	700

Or:

DR		Creditors' Ledger Control			CR
Date		£	Date		£
1.4.95	Balances b/d	100	1.4.95	Balances b/d	37,400
	Cash paid	87,100		Purchases	106,700
	Purchase returns	1,500			
	Discounts received	2,050			
	Bills payable	3,300			
	Contras	1,200			
30.4.95	Balances c/d	49,000	30.4.95	Balances c/d	150
		£144,250			£144,250
1.5.95	Balances b/d	150	1.5.95˙	Balances b/d	49,000

b i Advantages: avoids adding the individual accounts on a monthly basis, with a control account the individual balances need only be totalled annually; after the annual totals are arrived at, the control account highlights the full discrepancy, if any, and can be an aid in finding mistakes.

ii Contras arise where a supplier of goods is also a customer for the firm's product. The contra is needed because, in these circumstances, it would be wasteful to both send and receive cheques for the full amount and thus net cheques are usually paid by the party who owes more than he is owed.

Suggested solution 5.2

a

Jura Ltd

DR	£	Sales Ledger Control	CR £
B/d	63,010	B/d	130
Sales	309,079	Bank	335,426
Dishonoured cheque	683	Returns	4,342
Transport costs	700	Purchase invoice	103
Commission	48	Discounts	145
Credit balances	36	Bad debts	177
		Rebate	40
		Contra	1,562
		Balance c/d	31,631
	£373,556		£373,556
B/d	31,431		

DR	£	Purchase Ledger Control	CR £
B/d	85	B/d	41,530
Returns	3,529	Purchases	209,196
Bank	217,934	Refund	168
Contra	1,562	Purchase invoice	103
Discounts	390		
Balance c/d	27,497		
	£250,997		£250,997
		B/d	27,497

b Benefits of control accounts are:

i Location of errors by comparing control account balance with list of balances extracted from individual ledger accounts.

ii The normal ledger information is produced more quickly and in a more condensed fashion.

iii The control accounts are part of the double entry system and provide relevant figures for balance sheet purposes.

Suggested solution 7.1

Tom Blunderbuss
Trading and Profit & Loss Account for year ended 31 August 1994

	£	£
Sales		60,000
Opening stock	5,000	
Purchases (net of goods for own use)	49,000	
	54,000	
Closing stock (by balance)	9,000	
Cost of sales		45,000
Gross profit		15,000
Establishment expenses	6,000	
Administrative expenses	2,000	
Sales and distribution expenses	5,000	
Depreciation	3,000	16,000
Net loss		£(1,000)

Balance Sheet as at 31 August 1994

		£	£
Fixed assets:	Cost		30,000
	Depreciation		11,100
			18,900
Current assets:	Stock	9,000	
	Debtors	1,500	
	Bank (by balance)	600	
		11,100	
Current liabilities: Creditors		3,000	
			8,100
			£27,000
Financed by:			
Opening capital			19,000
Add:	Legacy, introduced		7,000
			26,000
Deduct:	Loss	1,000	
	Drawings: Cash	4,000	
	Goods	2,000	
			7,000
			19,000
Loan			8,000
			£27,000

Workings:
1

Creditors:

	£		£
Bank	51,500	Balance b/f	3,500
Balances c/d (By balance)	3,000	Purchases	51,000
	£54,500		£54,500

2

	£	Confirmation of bank:	£
Loan	8,000	Balance b/f	3,400
Legacy	7,000	Fixed assets	3,000
Debtors	60,500	Drawings	4,000
	75,500	Purchases	51,500
		Expenses: Estab.	6,000
		Admin.	2,000
		Selling	5,000
			74,900
		Balance c/d	600
	£75,500		£75,500

Suggested solution 7.2

a   To compute Carter's profit for the year it is first necessary to compute the capital both at the beginning and end of the year.

		30.6.94			30.6.95	
		£	£		£	£
Assets						
Shop:	Cost		12,000			12,000
	Less depn 4 years		2,400	5 yrs		3,000
			9,600			9,000
Fittings:	Cost	3,000			3,000	
	Less depn 4 years	1,200	1,800	5 yrs	1,500	1,500
Stock			2,000			4,600
Debtors			920			2,540
Cash			70			105
			14,390			17,745
Less liabilities						
Creditors		2,180			3,730	
Bank overdraft		695			1,350	
Loan		2,000	4,875		1,500	6,580
Capital			£9,515			£11,165

The increase in capital must represent:

a   capital introduced plus

b   profit for year minus

c   drawings.

Capital introduced amounted to £600 (the expenses paid from his personal accounts). Drawings amounted to £3,380 (cash from takings £2,600, insurance £30, furniture purchased through the business £750).

If capital 30.6.95 minus capital 30.6.94 = capital introduced plus profits minus drawings

then 11,165 – 9,515 = 600 + profits – 3,380 and profits = £4,430

b

Balance Sheet as at 30 June 1995

		Cost £	Depn £	Net £
Fixed assets:	Shop	12,000	3,000	9,000
	Fixtures	3,000	1,500	1,500
		£15,000	£4,500	10,500
Current assets:	Stock		4,600	
	Debtors		2,540	
	Cash		105	
			7,245	
Current liabilities:	Creditors	3,730		
	Bank	1,350	5,080	
Net current assets				2,165
				£12,665
Financed by				
Capital 1.7.94				9,515
Add: Capital introduced			600	
Profits			4,430	
				5,030
				14,545
Less: Drawings				3,380
				11,165
Loan				1,500
				£12,665

Suggested solution 7.3

Ben Dover
Revenue Statement for year to 30 June 1995

	£	£
Sales (note 2) 150,000 @ 15p		22,500
Cost of sales:		
Sausages (note 1)	5,700	
Bread rolls (note 3)	4,365	
Garnish 150,000 @ 1p	1,500	
		11,565
Gross profit		10,935
Expenses:		
Waste rolls (note 4)	582	
Rent	520	
Gas	230	1,332
Net profit		£9,603

Notes:

1 Sausages:

Value of sausages purchased = £ rebate/rate of rebate = 300 ÷ 5% = £6,000

No of sausages purchased = $\dfrac{\text{value}}{4 \text{ pence}} = \dfrac{6000}{.04} = 150{,}000$

Cost of sausages = value – rebate = 6,000 – 300 = 5,700

2 No. sausages sold = no. of sales.

3 Cost of sales of bread rolls = units sold × unit purchase price less rebate:

= 150,000 × .03 – 3% (150,000 × .03) = 4,365

4. Total cost of bead rolls:

$= \dfrac{£153}{3\%} = £153$ = £5,100 – 153

= £4,947

Less cost of sales: bread rolls   4,365
          £582

Note: this figure can be checked by deducting the number of bread rolls sold (150,000) from the number purchased:

$\dfrac{5100}{.03}$

and deducting 3 per cent of the value of the difference:

$\left(\dfrac{5{,}100}{.03 - 150{,}000}\right) 3 \text{ pence} \times 97\%$

= (170,000 – 150,000) 3 pence x 97%
= 600 x 97%
= £582

Suggested solution 7.4

a

C Jay
Statement of Affairs as at 1 May 1992

	£
Bank	3,000
Fixtures	4,000
Stock	7,750
Creditors	(1,750)
Depreciation – fixtures	(600)
Van and valuation	2,000
	£14,400

b

C Jay
Trading and Profit & Loss Account for year ended 30 April 1993

	£	£
Sales		41,935
Opening stock	7,750	
Purchases	22,600	
Closing stock	(8,500)	
Goods taken by proprietor	(1,500)	
Cost of sales		(20,350)
Gross profit		21,585
Wages	6,700	
Rates & rent (1,700 + 2,800)	4,500	
Telephone (550)	550	
Light & heat (1,100)	1,100	
Loss on sale	800	
Motor expenses	1,050	
Insurance	310	
Depreciation – fixtures	510	
– van	2,480	(18,000)
Net profit		£3,585

c

Balance Sheet as at 30 April 1993

	Cost	Depn	£
Fixed assets:			
Fixtures	4,000	1,110	2,890
Delivery van	12,400	2,480	9,920
	£16,400	£3,590	12,810
Current assets:			
Stock		8,500	
Current liabilities:			
Overdraft		(4,950)	
Creditors		(3,000)	
Net current assets			550
			£13,360
Capital:			
At 1 May 92			14,400
Introduced			3,250
Profit			3,585
			21,235
Drawings			7,875
			£13,360

C Jay
Creditors

DR	£		CR £
Bank	20,250	B/d	1,750
C/d	3,000	∴ Purchases trading a/c	22,600
Bank (o/s)	1,100		
	£24,350		£24,350

DR	Takings Account		CR
	£		£
∴ Total sales	41,935	Bank	31,250
Trading a/c		Paid out:	
		Wages	6,700
		Van	1,050
		Insurance	310
		Drawings	2,625
	£41,935		£41,935

DR	Drawings Account		CR
	£		£
Bank	3,750	Capital	7,875
Cash	2,625		
Goods	1,500		
	£7,875		£7,875

DR	Disposal Account		CR
	£		£
Cost	2,000	Allowance	1,200
		Profit & loss a/c	800
	£2,000		£2,000

DR	Van Account (new)		CR
	£		£
Part exchange	1,200	Depreciation @ 20%	2,480
Bank	11,200	C/d	9,920
	£12,400		£12,400

DR	Bank Account		CR
	£		£
B/d	3,000	Payments	41,350
Receipts	34,500	O/s Ch	1,100
C/d	4,950		
	£42,450		£42,450
		B/d	4,950

Suggested solution 8.1

a

Tuff Road Rugby Club Bar Trading Account
for year ended 31 August 1995

	£	£
Bar sales		15,510
Opening bar stocks	1,250	
Bar purchases (1,910 + 11,730 – 850)	12,790	
	14,040	
Less: Closing bar stocks	960	
Cost of sales		13,080
Bar gross profit		2,430

b

Income and Expenditure Account
for year ended 31 August 1995

	£	£
Subscriptions (note 1)		9,475
Bar gross profit		2,430
Interest on deposit account		480
		12,385
Less: Expenditures		
Groundsman	2,700	
Rent, rates and insurance	1,840	
Repairs to pavilion	425	
Postal (note 2)	90	
Rugby equipment	500	
Travelling	2,870	
Printing and stationery	560	
Depreciation (£100 cash register £800 pavilion)	900	
	9,885	
Less: Collections	1,280	
		8,605
Excess of income over expenditure		£3,780

c

Balance Sheet as at 31 August 1995

		£	£
Fixed assets:	Pavilion (NBV)		4,000
	Cash register (NBV)		300
			4,300
Current assets:	Bar stocks	960	
	Subscriptions due	720	
	Bank: deposit a/c	7,300	
	current a/c	4,250	
	Cash in hand	15	
		£13,245	
Current liabilities:	Subs in advance	55	
	Bar creditors	1,910	
		£1,965	
Net current assets			11,280
			£15,580
Financed by:			
Accumulated fund 1.9.94 (note 3)			6,800
Donations			5,000
			11,800
Excess of income over expenditure for year			3,780
			£15,580

Notes:

1

DR	Subscription Account			CR
	£			£
1.9.94 Balance due b/f	460	1.9.94 Balance in advance b/f		40
31.8.95 Subs income &		31.8.95 Receipts		9,230
expenditure a/c	9,475	31.8.95 Balance due c/f		720
31.8.95 Balance in advance c/d	55			
	£9,990			£9,990

2

DR	Petty Cash Account		CR
	£		£
1.9.94 Balance in hand b/d	30	Postage, income and	
31.8.95 Payments a/c	75	expenditure a/c	90
		31.8.95 Balance in hand c/d	15
	£105		£105

3

Accumulated Fund at 1.9.94

		£	£
Assets:	Pavilion		4,800
	Bar stocks		1,250
	Subscriptions due		460
	Bank: Deposit		700
	Current		450
	Cash in hand		30
			7,690
Liabilities:	Bar suppliers	850	
	Subs in advance	40	
			890
			£6,800

Suggested solution 8.2

a

Chaucer Theatre Club
Accumulated Fund as at 31 March 1993

	£	£
Premises at cost	85,000	
Less: Depreciation (3,400 x 9 years)	(30,600)	
		54,400
Fixtures at cost	16,000	
Less: Depreciation	(6,200)	
		9,800
Cash float		100
Bank overdraft		(380)
Arrears of subscriptions (4 x 20)		80
Subscriptions in advance (3 x 100)		(300)
Accruals: Printing		(320)
Repairs		(170)
Prepayments – insurance		120
Accumulated fund		£62,830

b

Chaucer Theatre Club
Income & Expenditure Account for the year ended 31 March 1994

	£	£
Income		
Subscriptions: Individual		3,940
Corporate		2,000
Ticket sales (52,880 + 50)		52,930
Sponsorship		12,500
Rents		3,900
Programme advertising		320
		75,590
Expenditure		
Light and heat (3,960 + 510)	4,470	
Insurance (120 + 1,820)	1,940	
Advertising	1,560	
Copyright costs (1,504 – 125)	1,379	
Caretaker's wages	8,016	
Printing (–320 + 1,575)	1,255	
Postage and telephone (610 + 85)	695	
General expenses	6,772	
Play performance costs	27,800	
Repairs and maintenance (–170 + 6,318)	6,148	
Equipment and costume hire	3,725	
Honoraria	200	
Depreciation: Premises (35,000 x 4%)	3,400	
Fixtures (9,800 x 10%)	980	(68,340)
Surplus of income over expenditure		£7,250

c

Chaucer Theatre Club
Balance Sheet as at 31 March 1994

	Cost	Depn	£
Fixed assets:			
Premises	85,000	34,000	51,000
Fixtures	16,000	7,180	8,820
	£101,000	£41,180	£59,820
Current assets:			
Bank		10,760	
Cash		150	
Debtors – subscriptions		140	
Prepayments		125	
		£11,175	
Current liabilities:			
Subscription in advance		120	
Accruals (85 + 510)		595	
Honoraria		200	
		£915	
Net current assets			10,260
			£70,080
Accumulated fund:			
As at 1 April 1993			62,830
Surplus			7,250
			£70,080

d Benefits and drawbacks of sponsorship.

The benefit to the sponsor would include:

i   Advertising in programmes, newspapers, etc.

ii   Taxation benefits.

iii Goodwill arising from association with a good cause.

The possible drawbacks are:

i   If the theatre shows any controversial plays, etc, this might give the sponsors adverse publicity.

ii

Thus, the benefits to the club would include:

i   Valuable source of additional income.

ii   If the sponsor is a local business this would encourage local people associated with the business to visit the theatre.

iii The sponsorship would probably require that the club maintained high standards.

The drawbacks would be:

i   If the sponsor has financial difficulties this may lead to sudden withdrawal of support.

ii   The sponsor may wish to be involved in club matters which may upset the club committee members.

iii Bad publicity attached to the sponsor may prejudice the club's reputation in the eyes of the public.

DR	Subscriptions Account		CR
	£		£
B/d (I)	80	B/d (C)	300
		Bank (I)	4,000
		Bank (C)	1,700
C/d (6 x 20) I	120	C/d (7 x 20)	140
Income & expenditure (I)	3,940		
Income & expenditure (C)	2,000		
	£6,140		£6,140

Suggested solution 9.1

Lowden Dealers Ltd
Profit & Loss Account for the year ended 30 September 1994

	£	£
Sales		120,000
Cost of sales		90,000
Gross profit		30,000
Establishment expenses	10,000	
Administration expenses	9,000	
Distribution expenses	6,000	25,000
Net profit		5,000
Proposed dividend		4,000
Retained profits for year		1,000
Retained profits brought forward		8,000
Retained profits as at 30.9.94		£9,000

Balance Sheet as at 30 September 1994

	Cost/ valuation £	Depn £	£
Fixed assets:			
Freehold property	30,000	–	30,000
Fixtures & fittings	20,000	10,000	10,000
	£50,000	£10,000	40,000
Current assets:			
Stocks		9,000	
Debtors		6,000	
Bank		1,600	
		16,600	
Current liabilities:			
Creditors		3,600	
Dividends		4,000	
		7,600	
Net current assets			9,000
Total assets less current liabilities			£49,000
Capital reserves:			40,000
Ordinary share capital			9,000
Profit and loss			£49,000

b i

Date	£	£
30.9.94 Sales	1,200	
T Goon		1,200

ii

30.9.94 Stocks	900	
Cost of sales		900

d i

30.9.94 Share premium account	5,000	
Revaluation reserve	15,000	
Ordinary share capital account		20,000

ii

30.9.94 Application account	2,000	
Dividends account		2,000

Suggested solution 9.2

Red Holley Ltd
Balance Sheet as at 30 September 1994

	£	£	£
Fixed assets:			
Freehold property	20,000	–	20,000
Plant and machinery	68,000	16,500	51,500
	£88,000	£16,500	71,500
Current assets:			
Stock		11,000	
Debtors	8,800		
Provision	(440)	8,360	
Bank		1,500	
		£2,0860	
Current liabilities:			
Creditors		9,000	
Proposed dividend		5,800	
		£14,800	
Net current assets			6,060
Deterred revenue expenditure			3,000
			£80,560
Share capital:			
Ordinary share capital			50,000
8% preference shares			10,000
			60,000
Reserves:			
General reserve			3,000
Profit loss account			17,560
			£80,560

Workings:

Profit loss account:

	£		£
Depreciation	1,500	Balance b/f	13,000
Dividend	1,000	Machinery	4,000
		Provision – doubtful debts	60
Balance	17,560	Deferred revenue	
		expenditure	3,000
	£20,060		£20,060

Suggested solution 10.1

i   Total gross profit on sales for the year

		£000
Factory profit		150
Warehouse profit		230
		380
Adjustment for profit in stock		
profit in warehouse stock 1.10.86	$\frac{80}{5}$ 16	
profit in warehouse stock 30.9.87	$\frac{60}{5}$ 12	
		4
Total Gross Profit		£384

ii Current Assets

		£000
Stocks:	Raw material	55
	Work in progress	141
	Finished goods $\left(30 + \frac{4}{5} \times 60\right)$	78
		£274

iii Stock turnover ratios

a   Raw materials stock turnover = materials consumed ÷ average R N stocks

$= 300 \div \dfrac{45 + 55}{2}$

= 6 times

b   WIP stock turnover = production cost ÷ average WIP stocks

$= 560 \div \dfrac{139 + 141}{2}$

= 4 times

c   FG stock turnover (at factory cost) = factory cost ÷ average FG stocks

$= 600 \div \dfrac{70 + 30}{2}$

= 12 times

d   FG stock turnover (at transfer price) = cost of sales ÷ average FG stocks

$= 770 \div \dfrac{80 + 60}{2}$

= 11 times

iv The purpose of transferring goods from the factory to the warehouse at a price higher than factory production cost is so as to be able to analyse the profits made between the two functions; manufacturing and trading.

If the transfer price is set to equate to the price at which the trading function could buy the product from a third party, the trading gross profit will be approximately the profit on merchandising the goods. Using this transfer price shows the profit which could have been gained simply from manufacturing.

In essence the purpose is to be more able to judge the effectiveness of these two

In essence the purpose is to be more able to judge the effectiveness of these two parts of the organisation independently of each other.

Suggested solution 10.2

a

Panchem Plc
Manufacturing Trading Profit and Loss Account
for the year ended 31 March 1994

	£000	£000
Raw Materials:		
Opening Stock	470	
Purchases	376	
Customs Duties	8	
Closing Stock	(420)	
Raw Materials Consumed		434
Manufacturing Wages		209
Prime Stock		643
Productions Overheads:		
Power (59 + 21)	80	
Indirect Materials (54 + 82 - 51)	85	
Chemists Salaries	48	
Non-production Wages	81	
Business Rates and Insurance (49 - 1 x 75%)	36	
Internal Transport Costs	34	
Safety Expenses	12	
Depreciation – Plant (60 x 90%)	54	
– Buildings (20 x 90%)	18	
Canteen Expenses (40 x 60%)	24	472
Cost of Production		1115
Work in Progress Adjustment:		
Opening	323	
Closing	(370)	(47)
Cost of Production of Finished Goods		£1068
Sales:		1436
Opening Stock – Finished Goods	398	
Cost of Goods Manufactured	1068	
Closing Stock – Finished Goods	(450)	
Cost of Sales		(1016)
Gross Profit		420
Office Expenses:		
Salaries	55	
Expenses (127 - 3 + 6)	130	
Canteen (40 x 30%)	12	
Rates and Insurance (49 - 1 x 12½%)	6	
Depreciation – Plant (60 x 5%)	3	
– Building (20 x 5 %)	1	(207)
Selling Expenses:		
Salaries	36	
Expenses (53 - 4 + 5)	54	
Canteen (40 x 10%)	4	
Rates and Insurance (49 - 1 x 12½%)	6	
Depreciation – Plant (60 x 5%)	3	
– Building (20 x 5%)	1	(104)
Net Profit		£109

b Four Limitations of Manufacturing Accounts

1   It is a financial statement and the apportionment of costs between manufacturing, office and selling may be arbitrary (as in the question). Similary deciding whether certain costs are direct or indirect may create problems.

2   The manufacturing account summarises the costs involved in the manufacturing process but does not provide any information about the efficiency of the manufacturing process and is therefore not useful for as a decision making tool.

3   Expenses are not compared to revenue received so it is inadequate as a performance statement.

4   It is a total account and does not analyse the costs of manufacturing the various products dealt with.

Suggested Solution 11.1

a

Thick, Thin and Stout
Capital Accounts

	Thick £	Thin £	Stout £		Thick £	Thin £	Stout £
				1.6.94			
Antiques taken	1,500			Balances b/f	15,900	10,600	
				Assets introduced			5,200
Goodwill				Profit on antiques	840	560	
adjustment	1,440	1,440	720	Goodwill			
Bank withdrawn	3,320			adjustment	2,160	1,440	
Balances c/d	12,640	12,640	6,320	Cash introduced		1,480	1,840
	£18,900	£14,080	£7,040		£18,900	£14,080	£7,040
				Balances b/d	12,640	12,640	6,320

b

Balance Sheet as at 1 June 1995

		£	£
Fixed assets:			
Land and buildings:	Cost		7,000
Fixtures etc:	Cost and valuation	14,400	
Depreciation		2,500	11,900
			18,900
Current assets:			
Trading stock		6,000	
Debtors		6,500	
Bank		2,000	
		14,500	
Current liabilities:	Creditors	1,800	
			12,700
			£31,600
Financed by:			
Capital accounts:	Thick		12,640
	Thin		12,640
	Stout		6,320
			£31,600

Suggested solution 11.2

a

Jack, Tom and Harry
Appropriation Account for year ended 31 December 1994

	9 months		3 months		Total	
	£	£	£	£	£	£
Profits		12,000		4,000		16,000
Add: Harry's salary				1,000		1,000
Rent				250		250
				5,250		17,250
Less: Interest on capital						
J	900		300		1,200	
T	600		200		800	
H	–	1,500	150	650	150	2,150
		10,500		4,600		15,100
Salary: Tom		2,250				2,250
		8,250				12,850
Profit shares:						
J $\left(\frac{2}{5}\right)$		4,950	$\left(\frac{1}{2}\right)$ 2,300		7,250	
T $\left(\frac{2}{5}\right)$		3,300	$\left(\frac{3}{10}\right)$ 1,380		4,680	
H		–	$\left(\frac{1}{5}\right)$ 920		920	
		£8,250		£4,600		£12,850

Capital Accounts

	J	T	H		J	T	H
31.12.94				1.1.94			
Balances c/d	12,000	8,000	6,000	Balances b/d	12,000	8,000	
				1.10.94			
				Assets			
				introduced			6,000
	£12,000	£8,000	£6,000		£12,000	£8,000	£6,000

Current Accounts

	J	T	H		J	T	H
				1.1.94			
Drawings:				Balances b/d	1,000	700	
Cash	5,000	6,000		Interest on			
Salary			1,000	capital	1,200	800	150
Rent			250	Salaries		2,250	
				Profits	7,250	4,680	920
31.12.94				31.12.94			
Balances c/d	4,450	2,430		Balances c/d			180
	£9,450	£8,430	£1,250		£9,450	£8,430	£1,250

Suggested solution 11.3

Capital Accounts, year to 31 March 1995:

Date			A £		B £		C £		D £
		£	£	£	£	£	£	£	£
1.4.94	Balance b/d		95,000		69,000		38,000		
	Loan interest								
	year to 31.3.93		1,200		1,500				
	Correction of								
	1993 profits	1,350		900		450			
	Loan interest								
	year to 31.3.94		1,200		1,500				
	Correction of								
	error	1,500		1,200					
Jan 94	Car taken over						1,200		
	Profit on car		75		50		25		
31.3.95	Bank								6,000
	Goodwill								
	adjustment		3,000		2,000		1,000	6,000	
31.3.95	Interest on loans		1,200		1,500				
31.3.95	Profits for year								
	(note 1)		32,535		21,690		10,845		7,230
31.3.95	Drawings								
	(note 2)	21,500		17,800		7,400		5,000	
		24,350	134,210	19,900	97,240	9,050	49,870	11,000	13,230
31.3.95	Balance c/d	109,860		77,340		40,820		2,230	
			£134,210	£134,210	£97,240	£97,240	£49,870	£49,870	£13,230	£13,230
1.4.95	Balance b/d		109,860		77,340		40,820		2,230

Notes:

1. Profit for year:

	£	£
per draft accounts		70,000
Add: D's salary		5,000
Profit for appropriation		75,000
Interest on loans A	1,200	
B	1,500	2,700
		72,300
Profits D$\frac{1}{10}$		7,230
		65,070
Remainder to: A	32,535	
B	21,690	
C	10,845	
in old profit sharing ratio		65,070

2. The drawings of £5,000 for D represent the salary he must have received during the year.

Suggested solution 11.4

a

Jim, Betty and Junior
Balance Sheets as at 31 May 1995

	Alternatives	
	(a)	(b)
	£	£
Goodwill	5,000	–
Fixed assets	15,000	15,000
Net current assets	16,000	16,000
	£36,000	£31,000
Financed by:		
Capital accounts: Jim	14,000	12,125
Betty	12,000	10,125
Junior	10,000	8,750
	£36,000	£31,000

Workings:
Capital accounts alternative (a)

	Jim	Betty	Junior		Jim	Betty	Junior
				Balances b/d	10,000	8,000	
				Revaluation of assets	1,500	1,500	
				Goodwill adjustment	2,500	2,500	
Balances c/d	14,000	12,000	10,000	Bank			10,000
	£14,000	£12,000	£10,000		£14,000	£12,000	£10,000

The only other entry required for alternative (b) is to write off the goodwill and hence the capital accounts will remain the same except:

	£	£	£
Goodwill adjustment	1,875	1,875	1,250
Balance c/d	12,125	10,125	8,750
	£14,000	£12,000	£10,000

Note: the above assumes Jim and Betty share profits equally but it could be argued that this benefits Betty more than Jim as he has invested more than her (10,000: 8,000) by 31 May 1995.

Suggested solution 11.5

a

		Alternatives			
		1		2	
		£	£	£	£
Fixed assets			21,000		21,000
Current assets:	Stock	9,000		9,000	
	Debtors	6,000		6,000	
	Bank	12,750		2,250	
		27,750		17,250	
Current liabilities:					
Creditors		19,500		19,500	
Net current assets/					
(liabilities)			8,250		(2,250)
			£29,250		£18,750
Financed by:					
Capital accounts:	X		10,000		–
	Y		5,000		–
	T		9,000		18,750 (w2)
			24,000		
Current accounts:	X (w1)	4,250			
	Y (w1)	1,000			
			5,250		
			£29,250		

Workings:
1

	X	Y		X	Y
			Current Accounts		
Balance b/d		500	Balance b/d	1,250	
			Profit on revaluation	2,000	1,000
Balance c/d	4,250	1,000	Goodwill payment		
			(bank)	1,000	500
	£4,250	£1,500		£4,250	£1,500

2 Under option 2 the capital account would be £18,750 only if goodwill of £1,750 is written off.

b

	£
Maintainable profit pa	9,000
Add: T's salary	6,000
	15,000
Add: Increase in profits	12,000
	27,000
Less: Loan interest	7,200
Estimated available profits	£19,800

Appropriation under		Offer no.	
		1	2
X		4,400	
Y		2,200	
T	$\left(\frac{2}{3}\right)$	13,200	19,800
		£19,800	£19,800

T's anticipated return on offer (1) is 13,200 pa for an investment of £10,500 (an annual return of 126 per cent) but under offer (2) he will gain an additional return of only £6,600 for an additional investment of £10,000.

Thus his marginal return on the additional money needed to take up offer (2) is 66 per cent. Thus he should only accept offer (2) if his cost of the marginal £10,000 is less than 66 per cent either in terms of direct interest.

Suggested solution 11.6

a

James, Charles and Harold

DR		Realisation Account			CR
	£				£
Plant and equipment	32,000	James capital a/c			
Stock	19,000	Goodwill			5,000
Debtors	17,000	Plant and equipment			18,000
Bank: Dissolution expenses	800	Stock			9,000
	68,800				32,000
		Bank: Plant and			
		equipment			12,000
		Stock			7,000
		Debtors			16,100
		Discount received			200
					67,300
		Loss on realisation:			
		James		750	
		Charles		500	
		Harold		250	
					1,500
	£68,800				£68,800

b

DR		Bank Account		CR
	£			£
Plant and equipment	12,000	Balance b/f		16,500
Stock	7,000	Dissolution expenses		800
Debtors	16,100	Creditors		9,300
James	5,750	Charles		7,500
		Harold		6,750
	£40,850			£40,850

c

Capital Accounts

	James	Charles	Harold		James	Charles	Harold
	£	£	£		£	£	£
Loss on realisation	750	500	250	Balance b/f	12,000	8,000	7,000
Assets taken over	32,000			Loan account	15,000		
Bank		7,500	6,750	Bank	5,750		
	£32,750	£8,000	£7,000		£32,750	£8,000	£7,000

Workings:

DR		Creditors	CR
	£		£
Bank	9,300	Balance b/f	9,500
Realisation account: Discount	200		
	£9,500		£9,500

Suggested solution 11.7

a

Brass & Smith
Profit & Loss Appropriation for year ended 31 December 1994

	1 Jan – 31 March	1 April – 31 Dec
Apportioned 3/9	12,000	36,000
Interest on drawings:		
Brass	–	360
Smith	–	240
Fender	–	150
		36,750
Salaries:		
(Smith (9/12 x 8,000)	–	(6,000)
Fender (9/12 x 12,000)	–	(9,000)
		21,750
Interest on capital:		
Brass (9/12 x 40,000 x 5%)	–	(1,500)
Smith (9/12 x 20,000 x 5%)	–	(750)
Fender (9/12 x 16,000 x 5%)	–	(600)
		18,900
Division of balance:		
Brass 2/3 / 4/7	(8,000)	(10,800)
Smith 1/3 / 2/7	(4,000)	(5,400)
Fender – / 1/7	–	(2,700)

b

(i) Partners' Capital Account for year ended 31 December 1994

Date		Brass	Smith	Fender
1.1.94	Balances b/f	38,000	19,000	–
1.4.94	Goodwill (2:1)	14,000	7,000	–
1.4.94	Cash introduced	–	–	19,000
1.4.94	Goodwill reversed (4:2:1)	(12,000)	(6,000)	(3,000)
		£40,000	£20,000	£16,000

(ii) Partners' Current Accounts for year ended 31 December 1994

Date		£	£	£
1.1.94	Balances b/f	–	–	–
	Drawings	(12,000)	(8,000)	(5,000)
	Interest on drawings	(360)	(240)	(150)
	Salaries	–	6,000	9,000
	Interest on capital	1,500	750	600
	Division of balance:			
	1 Jan – 31 March	8,000	4,000	–
	1 April – 31 Dec	10,800	5,400	2,700
	Balance c/f	£7,940	£7,910	£7,150

c

Brass, Smith & Fender – Partnership
Balance Sheet as at 31 December 1994

		Cost	Depn	£
Fixed assets:				
	Freehold land	65,000	–	65,000
	Foundry equipment	69,000	51,750	17,250
	Vehicles	32,000	24,000	8,000
		£166,000	£75,750	£90,250
Current assets:				
	Stock		7,920	
	Debtors		25,950	
	Prepayments		600	
	Cash in hand		1,250	
			£35,720	
Current liabilities:				
	Overdraft		4,800	
	Creditors		21,120	
	Accruals		1,050	
			£26,970	8,750
Net current assets				£99,000

	Brass	Smith	Fender	
Capital accounts	40,000	20,000	16,000	76,000
Current accounts	7,940	7,910	7,150	23,000
	£47,940	£27,910	£23,150	£99,000

d Three problems that are distinctive to the functioning of a partnership are:

i It is necessary to come to an agreement between the partners about division of profit, restrictions on drawings, amount of capital to be introduced, arrangements relating to interest.

ii On a change to the partnership, ie retirement, death, or introduction of a new partner, the agreements will have to be revised.

iii Partners must agree on the extent to which they are involved in the day-to-day running of the business.

Suggested solution 11.8

a

Smith & Khan
Profit & Loss and Appropriation Accounts for year ended 31 May 1995

	£	£
Commission on bookings		70,420
Commission on insurance		8,820
Loss on tours		(22,600)
		56,640
Salaries 31,000		
Postage & telephone (−150 + 3,850)	3,700	
Printing & stationery (+520 + 4,220)	4,740	
Sundry	2,100	
Rates (+ 600 + 2,800)	3,400	
Bad debt	830	
Depreciation: Fittings (10%)	4,000	
Cars (25%)	7,500	
		(57,270)
Net loss		£(630)

	1 June – 31 Nov	1 Dec – 31 May
Divided as to period		
Net loss	(315)	(315)
Salaries:		
S	–	(4,500)
K	–	(3,300)
C	–	(2,450)
Interest on capital @ 2%:		
S 100,000 x 2% x 6 months	–	(1,000)
K 55,000 x 2% x 6 months	–	(550)
C 35,000 x 2% x 6 months	–	(350)
Division of balance:		(12,465)
S 4/7 / 4/9	180	5,540
K 3/7 / 3/9	135	4,155
C – / 2/9	–	2,770
	–	–

b

Smith & Khan
Balance Sheet as at 31 May 1995

	£	£	£
Capital accounts:			
S			100,000
K			55,000
C			35,000
			190,000
Current accounts:			
S		(8,220)	
K		(5,940)	
C		(3,670)	(17,830)
			£172,170
Fixed assets:			
Freehold premises	160,000	–	160,000
Fixtures	40,000	26,000	14,000
Motor vehicles	30,000	16,500	13,500
	£230,000	£42,500	£187,500
Current assets:			
Debtors		16,400	
Prepayments		150	
		£16,550	
Current liabilities:			
Creditors		28,800	
Accruals (600 + 520)		1,120	
Overdraft		1,960	
		£31,880	
Net current liabilities			(15,330)
			£172,170

Suggested solution 13.1

a

Hardnails Ltd
Trading, Profit & Loss Account for the year ended 30 June 1995

	£000	£000
Sales		1,625
Stock 1.7.94	118	
Purchases	730	
	848	
Stock 30.6.95	185	
Cost of sales		663
Gross profit		962
Investment income		4
Profit on sale of fixed assets		2
		968
Less: Expenses:		
Wages	380	
Administration and selling costs	62	
Depreciation	34	
Debenture interest	18	
Provision for doubtful debts	2	496
Net profit for year		472
Proposed dividend		32
Retained profits for year		440
Retained profits b/f		48
		488
Discount on issue of loan stock written off		6
Retained profits as at 30.6.95		£482

b

Balance Sheet as at 30 June 1995

		£000	£000	£000
Fixed assets:	Land and buildings			1,300
	Machinery: Cost		211	
	Depreciation to date		75	
				136
				1,436
Investments				48
Current assets:	Stock		185	
	Debtors	160		
	Provision for doubtful debts	8		
			152	
	Cash in hand		2	
			£339	
Current liabilities:	Creditors		297	
	Loan stock interest		18	
	Dividends		32	
	Bank		44	
			£391	
Net current liabilities				(52)
				£1,432

Financed by:

	£000	£000
Share capital	Authorised	Issued
Ordinary 50 pence shares, fully paid	250	200
Reserves		
Revaluation reserve	150	
Retained profits	482	
		632
		832
12% Loan stock		600
		£1,432

c i Where the properties were revalued during the year the name or qualification of the valuer (surveyor in this example) and the basis used.

ii Quoted investments must be separately identified. Market value at the balance sheet date must be shown.

iii The aggregate of paid and proposed dividends will be disclosed and the amount of the proposed dividend must be shown under current liabilities.

iv In themselves administration and selling costs need will be disclosed in total as 'administrative expenses'.

v No disclosure required, unless qualifying as an exceptional item by virtue of the magnitude.

Suggested solution 13.2

a The justification for the provision of analysed information by companies with different classes of activities is that users of accounts are entitled to sufficient information to enable them to:

i understand the results and state of affairs of the company; and

ii be aware of the importance that changes in major component parts of a company's business may have on the company as a whole.

If a reader of a set of accounts is to be able to understand the trend of results in a diversified company, analysed information should be given. For example, an increase in overall turnover and profit might hide losses in certain activities, and unless analysed information is available users of accounts will not be able to form their own views on the effect of changing circumstances in the various areas on the companies future.

Also, readers of accounts should be aware of the sources of earnings in a diversified company so that they can form their own opinion on the quality and reliability of those earnings, especially if the activities are in high-risk areas.

A further point is that provision of analysed information shows up different rates of return on assets employed, and can be a pointer for management to take steps to improve returns in areas which have been below average in the past.

b There are three types of problem associated with providing analysed information. The first is purely practical – is the information available? This does not seem to be a major problem, as most companies large enough to have diversified operations have accounting systems adequate to provide the information. If they have not, then management must in any case be operating inefficiently, and new accounting methods should be introduced.

The second category of problems relate to the usefulness of such information:

Firstly, there is the point that even though a company may have different activities, it is still one unit as far as the investor is concerned. This does not seem to be a very forceful objection as overall performance depends on how well or badly individual activities perform. Any judgment as to the quality of earnings, level of risk and prospects for expansion must depend on the assessment of the earnings, risk and prospects of the components of the business and the size of these parts in relation to the whole.

Secondly, there is the objection that the information might be misleading on one of the following grounds:

i   It might give the impression that the activities of the company could be considered as independent businesses whereas this might not be the case. The answer to this may be that readers are not so unsophisticated as to jump to that conclusion, particularly if the analysed information is disclosed in tabular form and certain common costs not allocated.

ii   The basis of presentation would be purely judgmental and therefore not comparable between different companies.

     This is a valid point, but the answer is surely to establish guidelines for uniformity of disclosure by way of an SSAP rather than to refuse to disclose.

     Also, the primary purpose of analysed information is the comparison from one year of a business to the next, not one company with another.

iii The information may make companies accounts more complicated and therefore less readily understood: this depends on the care which is taken in presentation. The accounts of a large and diversified operation can never be simple, but they can be clear and precise.

The third category of problem is commercial. It can be argued that disclosure will weaken the company's position because competition, customes and suppliers will have more detailed information than previously. This might be particularly damaging to small companies, and also to international companies in their dealings with foreign governments.

Also, it is thought that management might be deterred from undertaking new ventures which although possibly profitable in the long term may show early losses which would have to be disclosed.

These arguments are advanced whenever new information is demanded; generally it is unlikely that it would be sufficiently detailed to be of great commercial use to a competitor. If the directors felt it was, then as in other areas now, they might feel strongly enough to risk a qualified audit report.

As far as new ventures are concerned, in the early years they would probably not be material enough to warrant disclosures. If they are significant then that is all the more reason for them to be closely monitored.

Suggested solution 13.3

a i   Share premium account: this is the fund that arises when shares are issued at an amount in excess of nominal value. It is a legal requirement that the excess over nominal value is credited to a share premium account and disclosed separately on the balance sheet.

It is a statutory reserve which is non distributable and can only be used for:

– the issue of bonus shares, fully paid, to existing members of the company;

– to write off expenses on the issue of shares/debentures;

– to write off preliminary expenses.

A share premium reserve is owned by the company shareholders.

ii   General reserve account: this is revenue profit set aside, to be retained in the business for use in the future, for a purpose as yet unspecified by the directors.

The reserve is legally available for distribution to shareholders as a dividend and could be used for a bonus issue, or to meet foreign exchange losses, etc.

A general reserve is owned by the company shareholders.

iii   Retained earnings account:

This is the total of the accumulated, undistributed profits of all past years. It is part of the shareholders equity.

Retained earnings are available for distribution to shareholders as dividend if required, can be used for a bonus issue or to cover future losses of the company.

Retained earnings are owned by the company shareholders

b i   Liquidity is a measure of the ability of a business to meet its liabilities. It indicates the extent to which a business has available cash resources or can turn its resources into cash quickly to meet its liabilities. Liquidity ratios are:

Current ratio: this is the ratio of current assets to current liabilities,

ie   66:17

or   3.9:1

The ratio appears extremely healthy.

Quick assets ratio: this is the ratio of current assets excluding stock to current liabilities,

ie   46:17

or   2.7:1

This ratio is also healthy, it demonstrates that the business has almost three times its level of liabilities in cash or near cash resources.

ii   Profitability is the ability of a company to utilise its existing capital employed and to increase it over a period of time. Profitability ratios are:

Return on capital employed (ROCE): this relates the net profit to the level of investment used to earn it. The ratio is calculated as net profit/capital employed with several variations of 'net profit' and the appropriate 'capital employed' figure. The ratio is 7.4/110 x 100 = 6.7 per cent. Theoretically, the higher the ratio the better, since a higher ratio suggests effective trading.

Gross profit margin: this relates gross profit to sales and is 12.8/30 x 100 = 42.7 per cent. It should remain constant unless the company has changed its pricing policy. Any unexpected variations must be investigated in case of fraud or stock valuation errors.

Net profit margin: this expresses the net profit as a percentage of sales and is 7.4/30 x 100 = 24.7 per cent. Any significant variations must be investigated to ensure that overheads are being properly controlled.

c i Annual dividend yield = dividend/price paid for shares = 2 per cent (400/20,000 x 100).

ii Total return on investment = increase in share value + dividend /price paid for shares = 42 per cent (8,000 + 400/20,000 x 100).

iii The annual dividend yield is poor at 2 per cent, a better return would probably be available from a bank or building society.

The total yield at 42 per cent is exceptionally good and more than compensates for the low return as long as the growth continues.

d Ordinary shares have no fixed rate of return so in theory in a time of high profit the dividends will be high. They are a risk investment since conversely in a time of low profit, or no profit, there may be no dividends. The market value of the shares will change in value and hopefully this will generate a capital profit.

Preference shares have a fixed rate of return so will not enjoy the benefits of high profits. They do however have priority over ordinary shareholders both as regards dividends and repayment of capital.

If Alice had invested £20,000 in preference shares at £1.20 per share she would have acquired 16,666 shares, and received dividends of £1,667, an 8.3 per cent return on the capital invested. Even though the dividend yield is better than on the ordinary shares the overall return, taking into account the capital growth, is better in the ordinary share investment.

It appears that in the short term the investment should remain in ordinary shares, but if the dividend does not increase and the capital growth slows down it might be advisable to consider a switch to preference shares later.

Suggested solution 14.1

a The goodwill referred to by Perry Ltd is inherent in the business but is only realised when the business is sold and until that time it must not be shown as an asset on the balance sheet.

Goodwill is an intangible asset that arises when the purchase consideration paid on the acquisition of a business exceeds the fair value of the assets at that date.

To take credit in the accounts for the 'goodwill' before it is realised would contravene the prudence concept of SSAP 2.

b Depreciation is the allocation of the cost of an asset over the period expected to benefit from its use. All assets with a finite life should be depreciated and the method of depreciation must be applied consistently, unless one of the estimates used in the original calculations is found to be incorrect. If the asset has genuinely risen in value it may be revalued. However, the revalued amount must continue to be depreciated over the remaining useful life.

Therefore the premises may be revalued but, in any event, must continue to be depreciated.

c Stock is to be valued at the lower of cost and net realisable value. Net realisable value is the selling price less any costs of sale, and applied to the stock in the question this would give a revised value of £750 (ie £850 - £100) for the damaged sweatshirts and the total stock figure should be £89,950 (ie £90,000 - £800 + £750).

This is an application of the prudence concept in that the loss resulting from the fall in value of the stock is taken into account as soon as the damage is discovered, rather than later at the point of sale.

Therefore the final stock figure must be reduced.

d The directors can declare a dividend provided the current profits cover past losses and that sufficient profit is available for distribution in accordance with the company's act.

It would be prudent to assess whether sufficient cash was available to pay the dividends, in view of the past history.

Debenture interest and bank interest are combined together and shown on the face of the profit and loss as a charge, before taxation.

Dividends must be shown as an appropriation of profit, disclosed after tax and must not therefore be added to the interest charges.

e The bad debt recovered must be credited to the profit and loss of the current period. The proposed treatment as a prior year adjustment only applies to the correction of a fundamental error and a change in accounting policy, and does not apply in this case.

It is advisable to write the recovery back through the customers' account so that his records are updated to take account of the repayment. If this is not done he will appear incorrectly to have a bad debt record.

Suggested solution 14.2

a

Convex Ltd
Manufacturing, Trading, Profit and Loss Account
for year ended 30 September 1994

	£000	£000
Direct materials		90
Direct wages		40
Prime Cost		130
Factory overheads:		
Overhead	30	
Depreciation	10	40
Cost of goods manufactured		170
Sales		120
Cost of goods manufactured	170	
Less Closing stocks $\left(\dfrac{170}{10,000} \times 4,000 \right)$	68	
Cost of Sales		102
Gross Profit		18
General overheads	7	
Advertising (6 x 25%)	1.5	8.5
Net Profit		£9.5

Balance Sheet as at 30 September 1994

		£000	£000	£000
Fixed Assets:	Plant and equipment cost			60
	Depreciation			10
				50
Current Assets:	Stock		68	
	Debtors		32	
			100	
Current Liabilities:	Creditors	62		
	Overdraft	15	77	23
Deferred Revenue Expenditure:				
Research and development			12	
Advertising			4.5	16.5
				89.5
Ordinary share capital				80
Retained earnings				9.5
				89.5

b a Depreciation
Convex Ltd can choose any method of depreciating its assets. Best accounting practice will be determined by the individual circumstances regarding the assets. Where it is estimated that the assets would lose most value in earlier years then a method such as reducing balance should be used and the rate given would be reasonable. However, another view is that all years' production benefit equally from the plant and machinery and that therefore, on the matching principle, each year should suffer an equal depreciation charge.

b Factory overheads and depreciation

SSAP 9 on Stocks and Work in Progress defines cost as inclusive of 'costs of conversion'. These costs of conversion include production overheads and applicable depreciation. Consequently the policy suggested in note b) is reasonable, provided that the production overheads are not abnormal, taking one year with another.

c It seems unwise to defer any part of either expense in these circumstances.

Regarding the advertising, there is no guarantee that the benefits will accrue after the programme is ended and thus deferral cannot be recommended.

Capitalisation of development costs in these circumstances is also wrong as the prototypes appear to have brought their benefit only to the period in which they are constructed, and the situation does not fall within the circumstances in which SSAP 13 regards capitalisation as advisable.

Suggested solution 14.3

a Purpose of Published Financial Statements:

1 To comply with the requirements of the Companies Act and Accounting Standards.

2 To provide clear information about company performance so that shareholders and investors can make decisions about their investment.

3 To provide uniform information about companies in a clear and easily understood format so that a variety of users can make decisions about their respective interests in the company.

4 To meet the requirements of the Stock Exchange in respect of public companies.

b Describe the problems that public companies must consider when preparing annual financial statements for publication:

1 The need to apply accounting standards and policies to events that occur during the accounting period to ensure they are correctly included in the financial statements. The cost of implementing the additional recording that is necessary may be excessive when compared with the benefit of the information so provided.

2 The difficulty of complying with the various legal and accounting requirements and at the same time preserving confidentiality to protect the company from competitors and to safeguard against possible takeovers.

3 The cost of gathering and presenting information for disclosure may be expensive particularly for smaller companies. In addition there is pressure for companies to provide information of a sociological and environmental nature which they may be reluctant to reveal.

4 Public companies with a large number of UK and overseas subsidiaries will have problems collecting information, agreeing inter-company

balances, translating foreign currency into sterling and coordinating the results for inclusion in the group accounts.

5   For many compliance with the legal time limits for publication of the accounts, filing annual returns and other statutory documents is often a major problem.

c Outline what you consider are the basic characteristics needed to produce effective financial statements:

1   Timely – It is important to produce the statements promptly otherwise time passes and the statements lose their usefulness.

2   Reliability – There is a need for an audit to confirm the credibility of the information.

3   Comparability – Information needs to be presented in such a manner that enables comparison to be made.

4   Completeness – This indicates that all items of current or potential interst should be revealed, but this aspect could clash with timeliness.

5   Understandable – Information should be in a form which gives the user easy knowledge of affairs.

6   Relevant – All information contained in the statements should be inter-related and applicable to the users's needs.

7   Objective – The statements should be free from bias and reveal a fair view of affairs.

Suggested solution 17.1

a The 'worth' of any share is determined not by the net assets underlying the share (net asset value per share) but by the price which someone else is willing to pay for it. On the stock exchange this will be the quoted price.

There are many factors which go towards determining the worth of any particular share, which could include:

i   yield per share;

ii   earnings per share;

iii performance of firm in relation to its industry group;

iv   risk of the industry;

v   risk/return preference of potential purchasers;

vi   future expectations regarding the share;

vii the value of the underlying assets.

Even if 'worth' were based on accounting information there are still several reasons why it cannot be computed from the published historical cost balance sheet.

One of the major reasons is that the accounts are prepared on the basis of 'going concern' and consequently the values shown in the balance sheet are a mixture of

i   historic cost;

ii   net realisable value (where lower than cost);

iii   something approaching replacement cost (for certain fixed assets which have been revalued).

Lastly, it is occasionally said that if the market price of a share falls below that of its net asset value it is 'under-valued' in stock exchange terms. Taking into account all the above difficulties, it is possible (and only possible) to say that the net asset value per share is its minimum 'worth'. However, it should be noted that there are many firms quoted on the stock exchange whose market valuation is far lower than their net assets.

b Gearing is the term applied to the ratio of fixed interest and fixed dividend bearing long-term loans and capital funds to the funds provided by ordinary shareholders. It is a measure of risk. The more highly geared a firm is, the more sensitive are the earnings of the ordinary shareholder to fluctuations in profit levels. That is, in a highly geared company the ordinary shareholders will benefit in a good year, but their return will be very low in a poor year.

The ratio can be expressed either as:

i $\dfrac{\text{fixed payment bearing securities}}{\text{ordinary shareholders funds}}$ or

ii $\dfrac{\text{fixed payment bearing securities}}{\text{total capital invested}}$

(*Note*: it has also been argued that bank overdrafts should be incorporated into the ratio.)

Whether it is a good or a bad thing from any ordinary shareholder's view will depend entirely on that person's risk/return preference and his/her perceptions and/or expectations regarding the (future) performance of the company. However, one can point to certain factors which result from high gearing, notably that the firm can only be 'highly geared' when compared to its industry group and consequently the reinvestment rate of this firm is likely to be lower than that of its peers. Hence if Stan Down is interested more in yield than capital growth then this may be a 'good' thing.

c There are two types of reserves:

i)   'non-distributable' reserves: those which *cannot* (by law) be distributed to shareholders;

ii)   'distributable' reserves: those which *can* be distributed to shareholders, which consist by law of *realised* profits only.

Consequently, the principal reserve which is distributable is retained profits and this reserve will have been built up over a period of time as a reinvestment of profit in the business. If any distribution took place to reduce retained profits (one year over the last) then the firm will have made distributions larger than the profits made during the year and as a result will have reduced the net worth of the company.

d In circumstances where more than one accounting basis is acceptable in principle, eg whether straight-line or reducing balance method of depreciation is used the accounting policy followed can significantly affect a concern's reported results and financial position. The view presented can be properly appreciated only if the policies followed in dealing with material items are explained. For this reason adequate disclosure of accounting policies is essential to the fair presentation of financial accounts (SSAP 2).

Matters to be disclosed might include:

i   a statement that turnover is net of discounts, intra-group sales and VAT or other sales taxes;

ii   a statement on depreciation policy, which since SSAP 12 will include the method and the rate used (or useful life);

iii a statement that stocks have been consistently valued at the lower of cost or net realisable value (SSAP 9);

iv   a statement to show the accounting policy in any of the following:

treatment of intangibles	repairs and renewals
long term contracts	consolidation matters
deferred tax	guarantees
hire purchase + leasing	conversion of foreign currencies

Finally, where the fundamental accounting concepts (going concern, accruals, consistency and prudence) have not been followed, a note to this effect must be included.

Suggested solution 17.2

a i

	A Ltd	B Ltd
Net profit to sales ratio	$\frac{12}{200}$ x 100	$\frac{57.2}{520}$ x 100
	6%	11%

ii

	A Ltd	B Ltd
Stock turnover ratio	$\frac{160}{12}$	$\frac{410}{22}$
	13⅓ times	18⅔ times approx

b

	£	A Ltd £	£	B Ltd £
Sales		200,000		520,000
Cost of sales		160,000		410,000
Gross profit		40,000		110,000
Rent	8,000		10,000	
Loan interest	1,200		8,400	
Other expenses	6,800		16,400	
Directors' salaries	10,000		15,000	
Depreciation	4,500		7,500	
		30,500		57,300
Net profit		£9,500		£52,700

c

s	£	A Ltd £
Sales		400,000
Cost of sales		300,000
Gross profit 25%		100,000
Rent	8,000	
Loan interest @ 12%	1,200	
@ 15%	9,000	
Other expenses	11,800	
Directors' salaries	10,000	
Depreciation	16,500	
		56,500
Net profit		£43,500

d (Any two of the following):

   i   age of freehold land and buildings;

   ii   age of plant and equipment;

   iii stock valuation method;

   iv analysis of other expenses/wages;

   v   industry statistics;

   vi breakdown of net current assets;

   vii history of industrial relations, unionisation, etc;

   viii character and background of directors;

   ix past R & D, expenditure, if relevant;

   x   any contingent liability;

   xi loan repayment terms.

Suggested solution 17.3

a Working capital (current) ratio:

	31 October	
	1994	1995
Stock	196	311
Debtors	82	129
Bank	30	
	£308	£440
Loan stock	150	–
Creditors	74	102
Dividends	26	39
Bank	–	35
	£250	£176
Current ratio	308:250	440:176
or	1.232:1	2.5:1

b A bank overdraft is repayable on call by the bank, which could be very short notice indeed. However, most firms with overdrafts tend to utilise them more as longer term borrowing, having little or no intention of repaying it.

Hence it can be considered to be part of long-term financing in certain circumstances, which will be individual to the companies themselves.

Suggested solution 17.4

Uthank Ltd
Profit & Loss Account for year ended 30 April 1995

		£	£
Sales	(note 2)		200,000
Purchases	(note 1)	176,000	
Closing stock		16,000	
Cost of sales			160,000
Gross profit			40,000
Expenses:	Administration	20,000	
	Establishment	2,550	
	Debenture interest	400	
	Audit fees	500	
	Depreciation:		
	Plant and machinery	800	
	Motor vehicles	2,750	
			25,000
Net profit			15,000
Dividend: Proposed			5,000
			10,000
Transfer to general reserve			2,000
Retained profit			£8,000

Balance Sheet as at 30 April 1995

		Cost	Depn	£
Fixed assets:	Freehold property	7,000	–	7,000
	Plant and machinery	8,000	800	7,200
	Motor vehicles	3,000	750	2,250
		£18,000	£1,550	16,450
Current assets:	Stock		16,000	
	Debtors		4,000	
	Bank (by balance) (note 3)		10,550	
			30,550	
Current liabilities:	Creditors	3,000		
	Dividend	5,000		
			8,000	
				22,550
				£39,000

Financed by:

		Authorised	Issued
Share capital		20,000	20,000
Reserves:	Share premium	5,000	
	General	2,000	
	Retained profits	8,000	15,000
			35,000
10% Debentures			4,000
			£39,000

Notes:

1

Payments for purchases	173,000
Creditors	3,000
Total purchases	£176,000

2 i   Sales – cost of sales = gross profit

   ii   Gross profit – expenses = net profit
or gross profit = net profit + expenses
Substituting (ii) into (i) gives:

   iii   Sales – cost of sales = net profit + expenses or
Sales – 160,000 = net profit + 25,000
In addition we are given

   iv   Net profit = $7\frac{1}{2}$ x sales
Substituting into (iii) we get

   v   Sales – 160,000 = $7\frac{1}{2}$% sales + 25,000
Sales – $7\frac{1}{2}$% sales = 25,000 + 160,000
$92\frac{1}{2}$% sales = 185,000
$$\text{Sales} = \frac{185,000}{92\frac{1}{2}\%}$$
= 200,000

3   Proof of bank balance:

	£		£
Share issue	25,000	Freehold property	7,000
Debenture issue	4,000	Plant and machinery	8,000
Sales	196,000	Motor vehicles	3,000
		Purchases	173,000
		Administration	20,000
		Establishment	2,550
		Debenture interest	400
		Audit fees	500
		Balance c/d	10,550
	£225,000		£225,000

Suggested solution 17.5

a

Jacques Dennett
Revised Revenue Statement for the year ended 30 September 1995

	£	£
Sales (950,000 – 27,000)		923,000
Cost of goods sold (485,000 – 24,300 + 26,000 + 13,870)		(500,570)
Gross profit		422,430
Rental income		5,000
Administrative expenses (120,800 – 25,000)	(95,800)	
Selling & distribution (81,700)	(81,700)	
Financial charges (12,500)	(12,500)	
Business premises – fall in value	(70,000)	
		(260,000)
Revised net profit		£167,430

Revised Balance Sheet as at 30 September 1995

	£	£
Fixed assets (426,000 – 40,000 – 70,000)		316,000
Current assets (149,000 – 27,000 – 26,000 + 5,000 + 5,000)		106,000
Current liabilities (71,000 + 13,870 – 20,000)		(64,870)
		£357,130
Capital	504,000	
Less: Draft net profit	(250,000)	
	254,000	
Add: Revised profit	167,430	
Add: Error in rent 1992	5,000	
Less: Drawings: Goods at cost	(24,300)	
Servicing cost	(25,000)	
Loan from friend	(20,000)	
		£357,130

b Report to Bank Manager. This must be in report style and should include the following:

i   Business entry concepts: goods supplied to family members must be treated as a gift by the proprietor ie drawings.

ii Prudence/conservatism concepts: stock must be valued at the lower of cost and net realisable value, profit must not be overstated.

iii Business entity concept: the servicing of private cars is not a business expense. It must be treated as drawings. In addition the vintage car bought for private use must not be included in business fixed assets nor depreciated. The related loan is treated as drawings.

iv Prudence/conservatism: if the fall in property values is regarded as permanent this must be written off the asset and deducted from the current profits.

v   Accruals concept: profit and loss must include the value of all services received/given in accounting period, irrespective of whether or not the invoice has been paid/received in cash. Therefore the rental income must be included for both years. For 1995 adjust profit and loss and for 1994 adjust opening capital.

vi Accruals concept: as for (v) the value of the unpaid invoices must be included in the trading account because the goods have been received during the accounting period.

c Assessment of liquidity and profitability.

Ratios:

Current ratio	$\dfrac{\text{current assets}}{\text{current liabilities}}$	$\dfrac{106{,}000}{64{,}870}$ = 1.63	
Quick assets ratio	$\dfrac{\text{current assets (less stock)}}{\text{current liabilities}}$	$\dfrac{41{,}000}{64{,}870}$ = 0.63	
Return on capital employed	$\dfrac{\text{net profit}}{\text{capital employed}}$ x 100	$\dfrac{167{,}430}{357{,}130}$ x 100 = 46.88%	
Gross profit percentage	$\dfrac{\text{gross profit}}{\text{sales}}$ x 100	$\dfrac{422{,}430}{923{,}000}$ x 100 = 45.77%	
Asset turnover	$\dfrac{\text{sales}}{\text{capital employed}}$	$\dfrac{923{,}000}{357{,}130}$ = 2.58	

Profitability is extremely good as evidenced by an excellent return on capital employed and gross profit margin.

However, the business would appeal to have liquidity problems with insufficient short-term assets to meet immediate liabilities.

Suggested solution 19.1

The limitation of financial accounting are set by the framework which has developed over the years which has resulted in the present set of accounting principles and conventions.

a The most obvious limitation is in the restriction of accounting data to those which can be expressed in monetary terms. This severely limits the usefulness of any balance sheet to a prospective purchaser, investor or creditor, as a number of very important factors are omitted from the accounts – eg the quality of labour relations, the calibre of management, internally generated goodwill.

b The historic cost concept also limits the usefulness of the accounts as the reader has no way of knowing the current value of the assets, although this conclusion may become less forceful with the advent of inflation accounting.

c The multiplicity of acceptable accounting policies renders easy comparison between businesses impossible, even though the consistency principle may ensure that within a company the apparent trends between one year and the next do in fact exist.

The above criticisms relate to the outside, the possibly lay readers views of the accounts, but while this may be important for the shareholders and creditors, from an economic standpoint there are more fundamental problems.

The major shortcomings of financial accounting from an economic view, that is, in its contribution to the profitability of the firm and thereby to the economy as a whole, lies in its original stewardship function.

Financial acocunts are essentially historical documents; the income statement records the revenue earned in the past period and the costs expended in order to earn that income, and the balance sheet records the state (or, rather, partial state according to convention) at one particular point in time. Moreover, not only are these documents historical in nature, they are probably also several months out of date by the time they are published.

A further consequence of this historical recording function is the lack of any explanation within the financial accounts. It may, for example, be apparent from the comparison of two consecutive years' income statements that profits have dropped because of an increase in wages. What will not be disclosed is any useful comment on this fact. Why wages rose, whether it could have been prevented, whether the rise will continue, whether economies can be made, productivity deals agreed etc. From the balance sheet it may be clear that the company's liquidity position has deteriorated due to acquisition of fixed assets; but there will be no indication of the reasons for the investment or the anticipated affect on turnover and profit.

Financial accounting, therefore, is limited in two major areas: firstly, in the accessibility, comprehensibility and reliability of the information provided, and secondly, and perhaps more importantly, in the deficiencies of useful information for profitable decision making.

Suggested solution 19.2

Traditionally, 'profit' in accounting terms has been held to mean the excess of revenue over expenditure. There is, however, also a view originating from the economists standpoint that profit is the increase in net wealth over a period. These two views are commonly called the revenue/expense basis and the asset/liability basis.

The problems arising from the revenue/expense basis are largely those of uncertainty. There is the problem of when revenue should be recognised and also the different methods of allocating expense.

Revenue recognition. There are three basic conditions for the recognition of revenue:

a it must have been earned;

b it must be objectively measurable;

c the most difficult process, the 'critical event' must have occurred.

In most cases, these conditions are fulfilled at the point of sale, but in such long-term processes as civil engineering and timber growing, this basis is clearly inappropriate and some proportion of the final profit must be brought in annually to avoid distorting the profit figures. Unfortunately, it is impossible to ascertain *what* proportion with any degree of certainty.

Similarly, on the expense side, costs can be recognised in three main ways:

a associating cause and effect, eg the cost of sales figures;

b systematic allocation, eg for depreciation;

c immediate write-off, eg for selling and administration costs.

The problem with (a) above is that it is very difficult to ascertain exactly – any method of depreciation is essentially arbitrary. (b) is dictated by prudence, but training cost, the recruitment costs, for example, may in fact have benefits over several years.

The asset/liability basis, unfortunately, does not escape these criticisms as the defining of profit as the increase in net assets over the period implies a high degree of accuracy in the measurement of the assets and liabilities, and it is one of the shortcomings of the traditional balance sheet that assets are stated at historic cost, not current value, and at cost less depreciation, an arbitary amount. Moreover, not all assets will be shown on the balance sheet – goodwill, know-how, etc are almost certain to be omitted – and certain liabilities, eg off balance sheet finance for leased assets, will also be omitted.

To a certain extent an ad hoc solution to difficulties surrounding profit has been reached by distinguishing between 'distributable profits' and 'non-distributable profit', the latter being such items as surplus on revaluation of fixed assets, and also by the introduction of the concept of 'extraordinary items' to distinguish non-trading profits. The root cause, however, seems to be the use of the single blanket term 'profit' to cover distinct and different meanings.

Suggested solution 19.3

a

Alternative A (note 1)	£
12% Interest on debentures £300,000	36,000
5% Discount on £300,000 over 10 years	1,500
10% Interest on loan of £215,000	21,500
	£59,000
Alternative B (note 2)	
Dividend on 800,000 shares	
800,000 x .625 x 11%	£55,000

Notes:

1 This alternative would reduce the taxable profits by £59,000 the net (after tax) cost would be £59,000 – 52% (59,000) or £28.

2 The dividend of £55,000 is not a charge against profits, but an appropriation of them.

Note: the timings of tax payments must also be taken into account, eg:

Alternative A:
Payment during year £59,000
Reduction in tax 9 months (minimum) later   30,680
Alternative B:
Payment of dividend (some time after year end)   55,000
Advance Corporation tax ¾ (approx)   24,000
                                                  £79,000
Reduction in mainstream corporation tax   24,000

b The factory would appear under the fixed assets category in the balance sheet, thus:

Fixed assets:
  Factory at cost   500,000

The methods of finance would appear thus:

	Alternative	
	A	B
Ordinary share capital		
800,000 shares of 50 pence		400,000
Reserves		
Share premium		100,000
Long-term liabilities		
12% Debentures	300,000	
Bank loan (note)	179,784	

Note:

Amount borrowed	215,000	
First year's interest	21,500	
	236,500	
Less first year's payment	56,716	(assumption: paid at end of year)
Amount still outstanding	£179,784	

Suggested solution 20.1

a

Pear Ltd
Journal

Date	Narrative	DR £	CR £
2.1.95	Freehold property	50,000	
	Provision for depreciation property	30,000	
	Revaluation reserve		80,000
5.1.95	Bank	200,000	
	Application and allotment		200,000
30.1.95	Application and allotment	50,000	
	Bank		50,000
30.1.95	Application and allotment	150,000	
	Ordinary shares of 50 pence		40,000
	Share premium		60,000
	Call account		50,000
25.3.95	Bank	10,000	
	Call account		10,000
25.3.95	Call account	60,000	
	Ordinary shares of 50 pence		60,000
29.3.95	8% Loan stock	100,000	
	Loan stock redemption		100,000
29.3.95	Loan stock redemption	102,000	
	Bank		102,000
29.3.95	Share premiums	2,000	
	Loan stocks redemption		2,000
29.3.95	Retained profits	15,000	
	Goodwill		15,000
29.3.95	Retained profits	13,000	
	General reserve (note)		13,000

Note: when loans/debentures are redeemed/repaid it is good accounting practice to transfer the amount redeemed to a general reserve. In this case it is possible to transfer only the amount of the retained earnings (£28,000) less the goodwill to be written off (£15,000) or £13,000.

b

Balance Sheet as at 31 May 1995	£	£
Fixed assets		
Property at valuation	200,000	
Plant and equipment: Cost	160,000	
Depreciation	(75,000)	85,000
		285,000
Current assets		
Stock	109,000	
Debtors	41,000	
Bank	24,000	
	174,000	
Current liabilities		
Creditors	(32,000)	
Net current assets		142,000
		£427,000
Capital and reserves		
Ordinary share capital (50p)		260,000
Reserves:		
Share premium	74,000	
Revaluation	80,000	
General	13,000	
		167,000
		£427,000

Suggested solution 20.2

	Putty Ltd		
Date	Narrative	DR £	CR £
May 1995	Freehold property a/c	15,000	
	Provision for depreciation	20,000	
	Revaluation reserve		35,000
10.5.95	Bank	330,000	
	Application and allotment a/c		330,000
12.5.95	Application and allotment	330,000	
	Ordinary £1 shares		30,000
	Share premium		60,000
	Bank		240,000
15.5.95	Goodwill	9,000	
	Asset a/cs	36,000	
	Ordinary £1 shares		15,000
	Share premium		30,000
20.5.95	9% Debentures 1980 a/c	15,000	
	Debenture redemption a/c		15,000
20.5.95	Debenture redemption a/c	15,150	
	Bank		15,150
20.5.95	Share premium	150	
	Debenture redemption a/c		150
20.5.95	Retained earnings	15,000	
	General reserve		15,000
May 95	Provision for repairs a/c	1,400	
	Retained earnings		1,400

Suggested solution 20.3

a

Pantile Ltd

Profit & Loss Account for seven days ended 7 May 1995

	£	£
Sales		23,700
Opening stock	34,000	
Purchases	nil	
	34,000	
Less: Closing stock (by balance)	14,600	
Cost of sales (by balance)		19,400
Gross profit $\frac{10,500}{5} + \frac{13,200}{6} = 2,100 + 2,200$		4,300
Goodwill written off		4,000
Net profit for week		300
Profits b/f		26,000
		£26,300
Transfer to capital redemption reserve		(26,300)

b

Summarised Balance Sheet as at 7 May 1995

	£	£	£
Fixed assets *less* depreciation			85,000
Current assets: Stock		14,600	
Debtors		44,500	
		59,100	
Current liabilities			
Creditors	25,000		
Bank (see workings)	17,900		
		42,900	
			16,200
Net current assets			£101,200
Share capital: 90,000 Ordinary 50 pence shares			45,000
10% Preference shares			13,700
			58,700
Reserves: Capital redemption reserve fund		26,300	
Share premium		16,200	42,500
			£101,200

Workings:

Bank

	£		£
Balance b/d	3,000	Creditors	14,000
Cash sales	13,200	8% Preference shareholders	40,800
Debtors	7,000		
10% Preference shareholders	13,700		
Balance c/d	17,900		
	£54,800		£54,800

Suggested solution 25.1

a

Sandforth Ltd
Cash Budget for three months ended 31 August 1994

		J	J	A
Income:	Cash sales	4,000	4,500	4,500
	Credit sales	5,600	6,700	8,200
		£9,600	£11,200	£12,700
Payments:	Creditors	9,000	9,500	10,000
	Wages	900	900	900
	General expenses	350	350	350
	Rent	1,800		
	Dividend		1,000	
	Capital		4,600	
		£12,050	£16,350	£11,250
Surplus/(deficit)		(2,450)	(5,150)	1,450
Balance b/f		5,300	2,850	(2,300)
Balance c/f		£2,850	£(2,300)	£(850)

b

Budgeted Profit & Loss Account, for three months ended 31 August 1994

	£	£
Sales		35,900
Opening stock	4,400	
Purchases	29,900	
	34,300	
Less: Closing stock (by balance)	5,580	
Cost of sales (by balance)		28,720
Gross profits (35,900 x 20%)		7,180
Wages	2,700	
General expenses	1,050	
Rent 3 months @ £150	450	
Depreciation (note 1)	270	4,470
Net profit from trading		2,710
Profit on sale of plant		200
Net profit		£2,910

Note:
1

	£
Cost of plant 1.6.94	5,000
Less: Disposals	2,000
	3,000
Additions	6,000
Cost at 31.8.94	£9,000
Depreciation = 1%/month or £270/qtr	

Suggested solution 25.2

a

Abba Ltd
Budgeted Trading, Profit & Loss Account for year ended 31 December 1994

	£	£
Sales		600
Opening stock	55	
Purchases (by balance)	490	
	545	
	95	
Closing stock (note 2)		450
Cost of sales (note 1)		150
Gross profit		
Wages	46	
Overhead expenses	18	
Depreciation	38	102
Net profit		£48

b

Budgeted Balance Sheet as at 31 December 1994

	£	£
Fixed assets:		
Cost		380
Depreciation		128
		252
Current assets:		
Stock	95	
Debtors (note 3)	150	
Bank (by balance)	20	
	£265	
Current liabilities:		
Trade creditors (note 4)	82	
Expense creditors (note 5)	3	
	£85	
Net current assets (by balance)		180
		£432
Share capital:		
Ordinary £1 shares		200
Profit & loss a/c		150
		350
Long-term loans		82
		£432

Notes:

1 Cost of sales:

Sales volume has increased by $\dfrac{600 \times 9}{300 \times 8} \times 100\% = 225\%$

∴ Cost of sales   = 200 x 225%
                    = 450

2 Closing stock:

Rate of stock turnover 1993   =   Cost of sales ÷ average stock

Average stock 1993   = $\dfrac{45 + 55}{2}$ = 50

Rate of stock turnover   = $\dfrac{200}{50}$ = 4

increased by 50% for 1994

therefore $\dfrac{\text{cost of sales}}{\text{average stock}}$ = 6

            average stock   = $\dfrac{450}{6}$ = 75

     $75 = \dfrac{55 + \text{closing stock}}{2}$

∴ closing stock = 150 – 55 = 95

3 Debtors:

Closing debtors is to be one month more than 1993

1993 closing debtors period   = $\dfrac{50}{300}$ x   12 = 2 months

1994 closing stock period   =   3 months

∴ closing stock   = $\dfrac{600}{4}$ = 150

4 Creditors (trade):

1993 creditors are $\dfrac{1}{6}$ of purchases

∴ 1994 creditors are $\dfrac{490}{6}$ or £82,000 (to nearest £000)

5 Creditors (expense):

1993 creditors are $\dfrac{1}{6}$ of expenses

∴ 1994 creditors are $\dfrac{18}{6}$ or £3,000

Suggested solution 25.3

a

Keensuppliers Ltd
Estimated Trading, Profit & Loss Account for the year ended 31 October 1994

	£	£
Sales		110,000
Opening stock	7,800	
Purchases	84,600	
	92,400	
Closing stock	4,400	
Cost of sales		88,000
Gross profit (note 1)		22,000
Expenses:		
Rates	4,000	
Salaries (including bonus)	11,100	
Administration	6,100	
Depreciation	800	
		22,000
Net profit		nil

Estimated Balance Sheet as at 31 October 1994

	£	£
Fixed assets:		
Freehold premises		20,000
Fixtures (NBV)		5,400
		25,400
Current assets:		
Stocks	4,400	
Debtors	5,000	
Bank	8,300	
	17,700	
Current liabilities: Creditors	14,100	
		3,600
		£29,000
Financed by:		
Ordinary share capital		30,000
Reserves:		
Share premium	4,700	
Profit and loss	(5,700)	
		(1,000)
		£29,000

b Required profits = £5,700

∴ required contribution = 5,700 + 20,900 = 26,600

If gross profit – $\frac{1}{20}$ gross profit = 26,600

then gross profit = $\frac{26,600 \times 20}{19}$ = 28,000

If gross profit = $\frac{2}{10}$ sales revenue

then sales revenue = $\frac{28,000 \times 10}{2}$ = £140,000

Note:

1

		£
SR (sales revenue)		110,000
COS $\left(\frac{8}{10}\text{ SR}\right)$		88,000
Gross profit $\left(\frac{2}{10}\text{SR}\right)$		22,000
Bonus $\left(\frac{1}{20}\text{ GP}\right)$		1,100
Contribution $\left(\frac{19}{20}\text{ GP}\right)$		20,900
Fixed costs:		
Rates	4,000	
Salaries	10,000	
Administration	6,100	
Depreciation $\left(\frac{19}{20}\text{ GP}\right)$	800	
		20,900
Net profit		nil

Suggested solution 26.1

a Two main reasons:
    ROCE   A: 50%   B: 12½%
    Reconciliation of A and B's profits.

A's profit	24,000
Cost of sales diff.	10,000
	14,000
Depreciation difference	1,000
	£13,000

i   Cost of sales: reason for difference: inflation (probably)

   –   possible that A is simply better at purchasing his supplies;
   –   more likely that as A purchased the supplies in prior accounting periods
       the price was lower.

   A's unit cost = £10/meg
   B's unit cost = £20/meg

ii Depreciation: reason for difference: inflation (certainly):

   –   question says that 'both A and B use similar premises and equipment';
   –   B's net capital employed exceeds A's by £56,000;
   –   ignoring the fact that A has £10,000 more stocks than B then B's costs
       of fixed assets must be far higher than A's;
   –   result must be higher depreciation charge.

b Not justified at all.

    i   B's profits more accurately reflect the 'true' profits;

    ii   COS adjustment to bring to replacement cost;

    iii Depreciation adjustment to bring to replacement cost;

    iv A is depleting the capital of the firm (in real terms).

Additional points:
Possible that depreciation is on equipment only (not premises) if this is true then likely that B's cost of premises far exceeds that of A hence such a high capital employed.

Index